Joseph Zobel
Négritude and the Novel

Contemporary French and Francophone Cultures, 51

Contemporary French and Francophone Cultures

Series Editor

CHARLES FORSDICK
University of Liverpool

Editorial Board

TOM CONLEY
Harvard University

JACQUELINE DUTTON
University of Melbourne

LYNN A. HIGGINS
Dartmouth College

MIREILLE ROSELLO
University of Amsterdam

DAVID WALKER
University of Sheffield

This series aims to provide a forum for new research on modern and contemporary French and francophone cultures and writing. The books published in *Contemporary French and Francophone Cultures* reflect a wide variety of critical practices and theoretical approaches, in harmony with the intellectual, cultural and social developments which have taken place over the past few decades. All manifestations of contemporary French and francophone culture and expression are considered, including literature, cinema, popular culture, theory. The volumes in the series will participate in the wider debate on key aspects of contemporary culture.

Recent titles in the series:

35 Martin Munro, *Writing on the Fault Line: Haitian Literature and the Earthquake of 2010*

36 Kathryn A. Kleppinger, *Branding the 'Beur' Author: Minority Writing and the Media in France*

37 Ruth Bush, *Publishing Africa in French: Literary Institutions and Decolonization 1945–1967*

38 Nicki Hitchcott, *Rwanda Genocide Stories: Fiction After 1994*

39 Sara Kippur and Lia Brozgal, *Being Contemporary: French Literature, Culture and Politics Today*

40 Lucille Cairns, *Francophone Jewish Writers: Imagining Israel*

41 Leslie Kealhofer-Kemp, *Muslim Women in French Cinema: Voices of Maghrebi Migrants in France*

42 Katelyn E. Knox, *Race on Display in 20th- and 21st Century France*

43 Bruno Chaouat, *Is Theory Good for the Jews?: French Thought and the Challenge of the New Antisemitism*

44 Denis M. Provencher, *Queer Maghrebi French: Language, Temporalities, Transfiliations*

45 Nicholas Hewitt, *Montmartre: A Cultural History*

46 Oana Panaïté, *The Colonial Fortune in Contemporary Fiction in French*

47 Jason Herbeck, *Architextual Authenticity: Constructing Literature and Literary Identity in the French Caribbean*

48 Yasser Elhariry, *Pacifist Invasions: Arabic, Translation and the Postfrancophone Lyric*

49 Colin Davis, *Traces of War: Interpreting Ethics and Trauma in Twentieth-Century French Writing*

LOUISE HARDWICK

Joseph Zobel

Négritude and the Novel

LIVERPOOL UNIVERSITY PRESS

First published 2017 by
Liverpool University Press
4 Cambridge Street
Liverpool
L69 7ZU

This paperback edition first published 2021

Copyright © 2017, 2021 Louise Hardwick

The right of Louise Hardwick to be identified as the author of this book has been asserted by her in accordance with the Copyright, Designs and Patents Act 1988.

All rights reserved. No part of this book may be reproduced, stored in a retrieval system, or transmitted, in any form or by any means, electronic, mechanical, photocopying, recording, or otherwise, without the prior written permission of the publisher.

British Library Cataloguing-in-Publication data
A British Library CIP record is available

ISBN 978-1-78694-073-5 cased
ISBN 978-1-80085-582-3 paperback

Typeset by Carnegie Book Production, Lancaster
Printed and bound by CPI Group (UK) Ltd, Croydon CR0 4YY

Contents

Acknowledgements	vii
Introduction	1
1 Zobel, Négritude, and the Novel	31
2 Earth, Ecocriticism, and Economics: *Diab'-là*	60
3 Nothing Happens, Twice: *Les Jours immobiles* becomes *Les Mains pleines d'oiseaux*	103
4 Rereading *La Rue Cases-Nègres*	142
5 Cultural Capital in the French Capital: From *La Fête à Paris* to *Quand la neige aura fondu*	187
Afterword	243
Bibliography	254
Index	267

Acknowledgements

I would like to record my thanks to all my colleagues, graduate students, and undergraduate students in the Department of Modern Languages at the University of Birmingham for their friendly support during the completion of this project.

This book was made possible by the Arts and Humanities Research Council through the award of an Early Career Leadership Fellowship between 2014 and 2016. The Fellowship allowed me to design and carry out an ambitious international project, and to undertake fieldwork and archival research throughout Martinique and metropolitan France; it also enabled me to spend a period developing my ideas as a Visiting Fellow in the Department of French and Italian at Emory University, Atlanta.

I would also like to thank colleagues throughout the College of Arts and Law at the University of Birmingham, and particularly the members of the Research and Knowledge Transfer committee and the North America Travel Fund committee for granting me internal institutional funding to support further periods of archival research in Paris, Aix-en-Provence, and Austin (Texas). Towards the completion of the manuscript, I was honoured to present a section of this research as a keynote speech at the Society for Francophone Postcolonial Studies annual conference. In addition, my election as an Associate Fellow of Homerton College, Cambridge, and the decision to profile me in the portrait exhibition 'Feminae Trinitatis' at Trinity College, Oxford, offered a welcome opportunity to discuss my work with colleagues and students at these institutions. My sincere thanks go to Anthony Cond and Chloé Johnson at Liverpool University Press for sharing my belief in this project, and to LUP's anonymous readers for their helpful comments on the manuscript. I am grateful to the entire LUP team for their outstanding professional support.

The specialist knowledge and assistance of librarians and curators has nurtured this research project, and I am most grateful to my colleagues throughout the world: in Martinique at Le Fonds Zobel and the Bibliothèque Schœlcher in Fort-de-France, and the Archives départementales in Schœlcher; at a European level, through the online database of The European Library; in the UK at the University of Birmingham (particularly the inter-library loans team) and the British Library in London, where I am especially grateful to the Eccles Centre; in the USA at the Stuart A. Rose Manuscript, Archives & Rare Book Library (MARBL) at Emory University and the Harry Ransom Archive at the University of Texas at Austin; and finally, in metropolitan France, at the Archives nationales d'outre-mer in Aix-en-Provence and the Bibliothèque nationale de France in Paris, including the INAthèque and the BNF Sindbad service, and also at the Bibliothèque Mazarine and the Bibliothèque du Musée du Quai d'Orsay.

Since 2013, I have been immensely privileged to work with members of the community of Rivière-Salée in Martinique, particularly in the preparation and delivery of the official events marking the centenary of Joseph Zobel's birth in 2015; it is my sincere wish that this book be part of the legacy of that memorable year. In Rivière-Salée, thanks are due to colleagues and friends at the *mairie* and the *médiathèque*, and to the staff and pupils of the Lycée Joseph Zobel and Collège Georges Elisabeth; it was an honour to work alongside people so dedicated to ensuring that Zobel's legacy is understood and celebrated, both within the local community of Saléens and beyond. In metropolitan France, the invitation from the Ministère des Outre-mer to speak at the Paris Salon du Livre in 2015 as part of the exceptional activities organised by the Passions partagées: Joseph Zobel network enabled me to embed wider public discussions about Zobel into the evolution of the research project.

My warmest thanks go to the Zobel family, who have been supportive of this project since its inception. Over the years, it has been a particular pleasure to meet and correspond with Jenny Zobel, Emily Marshall Zobel, and Charlotte Zobel, whose publications and wider activities on the life and work of Joseph Zobel have undoubtedly enriched my own study.

To paraphrase John Donne, no researcher is an island! Many more people than space permits me to name supported this project at various stages of its development, from in-depth discussions and reading suggestions, to participating in public engagement work, or supplying kind words of encouragement and camaraderie. I wish to express my sincere thanks to Mamadou Souley Ba, Moïse Benjamin (aka Benzo), Juliette Bertelot, Lyne-Rose Beuze, Liz Bonnin, Raphaëlle Bouville, Stewart Brown, Ruth Bush, Ginette Calmont, Suzy Cater, Patrick Chamoiseau, Yves Chemla, Gabrielle Chomereau-Lamotte, Richard Clay, Béatrice Clio, Jean-Daniel Clio, Martyn Cornick, Lisa Downing, Frantz Édouard, Rodolf Étienne, Romuald Fonkoua, Stephen Forcer, Charles Forsdick, Katharina Freise, Bob Garbutt, Toby Garfitt, Zbig Gas, Catherine Gilbert, Philip Hatfield, Isabelle Hertner, Nicki Hitchcott, Nicholas Hunter, Conrad James, Claude Jean-Laurent, Marie-Dominique Jeanne, Angela Kershaw, André Lesueur, Valérie Loichot, Ludovic Louri, Tiphaine Malfettes, Jonathan Mallinson, Rolond Monpierre, Raphaël Nicole, Manuel Norvat, Euzhan Palcy, George Pau-Langevin, Claire Peters, Jean-Marc Pulvar, Véronique Robbaz (née Tarrieu), Sir Ivor Roberts, Sheena Robertson, Cora Rodway, Jean-Marc Rosier, Sylvie Sainte-Agathe, Berny Sèbe, Yoshiko Shibata, Susan Smith, Rodolphe Solbiac, Patricia Thiéry, Joanna Trollope, Michael Whitby, Michael Wiedorn, and Antonia Wimbush.

My family, Elaine, George, and Rob, and Antonio (hero of the last act) have humoured me as I developed ideas, offered a sympathetic ear when the going got tough, and celebrated milestones. Thank you all for your precious support.

This book is dedicated to my mother, Elaine.

Introduction

Joseph Zobel, c'est LE romancier martiniquais.

Joseph Zobel is THE Martinican novelist.

Aimé Césaire[1]

La lecture de Joseph Zobel, plus que des discours théoriques, m'a ouvert les yeux.

Reading Joseph Zobel, more than any theoretical discourse, opened my eyes.

Maryse Condé[2]

At the Paris Book Fair in 2002, Aimé Césaire declared 'Joseph Zobel, c'est LE romancier martiniquais' (Joseph Zobel is THE Martinican novelist).[3] With these words, Césaire was deliberately drawing attention to the novels of a talented Caribbean author who was, and still is, often thought of as something of a 'one-hit wonder' because his literature has so far been incompletely studied, through the prism of just one novel. Joseph Zobel (1915–2006) has become one of the best-known authors of the Francophone Caribbean.[4] This is due to the international success

---

1 Jenny Zobel and Emily Marshall Zobel, '"Lorsque je vais dans mon village" (When I return to my village): Joseph Zobel's Visions of Home and Exile', *Wasafiri*, 26.3 (2011), p. 8.
2 Maryse Condé, *Le Cœur à rire et à pleurer* (Paris: Laffont, 1999), p. 103; *Tales from the Heart* trans. by Richard Philcox (New York: Soho Press, 2001), p. 111.
3 Zobel and Marshall Zobel, p. 8.
4 Throughout this study, the term 'Francophone Caribbean' is used when discussing Zobel's significance for, and status as a representative of, the

of his semi-autobiographical novel *La Rue Cases-Nègres* (1950),[5] which appeared in English translation as *Black Shack Alley* (1980).[6] The novel's renown was cemented in 1983 by Euzhan Palcy's celebrated film adaptation *Rue Cases-Nègres*, a global phenomenon released in English under two titles, of which Palcy's preferred version is *Sugar Cane Alley*.[7]

Yet, despite this international reputation, very little is known about Zobel's life or his transnational career. Moreover, the majority of scholarship dedicated to his work still focuses on *La Rue Cases-Nègres* and generates readings which consider that text in isolation. As a result, the significance of his novels within Caribbean and European literary traditions – for he undoubtedly makes pioneering contributions to both areas – has been downplayed and misunderstood. This has impeded deeper analysis of his wider body of sophisticated and ideologically radical novels, and it has also limited the academic understanding of the place of *La Rue Cases-Nègres* within that wider *œuvre*. Much of his other creative work across continents has gone unnoticed; in his lifetime, he was active in Europe, the Caribbean and Africa as a newspaper journalist, government press attaché, short-story writer, poet, spoken-word artist, radio broadcaster, sculptor, and painter.

The present study responds to this gap by re-examining Zobel's career, placing his substantial corpus of novels at the centre of the investigation, and using these works to generate new insights into his wider activities and roles. I draw attention to Zobel's considerable innovations within the genre of the novel, and to his significant contributions to the wider traditions of Caribbean, European, and Black Diasporic literature – and particularly to the Francophone tradition of Négritude. This is achieved through careful contextualisation of his works, and through a series of close readings which trace the ways in which his novels express radical new insights into racial identity, economic exploitation, gender, the environment, and immigration. I analyse the evolution of these themes in the six novels that Zobel published during his lifetime: *Diab'-là* (1945),

French-speaking space of the Caribbean most broadly defined (to include Haiti), while the term 'French Caribbean' indicates a more specific focus on the implications of his work for those areas of the Caribbean which are administratively French.

5 Joseph Zobel, *La Rue Cases-Nègres* (Paris: Éditions Jean Froissart, 1950).

6 Joseph Zobel, *Black Shack Alley*, trans. by Keith Q. Warner (Washington, DC: Three Continents Press, 1980).

7 Euzhan Palcy, *Rue Cases-Nègres*, 1983. English title: *Sugar Cane Alley*. An alternative English title is *Black Shack Alley*. I wish to record my thanks to Patrick Aglae, Euzhan Palcy's PA, for sharing this information with me.

Les Jours immobiles (1946), *La Rue Cases-Nègres* (1950), *La Fête à Paris* (1953), *Les Mains pleines d'oiseaux* (1978), and *Quand la neige aura fondu* (1979). In chronological order, these titles could be rendered into English as *Diablo*, *Those Timeless Days*, *Black Shack Alley*, *Adventures in Paris*, *Hands Full of Birds*, and *Once the Snow Has Melted*, and I return to the issues surrounding translations of Zobel's work in the following pages. *Les Mains pleines d'oiseaux* and *Quand la neige aura fondu* are rewritten versions of *Les Jours immobiles* and *La Fête à Paris*, and this leads me to consider the material conditions and artistic implications of this unusual and substantial rewriting project.

Zobel died in 2006, and his extensive personal archive is currently in preparation in Martinique, with considerable amounts of new, previously inaccessible information already available for researchers. My sustained archival work in Martinique, the United States, and metropolitan France has revealed numerous documents, dating from between the late 1930s until the end of the author's life, which cast new light on his career as a novelist, supporting my book's central argument that a rereading of Zobel's novels is both necessary and timely. Given the current paucity of biographical information about Zobel, this archival research also enables me to establish the first detailed account of the author's life and work.

A further important ambition of this study is to make Zobel available to the widest-possible readership, including those who cannot access material in French, and who come to Zobel via translations or through visual culture. To date, *La Rue Cases-Nègres* is the only novel by Zobel to be made available in English translation. The Trinidadian-born academic Keith Q. Warner's 1980 translation, *Black Shack Alley*, has played an essential role in ensuring that Zobel reaches new audiences. When discussing that novel, I quote from the published English translation, with my modifications when appropriate (indicated in the text). Quite remarkably, Zobel's other titles have yet to be translated into English, and to overcome that obstacle I include my own English translations of all previously untranslated French material. In a highly unusual achievement for a Francophone Caribbean novel, *La Rue Cases-Nègres* is available in translation in languages including Czech, Dutch, Italian, and Russian, and *Diab'-là* has also been translated into Czech.[8] The absence of any Spanish or Portuguese translations is notable, and is particularly regrettable given the clear significance of his work for Latin America and the Spanish-speaking Caribbean. This study thus also

---

8 Full details of Zobel's works in translation are provided in the bibliography.

contributes to urgent debates about the translation and circulation of French and Caribbean literatures across the world. In each chapter, I demonstrate that Zobel's novels are transnational works which perform an act of cultural translation of international importance. They invoke multiple frames of reference in complex and challenging ways, and their surprising translation history in Eastern Europe, and neglect in the Hispanophone and Lusophone worlds, indicates another layer of complexity in their reception and circulation.

As a black novelist from a humble background, Zobel is a trailblazer of Martinican, and indeed Caribbean, literature. Rather than writing in the dominant literary forms of the late 1930s and early 1940s – poetry and the essay – he instead turned to prose fiction, and this led him to develop black Martinican literature in a bold new direction: the novel. The originality of his novels lies in the way that they contest French cultural and political dominance by placing, for the first time, the lives of the poorest and most marginalised Martinicans at their centre. This, moreover, is undertaken from the viewpoint of a sympathetic insider, through accessible prose narrative. The issue of access and readability is paramount. A number of notable instances throughout this study demonstrate that Zobel's longevity as an author and cultural figure owes more to his enduring appeal in non-academic circles than to any official forms of academic consecration.

The scope and reach of Zobel's ambitious, subversive literary project has reverberations well beyond the island of Martinique, and can only be fully understood through detailed consideration of how his novels were inspired by, and in dialogue with, two major cultural phenomena of the time – here it is helpful to recall that Zobel was active as a novelist between 1942 and 1953 (he would not publish another original novel after *La Fête à Paris*). The first great source of inspiration is the transnational Francophone black consciousness movement of Négritude which aimed to radically alter conceptions of blackness, and which promoted and celebrated racial pride; the neologism is a contraction of the nouns *nègre* and *attitude*. In this study, when discussing the Négritude movement, the original form of the term with its French accent will be used throughout, to ensure that the reader is unavoidably confronted with the movement's Francophone heritage; when I quote secondary critics, I respect their individual spellings of the term regarding the use of capital letters and accents. The second great influence is also transnational in nature: the English-language North American Negro Renaissance movement, which has come to be known as the Harlem

Renaissance. At the time of its development in the 1920s and 1930s, this writing was referred to as the New Negro movement (itself a tradition with roots in the closing decades of the previous century) or Negro Renaissance. The term 'Harlem Renaissance' only became widely used in the 1960s, and as such it is an anachronism which I tend to avoid in favour of 'Negro Renaissance', which was in use at the time Zobel was writing novels.[9] Drawing attention to the American movement's historical name renders far more visible the close semantic relationship between the English terms 'New Negro' or 'Negro Renaissance' and the French term 'Négritude'; in the analysis that follows, the cross-fertilisation between the two movements is explored at considerable length to provide new insights into Zobel's literary career.

Zobel's originality as a novelist lies in his ability to take literary movements which were eliciting debate in elite circles, and make them relevant to the very people who had most at stake. His characters breathe life into abstract theoretic discussions about race, identity, gender, and oppression. Indeed, of all the authors to emerge from the Francophone Caribbean in the mid-twentieth century, none would surpass Zobel in his deliberate attempts to write literature that would reach a popular readership. For Zobel, writing presented a means to explore the realms of aesthetic experimentation, while always retaining an acute sense of social and political responsibility. This mode of socially engaged creativity produced a rich seam of literature which tackles, in a nuanced yet accessible manner, urgent questions about the development of modern societies in the Caribbean, Africa, and Europe in the twentieth century, and about the multiple and diverse roles, cultural and political, played by Francophone Caribbean citizens throughout the world.

Zobel's novels, and the film adaptation *Rue Cases-Nègres*, have taken fundamental yet marginalised aspects of Martinican culture, such as sugar cane plantations, and rendered them accessible to audiences across the globe, a remarkable achievement given that Martinique is all too often regarded as 'different' and 'inaccessible' to the wider Caribbean, and indeed the wider world. This difference stems in part from the island's historic development under French colonial rule. Martinique was first colonised by the French in 1635 and, along with Guadeloupe, French Guyana, and the Indian Ocean island of Reunion,

---

9 Ernest Julius Mitchell II, '"Black Renaissance": A Brief History of the Concept', *Amerikastudien / American Studies*, 55.4, special issue 'African American Literary Studies: New Texts, New Approaches, New Challenges' (2010), p. 651.

it transitioned from a colony into a *département d'outre-mer* or French Overseas Department on 1 January 1947. The island thus remained a fully integrated part of France at a moment when other former colonies were becoming independent, a controversial decision which is the subject of intense debate to this day. In 1993, with the creation of the European Union through the Maastricht Treaty, along with France's other overseas departments, the French island of Martinique became part of the EU. While living on a Caribbean island, then, Martinicans vote in French and EU elections and use the Euro.

Martinicans are at once Caribbean, French, and European. They embody contemporary debates on how personal and national identities may be defined in multicultural, multilingual, and transnational contexts. Unsurprisingly, given the island's political and administrative status, an overarching ideological shift away from concepts of insularity and isolation is a defining feature of late twentieth- and early twenty-first-century Martinican literature and cultural production, as exemplified by the work of a number of authors led by Édouard Glissant and his famous concept of *créolisation*. Prior to Glissant's work, however, a desire for cultural openness and dialogue was also a guiding feature of Zobel's literature. His novels seek nothing less than to reinscribe the agency of Caribbean identities, histories, and politics into the global history of humanity. Moreover, Zobel's achievement as one of a small group of leading twentieth-century figures whose cultural advocacy – particularly through the multimedia success of *La Rue Cases-Nègres* – has led to the increased global recognition of the Francophone Caribbean, must be understood as a defining moment in the struggle against the ongoing cultural and political isolation of Martinique.

Although Zobel is repeatedly referred to as a major figure in Caribbean literature, and as one of the rare Francophone Caribbean authors to have won global attention, there is a distinct lack of scholarship going beyond *La Rue Cases-Nègres*. Why is it that this author, who is so regularly referenced as a major Caribbean author in literary encyclopaedias, and who is studied in schools and universities across the Anglophone and Francophone world and in contexts as far afield as Japan,[10] has never before been the subject of a book-length academic study? Why is so

---

10 I am grateful to Professor Yoshiko Shibata for sharing with me her experiences of teaching Zobel, via Palcy's film, to students of Anthropology and Intercultural Studies at Kobe University, Japan, during our meeting at the annual Society for Caribbean Studies Conference held in July 2015 at The Drum in Birmingham.

little understood about Zobel's relationship to the Négritude movement? At the centenary of Zobel's birth, which was celebrated in April 2015, much of the author's life and work remained unanalysed. Tackling the enigma of how an author can at once enjoy such international fame, and yet remain largely a mystery, finally brings to light the full depth and breadth of Zobel's creative output, as well as the forces complicit in the making of his reputation. Only then can a more considered portrait of the author's work and life begin to emerge.

This study is bolstered by, and makes its own contribution to, recent approaches to Négritude. There is no single definition of the term 'Négritude', although scholars tend to agree that it refers to a literary movement launched by Léopold Sédar Senghor, Aimé Césaire, and Léon-Gontran Damas when they were students in Paris. Césaire first used the term in 1935 in the student publication *L'Étudiant noir*,[11] and all three authors rallied around it to different degrees in order to articulate a pan-African consciousness which fostered 'ways of imagining race and racism so that emphasis is placed on a reaction against colonial racism and assimilation'.[12] For Césaire and Damas, the movement offered a means to give voice to the trauma and ongoing consequences of transatlantic slavery, while Senghor's work – which became the most overtly political in focus when he was elected President of the newly independent Senegal and developed a Négritude-inflected politics – critiqued French colonial incursions into Africa. The movement also had important literary antecedents such as the work of sisters Paulette, Jane, and Andrée Nardal, Ousmane Socé, and René Maran, all of whom have been the focus of recent scholarship exploring both their literary contributions and the ways in which they have been excluded from literary and cultural historiographies.[13] Zobel's literature has

---

11 Christian Filostrat, *Négritude et Agonistes: Assimilation against Nationalism in the French-Speaking Caribbean and Guyane* (Cherry Hill, NJ: Africana Homestead Legacy, 2008), p. 119.
12 Bart Miller, *Rethinking Négritude through Léon-Gontran Damas* (Amsterdam: Rodopi, 2014), p. 20.
13 See for example T. Denean Sharpley-Whiting, *Negritude Women* (Minneapolis, MN: University of Minnesota Press, 2002); Brent Hayes Edwards, *The Practice of Diaspora: Literature, Translation, and the Rise of Black Internationalism* (Cambridge, MA: Harvard University Press, 2003); Shireen K. Lewis, *Race, Culture and Identity: Francophone West African and Caribbean Literature and Theory from Négritude to Créolité* (Lanham, MD: Lexington, 2006); Jean Khalfa, 'The Heart of the Black Race: Parisian Négritudes in the 1920s', *Wasafiri*, 23.4 (2008),

itself played a role in the rediscovery of the Nardals, particularly his short story 'Nardal', published in 1982, which discusses the exceptional family he knew in wartime Fort-de-France and pays homage to their role in strengthening his own racial pride as a black man.[14] Négritude is then currently subject to an urgent process of critical scrutiny and reappraisal. Kathleen Gyssels[15] and Bart Miller have drawn attention to Damas's marginalisation within the broader study of the movement, while Daniel Maximin, Anny Dominique Curtius, and others have drawn attention to the marginalised role of Suzanne Césaire.[16] This new criticism demonstrates the extent to which Négritude rewards closer analysis from new perspectives, to generate deeper understandings of the movement's historical, racial, gendered, economic, and political significance.

Zobel was not a founding member of Négritude, but he was of the same generation. In a crucial difference to Césaire, Senghor, and Damas, he did not set foot outside his native island of Martinique until after the end of the Second World War, and so was positioned at a physical and metaphorical distance from Négritude's bourgeois beginnings in Paris. As a result, Zobel developed his own conception of Négritude from an 'external' perspective – that is to say, far away from the Parisian universities and literary salons where the movement was being nurtured. Yet, paradoxically, his distance – literal and figurative – also meant that he developed an 'internal' understanding of Négritude, his experiences in Martinique serving as his guiding frame of reference. He was the only author of his generation to begin his publishing career in Martinique, and his first works appeared with local Fort-de-France

---

pp. 15–24; Mamadou Badiane, *The Changing Face of Afro-Caribbean Cultural Identity: Negrismo and Negritude* (Lanham, MD: Lexington, 2010); Jennifer Anne Boittin, *Colonial Metropolis: The Urban Grounds of Anti-Imperialism and Feminism in Interwar Paris* (Lincoln, NE: University of Nebraska Press, 2010).

14 Joseph Zobel, 'Nardal / En guise de postface', in *Et si la mer n'était pas bleue* (Paris: Éditions caribéennes, 1982), pp. 81–89.

15 Kathleen Gyssels, *BLACK LABEL ou les déboires de Léon-Gontran Damas. Essais* (Paris: Passage(s), 2016).

16 See Suzanne Césaire, *Le Grand Camouflage: Écrits de dissidence (1941–1945)*, ed. by Daniel Maximin (Paris: Seuil, 2009); *The Great Camouflage: Writings of Dissent (1941–1945)*, ed. by Daniel Maximin and trans. by Keith L. Walker (Middletown, CT: Wesleyan University Press, 2012); Anny Dominique Curtius, 'Cannibalizing *Doudouisme*, Conceptualizing the *Morne*: Suzanne Césaire's Caribbean Ecopoetics', *The South Atlantic Quarterly*, 115.3 (2016), pp. 513–34.

publishers, not Parisian publishing houses. His early novels are unapologetically and deliberately focused on depicting his own people; they are also unmistakably intended for local Martinican readers. Zobel made sustained attempts to give voice to marginalised groups and himself had intimate personal knowledge of their settings. In a documentary, Zobel stated that when he began to write, he was acutely aware of the need to bring an area into literature that had never been represented:

> Je regrettais de ne pas trouver à l'époque quand j'étais à l'école [...] des situations, des paysages et des gens, qui ressemblaient à ceux qui m'avaient entouré. Avec l'enseignement qu'on avait à l'école, qui était dans une pédagogie d'assimilation, même ceux qui auraient écrit, qui essayaient d'écrire, ils écrivaient jamais de la Martinique, ni créaient, ni racontaient une histoire dont les personnages étaient les gens de la rue, de Fort-de-France, les gens travaillant dans les champs de canne d'un petit village.[17]
>
> When I was at school, I wished I could find [...] situations, landscapes, and people who resembled those around me. With the teaching we received in school, which was a pedagogy of assimilation, even those who would have liked to write, who tried to write, well, they never wrote about Martinique, and they didn't create or narrate a story with characters who were everyday people in the street, from Fort-de-France, or people who worked in the cane fields in a small village.

His novels raise questions about representation and who is speaking for whom. As such, they make a significant contribution to the field of subaltern studies and to wider postcolonial debates about representivity, positionality, and audience.

Broadly defined, Zobel's novels can be divided into two groups. The first comprises *Diab'-là* (1945) and *Les Jours immobiles* (1946), along with a third, much later, publication, when, three decades after its original appearance, he rewrote and republished *Les Jours immobiles* as *Les Mains pleines d'oiseaux* (1978). This first group of novels consolidate and celebrate black racial identity. Through these works, Zobel pioneers a new kind of French Caribbean social realism which expands and develops the framework of Négritude, by placing those dispossessed groups which had previously been excluded or sidelined from the Négritude discourse firmly at the centre of his literary project. In other words, he turns the gaze on the poorest

---

[17] Dominique Gallet and Mona Makki, *Joseph Zobel: le soleil d'ébène* ('tv-francophonie' production, 2002).

members of Caribbean society. Zobel's first novels are extraordinary examples of 'home-grown' Négritude, and it is wholly significant that both *Diab'-là* and *Les Jours immobiles* share the same subtitle: 'roman antillais' (Antillean novel), which itself announces Zobel's ambition to forge a new genre of literature. They apply the movement's more abstract concepts about race to real settings by showing racial pride in black identity as an integral aspect of the everyday lived experiences of poor Martinicans. These first novels also introduce environmental themes. The uneducated but naturally intelligent character of Diab'-là is intended to serve as a role model for dispossessed groups, who are challenged, through the character's own processes of reflection which drive the narrative forwards, to reflect on why their society is constructed as it is – and to their detriment. *Diab'-là* accords considerable attention to the land, which is an equally important theme in *Les Jours immobiles*, and so Zobel also becomes the first novelist to subject the complex connection between Martinicans and the earth on which they live to deep interrogation. This had stark political consequences, and led to *Diab'-là* being censored (discussed at length in Chapter Two). The author's earliest novels, then, perform a radical critique of the colonial management and government of the Martinican land. This visionary direction of his work has long gone unexplored; my closer analysis demonstrates that Zobel's literary depictions of the land – in its political and spiritual dimensions – need to be brought into dialogue with postcolonial ecocriticism, an area which is only now, at the beginning of the twenty-first century, becoming the focus of serious scholarly attention, and to which Zobel's earliest novels make an important Caribbean intervention.

Zobel's second group of novels, *La Rue Cases-Nègres* (1950) and *La Fête à Paris* (1953), the latter of which was rewritten much later in his career as *Quand la neige aura fondu* (1979), continues and develops the author's ambition to create novels about working-class black heroes in extraordinary circumstances. Now the focus is on the character of José Hassam, Zobel's best-known and most enduring literary creation, a character inspired by his own life experiences (although, as I have previously demonstrated, the novel itself is not a straightforward autobiography).[18] The founding writers of the Négritude movement had not concentrated on foregrounding individual experience; instead,

---

18 Louise Hardwick, *Childhood, Autobiography and the Francophone Caribbean* (Liverpool: Liverpool University Press, 2013), p. 40.

they had provided more abstract and surreal impressions of groups of people or individual stereotypes. José Hassam became an emblematic character through whom Zobel could give flesh to the more abstract ideological and political battles mapped out by Négritude. In contrast to his literary forebear, the character of Diab'-là, whose appreciation of Négritude, although significant, is limited by the fact that he has received no formal education and does not participate in any cultural systems beyond those in his own village, José's progress through the education system enables him to move from the village of Petit-Morne to the urban context of Fort-de-France (the Martinican capital), and then to Paris. In *La Rue Cases-Nègres*, his trajectory through the French Caribbean intellectual system to some extent mirrors the trajectories of the Négritude authors, but with the highly significant difference that its hero begins from an extremely disadvantaged background. This difference in social status, or rather social class, is a gap which enables Zobel to mobilise José Hassam as a mouthpiece for a critique of the positive, emancipatory influence of Négritude for his own life and, by extension, to show its potential for a generation of marginalised people like him. In the sequel novel, *La Fête à Paris*, rewritten as *Quand la neige aura fondu*, José (like Zobel himself) is at last able to undertake the quintessential Négritude pilgrimage to study in Paris. It is in this final novel that the influence of Négritude is made most evident and is – for the only time in Zobel's novels – directly named and discussed by the characters themselves.

Zobel's novels about José Hassam illustrate the dilemma of the colonial *évolué* whose education has elevated him out of the social class into which he was born. He must choose between the humble society in which he originated, and that bourgeois world for which he is now 'qualified', where he is expected to apply his qualifications and seek a living in a professional role. But José cannot bring himself to conform to the behaviour of the stereotypical colonial *évolué*, which would dictate that he shun and disdain that part of society from which he originated, to embark on a life of 'social climbing'. This was Zobel's own dilemma. Throughout his career, as he became more and more successful, and increasingly distanced from the marginalised group into which he had been born, in his literature and in interviews he staunchly reiterated his admiration for the poorest members of society in the Caribbean, France, and Africa.

In Zobel's novels, it is racial pride rather than educational achievement which is essential to his characters' success as fulfilled, creative human beings. Moreover, his characters, particularly José Hassam, refuse to be constrained and trapped by overdetermined stereotypes of what constitutes 'black' behaviour. José's Négritude is a deeply rooted self-confidence contingent on racial pride, which has been forged over years of experiencing – and overcoming – racial discrimination. His is a deeply personal understanding of Négritude, and it is a way of life rather than a theoretical concept. This personal sense of Négritude allows him to face a number of challenging situations without succumbing to a racially induced inferiority complex. Zobel's exploration of race, particularly through the character of José, breaks down the binary oppositions which Jean-Paul Sartre had considered inherent to the Négritude movement in his (in)famous essay 'Orphée noir', which was placed at the beginning of Senghor's *Anthologie de la Nouvelle Poésie nègre et malgache de langue française*.[19] Indeed, Zobel's novels are remarkable for promoting an awareness of race and racism which goes beyond black-white dichotomies. In his final group of novels, Zobel audaciously expands his exploration of the sites of racial conflict to highlight the racism perpetrated in Martinique by the internal Martinican ethnoclass hierarchy itself. Through the José Hassam novels, he provides a searing and nuanced portrayal of the Antillean ethnoclass hierarchy, a hierarchy predicated on a complex intersectional system of social status and skin pigment. From José's marginal and interstitial position in the race-class matrix of the ethnoclass hierarchy, Zobel is able to present and critique in an unprecedented manner the full extent of the racial damage wrought by colonialism upon Martinican society. Writing against colonially induced systems of categorisation, Zobel's novels advocate a cultural politics which will lead to the appreciation of the inherent value of every human culture, on its own terms. His Négritude functions in his novels as an invitation to be curious about, and become acquainted with, black Caribbean culture, in a spirit of respect, compassion, and inclusivity; by extension, this same Négritude exhorts the reader to display a similar curiosity about other cultures around the world, and in particular to reappraise those cultures which have been marginalised and oppressed.

---

19   Jean-Paul Sartre, 'Orphée noir', in Léopold Sédar Senghor, *Anthologie de la Nouvelle Poésie nègre et malgache de langue française* (Paris: Presses universitaires de France, 1948), pp. ix–xliv.

Biography

Frédéric Joseph Zobel, known to all as Joseph Zobel, was born on 26 April 1915 in the small community of Petit-Morne within the boundaries of the Lapalun Plantation, near the town of Rivière-Salée in south-west Martinique. He was the son of Berthe Rocher and Richard-Eugène Zobel, who were unmarried. His mother was more commonly known as Man Célia, Acélia or the creolised form Asséli, and she worked as a wet nurse to the Des Grottes family, the owners of the Lapalun Plantation. The Des Grottes belonged to the group known as *békés*, the term used in Martinique to denote the white Martinicans descended from slave plantation owners. Zobel's father, Richard-Eugène, worked as a carriage driver on the same plantation, and was largely absent. This pattern of absence was established from birth, as Richard-Eugène Zobel only formally recognised his son on 21 June 1915, almost two months after Joseph had been born.[20] Berthe Rocher also had another son, Joseph's half-brother, Michel Rocher, who was four years younger and known affectionately to the family as 'le petit Michel'.

For much of his childhood, Joseph was raised on the plantation by his maternal grandmother, Marie Rocher, known as Man Marie, who like her daughter and Joseph's father also worked on the Des Grottes plantation. Little is known about his paternal relatives.[21] However, using recently digitised archival records, I have established that Richard-Eugène Zobel's father was probably a slave named Eugène Zobel. This man belonged to a generation who became – thanks to the efforts of Victor Schœlcher in metropolitan France, and because of numerous combats in the French Caribbean islands themselves – the first generation of Martinicans to be permanently emancipated from slavery in an historic ruling in 1848. For this momentous reason, this is a generation about whom extensive archival documents were kept. Records show that on 10 February 1849, the former slave Eugène Zobel received the *état civil*, the French Republican administrative process

---

20 'Acte de naissance de Joseph Zobel: extrait du registre des actes de l'État Civil de la commune de Rivière-Salée, 1915'. On display at the Écomusée de la Martinique (at the time of inspection in 2013), this document forms part of Le Fonds Zobel, Zobel's personal archive, which is based at the Musée régional d'histoire et d'ethnographie, Fort-de-France, Martinique.
21 In private correspondence with me, Joseph Zobel's daughter Jenny Zobel confirmed that family memory only goes back as far as Joseph's father, Richard-Eugène Zobel.

which conferred the status of 'citizen' on newly emancipated slaves. In the case of Eugène Zobel, this took place in the town of Trou-au-Chat, a town now called Ducos, 10 kilometres north of Rivière-Salée. Zobel is an uncommon name in Martinique, and it is highly plausible that Richard-Eugène Zobel was named after his own father; moreover, the geographical proximity supports the thesis that the former slave Eugène Zobel was Joseph Zobel's grandfather.[22]

As plantation labourers, both branches of Zobel's family came from poor, humble origins. Plantation slavery was still part of the family's collective living memory, as well as a structure which visibly continued to influence their present living conditions, and this was an experience which they held in common with the majority of black Martinicans. In contrast, many of Zobel's contemporaries who would go on to become authors were from far more affluent backgrounds, such as Césaire, whose father, mother, and paternal grandfather had been to school – indeed, his grandfather Nicholas Louis Fernand Césaire (1868–1896) was the first black man to be admitted to the École Normale de Saint-Cloud in Paris.[23] The significant social differences between Zobel and his contemporaries shaped his literary interrogation of the intersections of race and social class, an original approach quite without parallel among his peers.

In 1922, at the age of seven, Joseph Zobel had spent the majority of his days in Petit-Morne. The start of his formal education changed this, as he began to attend primary school in the neighbouring village of Petit-Bourg. The ruins of the modest two-room school can still be seen next to the church. On the other side of the church stands the presbytery, where several school scenes in *Rue Cases-Nègres* were filmed (the building is currently in a sorry state of disrepair). In the later classes, Zobel was taught by Stephen Rose, the head teacher. Archival photographs from the 1920s show Rose as a grave and immaculately dressed figure sitting proudly among his young charges.[24] Under Rose's tutelage, in 1928 at the age of 13, Joseph was awarded the *certificat d'études*, which certified that he had successfully completed his primary education. That same year, he sat a scholarship exam and won a partial scholarship to enter

22 Archive: Patrimoines Martinique. Record 2E8/19, actes 1384–1389, dated 1849–1857. See also record E_d_8/E30, actes 1384–1389, dated 1849–1857: http://www.patrimoines-martinique.org/?id=chercher&formulaire=etat_civil (accessed 8 January 2015).
23 Romuald Fonkoua, *Aimé Césaire* (Paris: Perrin, 2013 [2010]), pp. 26–27.
24 On display at the Écomusée de la Martinique (at the time of inspection in 2013), this document forms part of Le Fonds Zobel.

the *6ème* class, the first year of *collège* (middle school), at the Lycée Schœlcher, the island's most prestigious high school, in the capital city of Fort-de-France.

At this stage, it is helpful to once again compare the academic progress of Zobel and his peer Césaire, who was two years older. The Césaire family set great store by educating their children – particularly Césaire's father, whose zeal for his children's education was almost obsessive – and in 1924, the whole family relocated to Fort-de-France after 11-year-old Aimé won a scholarship to the Lycée Schœlcher.[25] In 1932, Césaire received his *baccalauréat* (the French secondary school qualification) and was awarded another scholarship to attend an elite French school, the Lycée Louis-le-Grand in Paris, as part of the prestigious *classe préparatoire* cohort. 'Preparatory classes' are an established feature of the French education system, advanced pre-university courses taught in elite high schools; only the highest achievers are admitted.

In contrast, Zobel entered the Lycée Schœlcher at the age of 13, joining a later class and therefore not benefiting from as many years at the institution as Césaire. Zobel's time in Fort-de-France at the *lycée* was a solitary experience. He was aware of the extreme financial burden that his education placed on his single mother, and this period of his life was shaped by his realisation of the stark socio-economic divide between himself and his classmates, experiences which are recounted in *La Rue Cases-Nègres* and throughout his interviews. In a documentary film, Zobel recalled the challenges of his time at the Lycée Schœlcher, commenting that it was:

> une très dure épreuve. J'avais été coupé de ma grand-mère [...] j'étais pas du tout chez moi, j'étais replié sur moi-même. Les élèves qui y étaient [...] appartenaient tous à la petite-bourgeoisie.[26]

> a very hard test. I had been cut off from my grandmother [...] I didn't feel at all comfortable, I withdrew into myself. The other pupils there [...] were all members of the petite bourgeoisie.

The significant differences in personal circumstances might explain why Zobel took slightly longer to complete his schooling than Césaire: in October 1934 Zobel received the first part of his *baccalauréat*, specialising in philosophy, obtaining the second and final part in 1935.

---

25 Fonkoua, pp. 30–32.
26 Kamel Kezadri and Olivier Codol, *Joseph Zobel, d'amour et de silence* (Mona Lisa, RFO, 1998).

By now, the educational gap between him and Césaire had expanded to three, rather than two, years (Césaire had completed his *baccalauréat* in 1932). This extra year suggests that the revealing episode in *La Rue Cases-Nègres* in which José fails the first part of the *baccalauréat* exam, a result of his disillusionment with the Eurocentric education system and his social isolation from his better-off peers, is likely to be based on real events in Zobel's life.

After earning his *baccalauréat* in 1935, Zobel's path diverged once more from the trajectories of the future literary and cultural elite of Martinique. He was prevented from leaving for France – and therefore from following in the student footsteps of fellow Lycée Schœlcher pupils Césaire and René Ménil – because he was refused a scholarship to study architecture at the École des Beaux-Arts (School of Fine Arts and Architecture) in Paris. In his literature, and in interviews given throughout his life, Zobel was categorical in his assertion that he was refused a scholarship because of discrimination against his identity as a *petit-nègre*, that is to say, a very dark-skinned and very poor member of Martinican society (the term is discussed in detail in the following chapter). The author felt certain that the colonial administrators on the scholarship committee had deemed his aspiration to study architecture to be above his social status. He recounted this devastating episode of his life in a documentary film in the following words:

> J'ai [...] commis l'imprudence de demander une bourse pour aller aux Beaux-Arts, parce que d'après la documentation que j'avais pu obtenir, c'était aux Beaux-Arts [...] qu'on pouvait se préparer à la profession d'architecte [...] ça a été un scandale auprès des messieurs au Conseil Général, il y en a qui se sont exclamés [...] 'Mais qu'est-ce qu'un nègre va faire aux Beaux-Arts?' Parce que les Beaux-Arts, c'était un lieu, une école [...] où c'étaient des gens dont les parents étaient fortunés, et ils pouvaient rentrer, et s'habiller d'une façon plus ou moins extravagante, fumer la pipe [...] Pour quelqu'un de mon extraction, ma condition, c'était vraiment fou et scandaleux.[27]

> I [...] made the mistake of asking for a scholarship to go to the School of Fine Arts and Architecture [in Paris] because, according to the information that I had read, that was where [...] you could train to become an architect [...] it caused a scandal among the panel at the General Council [of Martinique], and some of them were outraged, commenting [...] 'But what business would a negro have at the School of Fine Arts?' Because

---

27 See Gallet and Makki.

the school was a place, an institution [...] where everyone came from wealthy backgrounds, and they could attend, and dress in a more or less extravagant manner, and smoke their pipes [...] For someone of my social origins and my condition, it was truly crazy and scandalous.

Zobel was discovering that a successful education was no guarantee of a successful career, and in the above quotation, the term *nègre* is used by the scholarships committee in a deeply pejorative sense. Throughout his novels, Zobel repeatedly interrogates his origins and the limitations imposed on him by his condition as a 'nègre' and, moreover, a 'petit-nègre'.

True to the adage that every great success begins with a failure, however, this terrible disappointment actually led to new opportunities for the young man on his native island. Zobel found employment with the Martinican Department of Bridges and Highways, and spent two years working in the southern fishing village of Le Diamant. The south-western coastal regions of the island had already enchanted him as a teenager: in an interview with Radio France International, he explains that during his time at the Lycée Schœlcher, he had visited a cousin who worked as a primary school teacher in Anses d'Arlet. There, he was captivated by the traditions of the fishing villages, which were so markedly different in character from the rural inland areas and urban centres that had shaped his childhood and adolescence.[28] These experiences in Le Diamant and Anses d'Arlet were to play a formative role in his writing career, as they provided the setting for his first two novels.

In 1938, Zobel returned to Fort-de-France and his former English teacher Louis Achille, who was now the principal of the Lycée Schœlcher, appointed him to a post at the school as a *répétiteur*, an academic support role. The following year heralded the outbreak of the Second World War, and after the Armistice of 22 June 1940, Martinique came under the Vichy rule. Marshal Pétain appointed Admiral Georges Robert as the island's governor and Vichy High Commissioner for the Antilles, a role with considerable strategic and diplomatic significance for France in the Second World War. Under Vichy Martinique, there

---

28 'Joseph Zobel', presented by Maryse Condé, interview by Annette M'Baye d'Erneville. The interview is followed by readings of selections of *La Rue Cases-Nègres* by Jenny Alpha and Robert Liensol. Co-production CLEF – Radio France Internationale. Non commercialisé. En prêt au Service Culturel de l'Ambassade de France dans les États d'Afrique francophone et de l'Océan Indien (no date – Worldcat places the date between 1978 and 1980. See: http://www.worldcat.org/title/joseph-zobel/oclc/29033391).

were also important cultural implications which repay further analysis (and to which I turn here and elsewhere in this study), as they had a direct influence on Zobel's career as a novelist.

Just prior to the outbreak of war, Césaire had returned to Martinique and Fort-de-France. Now a graduate of the Sorbonne, he took up a teaching post at the Lycée Schœlcher in literature and the classics, and so the two men became colleagues. The first edition of Césaire's *Cahier d'un retour au pays natal* (*Notebook of a Return to the Native Land*) had just been published in the Parisian literary review *Volontés* (*Desires*) thanks to Césaire's contacts at the École Normale Supérieure in Paris, and his literary star was in the ascendant.[29] Again, it is worth noting that a metropolitan French publication vehicle such as this would have been quite out of reach for Zobel, who at this point had never set foot outside Martinique.

The refusal of a scholarship, and the very impossibility of being able to study in Paris alongside the leading authors of his generation, however, had the positive consequence of enabling Zobel to discover other aspects of his native island and to remain embedded in Martinican culture and society. As a result, he was the only major author of his generation to begin his publishing career *in situ* in Martinique, writing short pieces of fiction for the popular weekly newspaper *Le Sportif* (*The Sportsman*). Launched in Fort-de-France in May 1938, and edited by a man named Ferries Elisabeth, *Le Sportif* had positioned itself as more than just a sports rag, and carried the strapline 'organe hebdomadaire de propagande, d'information et de critique sportives' (weekly round-up of sporting propaganda, information, and criticism).[30] The ambiguous strapline hinted that as well as providing diverse 'sports news', *Le Sportif* would deliver a 'sporting' critique of current events in Martinique. Zobel thus made his literary debut in a politically engaged 'popular' newspaper which only circulated in Martinique, a fact that was highly significant for his development as an author. In contributing to the local press, he was required to write with a keen sense of the local audience, and with the express aim of reaching his fellow Martinicans.

The prose articles, mainly comprising short stories, which Zobel contributed to *Le Sportif* were to lead to his breakthrough as a novelist,

---

29 Fonkoua, pp. 52–53.
30 The earliest copy examined dates from Thursday 29 September 1938, and is listed as 'Premiere année no. 21', suggesting a launch in May of that year. See Archives départementales, Martinique. PER 156/1938-1950.

thanks to the encouragement and praise of his new friend Aimé Césaire. Césaire and Zobel had overlapped as pupils at the Lycée Schœlcher, although the two-year age gap between them, and Zobel's own admission that his time there was marked by great feelings of solitude and distance from his peers, meant that they had not known each other during their schooldays. However, once they became colleagues at the Lycée on Césaire's return in 1939, a deep and lasting friendship developed between the two men, despite the very different trajectories which their adolescent lives had taken. Césaire, the author published in Paris, was by this time attracting international interest and had a growing network of influential friends and contacts throughout the world. During the Second World War, the Lycée Schœlcher became a refuge for Martinican intellectuals such as Césaire and René Ménil, whose teaching activities went beyond the *baccalauréat* as they had the opportunity to teach groups up to *classe préparatoire* age (thus delivering teaching which bridged the gap between high school and university). They instilled in their pupils and in their compatriots a fervent belief in the potential for culture to awaken Martinicans politically. *Tropiques* (*Tropics*) became the best-known legacy of this period, a quarterly review which ran to 14 issues between April 1941 and 1945 (its intellectual legacy is analysed in greater detail in the following chapter).

Although Zobel did not contribute to *Tropiques*, his publications in *Le Sportif* had drawn Césaire's attention, and the two men began to discuss literature together whenever they crossed paths at the Lycée. These encounters were intense but brief, and in one interview, Zobel recollected that such moments were nothing less than 'fulgurants' (like flashes of lightening).[31] It was at one of these chance meetings that Césaire urged Zobel to write a novel. Zobel narrates this seminal encounter as follows:

> Un jour, Césaire m'a dit: 'je lis chaque semaine ce que tu publies dans *Le Sportif* et j'estime que tu es mûr pour écrire un roman; tu devrais écrire un roman.' Il m'a dit cela comme ça, m'a serré la main et est parti.[32]

> One day, Césaire said to me: 'Every week I read your articles in *Le Sportif* and I think that you are ready to write a novel; you should write a novel'. He said that to me just like that, shook my hand, and left.

31 'Zobel: sa vie, son œuvre', in *Les Cahiers de l'U.G.T.M. Education*, 6 (October 1985), p. 23 [transcription of radio interview with Radio Asé Pléré Annou Lité on 24 February 1985].
32 'Zobel: sa vie, son œuvre', p. 23.

The French term *mûr* carries connotations of being ready in the sense of being sufficiently mature. As a direct result of these words, Zobel began to write longer prose fiction.[33] Despite Césaire's encouragement, however, Zobel's attempts to progress from short-story writer to novelist were beset by difficulties. He finished writing *Diab'-là* in 1942, but in Pétain-controlled Martinique, the text had to be submitted to Vichy censorship controls. Censorship was rife in all areas of occupied France, and mainland French authors and publishers had to beware of falling foul of 'les listes Otto' (Otto's lists), named after Otto Abetz, the German Ambassador to Paris. These three notorious lists gave details of prohibited titles.[34] In the Antilles, a process of Vichy censorship was also implemented by Robert. The Vichy censors recognised the incendiary potential of Zobel's novel and imposed a publication ban (events which are discussed at length in Chapter Two of this study). The fate of Zobel's first novel anticipated that of the group of elite intellectuals who produced *Tropiques*; that review famously fell foul of the Vichy censor in May 1943.[35] The censors of the time, then, viewed Zobel's debut novel and the work of the *Tropiques* collective as equally subversive; yet in modern academic discourse, the political thrust of Zobel's literature has been all but forgotten.

Martinique would not remain long under Vichy control. On 18 June 1943, the second anniversary of De Gaulle's radio appeal on the BBC in London (an appeal which had also been broadcast in Martinique), a Liberation Committee led by the Fort-de-France mayor, Victor Sévère, placed a Cross of Lorraine in the main park in Fort-de-France, La Savane (Savannah Park). In a symbolic gesture, the Cross was placed at the site of the iconic *monument aux morts*, the memorial to the fallen Martinican soldiers of the First World War. Sévère appealed to the Martinican public to hold a demonstration on 24 June against Admiral Robert's Vichy administration.[36]

Realising that his position was no longer secure, on 30 June 1943, Robert announced his intention to retire and asked the United States

---

33 'Zobel: sa vie, son œuvre', p. 23.
34 Thomas Fontaine and Denis Peschanski, *La Collaboration, Vichy Paris Berlin, 1940–1945* (Paris: Tallandier/Archives nationales/Ministère de la Défense, 2014), p. 34.
35 Aimé Césaire et al., *Tropiques 1941–1945: collection complète* (Paris: Jean Michel Place, 1978), pp. xxxvii–xxxix.
36 Paul Butel, *Histoire des Antilles françaises, XVIIe–XXe siècle* (Paris: Perrin, 2007), p. 466.

to send an emissary to arrange for the change of administration. A delegation arrived in the neighbouring island of Dominica, which at the time was a British Crown Colony, to inform the French Consul of Martinique's decision to join Free France and to request the appointment of a new governor. The French Ambassador to Washington, Henri Hoppenot, arrived in Fort-de-France on 14 July 1943, having been mandated to take control of the French Antilles in the name of Free France. The Free French took over the Bank of France gold reserves, and regained control of the French naval fleet, both of which had been moved to Martinique during the war as a safeguarding measure, and had been kept intact under Robert's rule (a fact which became a main line of his defence when Robert was tried as a war criminal).[37]

For the remainder of the war, Martinique was under Free French rule. The new governor of the island was a brilliant young officer named Georges-Louis Ponton, who had received the Médaille de la Résistance (Resistance Medal) from De Gaulle.[38] Ponton was born in 1906 in Madagascar. He had already served across West Africa during the war, and had joined the Free French in 1940, working in Francophone and Anglophone areas and becoming involved with Radio Accra, the voice of Free France in West Africa, based in Gold Coast (present-day Ghana). Arriving in Martinique in 1943, Ponton's commitment to indigenous culture, and his belief that it should play a defining role in the island's future development, marked a radical break with previous governors. He had close and supportive contact with black Martinican authors, and it was he who granted Césaire permission to undertake a seven-month study visit to Haiti in 1944.[39]

---

37 In *La France aux Antilles (1939–1943)*, a memoir of his military service in the Antilles, Robert defends his actions under Vichy and cites comments by J. H. Hoover, the Vice-Admiral of the US Navy, that he had acted with unwavering loyalty to France (pp. 200–01). At the time of writing the memoir, however, Robert was being tried as a war criminal, and his entire publication must be viewed in that context. The focus is on military and political service and there is no mention of the censorship under Robert's rule of black Martinican culture: the names Césaire, *Tropiques*, and Zobel simply do not appear. See Amiral Jean Robert, *La France aux Antilles (1939–1943)* (Vaduz, Lichtenstein: Calivran Anstalt, 1978 [1950]).
38 Details gathered from the archival source Gouvernement de la Martinique, *Le Gouverneur Georges-Louis Ponton: sa carrière administrative et militaire. Sa mort et ses funérailles* (Fort-de-France: Imprimerie du Gouvernement, 1944).
39 Fonkoua, p. 81.

Through Ponton, Zobel was suddenly catapulted into a role at the highest level of Martinican administration. In an interview, Zobel recounted how he was unexpectedly invited to a dinner which Ponton had arranged for the island's intellectuals, including the Césaires, and notable Jewish émigrés who were in transit, including Gustave Cohen who had been Professor of Medieval Literature at the Sorbonne.[40] The invitation was an entry into another world for the young journalist:

> J'ai été foudroyé, moi qui n'avais jamais été invité dans cette sphère, ni même dans des sphères un peu inférieures [...] A ma grande surprise, le Gouverneur Ponton m'a présenté à ses invités en disant: 'c'est un Monsieur qui écrit des articles tout à fait remarquables dans *Le Sportif*.'[41]

> I was awe-struck; I had never been invited into that elite social circle, I hadn't even been invited to mix in circles close to it [...] To my utter surprise, Governor Ponton introduced me to his guests by saying, 'This man writes really remarkable articles in *The Sportsman*'.

Zobel's words testify to his amazement that someone from his social rank should suddenly be invited to mix with his island's intellectual elite. Ponton subsequently appointed Zobel as his press attaché. The budding novelist was suddenly exposed to a quite new sphere of culture and politics via his prestigious administrative role. As press attaché, Zobel came into contact with local radio, most likely encouraged by Ponton, who had already gained experience in wartime radio broadcasting in sub-Saharan Africa at Radio Accra. During this period, Zobel's friendship with the young governor opened up opportunities for a more visionary intellectual engagement with Martinican culture. Zobel was now an official guest at cultural events, and was charged with submitting event reports to Ponton. Moreover, there is a print legacy of this collaboration. Through archival research I have uncovered a neglected short-lived review called *Martinique: revue trimestrielle*, which ran to five issues between 1944 and 1946, printed by the Imprimerie officielle de Fort-de-France (Official Publishing House of Fort-de-France). It is astonishing that this significant publication has never been analysed by scholars. The first issue's contributing authors included none other than Césaire and Ponton, and Zobel is named as a

---

40 'Zobel: sa vie, son œuvre', p. 25.
41 'Zobel: sa vie, son œuvre', p. 25.

future contributor in the cover material.[42] He did indeed go on to supply pieces for the other four issues.[43]

Zobel's time working as part of this elite group was tragically curtailed. Ponton's projects to develop the island's infrastructure in tandem with his radical plan to acknowledge and develop an indigenous Martinican culture, and thus move away from the cultural stranglehold of France over Martinique, had left him increasingly politically isolated. Following a presumed suicide attempt, the governor was hospitalised at the Hôpital Colonial (Colonial Hospital) in Martinique. He died there on 31 July 1944 aged just 38, his death recorded as suicide by defenestration. In a radio interview given in Martinique in 1985, Zobel reflected on Ponton's suicide, commenting 'jusqu'à present, personne n'a jamais pu entendre dire pour quelle raison exacte' (even to this day, no one has been able to find out the exact reason).[44] Several decades later, then, the death of the visionary young governor still caused a deep sense of confusion in Zobel. Ponton's untimely death evidently came as a surprise to his close colleagues. Aimé Césaire was on his study tour of Haiti at the time of Ponton's death, and wrote a sincere and moving elegy which was printed as the first article in the twelfth issue of *Tropiques* in January 1945.[45]

Ponton's replacement did not share his predecessor's zeal for Martinican culture. Zobel realised that his position as press attaché was no longer required, and returned to his former post at the Lycée Schœlcher. Anxious to remain involved in the development of Martinican culture, Zobel took courses at the newly created École des Arts appliqués (School of Applied Arts) in Martinique, where he also taught French classes. In addition, he continued to write for Ponton's review *Martinique*, publication of which continued after the young governor's death. Zobel contributed short stories, the opening pages of *Diab'-là*, and a remarkable essay, 'Considérations sur l'art local' ('Considerations on Local Art'), which I analyse in Chapter Three.

42 *Martinique: revue trimestrielle*, 1 (March 1944). Fort-de-France: Service général d'information des Antilles françaises. Consulted in Paris at the Bibliothèque Mazarine: ANT 4°164.
43 Copies inspected at Musée du Quai Branly, Paris: Magasins P1660, PERIODIQUE, *Martinique*, 2 (1944)–5 (1946).
44 'Zobel: sa vie, son œuvre', p. 25.
45 Aimé Césaire, 'Georges-Louis PONTON, Gouverneur de la Martinique', *Tropiques 1941–1945: collection complète* (Paris: Jean-Michel Place, 1978), pp. 153–56.

The end of the war in 1945 brought new cultural opportunities and that same year, the first edition of *Diab'-là* finally appeared, three years after it had been banned under Admiral Robert's administration. *Diab'-là* was originally published by the Imprimerie officielle de Fort-de-France.[46] The place of publication suggests that Zobel was now more established, and had developed a network of contacts; it seems highly likely that this was a legacy of his time working with Ponton. A second novel with the same press, *Les Jours immobiles*, followed quickly after in 1946.[47] Also in 1946, the small Fort-de-France-based printing house Albert Bezaudin (named after its owner) published *Laghia de la mort* (untranslated: *Laghia of Death* would capture the original title's opacity, as a metropolitan reader will be unaware of the Creole term laghia, which refers to a dance), a collection of short stories, some of which Zobel had previously published in the journals *Le Sportif* and *Martinique*.[48]

In 1946, Zobel applied for a *congé administratif*, a leave entitlement for Antillean civil servants, which was granted. He was now allowed to leave Martinique for the first time, and he headed to Paris. His decision to emigrate resulted from a combination of ambition, and personal and professional dissatisfaction with Martinique, as he explained in an interview:

> je suis arrivé en France après quelques mois de réelles difficultés presque insurmontables [...] j'avais presque tout de suite juré de ne plus (jamais) remettre les pieds dans une colonie.[49]

---

46 Joseph Zobel, *Diab'-là* (Fort-de-France: Imprimerie officielle de Fort-de-France, 1945). Thus far, it has proved impossible to source a copy of this original edition. Archival documents (*Le Sportif* and *Les Cahiers de la libération*) held in Le Fonds Zobel include references to the 1945 edition [archival reference: DD:JZ.B.246]. The novel circulated beyond Martinique, and *The French Review*, based in America, received a copy for review. *Diab'-là*'s publication history is discussed at length in Chapter Two. Shortly before this book went to press, a copy of the original 1945 edition was located in Dakar, Senegal. See Charles W. Scheel, 'Introduction au dossier "Zobel" retrouvé dans la bibliothèque universitaire de l'UCAD à Dakar', *Continents manuscrits* 8 (2017), published 15 March 2017. See: http://coma.revues.org/857 (accessed 6 August 2017).
47 Joseph Zobel, *Les Jours immobiles* (Fort-de-France: Imprimerie officielle de Fort-de-France, 1946).
48 Joseph Zobel, *Laghia de la mort* (Fort-de-France: Bezaudin, 1946).
49 Zobel provided these comments in an interview with the Martinican academic Véronique Tarrieu. A copy of Tarrieu's handwritten notes is held in Le Fonds

I arrived in France after several months of real difficulties which had been almost impossible to overcome [...] almost immediately, I had sworn that I would never (ever) set foot in a colony again.

It is likely that some of the difficulties to which Zobel alludes here include the constant racial discrimination he experienced as a 'petit-nègre', the (related) refusal of his scholarship to study in Paris, and the loss of his position as press attaché after Ponton's death. The young man already had two novels and one short story collection to his name, but due to their place and manner of publication, he knew they were unlikely to circulate far beyond the island. Paris appeared to be the only place to develop his literary career. Zobel quickly secured a Parisian publisher for *Diab'-là*, and began to study at the Institut d'ethnologie and the Sorbonne.

In 1943, Zobel had married Pauline Ennare Cécina (also known as Enny or Paula) in Martinique, and in 1947 she and their three young children, Roland (b. 1944), Francis (b. 1945), and Jenny (b. 1947), joined him in France. Here, he wrote and published what was to become his best-known novel, *La Rue Cases-Nègres* in 1950. A sequel, *La Fête à Paris*, followed shortly after in 1953.[50] With the publication of these novels, in addition to a highly successful second edition of *Diab'-là* which had appeared in Paris in 1947,[51] Zobel became an author of some repute. His works were reviewed in both Martinican and international publications, and he was invited to international conferences and poetry readings, travelling to countries including Switzerland and Italy. He also took part in a number of radio broadcasts. This period of unprecedented success enabled Zobel to buy a modest country house in 1954, which became the family's holiday home, in Générargues, a small village in the Gard, not far from Anduze in the Cévennes mountains.

Unlike many of his peers, it appears that Zobel did not attend the First International Congress of Negro Writers and Artists held in 1956

Zobel, dated 1995 and marked for publication in the review *Indigo* [DD: JZ. B]. Tarrieu MS, 1995, p. 4. The interview was published, and I use the published page numbers throughout this study. Véronique Tarrieu, '"Je suis comme eux et ils sont comme moi": un entretien avec Joseph Zobel, Fonds Masson, 14 March 1995', *INDIGO: North American and Caribbean Studies Newsletter of the Université des Antilles-Guyane*, 22–23 (1999), p. 30. I would like to record my thanks to Véronique Robbaz (née Tarrieu) for her generosity in responding to my questions about this interview and for providing further details about *Indigo* (personal correspondence, November 2016).

50 Joseph Zobel, *La Fête à Paris* (Paris: La Table ronde, 1953).
51 Joseph Zobel, *Diab'-là* (Paris: Nouvelles Éditions Latines, 1947).

in Paris: the Martinican delegates whose names have been preserved are Césaire, Fanon, Glissant, and Louis-Thomas Achille, himself the son of Zobel's former English teacher, and then employer at the Lycée Schœlcher, Louis Achille. By then, Zobel was already living in Paris, where, after a promising start, he had not enjoyed the literary success for which he had hoped. Nor did Zobel attend the second and final congress, held in Rome in 1958; his absence here is quite unsurprising, however, as he and his young family had moved to live in Senegal in 1957, a move deeply influenced by his Négritude-inspired desire to reconnect with a lost African ancestry.

Zobel moved to Senegal to work as head teacher of a new high school in Ziguinchor. He had been recruited in Paris by Léopold Sédar Senghor, with whom he was personally acquainted. On arrival, however, Zobel found the school was still under construction. A year later, he transferred to Dakar, and subsequently left teaching to pursue a career in radio broadcasting. Zobel's cultural programmes were transmitted across Francophone West Africa. He also played an important role in the organisation of the Festival mondial des arts nègres (World Festival of Negro Arts) held in Senegal in 1966, an event of global significance which saw delegations from around the world converge in Dakar to debate black identity and Négritude. Zobel actively sought to increase the reach of the festival, and during the months preceding it he devised and presented the weekly radio broadcast 'Premier festival' ('First Festival') for Senegalese radio, which provided the public with an insight into the planned events.[52] In this period he had also contributed short stories to the first Francophone Senegalese magazine for African women, *Awa!*, which had a popular readership, and had made an abortive attempt to publish a novel, *Le Journal de Samba Boy* (*The Diary of Samba Boy*).[53] He had also published a collection of short stories, *Le*

---

52 Matt Schaffer, 'Interview with Joseph Zobel, 23 June 1969', (unpublished) original cassette recording (digitized) and transcript held at MARBL, the Woodruff Library, Emory University, Atlanta, p. 11. Audio cassette reference: ID: q4gtr (side A); ID: q4gvw (side B). MSS 755 Matt Schaffer Collection Box 2, Folder 4.

53 Following their collaborative publication of *Les Damnés de la terre*, Présence Africaine and Éditions Maspero founded a joint collection, 'Écrivains noirs du monde', to coordinate their publishing and distribution. Only two texts appeared with the collection, by Paul Niger and Léonard Sainville. The back covers of both books list a forthcoming title as 'Joseph Zobel, *Le Journal de Samba Boy* (roman)', but this novel was never published. See Ruth Bush, *Publishing Africa in*

Soleil partagé (*The Divided Sun*) in 1964, and a collection of poems, *Incantation pour un retour au pays natal* (*Incantation for a Return to My Native Land*) in 1965,[54] a title with an unmistakable nod to Césaire, which Zobel also released as a disc, known both by the same title as the printed collection and by the alternative title *Joseph Zobel dit trois poèmes de Joseph Zobel* (*Joseph Zobel Reads Three Poems by Joseph Zobel*).[55] The most significant literary event during this period, however, was the new edition of *La Rue Cases-Nègres*. Zobel's novel had slipped into obscurity until Présence Africaine obtained the rights and brought out a new edition in 1974; it has not been out of print since (I discuss the complex publication history of this novel at length in Chapter Four).[56]

On Zobel's retirement in 1976, the family returned to the south of France, electing to make the holiday home in Générargues their principal residence. Over a series of years, they had renovated the house, named 'Moun Oustaou', meaning 'my house' in the Provençal dialect. The fact that 'moun' is the Creole word for people compounded Zobel's sense of belonging to this area of southern France, where he felt he had rediscovered the mountainous landscapes and sun-drenched colours of his childhood in rural inland Martinique. In Générargues, he rewrote *Les Jours immobiles* and *Laghia de la mort*, which he republished with Présence Africaine as *Les Mains pleines d'oiseaux*[57] and *Laghia de la mort* respectively.[58] These were followed in 1979 by a rewritten version of *La Fête à Paris* entitled *Quand la neige aura fondu*.[59]

In 1982, Zobel published a new short story collection, *Et si la mer n'était pas bleue ...* (literal translation: *And what if the sea weren't blue ...*), with lavish illustrations by S. Mondésir. *Mas Badara* (*Badara House*), Zobel's last collection of short stories with Présence Africaine,

---

French: Literary Institutions and Decolonization 1945–1967 (Liverpool: Liverpool University Press, 2016), p. 79. I would like to record my thanks to Ruth Bush for discussing this matter, and Zobel's contributions to *Awa!*, with me.

54 Joseph Zobel, *Incantation pour un retour au pays natal* (Anduze: Imprimerie de Languedoc, 1965).

55 Joseph Zobel, *Incantation pour un retour au pays natal/Joseph Zobel dit trois poèmes de Joseph Zobel* (Voxigrave VX6845, no year). Bibliothèque nationale de France: FRBNF38067745, stamped 1966.

56 Joseph Zobel, *La Rue Cases-Nègres* (Paris/Dakar: Présence Africaine, 1974).

57 Joseph Zobel, *Les Mains pleines d'oiseaux* (Paris/Dakar: Présence Africaine, 1978).

58 Joseph Zobel, *Laghia de la mort* (Paris/Dakar: Présence Africaine, 1978).

59 Joseph Zobel, *Quand la neige aura fondu* (Paris: Éditions caribéennes, 1979).

appeared in 1983. In the same year, Euzhan Palcy's film adaptation *Rue Cases-Nègres* was released, and went on to win over 17 international awards, including a Silver Lion at the Venice Film Festival and the French César for best first feature. The film attracted new international attention to Zobel's literary career, and the author himself played a cameo role as a priest. In 1984, Zobel self-published the poetry collection *Poèmes de moi-même* (*Poems by Myself*), with the Martinican publishing house Désormeaux.[60]

After his return from Africa, Zobel became increasingly fascinated by Japanese and Chinese culture, particularly art and ceramics, and these influences are strongly felt in his later work, which comprises collections of poetry, visual art, and journal entries. In 1994, Zobel published *D'Amour et de silence* (*Of Love and Silence*) with Éditions Prosveta, again at his own expense.[61] This beautiful, original book of art, poetry, and journal entries displays his pronounced fascination with Japanese and Chinese culture.

In 2002, Zobel's last two publications appeared with the Caribbean-based publishing house Ibis Rouge: *Gertal et autres Nouvelles – Suivi de Journal 1946–2002* and *Le Soleil m'a dit. Œuvre poétique*.[62] These works have yet to be translated, and their titles could be rendered as *Gertal and Other Stories – Followed by Diary 1946–2002* and *The Sun Told Me: Collected Poetry*. These heterogeneous collections of short stories, selected diary entries, and poetry gather together the author's earlier material (some of which was now out of print), interspersed with new writings. That same year, Zobel was awarded the Grand Prix du Livre Insulaire for his collected works. Zobel passed away on 17 June 2006 in Alès, aged 91.

In 2015, in celebration of the centenary of his birth, two further publications appeared. The first, Roland Monpierre's graphic novel adaptation of *Diab'-là*, was launched at the Paris Salon du Livre.[63] The second, *Joseph Zobel: écrits inédits* (*Joseph Zobel: Unpublished Writing*), is a posthumous collection of three unpublished short texts which provide significant insights into the author's transnational career. The collection

60 Joseph Zobel, *Poèmes de moi-même* (Fort-de-France: Désormeaux, 1984).
61 Joseph Zobel, *D'Amour et de silence* (Fréjus: Éditions Prosveta, 1994).
62 Joseph Zobel, *Gertal et autres Nouvelles – Suivi de Journal 1946–2002* (Guyane: Ibis Rouge, 2002); *Le Soleil m'a dit. Œuvre poétique* (Guyane: Ibis Rouge, 2002).
63 Roland Monpierre, *Diab'-là, d'après le roman de Joseph Zobel* (Paris: Nouvelles Editions Latines, 2015).

was edited by Lyne-Rose Beuze and Gabrielle Chomereau-Lamotte and funded by the Région Martinique (Martinique Regional Government).[64] Most recently, in 2016, the author's granddaughter Charlotte Zobel published the bilingual book *Joseph Zobel Photographies (Joseph Zobel Photographs)*.[65] This collection of Zobel's own photographs interspersed with short entries from his personal diaries in French and in English translation is an important work which sheds new light on both Zobel's individual experiences and their significance for understanding the experiences of post-war migrants from the Caribbean to France more broadly.

* * *

The opening chapter of this book, 'Zobel, Négritude, and the Novel' discusses the relationship between Zobel's novels and the Négritude movement. By providing the first detailed contextualisation of the conditions in which he began to write novels, it also addresses the impact of the Negro Renaissance for Zobel, and demonstrates how his work engages – through conceptual and formal resonances – with the two movements. The second chapter, 'Earth, Ecocriticism, and Economics: *Diab'-là*', examines Zobel's first novel. The analysis focuses on the incendiary, revolutionary potential of this literary debut, situating it in its original context in the era of Négritude, colonialism, and Vichy occupation. This chapter also argues that *Diab'-là*'s radical content arises from the novel's profound appreciation of nature, and situates the text within the canon of the recently emerging field of postcolonial ecocriticism. In Chapter Three, 'Nothing Happens, Twice: *Les Jours immobiles* becomes *Les Mains pleines d'oiseaux*', I establish that Zobel's second novel continues the project he commenced with *Diab'-là* in as much as it centres on another Négritude-inspired depiction of a small local community in the process of becoming increasingly self-reliant. In addition, it extends the environmental themes which had been foregrounded in *Diab'-là*. In his retirement, Zobel rewrote the

---

64 Lyne-Rose Beuze and Gabrielle Chomereau-Lamotte (eds), *Joseph Zobel: écrits inédits* (Fort-de-France: Région Martinique Collection connaissance du patrimoine, 2015).
65 Charlotte Zobel, *Joseph Zobel photographies* (Graulhet: Charlotte Zobel/ Région Martinique/Escourbiac, 2016).

novel, and examination of the original reveals surprising insights into how Zobel's rewriting practices came to bear on the construction of his female characters.

The remaining chapters then move on to consider the second group of Zobel's novels. Chapter Four, 'Rereading *La Rue Cases-Nègres*', demonstrates that, read against the broader development of his career, this text is representative not of continuity, but of dissonance and rupture. Going beyond the existing analyses of the novel, this chapter argues that *La Rue Cases-Nègres* represents a discernible shift in Zobel's use of social realism and, by extension, of Négritude. Finally, moving away from works set uniquely in a Caribbean location, Chapter Five, 'Cultural Capital in the French Capital: From *La Fete à Paris* to *Quand la neige aura fondu*', discusses the original and rewritten versions of Zobel's novel of migration to metropolitan France, with particular reference to the theory of cultural capital as developed by Pierre Bourdieu.

My conclusion focuses on the afterlives and legacies of Zobel's novels across the world, and demonstrates that his reputation is subject to constant processes of redefinition. The multiple ways in which Zobel is figured is, I argue, an indication of the varied transnational and transdisciplinary contributions to literature, spoken word traditions, and the visual and plastic arts made by this overlooked, and quite remarkable, novelist.

CHAPTER ONE

Zobel, Négritude, and the Novel

Studies of Négritude have tended to focus on the founding triumvirate of Césaire-Damas-Senghor, thus creating the impression that during the most active years of the Négritude period, the novel was entirely sidelined by poetry and political and cultural essays.[1] Within that paradigm, Léon-Gontran Damas himself has often been neglected. Recent scholarship has begun to address the problems and blind spots inherent to this approach, and has cast new light on the wide range of thinkers, writers, and activists who played a part in both Négritude's genesis and its subsequent development. The work of Damas, Suzanne Césaire, Paulette Nardal, Andrée Nardal, and Jane Nardal, among others has been explored and reconsidered in recent scholarship by critics such as T. Denean Sharpley-Whiting, Brent Hayes Edwards, Shireen K. Lewis, Jennifer Boittin, Bart Miller, Kathleen Gyssels, Jean Khalfa, Daniel Maximin, and Anny Dominique Curtius.[2] It becomes evident, as a corollary of this rethinking of Négritude, that Zobel's novels also need to undergo the same process of rediscovery and reframing, and can in fact be understood as a series of experimental attempts to expand the movement's scope. The influence of Négritude, combined with Zobel's own intense experiences and observations of the complexity of race in Martinique, led him to pioneer a new kind of literature in the French Caribbean. Such a re-examination of Zobel's work leads to

1   Indeed, the novels which are most frequently connected with Négritude, such as Camara Laye's *L'enfant noir* (1953), Ferdinand Oyono's *Une Vie de Boy* (1956), and Cheikh Hamidou Kane's *L'Aventure ambiguë* (1961), were all written by African authors, and appeared significantly later than Zobel's novels. What I wish to draw attention to here is Zobel's unusual, and possibly unique, position as a writer influenced by Négritude whose career as a novelist began in the 1940s and was contemporaneous with the Négritude movement's heyday.
2   All works referenced in the previous chapter.

insights which challenge and alter the current understanding of French Caribbean literature during the Négritude period, in a development which is both timely and urgent.

It is not my intention in this study to argue for the straightforward classification of Zobel's novels as simply 'belonging' to Négritude. Rather, the aim is to contextualise and situate the development of Zobel's literature, and particularly his prose fiction, in the light of the contemporary movement of Négritude, which was still in its heyday in the ten years or so when Zobel wrote his four original novels. These novels irrefutably dialogue with and develop the Négritude project through prose fiction, a development which is discernible in the author's work from the early 1940s, through both direct and indirect references which I trace and analyse in this study. In the wider Francophone Caribbean, an introspective prose fiction form was already established in Haiti, largely thanks to the influence of movements such as Haitian Indigénisme and in works such as Jean Price-Mars's 1928 essay collection *Ainsi parla l'oncle. Essais d'ethnographie*.[3] Indigénisme shared Négritude's goal of depicting and promoting the specificities of black Caribbean culture and experience yet, unlike Négritude, it was not a specific riposte to French colonialism.

Without the advances of Négritude in the French Caribbean, it would have been impossible for Zobel to write the kind of literature he did. His novels present Martinique and Martinicans through a lens which is determinedly Caribbean, rather than French, in order to confront the legacy of the slave past and French colonialism in uncompromising detail. Moreover, his prose fiction is steeped in celebrations of the black body, black culture and social customs. Inspired in particular by the novelists of the Negro Renaissance (a movement now referred to as the Harlem Renaissance in a semantic shift which I discuss in the Introduction to this study), such as Richard Wright and Claude McKay, Zobel expands the scope of Négritude in order to depict the lived experiences of colonialism, race, and identity among the most humble strata of Martinican society.[4] As such, his work provides an essential and

---

3 Jean Price-Mars, *Ainsi parla l'oncle. Essais d'ethnographie* (New York: Parapsychology Foundation Inc., 1928).

4 While there are undoubtedly parallels between Zobel's prose fiction and contemporary novels appearing in Haiti, the archival evidence examined in the preparation of this study demonstrates that the North American literature of the Negro Renaissance exerted a greater influence on the author than Haitian

unexplored connection between the poetry and essays of Francophone Négritude and the Anglophone novelists, poets, and essayists of the African-American Negro Renaissance movement. As the Introduction to this study explains, in my historically sensitive reading I tend to prefer the original term 'Negro Renaissance', which was used when Zobel was active as a novelist, rather than the anachronism 'Harlem Renaissance', a term which only became widely used in the 1960s.

To understand the Négritude movement, it is essential to grasp how its authors sought to bring about a defiant reappropriation of the deeply controversial term *nègre*. It is a complex word to translate into English, and its particular nuances in the French Caribbean are integral to an understanding of the relationship between Zobel's novels and Négritude. In French, *nègre* may be employed as a noun or an adjective; neither usage is acceptable today, unmistakably freighted as they are with the weight of four centuries of physical and psychological racial violence. It is, however, essential to remain aware of, and sensitive to, the different historical developments between the vocabulary of race in English and French, as apparently similar terms are embedded in comparable yet also very different geographical and cultural contexts.

In the early 1900s, when used as an adjective, *nègre* underwent something of a transition and became part of an avant-garde cosmopolitan cultural vocabulary. It was used to denote *l'art nègre* and *la musique nègre*, as demonstrated by the name of the popular Parisian dancehall 'Le Bal nègre', which was attended by both black people and white people in Paris (the venue features in Zobel's *Quand la neige aura fondu*, as discussed in Chapter Five). This adjectival, descriptive use of *nègre* is most frequently translated into English as 'negro', a term that was also gaining a different cultural purchase, as exemplified by praise for 'Negro Spirituals'. However, the shift in the adjectival use of *nègre* and 'negro' was not a straightforward reappropriation of the term by black people themselves. It certainly helped to pave the way for a new, positive rethinking of blackness and identity, as demonstrated by journal titles launched between 1927 and 1932, which included *La Race nègre* (*The Negro Race*), *La Revue du monde noir* (*Review of the Black World*), *Légitime Défense* (*Self-Defence*), and *Le Cri des nègres* (*The Negro Cry*). While the adjective *nègre* was beginning to be reappropriated in new discourses on identity for political purposes

---

literature: for example, Zobel's interviews are peppered with references to North American authors.

by black people themselves, it was also being used to develop and perpetuate white stereotypes. To use *nègre* as an adjective, even in an apparently celebratory manner, still risked suggesting a stance of white 'negrophilia' of the kind mocked by Césaire in *Cahier d'un retour au pays natal* when he ironically observes: 'Ou bien tout simplement comme on nous aime! / Obscènes gaiement, très doudous de jazz sur leur excès d'ennui' (Or else they simply love us so much! Gaily obscene, doudou-crazy over jazz in their extreme boredom) (pp. 102–03).[5]

In contrast to the slippage inherent to the adjective, as a noun, *nègre* has unmistakably pejorative connotations. It can be translated into contemporary English by the anachronistic noun 'negro' or by the explicitly pejorative racial slur 'nigger'. In both English and French, these terms' origins lie in the vocabulary of slavery and the slave trade, and hold explicit connections to systematic oppression and brutality. In both languages, it is the context in which the term is used that ultimately determines its nuances, but these words are always loaded, and none are acceptable in twenty-first-century discourse. *Le nègre* may also be rendered as 'the black', a choice made by some translators. This is often a somewhat sanitising gesture, however, as it obfuscates the term's historical connotations. The more neutral term *le noir* does exist (colloquially, the use of *le black*, which has its own complex set of nuances, has also crept into the French language). In my critical analysis, I choose to refer to human beings as people rather than reducing them to a colour; as such, where skin colour is significant, I employ the terms 'black people' and 'white people'.

This discussion of racial terminology lies at the heart of any understanding of Négritude. The writers of Négritude set out to challenge the wide set of existing connotations of the term *nègre*, and to irrevocably alter them. Their bold reappropriation of the noun *nègre* and the decision to combine it with the noun *attitude* was an unapologetic declaration, and celebration, of blackness. Moreover, the Caribbean Négritude of Césaire and Damas explicitly engaged with that part of black Caribbean identity which was inherently associated with the specific connotations of *nègre* throughout the New World: slavery. Aware that their work had valence across a multilingual geographic expanse stretching across the nations of South America to the United

---

5 Aimé Césaire, *Cahier d'un retour au pays natal/Notebook of a Return to my Native Land*, trans. Mireille Rosello with Annie Pritchard (Newcastle upon Tyne: Bloodaxe, 1995 [1939]); my modified translation.

States, they addressed head-on the trauma of slavery, deliberately turning to that aspect of New World black identity which in polite society was most often disavowed. In a daring, triumphant affirmation of race and self, they reclaimed and celebrated the term *nègre*.

Nonetheless, critics generally agree that, for all the advances in thinking about race and identity it undoubtedly helped to catalyse, Négritude remained an elite rather than a popular movement. Its major figures were brought up under the *mission civilisatrice* (civilising mission) in French colonies, and their ideological terrain was the intersection of race and colonialism. The founding authors of Négritude were aware that, whether their origins lay in Africa, the South American continent, or on a small Caribbean island, their own particular struggles to establish a political identity involved communicating with the elite of metropolitan France. They had received the requisite education, and they belonged to an established tradition of elite black scholars in Paris for whom, as Philippe Dewitte has noted in his study of black intellectuals in France in the interwar years, 'la réflexion atteint [...] des cimes philosophiques capables de percer la carapace "ethnocentrique" des Français' (critical reflection reaches [...] philosophical peaks capable of piercing the 'ethnocentric' shell of the French).[6] The authors of Négritude were equipped to do battle with the French intelligentsia on their own terms, and they drew on recent European philosophy;[7] they also benefited from propitious conditions, as Parisian Négritude followed in the wake of other important Parisian black consciousness movements and publications of the 1920s and 1930s.

In his recent study of the theme of emigration in Caribbean literature, Malachi McIntosh describes Négritude as an 'emigrant elite-focused movement'.[8] The three men most closely associated with Négritude used their mastery of French culture as a lever, so that they could express a long-denied black civilisation which existed in the French

---

6 Philippe Dewitte quoted in Fonkoua, p. 50.

7 Recent research into Négritude has emphasised its development in relation to European philosophy, providing new insight into the influence of the work of Henri Bergson. See, for example, Donna V. Jones, *The Racial Discourses of Life Philosophy: Négritude, Vitalism and Modernity* (New York: Columbia University Press, 2010) and Souleymane Bachir Diagne, *African Art as Philosophy. Senghor, Bergson and the Idea of Negritude* (Chicago, IL: University of Chicago Press, 2011).

8 Malachi McIntosh, *Emigration and Caribbean Literature* (New York: Palgrave Macmillan, 2015), p. 112.

colonies. Yet they did so through the language of colonial domination, in publications (often elite student publications) originating in Paris. In his essay on Négritude, 'Orphée noir' ('Black Orpheus'), Sartre identified this linguistic feature as a marker of the success (or severity) of the alienating psychological mechanisms of the French *mission civilisatrice*. Here, comparison with the Negro Renaissance proves illuminating. The American movement, through novels such as Claude McKay's *Banjo* (1929) and Richard Wright's *Native Son* (1940) and *Black Boy* (1945), had pioneered a gritty and colloquial prose style to show how, through centuries of systematic oppression, black identity in the United States had become associated with abject poverty, violence, and fear. In contrast, Francophone Négritude was expressed in a formal French register and an abstract, surrealist style which owed a great debt to European surrealism. Négritude writing is void of the shocking, individual accounts of the lives of the poorest, most disempowered members of society who were at the core of the Negro Renaissance. The extent to which the rhetoric of Négritude was aimed at readers from the authors' places of origin is questionable. Césaire and Senghor aspired to give – and subsequently gave – speeches in the French Assemblée Nationale, and in the parliaments of newly decolonised countries and islands where they, and many of the authors in their wider networks, went on to obtain ministerial roles. This contrasted with the writers of the Negro Renaissance, whose immediate struggle in the United States was not one of decolonisation, but of racial equality and social opportunity, concerns that would later be articulated by Martin Luther King and his Civil Rights movement, then the Black Power and Black Panther movements, and in the present-day Black Lives Matter movement.

Négritude was an elite discourse nurtured in Paris, and a movement which resulted in brilliant yet largely abstract, theoretical poetry and essays. As such, its ability to reach the very people who were repeatedly referred to by the noun *nègre* was highly questionable. It is my contention in this study that Zobel's literary interventions through his novels are a direct response to this situation as he seeks to establish new pathways for communication between an elite discourse and a mass readership. When he decided to write a Martinican novel that would elevate *les nègres* to heroic roles through giving lived proof of their Négritude, that novel, *Diab'-là*, was the first of its kind and a radical new departure for French Caribbean literature.

The same defiance is at work when he decides to call a later novel *La Rue Cases-Nègres*. In a Martinican Creole inflection of French, both *cases* and *nègres* can function as nouns; literally, the title refers to the road with shacks for negroes – a space sometimes referred to in English-language material as 'the negro village'.[9] Such spaces existed on every plantation across the island, but the shacks had never before been the locus of a Martinican novel; indeed, internationally, this must be one of the first nuanced accounts of these spaces in World Literature. Zobel's novels, more than any other works of Négritude literature, signal a refusal to accept – any longer – the disavowal within Martinican society of the humanity of that group of people who were all too often reduced to the parameters of the racial slur *nègres*. Simply stated, Zobel put the *nègre* into Négritude.

The translation of these racial terms remains a vexed question. In this study, *nègre* has been translated, depending on its context, as 'Negro' or 'nigger'; where both English terms are possible, however, I have tended towards the use of 'Negro', itself a highly anachronistic term, but the one which most closely resonates with the period when Zobel was writing. When *nègre* is unequivocally intended as an insult, I have respected this in the wording of the translation. To do so is to defer to the time period in which Zobel wrote; nonetheless, the specific violence of both terms can still appear unacceptably offensive to some modern readers. Yet to translate *nègre* as 'black' would obfuscate the term's specific historicity. This translation dilemma resonates with contemporary politics. In May 2016, then US President Barak Obama signed the bill H.R. 4238, which eliminated the nouns 'Negro' and 'Oriental' from federal laws[10] – a bill which cast attention onto the specific historicity of these terms and reiterated the need to avoid such language in all future documentation. It is indeed a sense of time or rather, of the historical epoch, which must be observed in order to determine how the term is translated. For Zobel, who was writing in the 1940s and 1950s in direct dialogue with Négritude and the Negro Renaissance, his deliberate use of the word *nègre* was a historically situated reappropriation of a racist term, and a direct challenge to colonial racist discourse. To translate the word *nègre* in his novels by the term 'black' is problematically anachronistic, as it occludes the context of the racial struggles in which he and his fellow

---

9   See for example Thomas Cooper, *Facts Illustrative of the Condition of the Negro Slaves in Jamaica: with notes and an appendix* (London: J. Hatchard & Son, 1824 [1823]), p. 5.

10 See: https://www.congress.gov/bill/114th-congress/house-bill/4238/text (accessed 4 July 2016).

authors were engaged. Indeed, the fact that half a century later such language is regarded as unacceptable is a victory which must be ascribed to the work of activists including authors such as Zobel.

More than any other author writing at the time, Zobel reminds his readers that in 1930s and 1940s Martinique, the term *nègre* does not refer to a homogeneous mass of people; within the broader group, Zobel identified with the poorest and darkest members, who were known as *petits-nègres*. This term, with its prefix *petit*, infers a dark skin tone, poverty, lowliness, and insignificance: there is no doubt that to employ it is to evoke the colonial past and slavery. In the French Caribbean context, it refers to the group among whom the enduring effects of the economic and cultural structures of slavery were still most clearly visible. Interestingly, however, it is in this group that the nouns *nègre* and *négresse* are used as synonyms for man and woman to refer to members of the same community without stigma; this is demonstrated when Zobel's *petit-nègre* characters address and describe one another.

In the French language more broadly, through the legacy of French colonial discourse, the concept of *parler petit-nègre*, to signify broken or pidgin French, has come to demonstrate the link between language, poverty, lack of education, and pejorative connotations. To label someone's speaking patterns as *parler petit-nègre* immediately infantilises the speaker, magnifying their supposed inferiority and inability to speak 'correct' French. This racist language passes an implicit judgement on ability and disassociates non-white speakers from a specific white western concept of intelligence (in this case, the mastery of the French language). In fact, the broken, grammatically incorrect manner of using language which *parler petit-nègre* denotes is really a signifier of a lack of educational opportunity and economic disadvantage. All that is actually demonstrated is that the speaker has never formally learned French, as Fanon argues in *Peau noire, masques blancs* (*Black Skin, White Masks*). Fanon points out that whenever he meets a foreigner with an imperfect command of French, he does not automatically assume that the speaker is intellectually inferior. Instead, he recognises that this person is using a language in which they are not fully proficient, and assumes that there is another language in which the speaker is fluent.[11] He castigates those French people who automatically decide to *parler petit-nègre* to any black people they meet because they assume black people (whose use of

---

11 Frantz Fanon, *Peau noire, masques blancs* (Paris: Seuil, 1952), pp. 24–27.

French may indeed be imperfect) are incapable of sophisticated speech or thought in any language.

In choosing to illustrate the lives of *petits-nègres*, in their speech and activities, in their aspirations and dreams, Zobel confronts his readers with the uncomfortable truth that decades after abolition, there were still *rues cases-nègres* across Martinique where material conditions had evolved very little since slavery. He also dares to point out that it was here, in the world of these *petits-nègres*, far removed from the French *mission civilisatrice* which dominated urban settings, that another kind of Martinican culture existed. It was here, in this marginalised and oppressed group, that could be found a subculture in which African and Amerindian traditions were visible and unabashedly practised and celebrated by men and women who were comfortable with their identity as *nègres* and *négresses*. Decades before the work of the group of authors known as *les créolistes*, Zobel was striving to depict the dignity and integrity of the new culture that had been forged in the crucible of New World slavery, that same culture which since the 1990s has been celebrated as 'Creole'.

Despite the original ideology that is evidently at work in his novels, Zobel always disavowed any identity as a theorist, and he rejected invitations by interviewers to situate his work as part of Négritude. He was repeatedly asked for his opinion about predominant theoretical currents, and so questions on Négritude, Antillanité, and Créolité arise frequently in his interviews with academics and the popular press. Zobel consistently distanced himself from any specific movement, and expressed distaste for each of these labels (and others besides, such as 'Francophone'). The most important example of Zobel refusing to situate himself within any theoretical current occurs in an interview conducted by the Martinican academic Raymond Relouzat around 1970, and is reproduced by Relouzat at the end of a published set of notes for a lecture course on *La Rue Cases-Nègres* which he delivered at the Université des Antilles-Guyane.[12] Relouzat published the document privately with his own press, which had the motto 'Librairie Relouzat. Au

---

12 Raymond Relouzat, *Joseph Zobel: La Rue Cases-Nègres* (Fort-de-France: Librairie Relouzat, n.d.), p. 32. This rare document is a polycopy of Relouzat's lectures on *La Rue Cases-Nègres*. I have located and inspected two copies: one is part of the Michel Fabre collection at the Stuart A. Rose Library, Emory University, Atlanta, Georgia [Barcode: 010002394902]; the other is at the Bibliothèque Schœlcher in Martinique [843.009-2ZOB]. Although no date is given, there is a reference to the course running in 1969 on p. 19, and the Martinican

Service de Tous et de Chacun' (Relouzat Books. Serving Each and Every Person); a motto which chimed with the popular democratic ambitions of Zobel's own literature. This furnishes an interesting example of how the author's reputation has often survived thanks to the personal intervention of admiring individuals. At the time of his interview with Relouzat, Zobel had been living in Africa for over a decade; his books were not widely available in Martinique, metropolitan France, or Senegal, and he had slipped from public consciousness in Martinique. It is doubtful whether Relouzat's own students in Martinique would have even been able to acquire their own copies of *La Rue Cases-Nègres*, a novel which, at the time he was working, had had only two print runs, in 1950 and 1955 (the unusual publication history of this title is explored at length in Chapter Four of this study).

The limits of technology around the late 1960s and early 1970s make it likely that Relouzat's interview was a short telephone conversation, or a posted list of questions and answers, or at most a snatched conversation when Zobel was visiting Martinique. It is a brief and rather forced exchange which lacks the spontaneity of a lengthy oral discussion. Nonetheless, it is an extremely valuable document for understanding Zobel's development as a writer. Relouzat asks Zobel: 'Avez-vous le sentiment d'être d'une façon quelconque, à quelque degré que ce soit, le romancier de la "négritude" ou encore de "l'antillanité"?' (Do you feel that in some manner, to some extent, you are the novelist of 'négritude' or 'antilleanness'?). Another author might have seized such an opportunity to situate their work within the wider – and culturally acclaimed – movements of Négritude or Antillanité, but Zobel evidently did not feel compelled to align himself with theoretical movements. Instead, his response cautions against judging creativity according to specific contemporary theories:

> Non. Je suis un artiste créateur. Je n'ai pas le sentiment que ma négritude est un uniforme ou une fonction auxquels je dois sacrifier mon individualité, sachant fort bien du reste que, quelque subjective que puisse être toute démarche vers la beauté, je ne risque point d'y perdre mon âme de Nègre ou d'Antillais. (Relouzat, p. 32)
>
> No. I am a creative artist. I do not feel that my Négritude is a uniform or a function to which I must sacrifice my individuality, and in any case

---

copy is stamped 21 June 1972 (p. 3). The lectures, and interview with Zobel, must therefore date from between 1969 and 1972.

> I know full well that however subjective any attempt to create beauty might be, I am never at risk of losing my Negro or Antillean soul.

This important quotation, which might appear to be an outright rejection of Négritude, actually draws attention to Zobel's own ideology and the complex role of Négritude within it. The author's instinctive negation of any theoretical identification is immediately followed by his implicit acknowledgement that he has espoused Négritude in his own way, demonstrated by the possessive adjective 'ma'. The term 'ma Négritude' leaves the reader in no doubt about the extent to which Zobel felt solidly anchored in his racial identity as a black Caribbean man, an identity which he thinks through as a form of Négritude. Zobel's apparent rejection of being part of Négritude, then, was actually accompanied by the reiteration of his own unshakable identification with the Négritude movement.

In 1979, the author of the first scholarly article on Zobel's work, Randolph Hezekiah, who worked as a Lecturer in French at the University of the West Indies, was sensitive to this very same nuanced use of language, commenting: 'Zobel is an unmistakable advocate of the Black man's cause, but he pleads in subtle and quiet tones, without ranting and raving, without hurling too many accusations. He simply lets the evidence speak for itself'.[13] Working from Relouzat's lecture notes, which in 1979 constituted the only published critical document about Zobel, Hezekiah's article is the first to directly align Zobel with Négritude. Hezekiah points out the ambiguity of Relouzat's observation that Zobel is 'libre de l'hypothèque de la "négritude" telle qu'elle était vécue et exprimée par des contemporains' (free of the constraints of 'Négritude' such as they have been experienced and expressed by his contemporaries).[14] This enables Hezekiah to tentatively advance the argument that Relouzat's statement can actually function as a signpost to understanding Zobel's relationship to Négritude, allowing as it does for the possibility that the author was developing another kind of Négritude and applying the movement's ideas in quite new ways.

---

13 Randolph Hezekiah, 'Joseph Zobel: The Mechanics of Liberation', *Black Images*, 4.3–4 (1975), p. 44. Hezekiah received the honorary status of 'Chevalier dans l'Ordre des Palmes académiques' from the French Government in 1984. See: https://sta.uwi.edu/uwitoday/archive/february_2009/article3.asp (accessed 17 June 2016).
14 Hezekiah, p. 44.

This complex relationship can be understood as a form of modesty, or indeed as Zobel's own recognition that he was working at a different level to that of the founding Négritude authors. His social origins were quite unlike theirs, and his position in the ethnoclass hierarchy gave him a different, and indeed more complex and nuanced, perspective on race. It is this aspect which is homed in on by another Caribbean-born critic, Keith Q. Warner, in the introduction to his translation *Black Shack Alley*. Warner points out the Caribbean specificities of race and identity which Zobel set out to scrutinise by depicting 'the gradual awakening of the young narrator to the complexities of class distinctions and other social inequalities'.[15] While Césaire, Damas, and Senghor were writing as part of international aesthetic and political networks, and striving to change the perceptions of race in metropolitan France, Zobel was developing their ideas in a no less innovative manner, but from a grass-roots perspective, and applying them to his home island.

In an interview given in 1969, Zobel raises the topic of Césairean Négritude and its specific significance in Vichy Martinique. He figures himself as inspired by Césaire in the following terms:

> Césaire avait fondé une revue qui s'appelait *Tropiques* et cette revue était une arme terrible; justement cette revue était en somme l'étendard de la négritude et un certain nombre de jeunes écrivains et artistes dont moi-même ont emboîté le pas à Césaire pour protester justement contre cette politique, l'attitude de ces gens, en déclarant avec un certain défi qu'il était bon et beau et légitime d'être nègre, selon l'expression de Césaire même.[16]

> Césaire had founded a review called *Tropiques* and this review was a formidable weapon; indeed this review was the banner of Négritude and a certain number of young writers and artists, including myself, were following in Césaire's footsteps to fight against these politics, these people's attitudes, declaring with defiance that it was good and beautiful and legitimate to be a Negro, to use the words of Césaire himself.

Here, Zobel is adamant that he followed in Césaire's wake, and similar images of tutelage and admiration – from afar – abound in the comments which the author made about Césaire throughout his entire life. This relationship would prove decisive to the development of his career as a novelist, as fictionalised and immortalised in the preface to Zobel's

---

15 Warner, p. xv.
16 Matt Schaffer, 'Interview with Joseph Zobel, 23 June 1969'.

first novel, *Diab'-là*, when an anonymous speaker recalls a pivotal conversation with an unnamed interlocutor about black consciousness movements in the Caribbean. The two figures are identifiable as Zobel himself and Aimé Césaire (I explore this preface at length in Chapter Two), and the conversation places Césaire in the role of an inspirational yet distant mentor. In a clear nod to Négritude, the two men discuss the progress made thus far, and the voice which represents Zobel muses that it is time to move away from tragic stories 'où nègres, canne, sueur, misère, colère, rimaient affreusement' (where the words Negroes, cane, sweat, poverty, and anger were forever condemned to rhyme) (p. 11), and implement a new positive vision by working towards 'une autre histoire imaginée, de soleil, liberté, amour, joie' (a new visionary tale, of sun, freedom, love, and joy) (p. 11). This episode is based on an actual conversation during which Césaire told Zobel that he greatly appreciated his contributions to *Le Sportif* and that, in his opinion, Zobel was now ready to write a novel (discussed in the Introduction to this study). Zobel alludes to this important conversation, which inspired him to become a novelist, in several interviews given throughout his life, and the terms in which he recalls it are the same as are found in the preface to *Diab'-là*.[17] Zobel's debut novel, then, positions itself within a tradition of Négritude literature, both through its reverence of Césaire and in its aims to fundamentally change perceptions of black people. This was a constant theme of his literature, and in his final original novel, *La Fête à Paris*, Négritude itself is named and discussed as the defining characteristic of José Hassam's psychology.

Zobel was then always careful to identify with Négritude, while acknowledging that he was not one of the founders of the movement and that his relationship with it was a personal interpretation. He distanced himself from overly theoretical positions, and always acknowledged the debt he owed to Césaire, thus adopting the stance of a disciple of Négritude. Césaire and Zobel maintained a mutual admiration and respect for each other's work. In a poem written by Zobel towards the end of his life and included in the book which accompanies the DVD box set of Euzhan Palcy's three-part documentary *Aimé Césaire. Une parole pour le XXIe siècle* (*Aimé Césaire. A Voice for the 21st Century*), the younger author figures himself receiving Césaire's energy in reverential silence, commenting: 'Je respire ta présence en silence' (I breathe in

---

17 There is a striking similarity, for example, with the terms he uses in Kezadri and Codol's documentary; I return to this in the next chapter.

your presence in silence).[18] Yet Zobel's novels go much further than just emulating or echoing the work of Césaire. Indeed, when Césaire praises Zobel as the greatest Martinican novelist (at an event discussed at the opening of this book), there is a certain circularity and even hubris at play, as Césaire knows that he himself had encouraged Zobel to write novels, just as he knows that Zobel repeatedly referred back to this fact.

There is a fallacy to Zobel's complicity in positioning himself in Césaire's shadow; for all his positive intentions in imagining Césaire as the great orator, this has undoubtedly placed Zobel in a more silent, passive role. Closer attention to Zobel's novels reveals that the 'follower' author was not a mere disciple, but was actually developing the ideas of Césairean Négritude in quite new directions in novels which expand Négritude's framework. In Césaire's *Cahier d'un retour au pays natal*, the poet narrates a return from Europe and appraises with disdain what he perceives as a lack of development in his island in a poem which, from its opening, imagines an apocalypse in which the whole of his beloved Martinique will be made anew. This is constructed in an erudite, surrealist French which both dazzles and confounds the reader. In contrast, Zobel's first novels consider the same island, at the same historical moment, with a different gaze and different language. He homes in to depict – with real affection – the local communities forged in the crucible of slavery and poverty, and to celebrate the cultural heritage which endured into the post-slavery era.

While Zobel was adamant that he was not a theorist, he may be considered a practitioner of Négritude. His reluctance to theorise means that it is in his literary depictions of race 'in practice' – in fishing villages, plantations, cities, and in situations of immigration – that his own original thinking on race can be found. In particular, Négritude would have had a different significance for the rural population from the one it held for the educated town-dweller. Zobel explores this through a switch in focus unparalleled in Négritude writing which casts the authorial gaze onto the poorest section of Martinican society. One of Zobel's characters in *Quand la neige aura fondu* points out that whereas most Martinicans are referred to as 'gens' (people), there exists one group in Martinican society who are almost exclusively referred to as 'nègres' (p. 122) – a term intended to indicate their difference and distance from

---

18 Euzhan Palcy, *Aimé Césaire. Une parole pour le XXIème siècle / A Voice for the 21st Century* (Paris: JMJ productions, 1994–2006). Box set of three films, including the booklet *Aimé Césaire, un recueil de textes* (no place or editor, 1994).

the rest of the population. Through Zobel, those same people who were persistently and derogatively referred to as *nègres* became the main focus of novels. This draws attention to the problematic fact that thus far, the *nègres* themselves had been excluded from Négritude's primarily intellectual orbit. Now, in a major development, this same group were exhorted to revel in their own Négritude by Zobel, who granted them sympathetic and dignified literary representation. This testifies to his conviction that Martinican literature should represent not only the elite, but the *nègres*, or the *petit-nègres*, the group with which he most closely identified, and which found itself excluded from post-war narratives of modernity.

In his first novels, and even in his novels of immigration, Zobel's primary focus and audience was his countrymen and others sympathetic to their plight, not an elite audience. In an interview with Zobel conducted by Lilyan Kesteloot in Senegal in the late 1950s, excerpts of which are included in her 1963 ground-breaking study of black Francophone authors, *Les Écrivains noirs de langue française: naissance d'une littérature* (translated in 1974 by Ellen Conroy Kennedy as *Black Writers in French: A Literary History of Négritude*), Zobel stated that he wrote in an intentionally simple style. As cited by Kesteloot, the author 'déclare "n'employer jamais un mot qui ne soit pas dans le vocabulaire quotidien du people"' (declares [that he will] 'never use a word which is not in the everyday vocabulary of the people').[19] These stylistic choices and democratic aims appear to have hindered the broader understanding of Zobel's novels, as well as hampering a critical sense of the movements with which they are in dialogue. In 1982, the critic Hal Wylie wrote an article which asked directly why Zobel's work had not received greater attention, and expressed surprise at the 'meagreness of its critical reception'.[20] Wylie concludes that the likely reason is that Zobel's quieter style might be mistakenly understood as unpolemical by readers used to the 'polemical, argumentative' works of Négritude, which were 'full of denunciations and demands and [...] based on a sweeping analysis of the dialectics of race'.[21] Wylie

19   Lilyan Kesteloot, *Les Écrivains noirs de langue française: naissance d'une littérature* (Brussels: Université Libre de Bruxelles, 1963), p. 313. Translation by Ellen Conroy Kennedy, *Black Writers in French: A Literary History of Négritude* (Philadelphia, PA: Temple University Press, 1974).
20   Hal Wylie, 'Joseph Zobel's Use of Negritude and Social Realism', *World Literature Today*, 56.1 (1982), p. 61.
21   Wylie, p. 61.

reads Zobel alongside Négritude, while tacitly acknowledging that the author's literature displayed differences with the movement. Here, Wylie echoes Kesteloot – although he does not refer to her work in his study – who had commented that 'Certains [auteurs] d'ailleurs, comme J. Zobel, décrivent les sociétés coloniales sans intention polémique et sans rancune apparente: ce qu'ils montrent n'en est pas plus consolant pour la conscience occidentale!' (Certain [authors] moreover, like J. Zobel, describe colonial societies without polemical intention and without apparent rancour: nonetheless, what they depict is no more consoling for western consciences!).[22] Kesteloot is correct to draw attention to Zobel's considerable skill at depicting situations of abject poverty without an overtly aggressive or reproachful approach; indeed, this technique is all the more powerful as it invites readers from all over the globe, of different ethnicities, to come to his texts without feeling alienated. Zobel's inclusive manner of constructing his narratives mirrors the mode of inclusive intellectual activity identified by Edward Said as central to any intellectual undertaking to voice experiences of otherness and exclusion. Said expresses the hope that intellectual engagement is 'socially possible as well as desirable' (following Gramsci) and that such engagement must then avoid structuring 'analyses of historical experience around exclusions, exclusions that stipulate, for instance, that only women can understand feminine experience, only Jews can understand Jewish suffering, only formerly colonial subjects can understand colonial experience'.[23] There is a quiet yet articulate description of otherness and exclusion in Zobel's narrative which demands attention without excluding those whose own personal circumstances do not correspond to those which he is describing.

Yet there is also considerably more 'intention polémique' in Zobel's works than Kesteloot allows. As Wylie argues, the author was 'introducing brand new themes and subject matter into world literature'.[24] From his first novel, *Diab'-là*, Zobel's work unmistakably aims to spark a polemical debate and to voice unspoken truths about racial and social oppression, colonialism and slavery, and their effects on marginalised groups. Indeed, in one of Kesteloot's tabular surveys of black Francophone authors working in Africa, Zobel identifies himself as belonging to the category which Kesteloot defines as 'écrivains

---

22 Kesteloot, p. 304.
23 Edward Said, *Culture and Imperialism* (London: Vintage, 1993), p. 35.
24 Wylie, p. 61.

"engagés"' (writers 'with a cause') for whom 'contact avec la masse' (contact with the masses) was of fundamental importance.[25]

From his debut novel, Zobel sets out to write about, and denounce, extreme forms of exploitation: no easy task in a repressive context of fascist domination under colonialism and Vichy. To depict the situations around him with any degree of accuracy – and to have any hope of reaching a popular audience – the author was forced to forge his own unique linguistic style, which mixes 'standard' French with creolisms and is rich in neologisms, different registers, and code-switching. The lexical richness of Zobel's entire corpus has in recent years been subject to analysis by the linguistics researcher André Thibault and his collaborators. With the support of funding from the French Embassy in Canada, Thibault has used Zobel's work to discover more about the distinctiveness of French as spoken in the Antilles, and has commented on the astonishing lexical diversity of the author's work: 'les mots intéressants y foisonnent, et les contextes définitoires et variés vont nous permettre d'élaborer un glossaire qui devrait faire ressortir tout l'intérêt du français des Antilles pour l'histoire de la langue française' (it is teeming with interesting words, and its use of varied, defining contexts will allow us to develop a glossary which will reveal the full extent of the significance of the French of the Antilles for the history of the French language).[26]

Such recent research into Zobel's language is timely and contributes to the rethinking of the author's style and literary agenda. Though Wylie termed Zobel's style as the 'antithesis of the *avant-garde*' and 'rather staid',[27] he himself, and other critics besides, recognised in that steady, gentle and engaging prose a deliberately deceptive simplicity, which expresses nothing less than 'un discours militant' (a militant discourse) that is directly related to Négritude.[28] For Hezekiah, 'One of the author's chief preoccupations is the creation of heroes who symbolise the Negro's triumph over his destiny and the resultant pride in the Black race. It

25 Kesteloot, p. 308.
26 André Thibault, Patrick Drouin, 'Le lexique de Joseph Zobel, auteur antillais: extraction semi-automatique des particularismes lexicaux', paper presented at the *XXV Congrès International de Linguistique et de Philologies Romanes*, Innsbruck, 3–7 September 2007. See: http://www.rose.uzh.ch/seminar/personen/glessgen/actes_cilpr_Thibault_Drouin_section17.pdf (accessed 19 July 2016).
27 Wylie, pp. 61 and 64 respectively.
28 Amode Taher, *La Rue Cases-Nègres de Joseph Zobel: analyse critique* (Vacoas, Maurice: Le Printemps, 1989), p. 67.

is in this sense that we consider him to be a négritude writer'.[29] Wylie builds on Hezekiah's work, and his article draws heavily on Hezekiah, whom he praises for identifying Zobel with Négritude, both in the passages quoted above, and in his comment that Zobel contributes to the Négritude motif of a 'retour aux sources' (return to origins).[30] Moreover, Wylie perceives that Zobel is doing something different with Négritude: 'It appears that Zobel shares the same goals as the earlier Negritude writers but feels other methods are needed [...] He is aware of other variables which they swept aside or overlooked'.[31] There was, then, in the late 1970s and early 1980s an understanding that Zobel was innovating in truly significant ways at the boundaries of Négritude.

More recently, Martin Munro has considered *La Rue Cases-Nègres* to be a novel of the 'early post-Négritude period'.[32] Critics appear anxious to avoid labelling Zobel as a Négritude writer, precisely because, until very recently, Négritude was viewed as a defined set of three male authors, and their works. Recent scholarly exegesis of the movement points to the plurality of approaches to racial identity in the work of several overlooked authors who were writing under the inspiration of Négritude, such as Suzanne Césaire; in turn, it is now widely acknowledged that these authors themselves contributed new shape and texture to the movement. This advance in Négritude scholarship, and the availability of newly available archival documents relating to Zobel, means that the moment is opportune to reconsider Zobel's relationship to Négritude. He may be considered, following Munro, as an 'early post-Négritude' author, and yet he overlapped with Négritude chronologically, completing his first novel in 1942, and publishing his last original novel in 1953. Zobel would not have dared to position himself alongside the select founding triumvirate of authors. Yet recent publications support the argument that Négritude as an intellectual concern benefits when its scope is broadened to go beyond the three canonical authors. Zobel was dialoguing with Négritude through his novels, and they expand the movement's critical framework: if there is a novelist of Négritude, it is Zobel.

Zobel's affinities with Négritude go beyond an appreciation of the new discourses about race and identity pioneered by the movement.

---

29 Hezekiah, p. 44.
30 Hezekiah quoted in Wylie, p. 61.
31 Wylie, pp. 61–62.
32 Martin Munro, *Different Drummers: Rhythm and Race in the Americas* (Berkeley, CA: University of California Press, 2010), p. 149.

Zobel, Négritude, and the Novel 49

The effect of the authors of the Negro Renaissance on his own creative development was dramatic, just as for the other writers of Négritude. He immediately identified with this group of writers who were seeking to depict the marginalised problems of race – in history, economics, and politics – in North America. Many of Zobel's characters, from the uneducated Diab'-là to the Parisian student José Hassam, are depicted as readers, and the author strongly suggests that books, or at least the right kind of books, should not be a solo pleasure, but are best shared with sympathetic friends. This was the case in Zobel's own life; in Vichy Martinique, during a period when the island was under US blockade, and was more violently severed from metropolitan France than at any other time in its modern history, imports to the island, including books, were extremely rare. Books now became yet another commodity which could only be acquired through illicit, semi-clandestine networks. Zobel knew an underground 'dealer' named Bocage who received books from Canada and sold them to friends and contacts, often informally meeting his buyers at La Savane park in the heart of Fort-de-France because he did not have any physical shop premises.[33] Zobel's literary awakening to race occurred in these clandestine circumstances during the Second World War:

> Alors j'ai commencé par Claude McKay. J'avais une anthologie des écrivains négro-américains. Mais vraiment, pratiquement, physiquement, affectivement, chacun de ces livres que je lisais, c'était comme une espèce de breuvage que j'avais absorbé et qui avait immédiatement produit des transformations en moi [...] en commençant par *Banjo*, en commençant par *Native Son*, et tous ces extraits que j'avais dans l'anthologie. Il n'y avait rien d'équivalant dans tout ce que j'avais lu jusqu'à présent. [...] Qu'était-ce que Balzac et Maupassant à côté de cela? [...] Intellectuellement cela produisait sur moi l'effet que j'aurais ressenti, physiquement, si j'avais pris un breuvage ou un comprimé.[34]

> So I began with Claude McKay. I had an anthology of Negro-American authors. Well, really, practically, physically, emotionally, every book I read was like a kind of potion that I had drunk and which had produced immediate transformations in me [...] beginning with *Banjo*, beginning with *Native Son*, and all those extracts that I had in the anthology. It was unlike anything I had ever read before. [...] What were Balzac and

---

33 Zobel relates the story of his wartime book supplier Bocage in two interviews: Anonymous, 'Zobel: sa vie, son œuvre', p. 22 and in Tarrieu, p. 33.
34 Tarrieu, p. 33.

Maupassant compared to that? [...] Intellectually, it had the same effect on me that I would have felt, physically, if I had drunk a potion or taken a pill.

These encounters with Negro Renaissance authors through the printed page had an immediate, transformative impact which Zobel likens to the effect of a potion or illicit substance. Zobel does not name the anthology in question, nor does he comment on whether it was in the original English or in French translation (he was capable of reading either, as he excelled at English in school). His comments draw attention to the literary phenomenon of the black anthology, a literary form which played a decisive role in the construction and consolidation of a black literary canon across the Americas, and indeed across the globe. This tradition began with the seminal anthology *The New Negro: An Interpretation* (1925), by the African-American philosopher and literary critic Alain Locke, a collection which included poetry by McKay, but not *Banjo*, which was published four years after the anthology appeared.[35] With this anthology, Locke popularised the 'New Negro' movement, which itself had roots in an older tradition of black American writing. Moreover, in his chapter 'Negro Youth Speaks', he 'coined the term "Negro Renaissance," which he used in print and speech until his death'.[36] While Harlem was one reference point for Locke's writings, he did not use the term 'Harlem Renaissance'.[37]

If Zobel, rather than remembering the significance of anthologies in general, was thinking of one anthology in particular, it cannot be Locke's as *Banjo* was as yet unwritten. Yet, in the course of my research for this book, I have been unable to identify an anthology which does include *Banjo*, although other excerpts from McKay are frequently found. It seems more probable that Zobel enjoyed the passages from McKay which he found in an anthology, and then went on to read *Banjo* the novel. Indeed, *La Rue Cases-Nègres* shows José preferring *Banjo* to the texts prescribed for study at the Lycée Schœlcher (p. 287).

What of the circulation of these ideas in wartime Martinique itself? Until now, it has been widely believed that the Martinican journal *Tropiques* was responsible for bringing the works of the African-American Negro Renaissance movement to popular Martinican

---

35 Alain Locke (ed.), *The New Negro: An Interpretation* (New York: Albert and Charles Boni, 1927 [1925]).
36 Mitchell, '"Black Renaissance": A Brief History of the Concept', p. 644.
37 Mitchell, '"Black Renaissance": A Brief History of the Concept', p. 644.

attention. *Tropiques* was launched as the main vehicle for a black Martinican intellectual critique of Vichy Martinique, led by intellectuals Aimé Césaire, Suzanne Césaire, and René Ménil. Famously, the second issue, dated July 1941, includes an introductory article on 'Poètes nègres américains' (Negro American poets) by Aimé Césaire, followed by poems by James Weldon Johnson, Jean Toomer, and Claude McKay (in French translation). This issue is widely held to have cemented the connections between the writers of Négritude and their forebears, the Negro Renaissance writers. Such admiration had originated when the Négritude writers were students in Paris. As A. James Arnold has noted, for his *diplôme d'études supérieures* qualification at the École Normale Supérieure, Césaire had written a dissertation on the theme of the South in black American literature (completed in the academic year 1937–1938).[38] Prior to this, the pioneering cultural activities of Paulette Nardal had also celebrated the Negro Renaissance movement, and extracts of work by leading authors such as Hughes and Locke were reproduced in the *Revue du monde noir* (1931–1932).[39]

It is evident from Zobel's own testimony, however, that he and other educated intellectuals in Martinique were avidly reading Negro Renaissance authors prior to this. *Tropiques* was neither the first nor the only Martinican publication to encourage the public to become interested in the Negro Renaissance movement. By the time *Tropiques* appeared, Zobel was an established contributor to the Martinican newspaper *Le Sportif*, where he wrote under the pseudonym of 'Kay-Mac-Zo'. Zobel's pseudonym draws attention to the slippage within spellings of Claude McKay's name.[40] In the course of preparing this study, the earliest article signed Kay-Mac-Zo which I could trace is a previously unknown short story called 'Mon Village', published in *Le Sportif* on Friday 27 December 1940.[41] Zobel's use of the pseudonym Kay-Mac-Zo may of course precede that date.

Zobel had thus taken the strategic decision to write in a way that announced the significance of the Negro Renaissance movement at least

---

38 A. James Arnold, *Modernism & Negritude: The Poetry and Poetics of Aimé Césaire* (Cambridge, MA: Harvard University Press, 1998), p. 10.
39 Arnold, p. 11.
40 Although the correct spelling is 'McKay', to this day, a number of misspellings as 'MacKay' are in evidence on databases such as WorldCat.
41 Joseph Zobel, writing as Kay-Mac-Zo, 'Mon Village', *Le Sportif*, 138, 27 December 1940, pp. 3–4. Archives départementales, Martinique. PER 156/1938-1950.

seven months before the appearance of the second issue of *Tropiques*. Writing as Kay-Mac-Zo, he aimed to associate his name with the Negro Renaissance authors in the mind of the Martinican public, and to forge a link between black writing by Anglophone and Francophone authors from across the Americas. This is indicative of another, largely neglected current of black Martinican intellectual history during the Négritude period: the history of those authors who were not working in Paris, but were active in Martinique itself. The role played by Zobel and his contemporaries in Martinique has never been fully appraised or understood, and the only scholarly analysis of *Le Sportif* to date is by Jacques Dumont, in an article which considers the intersection of sport, identity, and politics but makes no mention of the contribution of prose fiction writers such as Zobel to the newspaper.[42]

Zobel's words about how he came into contact with Negro Renaissance authors are highly instructive, and they draw attention to the role of anthologies as a tool for the dissemination of ideas about race and identity, which he also fictionalised in his novels. One anthology of which he was certainly aware was the *Anthology of American Negro Literature*; it is read, with great enthusiasm, by a character in *Quand la neige aura fondu* (p. 136). Yet that work itself is ambiguous. It may refer to one of two anthologies which bore this title, both of which were available at the time when Zobel was writing. The first was edited by V. F. Calverton in 1929,[43] and includes an excerpt from McKay's 'Home to Harlem' and an essay by Locke, 'The Negro in American Culture'. In 1944, however, Sylvestre C. Watkins was given the remit to expand Calverton's work, and he published an updated edition with the aim of including even 'stronger and more stirring pieces of writing'.[44] His volume includes a short story, 'Truant' by McKay, and Locke's original essay, suggesting the timeless significance of that seminal anthology compiler. Given the publication date of Watkins's anthology, 1944, it is likely that this is the anthology in question, as it is feasible to assume that it would still have been fashionable among black students in Paris into the early 1950s. Was Zobel aware of the anthology's history, and

---

42 Jacques Dumont, 'La "famille" sportive aux Antilles françaises', *Outre-mers*, 96.364–65. Special issues 'Le Sport dans l'Empire Français. Un instrument de domination coloniale?' ed. by Driss Abbassi (2009), pp. 107–25.

43 V. F. Calverton, *An Anthology of American Negro Literature* (New York: The Modern Library, 1929).

44 Sylvestre C. Watkins (ed.), *An Anthology of American Negro Literature* (New York: The Modern Library, Random House, 1944), p. xi.

Calverton's earlier work? That is impossible to ascertain, but what the reference to *Anthology of American Negro Literature* does reveal is Zobel's enthusiastic participation in the transatlantic circulation of ideas about black identity in post-war Paris.

The significance of the black anthology genre was to further shape Zobel's own creative practice; in Paris in the late 1940s, Zobel prepared his own anthology, *Chants de la Négritude: 14 poètes, 20 poèmes de la Négritude* (*Négritude Songs: 14 Poets, 20 Poems of Négritude*), a previously unknown document which I became the first scholar to inspect in his personal archives in Fort-de-France in 2015.[45] The title and the ways in which the anthology are constructed reveal that Zobel was seeking to broaden Négritude beyond its founding triumvirate, and to open the concept so that it could accommodate a wider body of transnational authors. Again, it was a work of practice, rather than a work of theory, as Zobel used the anthology for the acclaimed poetry recitals which he gave across Europe and Africa. These recitals are another manifestation of his deep admiration for and commitment to the new literature of black consciousness, and the pivotal importance of this literature to his own development as an author.

In evidence of his own transnational understanding of racial struggles, in his anthology Zobel constructs his vision of Négritude along ideological rather than geographic or even linguistic lines, spanning across works originally written in French, Spanish, and English. He includes authors from the French- and Spanish-speaking Caribbean, such as Georges Desportes, Guy Tirolien, Nicolás Guillén, Césaire, Antoine Cupidon; from Francophone Africa, including Birago Diop, Paul Lorion, David Diop, Bernard B. Dadié, Lamine Diakhate, Léopold Sédar Senghor, Néné Khaly; and from the United States, namely the Negro Renaissance authors Langston Hughes and James Weldon Johnson. All were included in the original French, or in French translation. Zobel's own selection of 'Négritude' poets was a paean to pan-Africanism which traversed national boundaries, and gathered together Négritude authors broadly defined. The anthology is painstakingly prepared and includes the country of origin and publication references for each poet, although to date, it remains a personal, unpublished document.

At this juncture, it is helpful to return to my earlier arguments about Négritude. While the Negro Renaissance movement of 1920s

---

45 Le Fonds Zobel, Boite: Poèmes 2014.17.3; No. 2014.17.3.15. A.

and 1930s America set out to change perceptions of black people in western society forever, a goal shared by Négritude, there remain important differences between the two movements. The most significant is the social conditions which led to the production of this literature, and the anthologies draw attention to this very issue. For Locke, it was imperative that the literature of the Negro Renaissance reach the younger generation of African-American readers. The determination to improve the lot of his younger compatriots was evident in the dedication to his 1925 anthology, which is accompanied by a line of musical score: 'To the YOUNGER GENERATION: "O, rise, shine for Thy Light is a'com-ing. (Traditional.)' (original emphasis and punctuation). Locke's act of compiling an anthology of poetry, prose, and oral folktales testifies to a desire to communicate with and validate the experiences of African Americans, in literature which was designed for consumption in its place of production, that is to say, in America itself. This literary strategy is one which resonated with Zobel, who, in his desire to write novels that would reach his own people, was actually much closer to the Negro Renaissance movement than to Négritude.

In Zobel, an original combination of aspects of the Negro Renaissance movement and Négritude converge. In his first novels, *Diab'-là* and *Les Jours immobiles*, Zobel casts a spotlight on the lives of humble, everyday *nègres* and *négresses*. It was the first time that this social group would be depicted through literature that was neither exoticising nor condescending. In *La Rue Cases-Nègres*, a novel with a racially charged title which itself was only rendered viable through the advances of Négritude, Zobel carved out a literary space from which might emerge the voices of subaltern Martinicans who were oppressed both by the pigment of their skin and the socio-economic systems into which they had been born. In this, his Négritude refused what Gabriel d'Arboussier regarded in 1949 as the movement's 'mystification dangereuse' (dangerous mystification). D'Arboussier argued that Négritude had become a black consciousness movement which essentialised race and foregrounded skin colour, a strategy which eclipsed the equally urgent issue of social class (I return to this argument in Chapter Two).[46] From his earliest publications, Zobel's writing displays the same outright, unapologetic focus on questions of race, racial identification, and humanity which the three founders of Négritude had championed; but Zobel goes further,

---

46 Gabriel d'Arboussier, 'Une dangereuse mystification: la théorie de la négritude', *La nouvelle critique* (June 1949), 34–47.

by focusing on race and social class in a manner more reminiscent of the Negro Renaissance movement, which had produced destitute, dispossessed anti-heroes such as McKay's Banjo, and Wright's Bigger Thomas. If McKay's style and subject matter appealed to Zobel as a young man, decades later he professed to Relouzat his admiration for Wright's politically active work, confiding that 'Si l'action politique avait partagé ma vie, je n'aurais pas désavoué une comparaison avec Richard Wright' (If political action had marked my life, I would not have rejected a comparison with Richard Wright).[47] As Renée Larrier observes, in 1947, Marcel Duhamel's French translation of Richard Wright's *Black Boy* appeared with Gallimard, under the original English title with a subtitle in parenthesis: *(jeunesse noire)*.[48] This was just three years before the publication of *La Rue Cases-Nègres*, and the translation may have inspired Zobel's novel; indeed, Larrier notes a number of thematic and stylistic similarities between the two works.[49]

There are also significant differences, however: Zobel refrains from the explicit physical and sexual coarseness and violence of some Negro Renaissance writing; indeed, as his access to these texts was (at least initially) limited to anthologies, he may have been unaware of the more violent passages.[50] Instead, he focuses on the violence, not of individuals, but of systems – the social structures in which his characters are born, live, and will, in all probability, die. He gives voice to the experiences of the *petits-nègres*: plantation labourers who not only fight against the racial bias imposed upon them by white society, but are also forced to confront the racial prejudice of their economically advantaged black compatriots. In Zobel's literature, it is the struggle for dignity and

---

47 Relouzat, p. 32.
48 Renée Larrier, *Autofiction and Advocacy in the Francophone Caribbean* (Gainesville, FL: University Press of Florida, 2006), p. 33.
49 Larrier, p. 53, n. 18.
50 Nontheless, the references to sex in *La Rue Cases-Nègres* render the novel more 'adult' than some critics would allow. See Daniel Maximin's childhood narrative *Tu, c'est l'enfance* (Paris: Gallimard, 2004) for a discussion of how a schoolteacher, who was a friend of Maximin's parents, sent the family a copy of Zobel's novel with the cautionary explanation that she had indicated the passages which she deemed unsuitable for children due to their sexual content. I discuss this in a previous publication: see Hardwick, *Childhood, Autobiography and the Francophone Caribbean* (Liverpool: Liverpool University Press, 2013), pp. 136–37. Moreover, the reference to the fact that the teacher sends a copy to the family underscores just how difficult the novel had become to source (reinforcing my comments on its unusual publication history).

autonomy, for self-determination and independence in the face of abject, systemic poverty which shapes the development of black consciousness.

Moreover, these early novels demonstrate a profound appreciation of nature and the environment, and develop the stirrings of an environmental critique which is found scattered throughout Négritude writing. Césaire and Senghor wrote their native environments into literature in quite different ways; the Caribbean author used images of decay and squalor which aimed to destroy the clichés found in the sentimental and exoticising accounts of early twentieth-century *doudouiste* writing, while Senghor's depictions of the Senegalese landscape evoked tranquillity and a culture free of the yoke of colonialism. It is in the essays which Suzanne Césaire contributed to the review *Tropiques*, and which have only in recent decades been the focus of scholarly research, that Négritude's most engaging telluric analysis emerges. Suzanne Césaire repeatedly interrogates the relationship between topological space and Caribbean identity. Her 1945 essay 'Le Grand Camouflage' in the final issue of *Tropiques* forms something of a bridge between Négritude writing and Zobel's first novels, which were published in 1945 and 1946 (although *Diab'-là* had been completed and banned in 1942). Both sets of writing are linked by their pronounced concern with the Martinican environment.

An important direction in current scholarly research aims to situate the work of Suzanne Césaire as part of the emerging canon of postcolonial ecocriticism, an area to which Zobel's *Diab'-là* and *Les Jours immobiles* also make a significant intervention. In the late twentieth and early twenty-first century, ecocriticism became an important new field across the humanities and social sciences. The term is believed to have been coined in 1978 by William Rueckert in his essay 'Literature and Ecology: An Experiment in Ecocriticism',[51] and there is no single definition of this broad concept; it implies a sustained focus on interactions with and reactions to the environment in the literary sphere. For Cheryll Glotfelty, 'Ecocriticism takes an earth-centered approach to literary studies [...] despite the broad scope of inquiry and disparate levels of sophistication, all ecological criticism shares the fundamental premise that human culture is connected to the physical

---

51 William Rueckert, 'Into and Out of the Void: Two Essays', *Iowa Review*, 9.1 (winter 1978), pp. 62–86. Republished as 'Literature and Ecology: An Experiment in Ecocriticism', in Cheryll Glotfelty and Harold Fromm, *The Ecocriticism Reader: Landmarks in Literary Ecology* (Athens, GA: University of Georgia Press, 1996), pp. 105–23.

world, affecting it and affected by it'.[52] Ecocritical research is motivated by the troubling awareness that we are reaching an age of environmental limits, 'a time when the consequences of human actions are damaging the planet's basic life support systems'.[53] The ways in which people engage with the environment, and the knowledge they have about it, play an important role in both political and private life. Interactions with the environment, for work (financial profit), for survival (shelter and sustenance), and for pleasure (well-being), contribute to the construction of social identities which serve as an anchor for wider social and political discussions. Moreover, critics argue that a fully developed model of ecocriticism must bring postcolonial and ecological issues into dialogue as a means of challenging 'continuing imperialist modes of social and environmental dominance'.[54] From the opening pages of his first novel, Zobel is arguing for precisely these shifts in understanding. Moreover, his original depictions of the Martinican landscape also develop an aesthetic appreciation of what is now termed recycling. His works are rich in descriptions of repurposed objects, a recycling borne of necessity and a creative act which, the author argues, confers an intrinsic beauty and value of its own. This is carried to its logical conclusion in Zobel's fascination with the Japanese art of *ikebana* in his retirement. *Ikebana* places strict restrictions on the number of blooms used, and also requires a restricted number of leaves, fronds, and twigs. It teaches an artist to create a plenitude which emerges, paradoxically, from scarcity. The art form perfectly encapsulates Zobel's aesthetics of simplicity: an appreciation and celebration of the unexpected beauty he finds in discordant scenes which do not conform to modern ideas of beauty.

* * *

Zobel's choice of a literary and artistic career was unusual, if not exceptional, for an author of his humble social origins, particularly in conservative 1930s Martinique. To date, there has been no attempt to

---

52 Cheryll Glotfelty, 'Introduction: Literary Studies in an Age of Environmental Crisis', in Glotfelty and Fromm *The Ecocriticism Reader: Landmarks in Literary Ecology* (Athens, GA: University of Georgia Press, 1996), pp. xviii–xix.
53 Glotfelty, p. xx.
54 Helen Tiffin and Graham Huggan, *Postcolonial Ecocriticism: Literature, Animals, Environment* (London: Routledge, 2009), p. 2.

articulate the challenges for a working-class author writing in Martinique in the early twentieth century. In this respect, it is helpful to draw this chapter to an end by comparing Zobel's work with Albert Camus's analysis of the metropolitan author Louis Guilloux (1899–1980), another working-class French author known for his social realism.

Guilloux was born in Brittany and, like Zobel, remains best-known for his semi-autobiographical childhood narrative, *La Maison du peuple* (1927) (untranslated into English; a literal translation would be 'The House of the People'). Guilloux was also a published translator, and contributed to the global dissemination of black literature when he rendered McKay's seminal Negro Renaissance novel *Home to Harlem* into French, published in 1932 under the title *Ghetto Noir*. Albert Camus was a close friend of Guilloux, and provided a preface to a new edition of *La Maison du people* in 1953.[55] This essay proves a helpful theoretical framework for the analysis of novels about *le prolétariat* by authors who hail from this very group.[56] Camus begins by observing that authors from poor social backgrounds remain a rarity:

> Presque tous les écrivains français qui prétendent aujourd'hui parler au nom du prolétariat sont nés de parents aisés ou fortunés. Ce n'est pas une tare, il y a du hasard dans la naissance, et je ne trouve cela ni bien ni mal. Je me borne à signaler au sociologue une anomalie et un objet d'études.[57]

> Today, almost every French writer who claims to speak in the name of the proletariat was born to well-off or rich parents. This is not a defect; birth is a matter of chance, and I find this fact neither good nor bad. I am merely pointing out, for the benefit of the sociologist, an anomaly and a potential field of study.

Despite this claim that he is indifferent to the social origins of authors who depict poverty, and that he sees in social origin nothing more than a hazard of birth, Camus goes on to affirm that he prefers to read accounts by authors who have first-hand experience of the subject which they are depicting; his arguments in the preface thus reinforce the divide between his vision of *littérature prolétarienne* and Sartre's *littérature engagée*. Camus also acknowledges the difficulty of the task of writing literature

---

55 Albert Camus, 'Préface', in Louis Guilloux, *La Maison du peuple* (Paris: Grasset, 1953 [1927]), p. 11.
56 I would like to record my thanks to Mamadou Souley Ba for suggesting Camus's preface to Guilloux to me.
57 Camus, 'Préface', p. 11.

about poverty: 'rien n'est plus dangereux qu'un tel sujet qui prête au réalisme facile et à la sentimentalité' (nothing is more dangerous than a subject like this, which all too easily lends itself to facile realism and sentimentality).[58] He singles out Guilloux for praise as an author 'qui ne flatte ni ne méprise le peuple dont il parle et qui lui restitue la seule grandeur qu'on ne puisse lui arracher, celle de la vérité' (who neither flatters nor despises the people of whom he speaks, and who restores to them the only mark of greatness which cannot be stolen from them: the truth).[59] Moreover, he admires Guilloux's restrained style, with which he 'peint toujours avec les couleurs les plus justes et les moins crues, sans jamais rechercher l'amertume pour elle-même' (paints unfailingly with the most appropriate and least crude colours, without ever seeking out bitterness for its own sake).[60] Camus's words about an author who aims to depict the 'truth' about poverty without slipping into facile sentimentality could have been written for Zobel. The measured tones and careful avoidance of bitterness which Camus celebrates in Guilloux prefigure Kesteloot's praise of these same qualities in Zobel. Moreover, Camus finds that such stories can only have political resonance if they give voice to a wider history of suffering, and he argues that Guilloux 'n'utilise la misère de tous les jours que pour mieux éclairer la douleur du monde' (only depicts everyday suffering in order to better illustrate the suffering of the world).[61] This pattern of beginning with the local in order to tell a story which is global is also at work in Zobel's novels, to great aesthetic and political effect. It is an inherent part of the author's strategy in rendering visible the links between the perpetual poverty which is required of a *rue cases-nègres* in order to sustain the prosperity of middle-class and elite society in Martinique and, by extension, in France. These patterns of widening inequality are the touchstone of twentieth- and twenty-first-century global societies, and Zobel's ambition as a novelist who attempts to explain such structures cannot be underestimated.

58 Camus, 'Préface', p. 13.
59 Camus, 'Préface', p. 12.
60 Camus, 'Préface', p. 13.
61 Camus, 'Préface', p. 15.

CHAPTER TWO

Earth, Ecocriticism, and Economics
Diab'-là

On doit savoir gré à M. Joseph Zobel de son audace.

Joseph Zobel must be applauded for his audacity.

René Maran[1]

The legacy of centuries of violent conquests, the transatlantic slave trade, and indenture, all undertaken with the express aim of dominating and exploiting the land for maximum economic profit and with scant regard for human life, means that in the Caribbean basin, the connection between an individual and the soil on which they are living is subject to multiple tensions and interrogations. As a result, Martinicans have a complex psychological relationship with their *pays natal*. This anxiety is evident in a vast body of cultural work from Martinique which interrogates western concepts of origins and beginnings, particularly the writings of the philosopher, poet, and novelist Édouard Glissant, in which the notion of any fixed origin is constantly deferred and thwarted by overlapping, non-linear, cataclysmic histories which confront the legacies of genocide, slavery, and the mass forced transportation of human bodies to the Americas. Caribbean space, then, can all too easily be interpreted as a space of exile and isolation.

The notion of having a land to call home is further challenged by the legacy of the system of plantation slavery which required an unremitting supply of human hands, backs, muscles, and sinews to labour the soil and harvest its produce. Soil became synonymous with slavery, in a second

---

1 René Maran, 'Un Plaidoyer contre l'esclavage. Destins de l'empire' *Gavroche*, 11 October 1945, p. 6.

process of stigmatisation which came to shape the human relationship with the land. Critics of the pastoral 'plantation tradition', a term used to describe a type of American Southern Confederacy literature which promoted racial and class hierarchies by implying that only a strict biopolitical system could result in economic efficiency and a contented society, have drawn attention to the fact that the very word 'plantation' is a deceptively romanticised term.[2] In its place, they have argued that these spaces should more accurately be referred to as 'slave labour camps'. Such brutal, totalitarian structures were once the dominant order on plantations across the Deep South, Caribbean, and Latin America. Under the system of plantations or slave labour camps which continued in the circum-Caribbean area well into the post-slavery era, until the global collapse of the cane sugar and rum markets, working the land was synonymous with exploitation. A quotation from Patrick Chamoiseau's *Émerveilles*, an illustrated book of children's stories which the author co-produced with the artist Maure, draws attention to the psychology of black Martinicans who sought to abandon the canefields as soon as abolition was announced:

> Les nègres d'ici-là venaient d'abandonner l'esclavage des champs-de-cannes. Beaucoup d'entre eux s'étaient convertis en compagnons de la mer. C'était le beau moyen de s'éloigner de la terre, de la boue et des chiques, et des sueurs et des fouets qui s'en venaient avec. [...] Ces gens, venus des cannes, se transformaient très vite. La terre des champs leur avait abîmé le regard. Et recourbé l'échine. [...] Et, comme ils devaient chaque jour surveiller l'horizon (et empoigner la vie sans attendre une écuelle), cela leur redressait le dos d'un trait d'autorité.[3]

> The black men from hereabouts had just abandoned the slavery of the canefields. Many of them had chosen a new life on the seas. It offered the best chance to get away from the land, the mud, and the ticks, and the sweat and the whips which accompanied that life. [...] These people, who had come from the cane fields, rapidly began to change. The earth of the fields had damaged their vision, and curved their spines. [...] Now they had to watch the horizon every day (and seize hold of life, rather than waiting to be granted its scraps), and so their backs began to straighten out again, strengthened by this new-found authority.

2   Peter Wood, 'Slave Labor Camps in Early America: Overcoming Denial and Discovering the Gulag', in *Inequality in Early America*, ed. by Gardina Pestana and Sharon V. Salinger (Hanover, NH: University Press of New England, 1999), p. 231.
3   Patrick Chamoiseau and Maure, *Émerveilles* (Paris: Gallimard Jeunesse/Giboulées, 1998), p. 11.

In a new, post-slavery Martinique, Chamoiseau portrays the former plantation workers as deserting the back-breaking toil of the canefields and reinventing themselves at sea. Fishing emerges as an admirable and covetable occupation with the potential to forge a more positive relationship between black Caribbean people and their natural environment – but only, it should be noted, out at sea. The stigma of the land remains intact. The dehumanising effects of plantation slavery have rendered the very earth itself hostile not only to the workers' vision, in both a literal and metaphorical sense, but also to their bodies, which have become curved and deformed. These same ingrained prejudices against working the land, with their deep-rooted psychological origins which are traceable to slavery, were precisely what Zobel sought to address and dismantle in his first novel, *Diab'-là*.

A Martinican Novel for Martinican Readers

Zobel had commenced his publishing career by writing regular short stories for the Martinican newspaper *Le Sportif*, and by the end of 1940 he was a regular contributor. The newspaper's typical readers would have been middle-class black Martinicans who had received enough schooling to be able to read French, including those members of the black and mixed-race bourgeoisie who had left the island to study in France and had subsequently returned. With his short tales of Martinican life, in which Martinican readers could immediately recognise their own cultural customs and traditions, Zobel positioned himself as a fledgling author who wrote for a local Martinican audience. His short stories held up a mirror to the society around him, which was a Martinique in crisis, as the island had become part of Vichy France after the Armistice of 22 June 1940, and was governed by a repressive regime upheld by Admiral Robert, the Vichy High Commissioner for the Antilles. Among the readers of Zobel's stories in *Le Sportif* was the returnee Aimé Césaire, Zobel's colleague at the Lycée Schœlcher, who was so impressed that he urged Zobel to write a novel. Zobel would recount this pivotal moment in the 1998 documentary film about his life and career, *Joseph Zobel: D'Amour et de Silence* (*Joseph Zobel: Of Love and Silence*):

> Et un jour, comme cela [...] quand nous nous croisions dans un escalier, au Lycée Schœlcher, où Césaire avait été professeur à cette époque, il m'a dit 'Mais Zobel, je lis chaque semaine ce que tu écris, ce que tu publies

dans le journal *Le Sportif*. Mais j'estime que tu devrais écrire un roman, que tu es même mûr pour écrire un roman'. Et peu de temps après, je me suis mis à écrire *Diab'-là*.[4]

And one day, by chance [...] we bumped into each other in a stairwell at the Lycée Schœlcher, where Césaire was a teacher at the time, and he said to me, 'Well Zobel, every week I read what you're writing and publishing in the newspaper *Le Sportif*. Well, I think you should write a novel, you've matured enough to write a novel'. And a short while after, I began to write *Diab'-là*.

As a direct consequence of this conversation, Zobel graduated from short-story writer to novelist, and began work on *Diab'-là*, in which he attempted, for the first time, to apply the insights of Négritude to a novel. *Diab'-là* is also thematically innovative: its radical content arises from the novel's profound appreciation of nature, and the work must be situated as a pioneer of what is now termed 'ecocriticism' within the canon of Francophone Caribbean literature.

Diab'-là can lay claim to being the first Martinican novel aimed at local black and non-elite Martinicans, as it is irrefutable that Zobel's intended audience were the same local readers whom he had entertained in his columns for *Le Sportif*. The title alone makes this clear: *diab'-là* is a Creole term meaning 'devil', and Zobel was the first Martinican novelist to appeal directly to his own countrymen by electing to use a Creole word as a book title, a bold choice in early 1940s Martinique. The word *Diab'-là* is close enough to the metropolitan French *le diable* for all Francophone readers (including the metropolitan French) to make an educated guess at its meaning; however, the *diab'-là* in question is not a devil in the Christian sense. He is a character from Caribbean folklore whose behaviour ranges from mischievous to malevolent, and a current of magical realism runs through the novel. To this day, during Carnival in Martinique and Guadeloupe it remains popular to dress in red as a *diab'-là*. Although the novel's Creole title derives potency from a certain exoticism, publishers obviously felt it could also be a stumbling block as in Zobel's later novel *La Fête à Paris*, the title is glossed as *Diab'-là: ce diable d'homme* (*Diablo: This Devil of a Man*) in the list of works previously published.[5] The novel has yet to be translated into English and, as a result, has received very little academic attention, although in

---

4 See Kezadri and Codol. I have drawn attention to other instances of Zobel recounting this story in the previous chapters of this study.
5 Joseph Zobel, *La Fête à Paris*, p. 4.

1949 it was translated into Czech.[6] A possible English rendering of the title would be *Diablo* or *Diablo's Garden*, and throughout this chapter, I translate the character's name into English as Diablo.

Zobel's title employs a familiar Creole grammatical construction: it combines a noun with the word *là*, an adverb of place, meaning 'there'. Anyone familiar with the French Caribbean will have noticed the frequency with which this structure is used in everyday language, French or Creole. Creole grammarians such as Moïse 'Benzo' Benjamin have suggested that the common Creole structure of adding the suffix *-là* to the end of nouns is a pattern which arose because slaves would repeat their masters' orders to move objects, as illustrated by the following exchange: the master says, 'Donnez-moi cette chaise' (Give me that chair), to which the slave's reply might be 'Chaise-là?' (That-there-chair?).[7] Over the centuries, it has become habitual in French Caribbean Creole to add the *-là* suffix to nouns, even when it is devoid of meaning – at most, it denotes a slight emphasis on the noun to which it is attached. *Diab'-là* can be situated within the earliest tradition of Creole-inflected literature, which dates from the Guyanese author Alfred Parépou's *Atipa: un roman guyanais* (*Atipa: A Guyanese Novel*, 1885),[8] itself the earliest known novel to use a Creole word in its title (an *atipa* is a kind of fish), and a novel that was brought to new prominence by a host of scholars working in the 1980s, around the time of the Créolité movement.[9] In giving his first novel a Creole title, Zobel exploits what later postcolonial scholars have termed the metonymic gap, a technique which is described by Bill Ashcroft as 'a strategy of resistance, and […] a *refusal* to translate the world of the writer completely'.[10] The title *Diab'-là* ensures that the

---

6   Joseph Zobel, *Čertův chlapík: Román z Antil* (Praha: Pavel Prokop, 1949). Copy inspected via interlibrary loan from the University of West Bohemia University Library (Reference: 227.419) and located via the database of The European Library (www.theeuropeanlibrary.org/).

7   I would like to record my thanks to Benzo for our impromptu Creole grammar session at the Paris Salon du Livre in 2015.

8   Alfred Parépou, *Atipa: un roman guyanais* (Paris: Auguste Ghio, 1885).

9   See, for example, Marguerite Fauquenoy (ed.), *Atipa revisité ou les itinéraires de Parépou* (Fort-de-France: Presses Universitaires Créoles/Paris: L'Harmattan, 1989).

10 Bill Ashcroft, 'Bridging the Silence: Inner Translation and the Metonymic Gap', in *Language and Translation in Postcolonial Literatures: Multilingual Contexts, Translational Texts*, ed. Simona Bertacco (New York: Routledge: 2014), p. 25; emphasis original.

text's linguistic innovation and resolutely, unabashedly Creole context are proclaimed before its cover has even been turned, a defiant gesture from a debut novelist which was matched by Zobel's equally defiant subject matter.

Revolution in a Fishing Village

Completed in 1942, and first published in 1945, *Diab'-là* was, and remains, an audacious development in Caribbean literature. Its radical thesis resulted in several processes of censorship being applied to the work, and a detailed discussion of the novel's complicated publication history is given later in this chapter. The novel's plot is relatively straightforward: Diab'-là, a stranger from Martinique's agricultural interior, arrives in the southern village of Le Diamant and urges the members of this small fishing community to recognise and cultivate the most valuable unexploited asset which they have in their possession: the land.

In Le Diamant, the majority of the land has been carved up and privatised for wide-scale plantation exploitation, to the detriment of the wider population, who in turn have become estranged from it, and lost valuable skills and knowledge. The fishermen of Le Diamant identify with Diab'-là's desire for autonomy, but assume that he, as a 'terrien', a term which carries the twin pejorative meanings of 'country bumpkin' and 'land-lubber', must intend to seek work at the local plantation. Although the noun *la plantation* exists in French, Zobel's narrative uses the word *habitation*, the French Caribbean term for plantation, in another example of the bold insertion of a term which would immediately resonate with local Martinican readers, but which would disorientate readers from metropolitan France. The fishermen's assumption proves incorrect, and Diab'-là's violent reaction leaves them in no doubt as to his utter contempt for the loaded term *habitation* and all it denotes:

> L'homme parut violemment vexé:
> — Encore! s'écria-t-il. Mais j'ai échoué ici pour fuir *ça!* ... Messieurs, on dit y a pas de sot métier ni de métier des sots; eh bé, je vous assure que *ça*, dans les conditions les békés vous flanquent dedans, cé plus raide que la mort, cé plus raide que si on vous taillait le dos à coups de cravache de lundi à samedi soir! (p. 33)

At this, the man's face twisted in anger, and he exclaimed:
'Not again! I came here to escape *that*! My good sirs, they say that no job is truly foolish, just as no job exists that is only for fools; well, I can assure you that *there*, being worked to the bone by the *békés*, it's a fate worse than death, it's worse than having your back flayed by the whip from Monday to Saturday night!'

This eloquent attack on the *békés*' tyranny and the ignominy of working in the canefields of the plantation calls to mind Wood's comments, quoted at this chapter's opening, that plantations can more accurately be referred to as slave labour camps, which required a never-ending supply of human bodies to be put to work in the most dehumanising of tasks. Diab'-là's visceral hatred of the *habitation* leads him to equate it explicitly with slavery (even in this post-abolition era), and to comment that he would rather 'faucher les cheminées qui fument comme pour provoquer mon estomac vide' (tear down the chimneys which smoke away and goad my growling stomach) (p. 33). In the Caribbean, chimneys were only found on the *usines*, the factories where sugar was produced, and here, as in Antillean literature throughout the late twentieth and twenty-first century, the chimney serves as a potent dual symbol of exploitation and of the potential for vengeance. Diab'-là rejects outright the economic oppression of the plantations, in which workers' meagre pay is directly inverse to the hard physical labour they undertake: 'D'ailleurs, j'estime trop la force que j'ai là, pour que chaque samedi soir après la paie je sois encore plus triste que les cinq jours avant!' (Anyway, I know the strength I have here will save me from that sorry pay queue on Saturday evenings, waiting for a pittance that leaves the plantation worker in greater despair than the work itself!) (p. 33). This theme prefigures the famous pay scene in Zobel's later novel *La Rue Cases-Nègres*, where an incredulous plantation worker counts his meagre pay and exclaims: 'Qu'est-ce que j'attends pour crever, tonnerre!' (p. 62) ('What's keeping me from dying, God-damn-it!', p. 35). Zobel's first novel denounces the fact that the post-slavery plantation workers still live in the most brutal, inequitable of worlds, and introduces one character, Diab'-là, who has the audacity to envision an alternative system.

At Diab'-là's protests that he will not work on the *habitation*, the fishermen assume he must be intending to join them at sea: 'la mer est à tout le monde ici!' (here, the sea belongs to everyone!) (p. 34); water would indeed seem to present the liberty Diab'-là craves. Diab'-là, however, dares to differ: he has identified a need for locally grown vegetables and is determined to address this challenge. Unable to buy his own land, he offers himself as a casual labourer to any residents of Le Diamant who possess unused plots of land, with the promise that he will share all profits with the landowner. As Randolf Hezekiah has observed, Zobel's early novels tend to take the pattern of a hero arriving in a new environment, first experiencing alienation, and then gradually moving to assert himself and 'achieve some degree of recognition', and this pattern shapes *Diab'-là*.[11] Zobel's first novel is about the bonds which knit together communities, and how these communities can adapt to shape the environment around them, redefining their relationship with the land in the process.

Stylistically, Zobel's literary debut also displays a fluid manipulation of literary form and style which might surprise readers familiar with the more circumspect and pedestrian prose of his later novels. *Diab'-là* opens with a short text titled 'En guise d'introduction', (By Way of an Introduction), which is a flashback to a previous conversation between two unnamed men, and acts as a framing device for the story. It is written from the perspective of one of these men, who obviously represents the author of the story which follows – this man is evidently Zobel himself, although he is never named. He recalls drinking a rum punch in a coastal bar in the company of an esteemed, unnamed friend, who is addressed with respect using the formal French pronoun *vous*. The author refers to this friend as a mentor who has encouraged him to write: 'Vous devriez écrire, un nègre comme vous …' (You should write, a Negro like you …) (p. 11). The term *nègre* immediately positions the author as a man of the people, from a sugarcane plantation background, rather than a member of the elite. Its inclusion is indicative of the influence of Négritude in reclaiming and destigmatising a term which was at the time, and remains to some extent, synonymous with slavery (a fuller discussion of the term *nègre* is found in Chapter One of this study). Given Zobel's own documented comments on the genesis of *Diab'-là*, and in particular the chance conversation with Césaire at the Lycée Schœlcher which inspired the novel, the unnamed friend and mentor can only be Césaire himself. Roland Monpierre's 2015 graphic novel adaptation of *Diab'-là* is unequivocal on this point, and his opening frames Zobel on one side of the page – or, rather, on one side of the bar table – and Césaire on the other.[12]

11   Hezekiah, p. 45.
12   Monpierre, pp. 8–11.

In addition, the reference to this mentor-figure's recent return to Martinique (p. 12) further connects the mentor-figure with the notion of *retour*, in a nod to the first edition of *Cahier d'un retour au pays natal*, which Césaire had published in Paris just three years earlier, in 1939.

This metatextual device is set up in the most unaffected way imaginable: the two men are drinking together in a small bar which anticipates Les Sept Péchés (The Seven Sins), the bar where much of *Diab'-là*'s action unfolds. They sit staring out to sea and putting the world to rights. Indeed, the introduction to *Diab'-là* offers one of the most affectionate and alluring descriptions of drinking rum punch in any Francophone Caribbean text. The author lingers over his glass of 'rhum clair comme le soleil sur du sable, et une émeraude de citron' (rum, clear as sunshine on sand, and an emerald of lime) (p. 11). As the sun sets, he becomes introspective and stares at 'l'irisation du couchant au fond de mon verre' (the iridescence of the setting sun at the bottom of my glass) (p. 12). This bar setting is calculated to appeal to a popular readership who identify as *nègres*, like the author, a group who would not easily identify with traditional French literature, and for whom this novel was the first attempt to depict their everyday Martinican world.

Beginning with a familiar, popular setting is a skilful way of drawing the reader into the speaker's story, before broadening out to more challenging themes. For the real subject of the men's conversation is anything but anodyne: they are speaking of politics and Négritude, without ever directly mentioning the terms. The introduction includes a thinly veiled reference to Vichy: 'Il est vrai que depuis avant-hier on a volé toutes les lumières, mais ne dormons pas [...] Il s'agit de ne pas dormir, ni d'avoir peur, ni de rester muets' (It is true that the day before yesterday, someone put out all the lights, but that does not mean we have to sleep [...] Now is not the time for sleep, or to be afraid, or to remain silent) (p. 12). This is by far the most pointed political reference to Vichy in the novel, and is a poetic exhortation of the Martinican population to seek radical change in their society.

Diab'-là is a novel which aims to change black consciousnesses so that the political situation in Martinique can evolve. Prompted by his discussion with the unnamed mentor, the author decides that he will put their conversation into action, and write a new kind of story, which grants black Martinicans a different, positive destiny. In a playful gesture, the writer teases his readers by suggesting that in order to keep boredom at bay, the anonymous *vous*[13] – a pronoun which once referred to the single unnamed mentor, Césaire, but which by the preface's close appears to have taken on a collective dimension and to denote a much wider audience comprising the Martinican people – will sing the songs. From the outset, *Diab'-là* is figured as a collaborative novel, a story of the people, told with the participation of the people, with the aim of creating a new founding narrative for black lives in Martinique, in a mode directly inspired by Césaire and Négritude. With this, in a final deft touch, the traditional call and response Creole storytelling formula 'Cric!' 'Crac!' (p. 12) enthusiastically heralds the beginning of this unmistakably Martinican novel.

Diab'-là: The Personification of Négritude

The character of Diab'-là embodies Zobel's vision of a popular Négritude: he is a black hero who works for his own financial and spiritual liberation, who demonstrates solidarity with his wider community, and who displays both pride in his black identity and a wider racial curiosity about pan-Caribbean black history and politics. *Diab'-là* offers an overt celebration of blackness as a racial and cultural identifier, and continues Négritude's work of seeking to change the perception of blackness. From the hero's first appearance in the second chapter of the novel, he is defined by his colour and his impressive physique:

> A la patine générale de sa peau, et à la solidité de sa voix, c'était un nègre-rouge, d'environ trente-cinq ans [...] Sa mâchoire, très musclée, saillait un peu sous les oreilles, et sous sa veste kaki, fermée presque sous son menton dur, sa respiration soulevait lourdement sa poitrine bloquée entre les gonflements massifs de ses épaules. (p. 25)

> From the sheen of his dark skin, and the deep resonance of his voice, it was clear that he was born of a long line of Negroes, and was about thirty-five years old [...] His jaw was thick-set and jutted out a little under his ears, and under his kaki jacket, which was buttoned almost all the way up to his firm chin, every breath he drew made his broad chest rise and fall between his broad muscular shoulders.

---

13 In French, the pronoun *vous* (you) is used to address one person in a formal manner and also whenever a speaker is addressing more than one person at the same time.

The term 'nègre-rouge' denotes a man of African appearance, who does not appear to be of mixed race.[14] Throughout the narrative, Diab'-là is figured as a man whose ancestry is unabashedly African and Caribbean, rather than French and European; and he proclaims this identity with pride. Here again, the colour red subtly underscores the character's link to a devil.

The novel is Zobel's first sustained attempt at expanding Négritude's stylistic framework, moving beyond the movement's predilection for destabilising surrealism, *écriture automatique*, and sparse poetic verse. Instead, it offers a sustained creative exploration of the lives of black Martinicans who belong to the socio-economic group of *nègres* or *petits-nègres*, expressed now, for the first time, in deliberately engaging prose, and in the equally engaging genre of social realism. In so doing, Zobel aimed to broaden Négritude's readership, and to reach sectors of the population who had been excluded by the dazzling rhetoric of the movement's poetry but who might be enticed by a more 'applied' version. His novel demonstrates, in accessible prose, the practical potential of Négritude's abstract ideas. Diab'-là's first words appear intriguingly cryptic to the fishermen:

> L'homme [...] retroussa lentement sa manche et découvrit un bras noueux et dur, façonné comme de la chair forgée.
> — Y a du fer là dedans [sic], dit-il, en le martelant de son poing. Quand on a ça, cé pour le faire suer et manger sa patate où qu'on se trouve! (p. 24)
>
> The man [...] slowly rolled up his sleeve to display a sinuous, firm arm, which looked like cast-iron made flesh.
> 'That there is iron', he said, hammering on it with his fist. 'When you've got that, is sure you can use it to work up a sweat and feed your belly wherever you find yourself!'

Diab'-là's creolised speech immediately defines his social class: he is both black and poor, a worker, like the fishermen themselves. The novel includes long passages of dialogue which demonstrate Zobel's remarkable literary talents as he invents his own method of code-switching between French and Creole. For example, the terms 'cé' and 'ayen', for *c'est* (it is) and *rien* (nothing), abound in an attempt to

---

14 As explained on the website maintained by the Groupe Européen de Recherches en Langues Créoles http://creoles.free.fr/Cours/chabin.htm (accessed 17 May 2016).

faithfully transcribe the sounds of Creole speech, in a technique which is highly reminiscent of the idiomatic written dialogue style pioneered in the works of Negro Renaissance authors Claude McKay and Richard Wright. The 1989 Créolité movement, which was founded by three Martinican authors and champions Creole languages and cultures, generated a surprisingly limited amount of interest in rereadings of *Diab'-là*, of which the most significant legacy is an important 2006 article by Alfred Largange which is reproduced on the Potomitan website (the website associated with the 'CAPES de Créole', the teacher-training qualification in Creole). Largange's perceptive reading draws attention to the considerable appeal of the novel's style and content for a local audience, and he positions *Diab'-là* as 'le texte fondateur de la créolité' (the founding text of Créolité).[15] This critical interpretation draws attention to the revisionist nature of the claims to originality made by the founders of Créolité in the late 1980s. Indeed, Zobel's early style is infused with Martinican Creole and the rhythms, both spoken and sung, of Creole society. The novel is peppered with Creole terms which are glossed with footnotes, such as 'touaous' (seabird, p. 15) 'békés' (white creoles, p. 33), 'blaff' (spicy seafood stew, p. 68), 'toulou-lous' (small red crabs, p. 69), and 'iche' (child, p. 85). Other nautical Creole terms such as 'cayolis' (p. 11), meaning seaweed, and 'twart' (p. 17), a kind of boat, are not glossed, again employing the metonymic gap in a refusal to render this society entirely transparent to the uninitiated reader, who must ponder over these unfamiliar terms, and make an educated guess at their meaning. Zobel does not lay out his entire Martinican society for external scrutiny; some elements remain opaque, reminding the reader of their inability to ever entirely possess a foreign culture through reading alone.

This connection between Zobel and the writers of Créolité was pointed out to the ageing author; at this, he expressed his dissatisfaction with the movement due to what he considered its inauthentic reappropriation of Creole.[16] He agreed that there are clear similarities between the movement and his own attempts to represent the rhythms of spoken Creole on the French page, yet he was disdainful of the celebrity status which this had conferred on the group he disparagingly

---

15   Alfred Largange, 'Lire et relire Diab'-là', article published in 2006, and made available online at: http://www.potomitan.info/bibliographie/zobel/diabla.php (accessed 13 July 2015).
16   Tarrieu, pp. 36–37.

referred to as 'ces grands prêtres du créole' (these high priests of creole).[17] Moreover, Zobel reaffirmed his distance from all theoretical movements, commenting that decades earlier, he had indeed written literature akin to that of the authors of Créolité, but it would not have crossed his mind to claim that he was founding a new movement: 'à ce moment-là je ne m'étais pas porté comme celui qui était créateur d'une école' (at the time, I did not go around behaving like someone who was the founder of a new movement).[18] Zobel appears here to hold the staunchly Négritude line towards the 1990s literary movement, a position of antagonism due partly to the critique of Négritude and Aimé Césaire advanced by Créolité. There is, notwithstanding, a clear similarity between Zobel's literary innovations in the 1940s and the 1980s Créolité movement which made its founders literary superstars. Yet while the authors of Créolité used connections and publishing mechanisms to obtain a degree of international celebrity, and tapped into a more international cultural trend towards the rediscovery of local identities in order to examine a global/local tension, Zobel's locally published novel was so at odds with the *zeitgeist* of his time that he struggled to find editors willing to take the risk of publishing it.

Diab'-là's aural appeal and social realism are further enhanced by references to real songs. It is an experimental text which, much like early jazz poetry, infuses literature with music. In this way, it creates what can be thought of as its own soundtrack, which ranges from recorded discs to the work songs sung by the men and women as they labour the land. This soundtrack includes 'Ah Gade chabine-là' ('O Look at that Chabine'), the carnival hit of 1927 and a successful record by the famous clarinettist and bandleader Alexandre Stellio (1885–1939),[19] who was born in Martinique and was credited with bringing the musical style of the beguine to Paris. It also includes the infectiously catchy 'Dans trou crab'-là' ('Crab in a Hole'), which was recorded by the bandleader Ernest Léardée, a three-minute beguine in which the clarinet plays a jaunty tune to a break-neck tam-tam beat, released in the 1930s.[20] Through these popular references, Zobel heightens the verisimilitude of his text, and

17 Tarrieu, p. 37.
18 Tarrieu, p. 37.
19 Alexandre Stellio, 'Ah Gade chabine-là', *Au bal antillais: Franco-Creole Biguines from Martinique*, CD (1992).
20 Ernest Léardée, 'Dans trou crab'-là', *Quand Paris biguinait: orchestres créoles 1930–1940*, CD (1991).

further appeals to local readers who will recognise themselves and their culture on the printed page. More than just producing Creole-inflected language, Zobel was pioneering a multilayered style that Glissant would (much) later term 'oraliture', or oral literature.[21] *Diab'-là* breaks with existing literary conventions to build a story composed of words and sounds, printed text and voices.

The power of language and sound is nowhere more evident than in Diab'-là's speech. Although he speaks the local Creole, and is not a member of any social elite, he is an orator and his words create images and riddles which silence his peers, who find themselves repeatedly caught 'entre l'admiration et la méfiance' (between admiration and mistrust) (p. 24). The revelation of his name is itself highly dramatic:

> L'homme hésita un peu au fond de sa gorge:
> — Moi? fit-il, Diab'-là ...
> Il avait dit cela avec un écarquillement involontairement dramatique des yeux. (p. 24)
>
> The man's voice caught a little at the back of his throat:
> 'Me?' he said, 'I'm Diablo'.
> As he uttered these words, his eyes opened wide and flashed spontaneously.

His physical abilities are paired with his sharp intelligence, and he is singled out as a leader from his earliest days in Le Diamant: but he does not act alone. In Fidéline, who, as her name suggests, is loyalty or fidelity personified, Diab'-là finds his feminine counterpart. The meeting between the two, however, is far from conventional. On his first night in Le Diamant, Diab'-là confides in his new friend Jérôme that he needs a woman, and asks the local man to introduce him to one. He explains this direct attitude as ideologically and not just sexually motivated:

> — Je te demande pas de faire le maquereau [...] Quand on va dans un pays à l'aventure comme ça, sans même se demander pourquoi on laisse son patelin – parce qu'on a mare [*sic*] de certaines choses qui aigrissent la dignité – enfin je vais te raconter après [...] la première chose à faire, je te dis, faut commencer par se procurer une vaillante femme! (p. 27)
>
> I'm not asking you to be a pimp [...] When you head out to seek your fortune in new lands, without even stopping to ask yourself why you left home – because you're sick and tired of certain things which are an

---

21 Édouard Glissant, *Le Discours antillais* (Paris: Seuil, 1981), p. 778.

affront to your dignity – ah, I'll tell you another time [...] the first thing to do, I tell you, is to begin by finding a valiant woman!

Rather than seeking a single night of sexual pleasure, and using an unknown and temporary feminine body to satisfy his desires, Diab'-là makes it clear that he is placing a woman at the centre of his new venture in life, and that he sees her role as inextricably linked to his own. Above all, he values the emotional and spiritual fulfilment borne of a solid relationship:

> — Et je t'assure, appuya Diab'-là, cé de là il faut prendre son départ pour vivre dans le pays! [...] On a beau dire, cé une femme qui pilote un homme, cé une femme qui le mène à Dieu ou au tonnerre de Dieu! (p. 27)

> 'And mark my words', Diablo added, 'that's where you need to start if you really want to live well in this land! [...] As we tend to say, it's woman who guides man – in truth, it's woman who leads him to God, or to the wrath of God!'

Fidéline's first encounter with Diab'-là remains a rather clumsy plot inclusion at the beginning of a debut novel. It assumes a certain availability on the part of a single woman which is troubling, although it also acknowledges that women's own sexual desires are as powerful as those of men. This unconventional meeting, which foregrounds sexual attraction, results in a current of eroticism between Diab'-là and Fidéline which runs through the novel, and is present from their first scene together, when Fidéline is introduced, in bed, waking up next to Diab'-là:

> Alors, la jeune femme aspira l'odeur chaude de l'homme et s'allongea et se pressa contre lui, afin que sa joue, son flanc, sa cuisse, fussent, à travers sa mince chemise, accolés à ce grand corps endormi. Et elle resta longtemps, écoutant le délire fiévreux de sa chair. (p. 28)

> The young woman breathed in the man's warm scent and stretched herself out, pressing herself against him, until, through her thin nightgown, her cheek, leg and thigh were nestled against his large sleeping body. And she lay like this for some time, listening to the feverish delirium of her skin.

There are several references to Diab'-là's nudity, told from Fidéline's perspective, while the narrative refuses any such appreciation of Fidéline's own body. In contrast to his bare skin, she is wearing a chemise, again working to counter any impression that the novel's sexualisation of women is a blatant objectification. Instead, it is Diab'-là who is described in lingering detail by Fidéline as her admiring gaze snakes up his naked body (p. 30). Fidéline's admiration of Diab'-là's superior physical attributes is in line with Négritude's celebration of black physicality and black sexuality, and also conforms to the representation of a heteronormative reproductive couple; however, the narrative's emphasis on female sexuality and desire is quite atypical. From his earliest short stories in *Le Sportif*, Zobel is unusual in describing sexuality from a female perspective, as typified by the short story 'Défense de danser' ('Dancing not Allowed'), which is reproduced in his 1946 short story collection *Laghia de la mort*.

Fidéline's appreciation of her new partner owes some debt to her former lovers. Interestingly, it is the male villagers Jérôme and Asto, rather than female villagers, who are glimpsed gossiping about her sexual past. Fidéline is not chastised for slipping from an ideal absolute of chastity; rather Jérôme and Asto are sympathetic to the misfortunes she has suffered in her romantic life. She had a previous relationship with the ominously named Amant (Lover), who repaid her kindness by flirting with young women described as 'câpresses', a term which refers to mixed-race women with a light complexion. Fideline's reaction to this slight – which was both gendered and racial, containing the implicit suggestion of his preference for lighter-skinned women – was unambiguous, and she sent Amant packing. Another relationship with a partner named Léon ended just as badly, as he stole from her to feed his gambling habit:

> Faut dire cé une femme qui n'attend pas sur un homme pour manger. Loin de là, elle prop'tait Léon [...] et le salaud ne lui mordait-il pas les doigts pour lui prendre son argent et aller au pitt! (p. 32)
>
> You've got to say that she's not the kind of woman who relies on a man to feed her. Far from it! Why, she looked after Léon [...] and that bastard threw it back in her face, taking her money to go gambling at the cock pit.

Important here is the insistence that in her previous relationships, Fidéline has shown that she does not need a man to support her. Diab'-là and Fidéline rapidly form a strong bond which, after their initial encounter, is not directly dwelled on in the narrative. Towards the novel's close, there is a brief and elliptical reference to the fact that they have married, when Fidéline appears at a party 'au bras de son mari' (on her husband's arm) (p. 147). In the final chapter, her pregnancy, which reflects their garden's recovered fecundity, is announced in a similarly cryptic manner when she comments to a friend: 'Et puis nous avions encore une chose à dire … Ah! non, cé pas moi qui vais dire ça, parce que cé lui qui a fait ce beau travail-là!' (And we wanted to say one more thing ... Ah, no, I'm not going to tell you, because that good work is all down to him!) (p. 168).

The romantic love story between Diab'-là and Fidéline is not the main focus of *Diab'-là*, although it forms the backdrop to the narrative. What is foregrounded is their compatibility and the importance the narrative sets on a partnership between a *nègre* and a *négresse* which is based on strong physical attraction, affection, and a shared belief in the transformative potential of their own lived Négritude, a stance of dignity and ambition which influences their everyday behaviours. Fidéline is integral to the success of Diab'-là's agricultural venture. In the early stages, it is she who takes on extra work to keep the couple financially solvent: 'Fidéline, blanchisseuse de son côté, étayait le ménage' (Fidéline, who was a skilful laundress, took on work to prop up the household) (p. 47). The verb 'étayer', which translates as 'to support' or 'to prop up' makes it clear that Diab'-là's partner in life plays an equal role in his – or rather their joint – success, and that Fidéline can also be the lead breadwinner.

Indeed, Fidéline is the rarest of archetypes in Martinican literature: she is an active romantic heroine whose life is not beset by tragedy. There are few descriptions of Fidéline's physical traits, as she is almost always defined by her actions. Her beauty is equated with, and heightened by, her accomplishments at work, exemplified by a passage which marks her first appearance at the market in Le Diamant:

> Et c'est là, dans cet étalage de taches vives et fraîches, plus rayonnant qu'une parure, debout en sa robe d'indienne relevée et drapée par devant, la tête solidement nouée pour être bien à ses affaires, c'est là que Fidéline était belle. (p. 49)

> And it was there, among this charming display of lively and fresh colours, that she stood upright, gleaming brighter than a jewel, in her draped Indian dress, her headscarf firmly knotted so it wouldn't slip and fall in her way, it was there that Fidéline was truly beautiful.

In the female-dominated environment of the market, surrounded by produce which she and Diab'-là have grown together, Fidéline is at her most radiant. This scene derives erotic charge from Diab'-là's position as a voyeur, covertly watching her from his seat at the bar. Her beauty radiates from her self-fulfilment, and her satisfaction and joy at their joint achievements. This important passage has been discussed by Lyne-Rose Beuze, the head of Martinique's museums and a prominent critic of Martinican culture. Beuze suggests that the French painter André Maire's *Marchandes* (Female Market Vendors) series of paintings form the ideal illustrations to Zobel's novel, particularly *L'Approvisionnement du marché en plein air* (*Supplying the Open Air Market*), a lively market scene showing women at work, which Beuze equates explicitly with Fidéline's moment of triumph at the outdoor market.[22]

Relations between the sexes in the Caribbean have been complicated by the inhumane conditions of plantation slavery, where sexual violation was a frequent occurrence, either as a transactional encounter for profit where forced reproduction was systematically applied with the aim of producing more slaves, or to gratify the sexual appetites of a male whose position in the ethnoclass hierarchy enabled him to prey on the vulnerable. It would take the twentieth-century intervention of an African-American sociologist, Edward Franklin Frazier, to articulate the structures which had contributed to the different development of family units in plantation societies in the United States. In *The Negro Family in the United States* (1939), Frazier presented the plantation as a site of emasculation and discussed the development of a family structure which was held together by females, and which he termed the 'matriarchate'.[23] He described in detail a plantation system in which selective reproduction was enforced in order to supply new slaves, and where men were instructed to procreate without having any subsequent responsibility for the women they had impregnated, or for the children born of these encounters. Male slaves were stripped of power and compelled to defer to the overseers and slave drivers, who upheld a system in which the plantation owner and master was the ultimate patriarch, holding the power to decide the fate of slave men, women, and children. Such a system can, after Foucault, be understood as a biopolitical system for the governance of human life.[24]

---

[22] André Maire (1898–1984) travelled to Martinique in 1968 at the age of 70 and spent time painting in Le Diamant, which was then still a small fishing town of just 2,000 inhabitants, very similar to the society Zobel describes in *Diab'-là*. See Lyne-Rose Beuze, *André Maire (1898–1984): un peintre voyageur à la découverte de l'Ame Martiniquaise* (Fort-de-France: Musée Régional d'Histoire et d'Ethnographie, 2006), p. 22.

[23] Edward Franklin Frazier, *The Negro Family in the United States* (Notre Dame, IN: University of Notre Dame Press, 2001 [1939]).

[24] I explore Caribbean biopolitics in another publication. See my contributions to 'Race, Violence and Biopolitics', a special issue of the *International Journal of Francophone Studies*, 17.3–4 (2014), guest ed. by Louise Hardwick and Alessandro

Zobel's first novel, which holds the bond between a man and a woman sacrosanct, suggests that an alternative Caribbean narrative for gender relations is possible. Diab'-là's conviction that a woman will lead a man to success or failure in life, and that a strong relationship is the bedrock of happiness, is an indication of his respect for the place of women in Caribbean society, and for the specific challenges faced by Caribbean women. Indeed, Zobel accords women a more active role than is generally found in the Négritude writing of Césaire, Damas, and Senghor. Their poetry venerated the black woman's attractiveness and erotic appeal, but simultaneously placed her in a passive role, and objectified her. In contrast, Zobel underscores his heroine's agency, and figures her as quite capable of operating independently of any man. Moreover, a successful match will harness the couple's agency to produce a formidable co-created power. Diab'-là and Fidéline work together for the same goals; one cannot succeed without the other, and they enable each other to reach their potential.

The Politics of Place and Race

In *Diab'-là*, Zobel drew on his own first-hand experiences in the southern coastal village of Le Diamant, where he had worked as an employee of the Department of Bridges and Highways (Ponts et Chaussées) between 1937 and 1938.[25] The novel's setting is significant for the parallels it invites with Zobel's biography – the young stranger from inland arriving in a fishing village – but it also has a wider significance. Le Diamant is one of the island's most symbolically charged locations, and is famous for 'le rocher du Diamant', known in English as 'Diamond Rock'. Rising some 176 metres out of the sea, this volcanic rock is one of the island's most famous landmarks, and is said to be named for its indestructibility and its chiselled shape. The last in a chain of extinct volcanoes which runs across Martinique, the rock's geological composition means that it is able to withstand the onslaught of the Caribbean Sea (the waves around Le Diamant are notoriously rough). At the novel's opening, Diab'-là arrives in Le Diamant and contemplates the famous rock, as though to draw inspiration from its resilience:

Corio. See in particular: Hardwick and Corio, 'Introduction' (pp. 285–304), and Hardwick, 'Creolizing the Caribbean "Coolie": A Biopolitical Reading of Indian Indentured Labourers and the Ethnoclass Hierarchy' (pp. 397–420).
25 'Zobel: sa vie, son œuvre', p. 20.

> Diab'-là achevait une cigarette en regardant le rocher qui trempait là, tel un caillot dur picoré d'oiseaux noirs et gris. Il regarda aussi l'Anse Cafard où l'embrun faisait une buée violine à la racine du Morne. (pp. 34–35)

> Diab'-là finished his cigarette, gazing out at the sea-battered rock, which looked like a solid stone that had been pecked away by the black and grey birds. He looked towards Anse Cafard, too, where the sea spray rose in a violet mist at the base of the Morne.

The description of Diab'-là's new environment begins at the symbolic Diamond Rock, and then scans along the horizon to the Anse Cafard, a cove situated at the far end of the beach, and the Morne (the French Caribbean term for a volcanic hill). This is one of Martinique's best-known vistas, instantly recognisable to Martinicans and visitors to the island alike. Le Diamant is an important site of memory. The seas around the rock were the site of fierce naval battles between the French and the English during the Napoleonic wars, and in 1925 the area was the scene of a massacre which the anthropologist Richard Price focuses on in *The Convict and the Colonel: A Story of Colonialism and Resilience in the Caribbean*,[26] an account of a political scandal and a massacre of poor black workers which, as Price observes, has all but slipped from modern consciousness. Today, one of the island's most important historical monuments to slavery is found at Anse Cafard. The clifftop above the cove marks the site where the last slave ship was shipwrecked in Martinique. More recently, this tragedy was commemorated by Laurent Valère's magisterial *Mémorial Cap 110* sculpture comprising 15 giant stone torsos, each facing towards the Gulf of Guinea in Africa, inaugurated in 1998 to mark the bicentenary of abolition.[27]

Le Diamant is an exceptional location where Martinican history, culture, and the natural environment are entwined with particular intensity. It is fitting, then, that Zobel places Diab'-là in this highly symbolic and mythical landscape to harness his extraordinary powers and forge a new legend about the relationship between humans and their environment. The shift is clearly influenced by Négritude; throughout the novel, Zobel uses imagery to suggest parallels between the agricultural revolution which Diab'-là is leading in Le Diamant, and past slave rebellions. At pivotal moments, a conch call (the act of blowing into a conch shell to produce a muted but resonant noise) is

---

26 Richard Price, *The Convict and the Colonel: A Story of Colonialism and Resilience in the Caribbean* (Durham, NC: Duke University Press, 2006).
27 See: http://www.laurentvalereartstudio.com/cap-110-1 (accessed 29 June 2017).

evoked, in a subtle narrative suggestion of revolt. This sound is symbolic of the *esclave marron*, or maroon, the escaped slave who revolts and resists, for whom the conch was an important means of communication. As Diab'-là explains his vision to work the land to Jérôme, the characters both hear a distant conch call (p. 36). When this plan takes shape because Ti-Jeanne asks Diab'-là to tend her plot of land, this significant moment is heralded by a mysterious sound, or even a gut feeling, which is likened to a conch call: 'Soudain, on eût dit une conque qui soufflait' (Suddenly, it seemed a conch was being sounded) (p. 61). This implied call is a metaphor for the freedom represented by Ti-Jeanne's offer of land. In a later scene, two men look out to sea and discuss the sound of the conch used by the fishermen, and its ability to elicit an instinctive response in them (p. 82). Finally, once the garden is in full bloom, Diab'-là cups his hands and makes a sound like a conch call to attract Fidéline's attention, and she responds in kind (p. 136). These subtle references to the conch incorporate the specific symbolism of Caribbean revolt and autonomy into the narrative; their significance might not be grasped by a European, but would have been immediately accessible to Martinican readers.

Diab'-là was written during the Second World War at the historic moment when Martinicans were forced to re-evaluate their relationship to their own land, because the Vichy-controlled island was blockaded by the Allies. In a short note added for the 1945 publication, Zobel explains his novel's fraught pathway to publication:

> Voici le roman que j'avais écrit en 1942 à l'intention de mes compatriotes gémissant dans les ténèbres de la « Révolution nationale ».
> Pour cause, il fut interdit par la censure du représentant du gouvernement de Vichy aux Antilles, l'amiral Robert.
> Aujourd'hui, à la faveur des libertés retrouvées, je le livre au public tel que l'amour de mon pays et de mes congénères me l'avait inspiré.
> Fort-de-France, le 15 avril 1945.

> Here is the novel that I had written in 1942 for my compatriots who were languishing in the gloom of the 'National Revolution'.
> With good reason, it was banned through the censorship of the government representative for Vichy in the French Antilles, Admiral Robert.
> Today, to honour freedoms so recently restored, I am making it available to the public in its original form, which was inspired by my love for my country and my kinsmen.
> Fort-de-France, 15 April 1945.

Zobel underscores the fact that his novel is destined primarily for internal audiences, and that these audiences were deprived of his work in 1942 by Vichy censorship (discussed in detail below). Indeed, the paratextual note contains the novel's only direct references to the Vichy government and their 'National Revolution'. This 'revolution' was spearheaded by Pétain and promoted a return to the land, ostensibly to recover lost knowledge, but in fact designed to reintroduce exploitation and submission and to force the many to labour for the few. Zobel's arguments for a return to the land had quite the opposite intention: he urged poor black Martinicans to reclaim their native soil as a means to cast off the shackles of over three centuries of colonial domination.

Intriguingly, on its publication in Paris in 1947, discussed in detail in the following pages, *Diab'-là* was immediately recognised as a novel which had particular significance for understandings of the human relationship to the land. In 1948, it was the joint winner of the Le Prix littéraire Sully-Olivier-de-Serres, a prize for literature of particular agricultural merit, along with *Le Galvaudeux: récit de la vie d'un berger (The Vagabond: The Life Story of a Shepherd)* by Alps-based author and shepherd Pierre Melet. Each author received the considerable sum of 5,000 *francs*.[28] Zobel's debut novel was ahead of its time in recognising Martinique's exceptional biodiversity. *Diab'-là* provides the first sustained description of the Martinican soil's fertility and its potential to engender new life; the soil and the growing cycle are as essential to the narrative as any of the characters. Coaxed back from a state of disorder, as weeds are replaced by seedlings, the soil reveals itself to be a priceless asset and, for the first time, the market at Le Diamant is supplied with vegetables which were, to the amazement of all, 'produits par cette rocaille de Diamant!' (produced by the gravelly soils of Le Diamant!) (p. 50). For these reasons, the novel must be recontextualised as an important contribution to a genre of writing which is now referred to as ecocriticism, a term which implies a pronounced focus on the environment and the human relationship to it.

The Haitian Jacques Roumain's *Gouverneurs de la rosée* (translated by Mercer Cook and Langston Hughes as *Masters of the Dew*) (1944)[29] is held to be the defining work of mid-century Francophone Caribbean

---

28 'Echos des lettres et des arts', *La Croix*, stamped 15 and 16 February 1948. Le Fonds Zobel: DD:JZ.B.246.
29 Jacques Roumain, *Gouverneurs de la roseé* (Port-au-Prince: Imprimerie de l'état, 1944). Translation by Mercer Cook and Langston Hughes, *Masters of the Dew* (New York: Reynal & Hitchcock, 1947).

ecocriticism. Roumain completed his novel shortly before his death on 18 August 1944, although he had been working on the project for several years prior to its completion. The manuscript of *Diab'-là* was completed on 12 August 1942, a date Zobel provides at the end of the novel (p. 174). That both authors were turning to their native soil and reimagining its potential for liberation of a literal and metaphorical nature, at around the same time, is significant. For Roumain, it can be read as a response to US incursions into his nation's sovereignty; for Zobel, as a similar response to the indignities of Vichy rule. There is a further potential connection. During his study visit to Haiti in the summer of 1944, it is possible that Césaire might have been charged by Zobel with seeking a publisher for *Diab'-là*. A letter dated 17 July 1944 and sent by Césaire from Haiti to Martinique's Governor Georges-Louis Ponton bears the postscript 'dis à Zobel que je ne l'ai pas oublié!' (tell Zobel I haven't forgotten him!),[30] although it is impossible to gauge the full significance of this brief comment. Had Zobel, still seeking a publisher for *Diab'-là*, asked Césaire to enquire whether a Haitian press might agree to publish the manuscript? At the time, Haiti had a more advanced publishing industry than the then French colony of Martinique. The full significance of the footnote is lost to time, but the postscript certainly demonstrates the close complicity between Césaire, Ponton, and Zobel in 1944, and suggests that Zobel had entrusted an unknown task to Césaire in Haiti.

The narrative arcs of Diab'-là and Roumain's Manuel bear striking similarities: both men make a mysterious entrance into small Caribbean communities, and proceed, by dint of their iconoclastic vision, to alter the very structure of these communities – a change which hinges on introducing a new set of interactions with the natural environment. They both form strong romantic relationships, and each novel ends with the promise of new life as their partners are pregnant. Yet the change in behaviours in *Gouverneurs de la rosée* is predicated on a dramatic, and symbolic, discovery of a spring at a critical time of human-induced drought, and the discovery of water allows a change in agricultural patterns. Roumain's more sensational novel includes intense sexual rivalry and jealousy, and ends in tragedy and bloodshed. Moreover, Manuel's anger at the exploitation of black men is attributed in part to the horror he has witnessed externally, elsewhere, on the massive

---

30 Aimé Césaire, letter to Georges-Louis Ponton, dated 17 July 1944, ANOM: FP 173APOM/1 PONTON.

plantations in Cuba. In contrast, unlike Manuel, who meets a tragic end, it is Diab'-là himself who leads events to a triumphant conclusion in Zobel's novel, and Zobel's more optimistic narrative does not rely on the miraculous discovery of a new water source, but on a series of small and gradual changes. *Diab'-là* does not include sensationalist plot lines, in keeping with Zobel's aspiration to produce a literature that would inspire his fellow Martinicans. Read in the context of the era, his is the more politically daring of the two novels, as it takes direct aim at the internal exploitation endemic in Martinique itself, and thus confronts the paradoxical dilemma of how to love a native land where the very social fabric is one of exclusion, domination, and exploitation.

J. Michael Dash has argued that *Gouverneurs de la rosée* belongs to a phase of Caribbean modernism in which authors sought to create foundational narratives based on 'a dream of liberation from an oppressive Western system of knowledge'; for Dash, however, these works do not bring about meaningful change, as they only '[end] up asserting a new, closed, hegemonic system of values'.[31] The question remains, however, as to whether the new systems explored in works such as *Gouverneurs de la rosée* and *Diab'-là* are indeed unsuccessful because they are closed and hegemonic, or whether they actually operate as purposely local circuits, in which individual participants can work together and make a tangible contribution to their everyday lives and communities. Given the increasingly prominent contemporary concerns about local autonomy and quality of life being sacrificed at the altar of international supra-structures which operate according to the neoliberal logic of profit margins and at the expense of all else, the 'local' turn signified by both novels appears more paradigmatic and more in harmony with an early twenty-first century drive towards localised collective actions across the globe. The systems proposed in the novels are localised actions able to target one or two specific problems and issues and lead to demonstrable benefits in these areas, although they remain countercurrents within a tide of global modernity, rather than possessing the power to turn the tide itself.

The most striking parallel between the two novels is the emphasis they both lay on collective labour. Diab'-là comments that he is following the conventions of his home region of Morne-Vent, and the group

---

31 J. Michael Dash, *The Other America: Caribbean Literature in a New World Context* (Charlottesville, VA/London: University Press of Virginia, 1998), pp. 79–80.

structure he sets up is reminiscent of the Haitian *coumbite* depicted in *Gouverneurs de la rosée*. Both works exemplify the survival of African cultural practices throughout its diaspora: the *coumbite* is an African structure of reciprocal group labour. Exactly the same dynamics are in evidence in Zobel's novel, as a group of men gather to 'éventrer la terre rebelle' (rip open the rebellious earth) (p. 77). Working the land thus ceases to feel like heavy labour, and instead takes on a playful aspect:

> Ils s'étaient répartis en plusieurs équipes sur les endroits les moins pénibles, et ils œuvraient tous les trente, sans geignement, au même rythme du tam-tam excitant. C'était une lutte amusante à qui surpasserait les autres, à qui prendrait la tête de son équipe, à grands coups cadencés, pour fouetter la queue de provocations stimulantes et joviales. (p. 77)

> They had split into several teams and set to work in the least difficult spots, and all thirty laboured, without any grumbles, to the tam-tam's encouraging, stimulating beat. They competed happily to see who would outdo the others and who would emerge as each team's best worker. They dug with great rhythmic strokes, and the stragglers were whipped with words of encouragement and mirth.

This scene, so closely resembling slave plantation labour, deliberately replaces the misery of working for another with the joy of working for aligned individual and collective goals. The link to slavery is made clear in the deliberate choice of the verb 'fouetter' (to whip), but now it is used to describe teasing words, which are unmistakably terms of frivolity and friendship. Everyone has a role to play – women prepare food and rum, and even the children are actively involved: 'Les enfants écartaient les souches évulsées [*sic*], entassaient les cailloux avec une activité de fourmis' (The children took away the torn-up roots, and piled up the stones, with ant-like assiduousness) (p. 77). The striking dental image of 'les souches évulsées' (torn-up roots) owes a debt to the surrealism of the Négritude authors, particularly Césaire, and is an example of the subtle use of surrealism and metaphor at work in Zobel's novel.

Diab'-là's young friend Asto is the next member of the group to benefit from the collective action. A nocturnal meeting is held to dig the foundations for his house so that he can marry, and once again, events take a distinctly festive turn: 'C'est exactement pareil à lorsque la marmaille s'amuse un soir quelconque, simplement pour s'éjouir [*sic*] d'une bonne semaine. Tout le village en est' (It's just like those evenings when the children spontaneously decide to play, for no other reason than to mark the end of a happy week) (p. 91). Building Asto's house is a musical affair, in one of the novel's most aural passages, rich with the sounds of tambour drums, singing voices, and the rhythmic noise of shovels digging into the earth (pp. 91–95). Two men dance an unnamed combat dance which is recognisable as a *laghia* to readers of Zobel's short story 'Laghia de la mort' (from the collection *Laghia de la mort*). By steeping this scene in musicality and physicality, Zobel foregrounds the characters' unabashedly African heritage – that is to say, their Négritude. The boldness of this gesture is illustrated by Zobel's comments on the popular prejudices surrounding the tambour drum at the time. In an interview, he recalls how when he was working in radio during the war, drums were taboo:

> Je me rappelle que pendant la guerre, pendant que j'étais l'attaché de presse du Gouverneur Ponton, il y avait quelqu'un qui était responsable de la radio et qui avait trouvé que c'était un petit peu anachronique de commencer les émissions par la Marseillaise ou par la Marche Lorraine. Il avait dit: 'par exemple, on pourrait ouvrir la radio par un roulement de tambour'; mais on lui a répondu: 'ici nous ne sommes pas en Afrique, le tam-tam c'est pour l'Afrique; nous ne sommes pas des Africains'. Les Martiniquais surtout tenaient à ne pas être pris pour des Africains.[32]

> I remember that during the war, when I was press attaché to Governor Ponton, someone who worked for the radio commented that it was a little anachronistic to begin the radio broadcasts with the Marseillaise or the Lorraine March. He said, 'We could begin with a tambour drum roll'. But the only response he got was: 'We're not in Africa, leave the tam-tam to Africa, we are not Africans'. Martinicans absolutely did not want to be mistaken for Africans.

In his own writing, the tambour drum is destigmatised and depicted as a purveyor of physical and psychological strength. Celebrating the connection with music which has evolved in black Caribbean popular society is an intrinsic part of Diab'-là's own lived Négritude, and the character's attitude stands in direct defiance of the widespread contemporary bourgeois disdain for the black Martinican musical heritage.

For all these positive depictions, the novel does not naively present rural life as a pastoral idyll; working the land is an arduous, unforgiving process, and success is contingent on the extraordinary efforts made by Diab'-là, Fidéline, and the wider community. When the couple finally

---

32 'Zobel: sa vie, son œuvre', pp. 29–30.

begin to harvest their crops, they remember that this is why they had worked so hard, and that the food itself is:

> Ce pour quoi ils avaient écorché le sol rétif.
> Ce pour quoi ils avaient imploré tantôt la pluie, tantôt le soleil.
> Ce pour quoi ils avaient eu des nuits entières d'anxiété et d'insomnie, après des journées de labeur passionné. (p. 138)

> The reason why they had flayed apart the reluctant soil.
> The reason why they had implored either the rain, or the sun.
> The reason why they had spent whole nights in the grip of anxiety and insomnia, after long days of enthusiastic labour.

This anaphoric structure, reminiscent of Césaire's use of anaphora throughout the *Cahier d'un retour au pays natal*, is a device that Zobel employed repeatedly at the beginning of his prose career, particularly in the short stories of *Laghia de la mort*. Here, the repetitive structure aptly sums up the cumulative efforts which, by the novel's close, have transformed the relationship with the land from troubled and fraught to benevolent and bountiful. This is symbolised by one of the final images of Diab'-là's contentment and harmony with nature:

> La vigueur de la végétation, l'ardeur des bêtes, la sérénité du ciel, éveillaient en lui un flux de vie si intense de beauté virile, une sérénité si pleine! (p. 152)

> The vigour of the vegetation, the vivacity of the animals, the serenity of the sky, awakened in him an intense appreciation of life, in a rush of pure creative beauty, and complete serenity!

Working the garden and coaxing it back to life has led Diab'-là to a sense of well-being and spiritual exaltation, a fertile and virile bond between humans and nature which reaches a climax with Fidéline's pregnancy at the novel's close. The uncanny timing of the pregnancy is another example of the rich magical realism that runs through the novel. The genre, characteristic of novels from the Americas and particularly Latin America, is used by Zobel to underscore his hero's proximity to non-French culture, as Diab'-là's supernatural abilities to work the land are attributed to his expertise in 'magie ancestrale' (ancestral magic) (p. 133). While this aids him in his agricultural project as it endows him with a heightened state of harmony with the island and its nature, his unprecedented success in tending the land is still clearly intended to set an example which could be emulated by any Martinicans with enough determination.

Diab'-là exhorts Martinicans to realise that whatever their social status, the land is their most precious asset, and implores them to look with fresh eyes at the natural world around them, and to regard it as a rallying point around which whole communities can be constructed. Once the foundations of Asto's house are dug, Diab'-là says he will call on the community again for further assistance. This collective action is essential, he comments, because:

> Faut toujours une entente. Faut faire en commun tout ce qu'y a à faire. Quand on fait ensemble une chose pour le bonheur d'un seul, cé le bonheur de tous en même temps. Et puis la chose est plus solide. Et le bonheur est plus durable … (p. 95)

> You always need an agreement. Every important job should be done as a group. When we do something together that will create happiness for one person, it's also a way to make the whole group happy. And what we've made is more solid. And the happiness lasts longer …

While Négritude poetry had called for change in abstract terms, Zobel's novel offers a blueprint for social change. It sets out a pattern of collaborative labour with clear beneficial outcomes for society. Collective action forges closer communal ties, and leads to a sense of empowerment. Moreover, it offers economic liberation from the *békés*' stranglehold. In farming his own land, Diab'-là is advocating a move away from capitalist accumulation, in a return to a barter economy where plants can be exchanged for animals, which in turn can be exchanged for more land, in a self-sustaining cycle. He has nothing but disdain for the language of money, which he finds utterly hollow: 'des mots qui n'évoquaient rien de beau, ni de vivant. C'étaient des mots sans chaleur' (words which did not mean anything beautiful, or living. They were words without warmth) (pp. 157–58). In his world view, money's place in life is reduced to a physical presence, something to be kept in a small container for emergencies, but not something to covet, because 'l'argent, ça durcit le cœur, et le rend comme la chair des lépreux, et le pourrit' (money hardens the heart, and makes it like a leper's skin, and rots away at it) (p. 159).

The forms of empowerment being expressed are all intrinsically linked to altering perceptions of blackness, but the novel does not openly preach its politics. Diab'-là leaves it to the villagers to come to this realisation themselves, a fact grasped by Asto: 'Messiés! Si un beau jour tous les nègres du monde voulaient se donner un coup de main comme ça, les uns aux autres, quelle sacrée victoire, hein!' (Gentlemen!

If one fine day all the Negroes of the world decided to help each other like this, one man helping the next, what a triumph that would be, eh!) (p. 78). Rather than unleashing philosophical terms on a population not yet ready to engage with them, Diab'-là's method of leadership is to take action, and then build on this momentum to encourage others to reflect on how to realise their full potential. His project (and, by extension, Zobel's own project with the novel) is intrinsically linked to Négritude's desire to change black consciousness and politically awaken black Martinicans, so that they might strive for greater autonomy.

Once significant progress has been made among the villagers of Le Diamant, the character of Capitain'-là is introduced and becomes the device through which the ideas of Négritude are more explicitly broached. In contrast to Diab'-là, he has retired from village life and, as Hezekiah has noted, 'devotes his energies, somewhat like old Gisors in *La Condition Humaine*, to an appraisal of the Black man's problems'.[33] Capitain'-là only appears in Chapter 11, just four chapters before the novel's close. The bipartite composition of his name confirms him as one of a line of Creole characters who have a special status in the text, from Diab'-là himself to the 'crab'-là', the subject of the hit record which almost causes a scuffle in the village (p. 54). Capitain'-là introduces an important pan-Caribbean dimension: he is of undetermined origin, but hails from one of the nearby British Caribbean islands, and was at one time referred to as 'l'Anglais' (p. 121). On his retirement, he returned to marry a Martinican girl he had met during his travels and took a house in Le Diamant.

Capitain'-là first appears in full flow discussing abolition at the bar Les Sept Péchés, midway through a conversation about Caribbean autonomy and self-determination. His radical political position emerges as he comments that the abolitionist Victor Schœlcher was only doing what any black man would have done: 'c'eût été moi si Schœlcher n'était pas venu [...] Je suis un nègre, né avec la liberté dans le sang!' (It would have been me if Schoelcher hadn't come [...] I am a Negro, born with freedom in my blood!) (p. 120). Zobel wrote Capitain'-là's comments exactly one decade before Fanon would publish *Peau noire, masques blancs* in 1952, but the captain's words draw attention to the same psychological phenomena discussed in Fanon's penultimate chapter, 'Le Nègre et la reconnaissance', where he posits recognition as the fundamental unresolved psychological tear in Antillean society.

---

33 Hezekiah, p. 46.

Fanon identifies a pathological desire for recognition in Antillean society which, for him, stems from the unarticulated trauma of the abolition of slavery, and traces the cause of the malaise to the fact that in 1848, abolition was bestowed by the French, rather than being won outright through revolutionary struggle by the slaves:

> Il n'y a pas de lutte ouverte entre le Blanc et le Noir.
> Un jour le Maître Blanc a reconnu *sans lutte* le nègre esclave.
> Mais l'ancien esclave veut *se faire reconnaître*.[34]
>
> There is no open conflict between White and Black.
> One day the white master recognised *without a struggle* the black slave.
> But the former slave wants to *have himself recognised*.[35]

Fanon's account, however, significantly underplays the history of revolt, *marronnage*, and resistance by Antillean slaves in the long struggle for abolition, and the fact that slave uprisings in Martinique meant that the 1848 decree was put in place two months earlier than the French administration had originally planned. In contrast, Capitain'-là's words are part of an important current in Martinican literature and thought which strives to assert the agency of Antilleans themselves in winning abolition. His outburst prompts Jérôme to describe Diab'-là as a model for dignity and action:

> cet homme qu'on dit Diab'-là, cé pas un nègre qui farniente sous les cocotiers, ni un homme qui s'agenouillerait jamais pour dire: 'Pardon, maît'! (p. 120)
>
> this man they call Diab'-là, he's not a Negro who lounges around under the coconut trees, and he's certainly not a man who would ever kneel down and say 'Sorry, Masser'!

Here, Diab'-là's heritage is aligned not with the submissive attitude of the slave, but rather with the rebellious attitude of the resistors of slavery. This description perplexes Capitain'-là, and his reaction leads Hezekiah to suggest that he represents 'an older generation of Black leaders, given to dreams of liberation, who failed to translate their ideas into action', which initially makes him react to hearing of Diab'-là 'with a feeling of disbelief and jealousy'.[36] When the two men meet, however, it

---

34 Fanon, *Peau noire, masques blancs*, p. 176; emphasis original.
35 Frantz Fanon, *Black Skin, White Masks*, trans. by Richard Philcox (New York: Grove Press, 2008), p. 191; emphasis original.
36 Hezekiah, p. 46.

is immediately clear that there is no animosity between them, but rather a mutual desire to exchange and learn.

From their first conversation, Capitain'-là implicitly equates Diab'-là with other moments of Négritude across the Caribbean. Césaire had declared in 1939 that it was in Haiti that 'la Négritude se mit debout' (Négritude got to its feet).[37] Similarly, Capitain'-là (a character first created in 1942) finds Diab'-là's words akin to Haitian King Henri Christophe's declaration to his people, which the old man then recites by heart:

> Il faut que nous construisions quelque chose qui nous fasse respecter, et nous respecter nous-mêmes ... et ce monument de notre orgueil, je veux que mon peuple le réalise, dussé-je lui briser les reins de travail. (p. 123)

> We must construct something that makes us respected, that makes us respect ourselves ... and this monument to our pride must be created by my people, that is my desire, even if I have to break their backs with toil.

This quotation, attributed in the novel to Henri Christophe, argues that black people needed to be psychologically and physically taken apart, dismantled, or even un-made and broken, so that they might be reconstructed in a new way. It is, in one respect, a naïve comment which displays no awareness of the dictator which Henri Christophe became. Yet it clearly reflects Capitain'-là's admiration of Diab'-là's potential to transform the lives of everyday black people. The quotation comes from an unnamed book in Capitain'-là's multilingual library, which includes texts written 'en français, en anglais, en espagnol' (in French, in English, and in Spanish) (p. 124). So begins a series of conversations between the two men in which they discuss black civil rights across the world. Capitain'-là is the only reader mentioned in the novel, and this status is significant, as he encourages Diab'-là – a character whose own literacy is questionable, as demonstrated by his anxiety about spelling (p. 139) – to take an interest in books as transmitters of ideas, an allegory for the function which Zobel hoped his own book would perform.

Diab'-là includes the first permutation of an idea which Zobel would refine and hone throughout his career – the conviction that black people's struggle requires a reinvention which is fundamentally psychological. This idea is explicitly stated by Diab'-là in one of his discussions with Capitain'-là: 'je trouve que cette lutte, nous n'avons qu'à y penser pour la gagner, car cé pas une lutte à coups de coutelas, cé une lutte contre

---

37 Césaire, p. 90.

nous-mêmes' (I think that with this struggle, once we set our minds to thinking it through, it's already won, because it's not a struggle that must be fought with a cutlass, it's a struggle against ourselves) (p. 124). It is time for a new understanding of black people's worth, a new-found self-respect and, above all, an awareness that they have played an active, not passive role in history: if black people can internalise these positive messages, which run counter to western hegemonic discourse, then they will have made major progress in the racial struggle. Such moments are evidence of Zobel's affinities with Négritude, as noted by Hezekiah, who finds that 'in Zobel's world of fiction, it is by a conscious act of liberation that the Martinican Negro moves from a disadvantaged position to a feeling of self-confidence and hope'.[38] For all the challenges and setbacks which the protagonists must endure, there is undeniably a forward motion in *Diab'-là*, as the black characters display keen intelligence – although not of the kind which is taught and valued in French schools – which they harness in order to achieve new levels of independence. Diab'-là's vision of black solidarity is something he manages to put into words, and he is convinced it is time to 's'aimer bien fort pour ne pas mollir' (love each other truly, so we do not falter) (p. 124), a phrase which is a recognisable French adaptation of the popular Creole proverb 'tchimbe rèd, pas moli' (stay strong, don't falter). Significantly, however, for the more mature Capitain'-là, what matters most is not succumbing to the temptation to 'trahir' (betray) (p. 124). The concept of racial betrayal is returned to when the men overhear a young black boy reciting his French school lessons about the Seine. This pushes Capitain'-là to expand on the concept of racial betrayal, in the earliest example of a critique of the French colonial education system in Zobel's novels. The theme would of course become a leitmotif of his later works. In *Diab'-là*, education is already being figured as a force for perpetuating a French colonial order and exacerbating class divisions, rather than bringing about real social change. And so Capitain'-là comments:

> Pourvu qu'après cela il n'oublie pas qu'il a des charges ... Mais oui, nos nègres ici se contentent de franchir quelques barrières et de tourner le dos aux leurs ... Il faut jeter les barrières, élargir la trouée pour permettre la ruée en avant! (p. 127)

> As long as, after all that, he doesn't forget that he has responsibilities ... Yes, our Negroes from round here are all too happy to overcome a few

---

38 Hezekiah, p. 45.

barriers, and then turn their back on their own ... We need to knock down these barriers, and make the breach even bigger, to make way for the great charge forward!

The chapter closes with the image of Capitain'-là attempting to overcome the anger which threatens to consume him each time he thinks about the current education system, which so evidently fails to meet the needs of average Martinicans. This colonial system produces a stream of young pupils, and qualified teachers, who are conditioned to prefer French culture above all else, and thus to denigrate and deny their own Creole culture. Here, the first stirrings of passionate educational critiques which run through Zobel's works, and which reach their apogee in the novel *La Rue Cases-Nègres*, can clearly be discerned – critiques of an alienating education system, and of the 'betrayal' which the narrator, and indeed author, associates with certain kinds of social mobility that promote individual advancement over meaningful change across a whole society.

The incendiary potential of the discussions between Diab'-là and Capitain'-là is evident. Zobel must have been aware of the murder of the journalist André Aliker (discussed below in greater detail) when he followed in Aliker's path and began working for a Fort-de-France newspaper. Seven years after the older man's murder at the hands of a *béké*-led conspiracy, Zobel penned a novel which refrained from naming any specific *béké*, but certainly made a persuasive case as to why the black Martinicans' contemporary suffering could be traced to the *béké* plantocracy:

> Sans doute on avait soumis les nègres à cet état afin de les civiliser, n'est-ce pas? ... Mais je crois qu'à force de fabriquer des fortunes pour ceux qui s'étaient chargés de leur destin, ils sont civilisés maintenant ... Eh bé! Capitain', ce que je veux dire, cé que ça doit changer à partir d'aujourd'hui! ... Cé moi qui vous parle ici, mais je sens comme si je suis un peuple, tout un peuple. Et quand tout un peuple refuse une chose et demande une autre! (p. 173)

> Negroes were oppressed in this manner in order to civilise them, so they say? But I believe that by making a fortune for those who had absolute power over them, they have shown proof enough of their civilisation now ... Ha! Captain, what I mean is that things need to change, and that must start today! I am just one voice, but I feel as though I am a nation, an entire nation. And when an entire nation refuses one thing, and demands another!

This pointed rhetorical attack on the *béké* ruling elite is an unmistakable call to arms. Zobel is calling for a new racial consciousness that will go hand in hand with a new political consciousness. As the closing lines of the novel build to a climax, both Diab'-là and Capitain'-là agree that change must come now, either as 'un coup de surprise' (a surprise) or as 'un coup de tonnerre!' (a roll of thunder) (p. 173). The novel's final words demonstrate Zobel's skilful use of poetic imagery, returning to the figure of the maroon to lend a metaphorical, historically loaded charge to the discussions between Diab'-là and Capitain'-là: 'Et leurs paroles avaient des bruits de combat et de chaînes brisées' (and their words were like the sound of combat and broken chains) (p. 173). This unexpected juxtaposition of terms is nothing less than a poetic incitation to revolt, and to continue the slave struggles of the past for liberation.

Diab'-là – A Banned Novel: Literary Debuts in Martinique and Paris

Diab'-là's calls for change in Martinique must be read in the context of the growing popularity of the Communist Party on the island in the years preceding the Second World War. In *'Le Communisme est à l'ordre du jour': Aimé Césaire et le PCF, de l'engagement à la rupture (1935–1957)* ('Communism is the Agenda': Aimé Césaire and the PCF, from commitment to rupture: 1935–1957), David Alliot analyses the currents of communism which prevailed in black student circles in Paris, among not only French colonial students, but also the black American writers of the Negro Renaissance such as Richard Wright, and in Martinique, particularly at the Lycée Schœlcher, where Zobel worked, and would have been aware of these currents.[39] Diab'-là is unequivocal in its beliefs that a more socialist, locally based, and indigenous governance is needed, and the novel's emphasis on community and autonomy resonate with the communism of the era. There is, however, no record of Zobel himself having ever been a member of the Communist Party. Later in his life, in the 1960s, he explicitly did not identify himself as Marxist-Socialist in a survey of black authors working in Africa carried out by Lilyan Kesteloot.[40]

The Martinican Communist Party had been established in 1919 by a group led by Jules Monnerot, a philosophy teacher at the Lycée

---

39 See David Alliot, *'Le Communisme est à l'ordre du jour': Aimé Césaire et le PCF, de l'engagement à la rupture (1935–1957)* (Paris: Pierre-Guillaume de Roux, 2013).
40 Kesteloot, p. 288.

Schœlcher, and in 1920 the group launched the communist newspaper *La Justice*. In late 1933, when Zobel was 18 and preparing for his *baccalauréat*, *La Justice* triggered a political scandal by revealing that a rich *béké*, Eugène Aubéry, had committed fraud. The revelation proved fatal. The paper's editor, André Aliker, survived two attempts on his life but on 12 January 1934 his body washed up on a beach near the town of Case-Pilote. Aliker had undoubtedly been murdered: he was found drowned with his arms tied behind his back. Aliker's colleague at *La Justice*, the agricultural union leader Léopold Bissol, went on to be elected as Conseiller Général (General Councillor) in Fort-de-France in 1937.

It is highly likely that Zobel would have had some awareness of the Aliker affair as a pupil at the Lycée Schœlcher, and as a young man living in the island's capital city. The affair demonstrated the very real danger to which writers were exposed in 1930s Martinique if they dared to challenge and denounce the ruling powers. Zobel was also likely to have been aware of the mass protests organised by the Martinican Communist Party against the exploitative *béké* rule, of which the most famous example was a march during a period known as 'La Grève de la Faim' (the hunger strike), in which striking cane-cutters descended on the streets of Fort-de-France in 1935.[41]

It is little surprise, then, that the inherent challenge *Diab'-là* presented to the island's strict hierarchy almost prevented the novel's publication. Although the preface written by Zobel alludes to the fact that the text was censored by the Vichy regime, *Diab'-là* also fell foul of an earlier instance of censorship. In a radio interview, Zobel revealed the double censorship of his novel, explaining that when he was seeking to publish *Diab'-là*, he initially sent the manuscript to the local newspaper *Le Courrier des Antilles* (*The Courier of the Antilles*), in the hope that they might serialise it. The editor's reaction took Zobel completely by surprise:

> Je me suis fait littéralement houspiller et on m'a dit: 'vous vous rendez compte; si vous publiez ce livre, ce n'est pas un service que vous rendrez à la Martinique parce que dans votre livre il y a des gens qui mangent avec leurs doigts dans des *coui* et qui marchent nus pieds [*sic*], qui sont en haillons. Mais l'étranger qui lira ce livre nous prendra tous pour des sauvages!'[42]

---

41 Butel, p. 449.
42 'Zobel: sa vie, son œuvre', pp. 23–24.

> I was given a complete dressing down, and was told: 'You do realise that if you publish this book, you'll be doing a disservice to Martinique, because in your book there are people who eat with their fingers from *coui* bowls and who walk barefoot, wearing rags. Any foreigner who reads this book will take us all for savages!'

Zobel's first virulent rejection, then, came from his compatriots. This was to mark the beginning of his uneasy relationship with the Martinican intelligentsia. The anecdote reveals the alienating tensions at work within non-white Martinican society itself, the legacy of colonialism and the *mission civilisatrice*, and tensions which Zobel would explore and decry throughout his career. Disheartened, but still determined to find a publisher, Zobel submitted his manuscript to the Vichy Censor, an event to which he refers in his short preface. This led to a meeting with Lieutenant Henri Bayle, Admiral Robert's director of censorship. Bayle condemned the novel for what he perceived to be its negative portrayal of Martinican society. Zobel's account of Bayle's comments bears reproduction:

> Mais qu'est-ce que c'est ce livre? Qu'est-ce que c'est que ça? Vous n'aimez personne, vous en voulez à tout le monde: vous tapez sur les mulâtres, vous tapez sur les nègres, personne ne trouve grâce devant vous.[43]
>
> What kind of a book is this? What do you think you are doing? You dislike everyone and bear a grudge against one and all: you criticise the mulattoes, you criticise the Negroes, you don't spare anyone.

This strident critique left Zobel, in his own words, 'sidéré' (aghast).[44] Bayle's accusation of disloyalty towards his own people seems calculated to silence Zobel into mute humiliation. Permission for the novel to be printed was refused, and so Bayle ensured that its ideas could not circulate. Despondent and confused, Zobel nonetheless remained convinced that he had not produced a novel that would attack his own people, and that his motives had been quite the opposite: 'je l'avais écrit pour exalter' (I had written it as a celebration).[45]

The fall of Vichy Martinique in summer 1943 brought new cultural opportunities. In spring 1945, *Diab'-là* finally appeared, three years after Robert's administration had banned it. The first edition was published

---

43 'Zobel: sa vie, son œuvre', p. 24. The interview, which is a transcription of a radio interview, incorrectly spells Bayle's name as Bell.
44 'Zobel: sa vie, son œuvre', p. 24.
45 'Zobel: sa vie, son œuvre', p. 24.

in Fort-de-France by the Imprimerie officielle de Fort-de-France. The place of publication suggests the backing of a powerful patron, and is likely to be part of the legacy of Georges-Louis Ponton (1906–1944), who in 1943 had replaced Admiral Robert as Governor of Martinique. The young, idealistic new governor fervently believed that the recognition of local culture was a means of social development, and he appointed Zobel as his press attaché. After Ponton's premature death in 1944, Zobel returned to work at the Lycée Schœlcher. Ponton received a glowing eulogy from Césaire in *Tropiques*, which closes with a striking vignette foregrounding Ponton's significance for the Martinican *paysan* or country peasant:

> C'était que, de temps en temps, sur la croupe d'un morne, un paysan, machète en main, s'arrêtait, déplissait son front de la petite vérole de sa sueur, secouait sa vieille lassitude et reprenait le sentier d'un pas plus ferme en songeant qu'il y avait quand même, loin là-bas, du côté de Fort-de-France, du côté 'bureau', un homme qui, tant qu'il serait là, nous éviterait le scandale de la Réaction triomphante: Georges-Louis PONTON, un pur.[46]

> Because, from time to time, on the rump of a hillside, a country peasant, machete in hand, would stop to wipe the smallpox-drops of sweat from his brow, and to shake off his ancient fatigue, before continuing on his way with bolder steps, in the knowledge that there was after all, far away down there in Fort-de-France, in the 'administration', a man who, as long as he was there, would save us from the scandal of the Triumphant Reaction: Georges-Louis PONTON, a man who was pure.

For Césaire, Ponton had acted as a barrage against the 'Triumphant Reaction', a reference to Trotsky's description of a global shift to the political right. Césaire is passing comment on the increasingly reactionary politics of Martinique which had thrived during Robert's Vichy era. Ponton had sought, unsuccessfully, to bring about a more liberal politics. Césaire's description of the Martinican peasant (or, the machete might suggest, cane-cutter), who for a brief period experienced a new faith that the island's governing powers were working in his interest, presents a rural figure who anticipates Diab'-là himself.

Yet, even after his death, Ponton's programme of cultural development continued, both through the review *Martinique*, and in Zobel's work.

---

46 Césaire, 'Georges-Louis PONTON …', *Tropiques 1941–1945: collection complète* (Paris: Jean Michel Place, 1978), p. 156.

Having enjoyed access to more elite circles when working for Ponton, Zobel now had the contacts that would pave the way for the publication of *Diab'-là*. He recounts in an interview that the Imprimerie officielle was the only publishing house at the time in Martinique which had the equipment to publish novels.[47] The director, Eustache Lotaut, was a personal friend who agreed to publish *Diab'-là* if Zobel could raise the funds, which Zobel duly did by selling his prized radio set to a friend.[48] Original copies of *Diab'-là* are extremely rare (the only known copy was identified in 2017 in Dakar, Senegal); it was printed as a special limited edition, and was not available in bookstores.[49] However, international press reviews from 1945 confirm the existence of this first edition, and the novel's opening pages were reproduced in the Martinican newspapers *Le Sportif* and *Les Cahiers de la libération (The Liberation Notebooks)*,[50] as well as in the review *Martinique*.[51] This edition was also listed as a received book available for review in an American scholarly publication, *The French Review*;[52] a review by Paul Langellier was subsequently published in the journal.[53] In 1945, the year it was published, *Diab'-là* received Le Grand Prix Littéraire des Antilles (the Grand Literary Prize of the Antilles),[54] clear evidence of local recognition of its literary impact.

Presently, the only available versions of *Diab'-là* are all reprints of the second edition, which was published in Paris in 1947 with Nouvelles Éditions Latines, with a preface by Georges Pillement. This second edition itself has caused further confusion as to *Diab'-là*'s publication dates. The year when copyright was granted, 1946, appears in the book's opening pages, and no year of publication is given on the title page. The standard convention adopted by the Bibliothèque nationale de France in

---

47 'Zobel: sa vie, son œuvre', p. 26.
48 'Zobel: sa vie, son œuvre', p. 26.
49 For details of the Dakar find, see Scheel; on the print run, see: *'Diab'-là* par Joseph Zobel', *Le Sportif*, 24 mars 1945, p. 3. Le Fonds Zobel: DD:JZ.B.246.
50 Copies inspected at Le Fonds Zobel, Fort-de-France: DD:JZ.B.246.
51 Copies inspected at the Musée du Quai Branly, Paris: Magasins P1660, PERIODIQUE, *Martinique*, 2 (1944)–5 (1946).
52 'ZOBEL, J., *Diab'-la, roman antillais* [sic] (Imprimerie officielle de Fort de France, 1945)'; the listing appears in *The French Review*, 19.4 (1945), p. 244.
53 Paul Langellier, 'Review: *Diab'-la, roman antillais* [sic] by Joseph Zobel', *The French Review*, 19.5 (1946), p. 322.
54 René Maran, 'Le Mouvement littéraire aux Antilles et à la Guyane', *De West-Indische Gids*, 33 (1952), p. 16. The article was reproduced with the permission of the review *Eldorado*, where it had originally appeared in 1949.

such cases is to take the 'achevé d'imprimé' (publication) date, which is found at the back of a text, as the year of publication. This establishes that although copyright was granted in 1946, the Parisian edition of *Diab'-là* appeared in 1947.[55] A letter written by Zobel (who at the time, had recently immigrated to Paris) which discusses the Parisian launch of *Diab'-là*, corroborates this date and states that the launch party was held on Friday 26 March 1947.[56] All editions currently in print are labelled as the second edition, as the first edition comprises those copies published in 1945 in Fort-de-France.

Pillement was a late choice to write the preface, and the task only fell to him due to the death of the prominent journalist Pierre Bénard, the former editor of the leading satirical newspaper *Canard enchaîné* (*The Chained Rag*; 'canard' is slang for newspaper). The previous year, Pillement had provided the preface to a collection of stories, *Bleu des îles: récits martiniquais* (*The Blue of the Isles: Martinican Tales*),[57] by another Martinican author, Raphaël Tardon, who was an acquaintance of Zobel. The paternalistic, exoticising tone of Pillement's preface to *Diab'-là* can be explained by this connection. Pillement's knowledge of Antillean literature was evidently shaped by Tardon, a Martinican author based in Paris who wrote fantastical tales of Martinique in a more conventional exoticist style; tales which, from their inception, were designed for the metropolitan French public. So Pillement's preface to *Diab'-là* praises the novel's 'qualités de terroir' (local flavour) (p. 7), and the naivety of Zobel's characters, and completely overlooks the novel's dialogue with politics and Négritude; instead, he is content to make the insipid observation that *Diab'-là* is arguing for black Martinicans to achieve 'la place qui leur est due' (the place which is due to them) (p. 8) in the world. This misreading completely underplays the novel's audacious tone and objectives. Zobel was said to loathe the preface.[58]

Despite Pillement's patronising and paternalistic preface, *Diab'-là* rapidly received more astute attention in metropolitan France, notably winning the Sully-Olivier-de-Serres prize (which has specific relevance for ecocritical readings of the novel, discussed above). Its fame was also enhanced by the intervention of the author and critic René Maran,

---

55   I record my thanks to the librarians of the Bibliothèque nationale de France for assisting me in clarifying this matter.
56   'Letter dated 1 April 1947' reproduced in Monpierre, p. 5.
57   Raphaël Tardon, *Bleu des îles: récits martiniquais* (Paris: Fasquelle, 1946).
58   Largange, 'Lire et relire Diab'-la'.

the first black winner of the Prix Goncourt for his novel *Batouala: veritable roman nègre* in 1921. Maran praised Zobel's novel in articles for the Parisian weekly newspapers *Gavroche* and *Les Lettres françaises* (*French Literature*).[59] He found *Diab'-là* exceptional in its depiction of an impending black revolution which, he commented, 'obligera peut-être bientôt les gros planteurs et les seigneurs du rhum à ravaler le racisme héréditaire dont ils ont eu tort d'abuser' (may soon oblige the big planters and rum barons to swallow the hereditary racism which they have so wrongly abused).[60]

In 1949, Maran welcomed *Diab'-là* as an artistic innovation and Martinican literary landmark, noting that Zobel was 'le premier écrivain martiniquais qui ait songé à tirer de sa terre natale un roman strictement régionaliste' (the first Martinican novelist to consider drawing inspiration from his native land to create a truly regionalist novel).[61] Similarly, the Martinican paper *Le Clairon* (*The Bugle*) had praised Zobel for moving beyond 'littérature à la Baedeker' (travel guide-style literature) to produce a 'vision de notre vie [...] nette, précise, aiguë. Aiguë comme celle de l'auteur de *Banjo*. [...] A lui seul donc, Diab'-là nous console de toute l'insipidité des pseudo-romans antillais, écrits depuis ce dernier quart de siècle' (a clear, precise, pointed vision of our life [...] Pointed like that of the author of *Banjo*. [...] Only Diablo offers consolation for the utter insipidness of the pseudo-novels from the Antilles which have been written in the last quarter of a century).[62] If Maran, writing for a Parisian public, highlighted the novel's denunciation of white racism, the *Clairon*, with its Martinican readership, suggested Zobel's affinities with the Negro Renaissance movement and the author of *Banjo*; the Martinican reviewer would have been aware of the pseudonym Kay-Mac-Zo which Zobel had chosen for his contributions to *Le Sportif*.

The contemporary reviews are quick to point out the political and social significance of Zobel's innovations in *Diab'-là*, although they do not consider how the Négritude movement might have inspired him, ignoring entirely the significance of the opening preface with Césaire, and the character of Capitan'-là. At the time, the leap from the

---

59 Maran, 'La Martinique, bastion littéraire française des Antilles', *Les Lettres françaises*, 3 May 1946, p. 5, and 'Un plaidoyer contre l'esclavage'.
60 Maran, 'Un plaidoyer contre l'esclavage', p. 6.
61 Maran, 'Le mouvement littéraire', p. 16.
62 'Le beau livre que voilà', *Le Clairon*, 10 July 1945. Le Fonds Zobel: DD:JZ.B.246.

surrealist poetry of the movement to Zobel's social realist prose might have appeared too great for such comparisons to be drawn, although Hezekiah would point out the obvious affinities several decades later. *Diab'-là*'s discussions of the black man's sense of place and value in the world furnish clear evidence that Zobel's debut novel was inspired by, and attempts to dialogue with, Négritude. *Diab'-là* can perhaps best be understood with reference to certain criticisms of late Négritude's insistence on highlighting racial differences, in contrast to its earlier preoccupation with class and the oppressed proletariat of any colour. In 'Les Étudiants noirs parlent' (Black Students Speak), a special issue of *Présence Africaine* published in 1953, Togolese student Albert Franklin contributes an article entitled 'La Négritude: réalité ou mystification?' (Négritude: Reality or Mystification?).[63] Franklin systematically refutes the characteristics which Sartre claimed were inherently linked with Négritude: anti-racist racism, a sense of collectivity, rhythm, sexual prowess, and ancestor worship. For Franklin, as Belinda Jack has observed, these characteristics can be accounted for 'either in terms of the material conditions of the black man's circumstances or in terms of white misconception, myth and prejudice'.[64]

Franklin is concerned that Négritude is employing a rhetoric of racial mystification in order to radicalise black populations against white socialism, and that rather than constituting an act of racial consolidation, the movement is encouraging a withdrawal into racial identities, to the detriment of a global socialism. This article can be aligned with communist critiques of Négritude found as early as 1949 in the work of Gabriel d'Arboussier, who published the article 'Une dangereuse mystification: la théorie de la Négritude' (A Dangerous Mystification: The Theory of Négritude) in *La Nouvelle critique* (*The New Critic*), a journal sponsored by the French Communist Party.[65] For Franklin, improving the material conditions of black people should be any cultural movement's primary political goal, and he declares that:

> les opprimés de tous les pays doivent, à travers le monde entier, créer et renforcer une solidarité effective. C'est un crime quand, à la faveur

---

63 Albert Franklin, 'La Négritude: réalité ou mystification?', *Présence Africaine*, 14 (1953), pp. 285–303.
64 Belinda Jack, *Negritude and Literary Criticism: The History and Theory of 'Negro-African' Literature in French* (Westport, CT: Greenwood Press, 1996), p. 78.
65 D'Arbousier, pp. 34–47.

d'un nationalisme légitime [...] certain [sic] veulent amener les Nègres à repousser la main tendue du prolétariat blanc, c'est une des raisons pour lesquelles nous la dénonçons.[66]

[...] the oppressed of every nation ought to create and reinforce an effective solidarity, across the entire world. It is a crime when, to favour a legitimate nationalism [...] some wish to encourage Negroes to brush aside the hand offered by the white proletariat, and that is one of the reasons why we are denouncing it.

By working alongside, but separately from, the main triumvirate of Négritude writers, Zobel develops his own understanding of Négritude in a direction which has clear affinities with Franklin's arguments that literature has a duty to raise political awareness and improve the lot of the oppressed masses. The novelist had not yet set foot outside Martinique, and *Diab'-là* is bereft of any comments on the need for solidarity between oppressed groups which Franklin urges: Zobel is certainly thinking about class but, unsurprisingly, at this stage, only in the context of his native island and its neighbours. Yet, as his work develops, he will display an increasing awareness of the intersectional forces of race and class, and this becomes particularly pronounced in his final two novels, *La Rue Cases-Nègres* and *La Fête à Paris*.

* * *

In *Diab'-là*, the clarity and accessibility of Zobel's prose style, and the vision of how an everyday Négritude might be lived out by his protagonists and, indeed, by his readers, provide evidence of his aim to transmit a philosophical and political message of courage, compassion, and resistance to those same oppressed groups who were most in need of it. Zobel's first novel pioneers a new literature that makes innovative use of Creole to create an idiom which, as the narrator explains in the short introduction, was intended to awaken the political conscience of his fellow Martinicans. Diab'-là's incessant energy and creativity, and charismatic, and even supernatural, powers of leadership, enable him to take up his calling as 'un maître parmi les hommes' (a master among men) (p. 119). Moreover, *Diab'-là* undertakes an incredible attempt to dissociate working the land from the trauma of centuries of plantation slavery.

---

66 Franklin, p. 303.

The novel, which demonstrates a profound appreciation of nature, and aims to alter how Caribbean people consider their natural environment, deserves inclusion in the emerging canon of postcolonial ecocriticism. In an era of increasing concern about Martinican vulnerability to environmental crises, demonstrated by the Caribbean's designation as one of 25 global biodiversity hotspots 'where exceptional concentrations of endemic species are undergoing exceptional loss of habitat',[67] Zobel's first novel may still come to play a revolutionary role. The rediscovery of this novel might yet change the ways in which Martinican people think of, and interact with, their local environment, suggesting as it does ways to unlock the full potential of the landscape through a model of modest self-sufficiency, which promises an abundance of self-fulfilment.

---

[67] Norman Myers, Russell A. Mittermeier, Cristina G. Mittermeier, Gustavo A. B. da Fonseca and Jennifer Kent, 'Biodiversity Hotspots for Conservation Priorities', *Nature*, 403 (24 February 2000), pp. 853–58.

CHAPTER THREE

Nothing Happens, Twice
Les Jours immobiles becomes *Les Mains pleines d'oiseaux*

As the famous quip about Samuel Beckett's play *En attendant Godot* goes, '*nothing* happens, *twice*'.[1] The transformation of Zobel's second novel, *Les Jours immobiles* (1946), into *Les Mains pleines d'oiseaux* (1978) might draw a similar comment. Both iterations of the novel describe, in lingering detail, the tranquil social customs and seasonal activities which punctuate life in a small fishing village in southern Martinique. For vast swathes of both novels, the original title *Les Jours immobiles*, which might be translated as the 'unmoving days' or 'never-changing days' – rings true. A more poetic rendering would be *Those Timeless Days*, and indeed, the narrative evokes the slow, seemingly eternal rhythms and cycles of simple lives led far away from urban centres.

In his second novel, Zobel was continuing the project he had commenced with *Diab'-là*: turning the gaze inwards in order to depict the everyday lives of humble black Martinicans. While in *Diab'-là*, working the land was an act of defiance, in *Les Jours immobiles* it is a far more organic, gentle gesture. In this novel, rather than being barren and rocky as in *Diab'-là*, the fertile land offers itself and its bounty to those fortunate enough to live in the sleepy paradisiacal region where the narrative unfolds. Yet there is also a subtle, deeper political message in the novel. Significantly, characters are depicted in the process of reconnecting with 'forgotten' patterns of living off, and with, the land

---

1 Vivian Mercier, 'The Uneventful Event', *The Irish Times*, 18 February 1956, p. 6; emphasis original.

– knowledge which is implicitly linked to that part of Antillean culture which does not descend from French colonialism, but rather from the interlinked heritages of slavery and Amerindian culture. The novel raises urgent questions about the potential for the arts to play a political role in social change, and my analysis is deepened through reference to Zobel's only known published essay, which the author was working on at the same time as *Les Jours immobiles*. This essay, 'Considérations sur l'art local' (Considerations on Local Art),[2] appeared in 1946 in the review *Martinique*. I discovered this previously unknown work in 2015, during research in the archives of the Musée du Quai Branly in Paris. It is a valuable document which sheds new light into the author's wider cultural ambitions in 1946.

The two different versions of Zobel's second novel were produced in radically different material conditions: *Les Jours immobiles* was printed in Martinique in 1946 at the Imprimerie de Fort-de-France, where he had published the first edition of *Diab'-là* just one year earlier. However, while *Diab'-là* enjoyed a second lease of life outside Martinique thanks to the second edition which was published in Paris, this was not the case with *Les Jours immobiles*. After the limited 1946 print run, which Zobel had funded himself,[3] the novel was never republished in Martinique or in Paris. As a result, copies of *Les Jours immobiles* are now extremely rare.

When Zobel retired in 1976 after 19 years in Senegal, he made 'Moun Oustaou', the holiday home in the south of France which he had purchased in 1954 and slowly and painstakingly renovated, his main residence. He and his family settled at the house in the village of Générargues, near Anduze. In an interview recorded shortly after his retirement for *Radio France Internationale*, he commented that he now wished to take advantage 'de l'indépendence, du calme et du repos'[4] (of the independence, the calm, and the rest) which Générargues offered him, and return to his literary career, a career which, by his own admission, he felt he had had to neglect due to the more pressing material necessities of earning a living. In the interview, Zobel's opening

---

2   Joseph Zobel, 'Considérations sur l'art local', *Martinique*, 5 (1946), pp. 33–38. Musée du Quai Branly, Paris: Magasins P1660, PERIODIQUE, *Martinique*, 2 (1944)–5 (1946).

3   Zobel comments, 'ce livre, je l'ai publié à compte d'auteur' (I funded the publication of this book myself) in an interview with Annette M'Baye d'Erneville for Condé's radio programme, 'Joseph Zobel'.

4   Condé, 'Joseph Zobel'.

presentation of himself, which he gives in the third person, foregrounds his desire to return to writing in order to:

> poursuivre une œuvre littéraire qui est, en ce moment, à son avis, incomplète puisque le souci de gagner sa vie, assumer des responsabilités administratives, ne lui ont pas permis d'écrire tous les livres qu'il a en projet, même de terminer tous ceux qu'il a déjà commencés.
>
> continue a literary œuvre which is, at the moment, in his opinion, incomplete, because practical concerns such as earning a living and carrying out administrative duties have not allowed him to write all the books which he intends to write, or even to complete all those that he has already begun.

On the one hand, then, the decision to return to *Les Jours immobiles* some 30 years later sprung from necessity: the novel had fallen into obscurity, and it is evident that Zobel regretted this. However, rather than republishing the original work with another publisher, he took the unusual decision to completely rewrite the novel. This uncommon decision may be read as evidence of Zobel's dissatisfaction with his existing body of work which, as he comments in the interview above, he considered to be underdeveloped and incomplete. Having enjoyed some level of public and critical attention, including several prestigious literary awards, between 1945, when *Diab'-là* came out in Martinique, and the early 1950s, when *La Rue Cases-Nègres* was published, the move to Africa had somewhat curbed the author's literary creativity. During this period, he had published just one original prose work, the collection of short stories *Le Soleil partagé* (1964) and a slim volume of new poetry, *Incantation pour un retour au pays natal* (1965); the most significant development was the new edition of *La Rue Cases-Nègres* (1974). On retirement, Zobel sought to revive his literary ambitions. Two of his novels, *Les Jours immobiles* and *La Fête à Paris*, were no longer available in print, and he set about rewriting them. Inspections of the manuscripts of poems, short stories, and novels which are held in the Fonds Zobel, Zobel's personal archives in Martinique, reveal an author for whom the process of writing was extremely laborious. He would rework sections of text multiple times, in a meticulous quest for the right phrase. This painstaking approach can also be observed in his published rewriting; the changes between the original and rewritten versions are often minuscule additions or deletions, or are only evident in a subtle change in perspective.

This kind of rewriting is both illuminating and problematic. Rachel Douglas has identified rewriting as a significant feature of Caribbean literature.[5] Douglas concentrates on the specific case of the Haitian author Frankétienne (born in 1936), and also discusses instances of rewriting in the work of the Martinican authors Aimé Césaire and Édouard Glissant. Following the work of the French critic Gérard Genette, she suggests that the terms 'hypotext', denoting the original version, and 'hypertext', to denote a later, modified version, are useful tools enabling literary critics to distinguish the kinds of intertextuality and rewriting which are at work in an author's *œuvre*. Investigating why Caribbean authors feel compelled to return obsessively to their literature through reworkings, Douglas points out that while the French approach to the field of narratology has generated studies of rewriting, hypertextuality, and intertextuality which have a tendency to 'view their subject with often almost no reference to anything outside the text', Caribbean rewriting cannot be approached in such a distant, decontextualised manner, because 'rewriting in the Caribbean serves as an important marker of the changing political, social, economic, and historical contexts in which the texts are embedded'.[6]

The revised 1978 version was the novel that Zobel intended to be his lasting legacy to readers. For this reason, the present chapter commences with an analysis of the hypertext, *Les Mains pleines d'oiseaux*, which is also the only edition that is currently widely available to contemporary readers. After analysing that work, the chapter turns to the original hypotext, *Les Jours immobiles*. Zobel's decision to rewrite the novel bears examination in the light of the contextualising processes to which Douglas has drawn attention; as such, when comparing the texts, I consider a number of contextual issues which reveal subtle shifts in the author's thinking between the two versions. I also identify the tropes to which the later, more mature Zobel wished to draw attention.

Most importantly, this process of comparison makes it possible to interrogate the narrative inconsistencies of the hypertext *Les Mains pleines d'oiseaux*. How do the narrative dynamics suffer as a result of the rewriting? Does the final version stand alone, or does it become an amalgam, an incomplete fragment of the first version? I consider whether this later version might become trapped in a timeless and contextless space between the original *Les Jours immobiles*, which arose from a particular social and political environment – Martinique – which Zobel,

---

5 Rachel Douglas, *Frankétienne and Rewriting: A Work in Progress* (Lanham, MD: Lexington, 2009).
6 Douglas, p. 1; p. 2.

at that point in his life, had never left, and the revised novel. *Les Mains pleines d'oiseaux* was produced by a decidedly more cosmopolitan Zobel who had at the point of rewriting spent ten years in metropolitan France, and almost 20 years in Africa. The dynamics of Zobel's rewriting are explored in this chapter, paving the way for me to return to these same questions in Chapter Five, when I consider how Zobel's last original novel, *La Fête à Paris* (1953), becomes *Quand la neige aura fondu* (1979), his final rewritten novel, and his final published novel.

Timeless Days

Les Mains pleines d'oiseaux, like *Diab'-là*, owes a great debt to the time Zobel spent living and working on the south-west coast of Martinique, and the novel is set in the scenic area known as Les Anses d'Arlet (p. 27), which lies just a few kilometres to the north of Le Diamant, the setting of his first novel. Zobel felt great affection for this region of Martinique, as he explains in a radio interview:

> Moi, je suis de l'intérieur [...] la vie des pêcheurs, la vie des gens de la mer, cela m'avait tellement émerveillé. Plus tard, je n'ai pas pu résister à l'envie d'écrire un livre qui reflétait cette vie.

> Me, I'm from the interior [...] the life of these fishermen, the life of these people living by the sea, it completely enchanted me. Later, I couldn't resist writing a book which reflected that life.

In the same interview, Zobel goes on to name the novel in question as *Les Jours immobiles*.[7] In Kezadri and Codol's 1998 documentary *Joseph Zobel: D'Amour et de Silence*, Zobel comments that the novel is set in 'Petite Anse' (Small Bay). This is a tranquil and picturesque area flanked by verdant *mornes*, volcanic hills; at the shoreline, a sheltered arc of golden sand slopes down into the gentle waves of the Caribbean Sea. *Les Mains pleines d'oiseaux* continues the process of environmental rapprochement which Zobel had commenced in *Diab'-là*, to argue for the same radical shift in how Martinicans view their own country. In this second novel, as in Zobel's literary debut, the land plays an active role in the narrative, as the main protagonists' decisions and lifestyles are inseparable from the landscape in which they live. The choppier waters of Le Diamant, where revolution was brewing in *Diab'-là*, are replaced

---

7   Condé, 'Joseph Zobel'.

by the calmer seas of Les Anses d'Arlet, where a more moderate, but no less significant, change is depicted.

The novel's plot revolves around an old woman, Cocotte, who is the single turbulent force in an otherwise overwhelmingly gentle narrative; indeed, in one version of Zobel's 1977 manuscript revisions, she was to lend her name to the book through the title *Cocotte ou les jours immobiles*.[8] The actual rewritten title, *Les Mains pleines d'oiseaux*, is a direct reference to a scene in which Cocotte is surrounded by birds, which the villagers suspect she may have called to her through supernatural powers. Cocotte and her grandson, Géo, form a grandmother-grandson pairing, and the dynamic between the cantankerous old lady and her introverted and reflective grandson is the prototype for M'man Tine and José in Zobel's next novel, *La Rue Cases-Nègres*. Throughout *Les Mains pleines d'oiseaux*, Cocotte is secretly making arrangements for her own funeral: she has a dress made in anticipation of being laid out at her traditional Caribbean wake, and sets some coffee and a fine bottle of rum aside for the same event. In a deft comic touch, both these treasured liquids will be drunk, and very much enjoyed, during her lifetime!

The novel's exposition covers a great deal of ground and explains Géo's current bachelor status: he is a fisherman whose long-term partner, Cidalise, died in pregnancy, which is why he now lives with his grandmother, Cocotte. Their neighbour is Maïotte, a beautiful *poissonnière* or fishmonger who used to sell Géo's catch for him in the town. Following Cidalise's death, Maïotte moved to Petite-Anse because she is in love with Géo. Before long, Géo decides to live with her, but their relationship has a suggestion of scandal because it is hinted that she may have been involved with Géo while Cidalise was still alive. Moreover, the villagers judge Géo harshly for being involved with an 'outsider' and, by extension, for daring to bring change into the small 'immobile' community. As a result of this social pressure, Géo abruptly decides to leave Maïotte, and returns to live with his grandmother Cocotte. It is at this point that the novel's action begins.

Les Mains pleines d'oiseaux is remarkable for its subtle tableaux of coastal Martinican society in the 1940s, although the deliberate absence of specific temporal markers in both versions of the novel lends the sedentary work a timelessness or atemporality suited to its original title. As in *Diab'-là*, the narrative intertwines two main strands; the first socio-economic, in the detailed descriptions of how the characters

---

8 Manuscript inspected at Le Fonds Zobel: 2014.17.4.9.

live, and try to make a living, in the sleepy *anse* (cove), and the second romantic, in the unresolved relationship between Géo and Maïotte. This is mirrored by the budding and more straightforward relationship between two young people, Amboise and Françoilise.

More generally, the novel investigates the dynamics of a small village community: one significant subplot relates the burgeoning friendship between Géo, who is in his early thirties, and Amboise, a young man of about 19, whom Géo hires as an apprentice fisherman on his 'pirogue', a small fishing boat (p. 37). This slowly evolving subplot about male friendship finds its counterbalance in the second subplot, which focuses on the comic animosity between Cocotte and her male first cousin Sylva. The cousins' mutual antagonism is so long-standing that it has become part of local folklore: 'Cela devait remonter à Marquis d'Anterre, comme disent les vieux pour situer des faits dont aucune mémoire ne permet de témoigner' (It must have happened in the time of the Marquis of Yore, as old people say to situate events which no living soul can actually remember) (p. 40). Importantly, in a novel about the stability and fixedness of life in Petite Anse, the reliability of the patterns of social relations – amicable or antagonistic – plays an essential role in creating the impression that nothing here will ever change.

In line with Zobel's complex depictions of female characters throughout his novels, Cocotte is a complicated, paradoxical figure. She is at once maternal and compassionate, and aggressive and cantankerous. Her name is a gendered term of endearment which also equates women with the act of cooking (a *cocotte* is a French term for a saucepan or pot), a significant detail in a novel which questions how Martinicans prepare and source their own food. Cocotte is the forerunner of another formidable grandmother, M'man Tine in *La Rue Cases-Nègres*. Both grandmothers have *béké* (white slave owner) ancestry, but Cocotte's white forebear recognised his mixed-race family, with the result that they were able to inherit his money. This *béké* wealth has been transferred down through the generations. Cocotte owns land and, according to rumour, she 'aurait de l'argent caché sous les fondations de sa case' (is said to have money hidden in the foundations of her shack) (p. 42); the practice of burying money under a house is commonly associated with *békés*, who turned to this method of storing their wealth in remote areas of the island, given the absence of accessible or reliable banks. Cocotte's comfortable situation means that she enjoys a far more indulgent and indolent life than her *La Rue Cases-Nègres* counterpart, M'man Tine; indeed, she is something of an alter ego for M'man Tine, who herself mentions in *La Rue Cases-Nègres* that her uncle cheated her out of a modest amount of agricultural land that her *béké* grandfather had left her mother (p. 43).

Cocotte does not just rely on inherited wealth; she is also a canny businesswoman and an economic dynamo. Her careful money management allows her to subtly help Géo and Amboise make their own financial way in the world; she also provides Maïotte with a valuable stream of income through sewing commissions. While proud of her social standing and keen to remind her neighbours of her status with her grand gestures and fine outfits, the old lady also understands the importance of reinvesting in her own community, and in its young people in particular. Yet the name Cocotte, with all its sweet and nurturing inferences, is also laden with irony as she succumbs to frequent bursts of temper, and never more so than when confronted by her cousin Sylva.

The origin of the rivalry between the cousins is rooted in social reality: the scarcity of water. To this day, Les Anses d'Arlet remains the most arid part of southern Martinique; water is still a particularly precious commodity despite the arrival of modern plumbing. In Zobel's novel, the villagers' water needs are served by a communal spring and just two wells, one which belongs to Cocotte, and the other to Sylva (in a further subtle indication of the family's inherited wealth). Each well's water has a different taste, and in the dry season, once the communal spring has dried up, villagers must make the tactical choice of which well they will use. This social decision effectively splits the villagers into two camps as 'le choix de l'eau du puits de Sylva ou de celui de Cocotte devient presque aussi déterminant qu'une option politique' (the choice of well – Sylva's or Cocotte's – becomes almost as important as a political allegiance) (p. 41). The cousins' feud provides the overarching narrative arc, and leads to the climactic events at the novel's close, where their relationship comes to a tragic-comic conclusion.

The novel, then, devotes a great deal of its plot to the depiction of what might now be termed the management of natural resources. Contemporary Anses d'Arlet, where modern sanitation and running water have long since rendered the old wells obsolete (although the area still suffers from drought), has conserved the memory of this period in its monuments. In Grande Anse, the largest and most developed of the bays, a series of raised sculptures with round circular forms mark the locations where wells used to be; they stand as a reminder of past generations' interactions with nature, and of the social prominence that these structures once held for the local community.

In *Les Mains pleines d'oiseaux*, Zobel argues, in a subtler manner than he had done in *Diab'-là*, for a reassessment of Martinicans' interactions with their environment. The detailed descriptions of the splendour and interconnectedness of the natural world mirror the precious network of social interactions which bring the community together. Zobel's novel argues that these humble coastal dwellers, with all their peccadilloes, and for all their petty feuds, exemplify the essence of humanity. Orphaned children are welcomed in by their neighbours, disabled villagers and the elderly are cared for by the wider community, and the Anse is one large extended family. This emphasis on the incredible sense of community which the author perceives in marginalised groups anticipates the affectionate and genuine admiration in the depictions of sugar cane workers in his next novel, *La Rue Cases-Nègres*.

Although on the one hand, this sense of community triggers an almost pathological desire to protect the village body from foreign 'invaders' like Maïotte, it also allows for the complete integration of characters who do not conform to social views of normativity. This is exemplified by the deft vignette of the blind fisherman Marceau. His neighbours are on hand to help him out when necessary with small tasks, and rather than pitying him, they admire his physical and moral strength, as well as his extraordinary musical talent on the accordion:

> Marceau est un des plus aimés. En réalité il n'y en a pas un qui ne voudrait être ses yeux pour le délivrer de la nuit qui pourtant ne lui fait pas peur. [...] Ainsi, Marceau n'a jamais vu la mer dans laquelle il se baigne et nage, ni une pirogue dont pourtant il sait tirer les avirons avec une cadence et une vigueur que beaucoup lui envient; jamais vu le visage de sa femme ni le sourire de ses enfants. (p. 55)

> Marceau is one of the most well-liked villagers. Truth be told, there is not one of them who would not wish to be his eyes, and so deliver him from that eternal night which he, however, confronts without fear. [...] Marceau has never seen the sea in which he bathes and swims, nor the *pirogue* which he manoeuvres with such rhythmic and deft oar strokes, to the envy of many a villager; moreover, he has never seen his wife's face, nor his children's smiles.

Although the villagers feel great compassion for Marceau's lack of sight, this is tempered by their poetic, philosophical conviction that their blind neighbour's perception of the world is rich in quite different ways:

> Alors, on se console parfois en se disant que peut-être, il y a au-dedans de

> lui une grande clarté qui éclaire tout ce qu'il entend, tout ce qu'il touche, et leur donne une réalité dont la perception se passe de la vue. (p. 55)

> So sometimes, to console each other, the villagers say that there is perhaps a great brightness inside him which lights up everything that he hears and touches, and creates a heightened reality far superior to the perception offered by mere human sight.

In this self-supporting community, Marceau is able to play an active role and be a valued and cherished member of society. His disability elicits compassion but is not pitied; it is recognised as the source of his unique set of strengths.

Diab'-là had presented one man, a stranger, as the agent of change. In contrast, it is the collective nature of the community which brings about change in *Les Mains pleines d'oiseaux*, when a group of villagers come together spontaneously to consider the natural resources which are already at their disposal, and how together they might use them in a new, ingenious way to improve their material fortunes and achieve an enhanced sense of self-fulfilment. Crucially, both novels propose that change can only come from a re-examination of marginalised groups' relationship with the land. *Les Mains pleines d'oiseaux* is a quiet celebration of life far from Martinique's urban areas. Although the inhabitants of Petite Anse are shown to be poor in material terms, they enjoy an autonomy and self-determination which leaves the narrator in awe. This is explicitly linked to the fact that the villagers work for themselves, rather than being employed by the large industries which dominated Martinican life:

> somme toute, la vie n'est pas douloureuse dans l'Anse. Elle pourrait être belle pour tous et au gré de chacun. L'effort des hommes n'est voué à aucune plantation, aucune rhumerie ou sucrerie; on y travaille selon son tempérament, et, peu ou beaucoup, on a pour soi tout le produit de sa peine [...] Mais l'Anse, c'était l'endroit où, seuls, nous pouvions vivre, nous qui n'étions ni plus riches ni plus pauvres que les autres mais plus livrés à nous-mêmes – et certainement moins dépossédés. (p. 45)

> all in all, life is not painful in the Anse. It has the potential to be beautiful for everyone, in their individual way. Men's labour is not destined for any plantation, rum factory or sugar plant; instead, people set their own working patterns, and they reap the full harvest of their toil, be it a little, or a lot [...] The Anse was the only place where, as individuals, we could live, we who were no richer or poorer than the next man, but much freer to follow our own impulses – and certainly less dispossessed.

In a rare and telling moment, the subtle slippage between the third person and the first person directly involves the narrator, who does not intervene in this manner throughout the novel, in the plot. Letters released after Zobel's death reveal that he drew on his first-hand knowledge of real-life people in his books,[9] and this suggests that for the narrator/author himself, Les Anses d'Arlet was a privileged location where he found that life unfolded to a different rhythm to that which he had previously experienced.

In short, life in the Anse is rich in a way which cannot be measured by modern western standards. Wealth and value are derived from individual fulfilment, social engagement, and a model of inclusion which works against social dispossession. As Hal Wylie observes, 'one has the feeling that if outside forces would just leave the village alone, the simple people there could develop an almost utopian existence'.[10] Language, too, is stripped of its taboos, as exemplified when a young idealistic *institutrice* – a female primary school teacher – pays *visites de courtoisie* (courtesy visits) to all the villagers, including the old lady Cocotte even though there are no school-age children in her household:

> Elle [l'institutrice] parlait français, mais il y avait si longtemps que Cocotte n'avait pas prononcé deux mots de français, que sa langue fonctionna mal quand elle voulut répondre [...] et ce fut comme si elle et son parler avaient fait une culbute qui aurait pu être fâcheuse, voire grave, si l'institutrice ne l'avait pas aussitôt secourue avec un mot de patois, par quoi l'une et l'autre abandonnèrent le français. (p. 125)

> She [the primary school teacher] spoke in French, but it had been such a long time since Cocotte had uttered two words of French that her tongue wouldn't work properly when she tried to answer [...] and it felt as though she and her speech had made a grievous error which could have been embarrassing, or even serious, if the teacher hadn't immediately come to her rescue with a word of patois. At this, they both abandoned French altogether.

Old meets new in this exchange, as the urban values of formal education collide with traditional Creole culture; yet there is evidence of humanity,

---

9 Petite-Anse is mentioned directly in a letter dated 23 October 1947 which Zobel sent from Paris, where he was living at the time, to his friend Valbrun in Martinique, written in response to Valbrun's latest letter, a highly amusing account which had updated Zobel on the latest goings on in Petite-Anse. See Charlotte Zobel, *Joseph Zobel Photographies*, pp. 45–46.
10 Wylie, p. 63.

shared understanding, and adaptation. *Les Mains pleines d'oiseaux* depicts the culture clash between rural Creole values and modern French colonial education, and provides an idealised scene of how successful communication and mutual compassion might reduce the chasm between the two worlds. This is represented at a linguistic level, as the teacher puts Cocotte at ease by using Creole with 'une douceur de voix, une finesse d'expression!' (a soft voice and such a refined way of speaking!) (p. 125). Cocotte replies in 'son meilleur créole, qu'elle rehaussait de son mieux avec des "mademoiselle", des "bien merci" des "effectivement", des "s'il vous plait", articulés avec toute la grâce dont elle se savait capable [...]' (her best Creole, which she did her best to refine by peppering it with the French terms 'mademoiselle', 'thankfully', 'certainly', and 'please', which she pronounced as gracefully as possible) (pp. 125–26). This highlights the French-Creole diglossia in Martinique and the spectrum of Creole language, in an early literary recognition that while the language can be a tool for the cruder practical communication which developed in plantation society, it also has a more polished, nuanced form, as represented by the teacher's graceful, elegant Creole. The scene is a rare early example – and, quite possibly, the first example – of Creole being tolerated by a French Caribbean schoolteacher, albeit in an out-of-school context. Zobel's cousin, who worked as a primary school teacher in Les Anses d'Arlet, and who introduced him to the region,[11] may have served as the inspiration for this important scene.

As the women's meeting becomes increasingly cordial, Cocotte suggests they enjoy a glass of rum together, reassuring the school teacher that it is not strong; at this, 'Mademoiselle rit de bon cœur et finit par accepter' (Mademoiselle laughed heartily and accepted) (p. 126). So the rum which Cocotte had intended to preserve for her funeral is uncorked and liberally enjoyed! This portrait of a young female teacher who is able to reconcile traditional Creole society with French colonial education remains one of Zobel's most endearing representations of how French education might successfully be introduced in Martinique in a way which still upholds Creole cultural specificities. The insistence on the scene's exceptionality – it is 'la première fois!' (the first time!) (p. 125) that such a visit has taken place – suggests, however, that Zobel's overriding view of education in rural Martinique was that it upheld a framework of French domination, rather than allowing for Creole cultural accommodation.

11 Condé, 'Joseph Zobel'.

This significant moment in *Les Mains pleines d'oiseaux* also resonates with Zobel's wider novels, and their afterlives in film. In her important study of Euzhan Palcy's adaptation, *Rue Cases-Nègres*, the critic Sylvie César points out that the film includes an inserted scene which makes a marked departure from the original novel's outright criticism of French colonial schooling. In the novel, when José Hassam is accused of plagiarism by a racist black male teacher who refuses to believe that a *petit-nègre* could have produced such an eloquent literary account of Médouze's funeral wake, the young boy is too despondent and disillusioned with the school system even to protest (a scene explored in detail in the next chapter of this study). In contrast, the film *Rue Cases-Nègres* invents a new scene in which the same teacher later visits M'man Tine to say that he has realised his error, and to apologise for having doubted José.[12] This major concession from the bourgeois teaching class to the poorer sections of society has always been interpreted as Palcy's pure fabrication. Yet Zobel's own scene in *Les Mains pleines d'oiseaux* between Cocotte and the primary school teacher (which is also present in the original 1946 novel), directly anticipates the inserted scene in the film *Rue Cases-Nègres* because it promotes a model of direct and compassionate contact between educators and the families of the children in their charge, showing how important such a link could be for children from disadvantaged, non-traditional backgrounds.

In *Les Mains pleines d'oiseaux*, then, there is a celebration of the humble lives of Martinique's *nègres* and *négresses*. Another example of the novel's celebration of blackness occurs when Amboise and Géo decide to celebrate the end of the dry season by bathing together in the newly flowing spring:

> Amboise, qui s'était penché en avant pour dégager ses talons de sa culotte, se redresse et s'étire comme un jeune animal qui s'éveille, et, tout en continuant de siffler, se gratte l'aine en faisant crisser ses ongles sur la pilosité fauve qui lui ombre la peau, et des deux mains, en se tordant, il se gratte le ventre, et plus vivement encore la ligne creuse dont le bout de fibre torsadée avec quoi il retient sa culotte a marqué sa peau. (p. 71)

> Amboise, who had leaned forward to untangle his trousers from his heels, stood upright and stretched out, like a young animal awakening, and, still whistling, scratched his groin, his nails raking through the coarse hairs which shaded his skin, and then began to rub his stomach

---

12 See Sylvie César, *'Rue Cases-Nègres' du roman au film, étude comparative* (Paris: L'Harmattan, 1994), pp. 101–02, 132.

with both hands, before twisting round to rub with renewed vigour along the deep furrow left on his skin by the twisted cable that he used as a belt.

The social realism of a young man relaxing and scratching his groin is rendered in natural brushstrokes, and the reader is invited to share in Amboise's utter sense of repose, rather than read this as an uncouth gesture. These celebrations of working-class black bodies, another direct continuation of Zobel's work in *Diab'-là*, were both original and radical at the time when Zobel was writing. Such descriptions derive additional political agency from the influence of Négritude on Zobel's work, as they represent the author's Négritude-inspired ambition to cast the gaze, for the first time, onto that group which Martinican society referred to as *nègres*. No other author writing about the French Caribbean at the time undertook to document dirty, sweaty working-class black bodies with admiration and dignity. This group was excluded from dominant discourse, to the extent that their very bodies were disdained, excluded, and rejected; they were unwelcome in modern bourgeois spheres of life in the island, and reduced to the role of objects of shame or ridicule in Martinican literature and culture. In the bathing passage, the novel's simple but lingering detail, with its focus on parts of the body which are usually not displayed (the groin, the pubic hair), is a celebration of these black men in their full corporeality. The mention of Amboise using a twisted cable as a belt serves as a reminder of their poverty, but by acknowledging it in a matter-of-fact manner, poverty too is destigmatised, and the narrative suggests the men's ingenuity in improvising items which they cannot afford to buy.

When, in the same scene, Amboise and Géo begin to dance a *laghia* combat dance, it is rendered in terms that directly recall the slave past, and offer praise of the unique human culture which was created out of the inhumanity of plantation slavery. Elsewhere in Zobel's work, the *laghia* is an important cultural element which reconciles past and present, and this is nowhere more evident than in his first collection of short stories, *Laghia de la mort* (1946), originally published the same year as *Les Jours immobiles*. In *Les Mains pleines d'oiseaux*, during the dance, Amboise is described as trying to form a 'carcan' out of his own arm: the term was used under slavery to refer to objects such as an iron collar, a yoke, and a shackle. Thus, a loaded word which has unmistakable resonances of slavery is inserted in a playful, positive manner: the two men can imagine their own bodies in ways that recall their slave lineage without shame or embarrassment, free of any complexes or alienation caused by that painful history. This is another example of the lived Négritude embodied by Zobel's characters: the residents of the Anse, who are secure in their autonomy and self-determination, are also psychologically liberated, and as a corollary they do not have a traumatic relationship with Martinique's slave past. As Amboise and Géo fight and frolic, the constant reminders of their dark skin and their material poverty are related with no sense of stigma; rather, their skin colour is celebrated, and the rags they wear are of no consequence. The social fabric of this tight-knit community is where true wealth resides.

Throughout the novel more generally, dance and songs carry the memory of slavery in an open manner, as is evident in this comment on Cocotte's constant singing:

> On ne savait pas d'où venait [sic] la plupart de ses chansons. Comme les paroles en étaient en français, c'étaient peut-être des chansons que chantaient les femmes blanches, dans le temps, dans le jour filtrant à travers les persiennes de leurs salons ou de leurs chambres pendant que de jeunes négresses leur démêlaient les cheveux ou leur rafraîchissaient l'air à lents coup[s] de punka. (pp. 78–79)

> Nobody knew where most of her songs came from. As the words were in French, they were probably songs sung by white women, in the past, sitting in the rays of light which slanted through the shutters of their *salons* or bedrooms, while young Negro women combed their hair or slowly fanned them with a *punka*.

Cocotte's songs are in French, not Creole, yet here the French language is not a marker of an advanced civilisation or the vehicle of the *mission civilisatrice*, but a direct signifier of the slave past of racial domination and exploitation. The female slave tends to the hair of her mistress, or fans her with a *punka*, a fan made of a palm frond which was hung from the ceiling and moved by a slave or servant (this kind of fan was often used in India). The description acknowledges the slave past without acrimony, although the *tableau* Cocotte imagines can certainly be charged with being a romanticised version of history.[13] Writers such as bell hooks have argued that the female house slave, although shielded from physical plantation labour, did not enjoy the

---

13 See, for example, two comprehensive studies of women's experiences of slavery in the French Caribbean: Bernard Moitt, *Women and Slavery in the French Antilles, 1635–1848* (Bloomington, IN: Indiana University Press, 2001) and Arlette Gautier, *Les Sœurs de Solitude: femmes et esclavages aux Antilles du XVIIe au XIXe siècle* (Rennes: Presses universitaires de Rennes, 2010).

position of privilege which some authors and critics have claimed, as they were highly vulnerable to the caprices of their white owners – male and female – within the private space of the plantation house.[14] House slaves were under constant pressure as they had to navigate a complex psychological landscape of partial inclusion into white society. This fragile balance threatened at any moment to tip into complete exclusion, which in its ultimate expression would be their murder, in the event that they were not deemed sufficiently compliant to the demands – physical, psychological, or sexual – made of them. Yet there is more at work in Zobel's novel than might first meet the eye. Cocotte actually sets up this bucolic image of plantation life in order to immediately challenge it; she is adamant that her knowledge of French songs does not begin in the white French plantation, and claims that these songs actually came from mermaids who witnessed the Middle Passage 'naguère' (in times long ago) (p. 79). These same mermaids terrorised the white sailors who were engaged in slavery:

> Elles se hissaient à la pointe des lames, au passage d'un navire qui allait acheter, revendre ou voler des nègres d'un côté ou de l'autre de cette mer immense. Elles déchaînaient la tempête. Alors, l'équipage leur jetait des peignes et des barils vides qui avaient contenu du vin ou de la viande salée. Alors elles s'installaient sur les barils, livraient leur chevelure au vent en jouant comme d'un instrument avec le peigne, et se mettaient à chanter. Bien sûr, la cargaison de nègres qui gémissaient de douleur et de chagrin dans la cale du bateau ne pouvait assister à ce spectacle! (p. 79)

> Whenever a boat sailed past which was going to buy, sell, or steal Negroes from one side or another of this immense sea, the mermaids swam up to the crests of the waves. Then they unleashed a tempest, and the crew began to hurl combs and empty barrels, which had contained wine or salted meat, at them. At this, the mermaids climbed on to the barrels, letting their hair flow freely in the wind and playing the combs like musical instruments, and they began to sing. Of course, the cargo of Negroes who were moaning with pain and sorrow in the boat's hold could not see any of this!

The mermaids' agency over the sailors is a form of vengeance for the captured Africans, who have lost their old identities and are already transformed, as the novel shows, from people into an amorphous mass of *nègres*: objectified, profitable cargo bound for the New World. The

---

14 bell hooks, *Ain't I a Woman? Black Women and Feminism* (Boston, MA: South End Press, 1981), pp. 23–24.

old woman demonstrates her awareness of the traumatic origins of her black ancestors' arrival in Martinique; she pictures this history as an ancient folkloric tale of good against evil, in which the earth itself is inhabited by non-human forces which have witnessed, and sought to punish, the evil act of transatlantic slavery. Inherent to the kind of Négritude being developed by Zobel through his black villagers is an understanding of the horror of transatlantic slavery, and the acknowledgment that its legacy is still in evidence around them, and in the ways they comprehend the world; yet, crucially, it is also an understanding that does not prevent his characters from living with their past, while looking to the future.

Les Mains pleines d'oiseaux is also remarkable for the way in which it demonstrates how race is not a black-white binary in Martinique, but rather a spectrum. In contrast to *Diab'-là*, a novel in which no specific *békés* were named, and in which there is more of a binary divide between black and white Martinicans (the latter group being defined through their absolute physical absence in the novel), *Les Mains pleines d'oiseaux* shows how over generations, all Martinicans had become inextricably linked by history as well as by genetics. Cocotte's wealth is used as a way to trace these relationships and render them more visible. She herself claims that her well was built

> autour de la résidence de l'arrière-grand-père d'Eugène Larcher, son grand-oncle, dont le père, dans le temps – peut-être bien au temps du Marquis d'Anterre, précisément – avait d'immenses propriétés, des plantations, une sucrerie, des esclaves. (pp. 40–41)

> beside the great house belonging to the great-grandfather of Eugène Larcher, who was her great-uncle, and whose own father, long ago – maybe back in the time of the Marquis d'Anterre himself – had immense properties, plantations, a sugar refinery, and slaves.

Cocotte becomes emblematic of the island's past, with her mixed black and white ancestry, descended from slaves and slave owners.

The reference to the Larcher family is loaded with historical significance, as it places Cocotte as part of a notorious real-life mixed-race family from Les Anses d'Arlet. The family's notoriety did not result from having crossed the colour lines of Martinican society, as mixed-race unions were relatively common. This fact is demonstrated by *Le Code noir* of 1685, which legislated for such unions. In 1768, however, the Larchers became infamous for being the first family in which a mixed-race relationship resulted in an official marriage. Through his marriage to an *esclave affranchi* (freed slave), the 'mulatto' woman Madeleine Roblot, Larcher acknowledged the six children she had previously borne him, who were then aged between seven and 25 years old. In a further dramatic and unusual development, after Larcher's death, Madeleine won the right to his inheritance in a trial which scandalised white Martinican society:

> Barthélemy Larcher fut le seul créole blanc, au XVIIIe siècle qui épousa une fille de couleur et reconnut les enfants nés avant son mariage. Un procès célèbre fut soutenu et gagné par sa femme et ses enfants contre ses neveux et nièces.[15]

> Barthélemy Larcher was the only white Creole in the eighteenth century who married a girl of colour and recognised the children born before the marriage. An infamous trial was brought, and won, by his wife and children against his nephew and nieces.

This mixed-race marriage means that the narrative's casual reference to Cocotte's relationship to a *béké* family will, to a reader with local knowledge, immediately call to mind the Larcher story. Cocotte, who may well have been inspired by a real person, can be situated in a real-life Martinican history: moreover, her dynamism and determination recall the extraordinary actions of her purported ancestor Madeleine Roblot, who took on the Martinican legal system to provide her own mixed-race children with an inheritance – albeit one which would have included black plantation slaves. Like a significant proportion of Martinicans, Cocotte descends from both slave owners and slaves, with a heritage which includes the victims of exploitation and the perpetrators of domination. The physical benefits of this ancestry are evident in the lands which the old lady has inherited; moreover, the slave-owning part of her family would have been further enriched by the compensation monies paid out to former slave owners after abolition.[16]

---

15 Émile Hayot, *Les Gens de couleur libre du Fort Royal (1679–1823)* (SFHOM, 1971, re-edited in 2005), p. 115.
16 There is an interesting parallel here with the story of science presenter Liz Bonnin, whose ancestry was traced by an episode of the BBC1 programme *Who Do You Think You Are?* broadcast on 9 December 2016. Bonnin discovered that one Martinican ancestor, Pauline Zoé, a former slave, inherited her *béké* husband's slave plantation and, after 1848, subsequently received compensation for the loss of the slaves she had inherited. At the invitation of the production team, I contributed to the programme's preparatory research.

It is historically and geographically consistent that the fabled Larcher family is interwoven into the narrative, as Larcher had a property in the area, and the beauty spot Morne Larcher, the hill where Larcher had a house, forms a natural boundary between Les Anses d'Arlet and Le Diamant (the *morne* is described, but not named, in *Diab'-là*). Indeed, the landscape in *Les Mains pleines d'oiseaux* is a living, tangible entity with which the villagers enthusiastically interact. For a reader of the original 1946 text, descriptions of the rhythms of daily rural Martinican life such as *jeter la senne* (which refers to a traditional method of 'casting a fishing net' that requires several men in a collective, communal practice), harvesting food, or following a forest 'trace' or path through the *mornes* would have been striking in their novelty. No other writer at the time was choosing to focus on these elements of rural Martinican life in a way that de-exoticised them. Zobel was arguing that the island's natural diversity and, in particular, the way in which geography and the environment shape local everyday customs and practices, must be appreciated and celebrated. In today's modern era, the novel's pastoral scenes are reminiscent of a recent, yet psychologically distant age in which people experienced their natural environment first-hand, relying on it for food and shelter, rather than rapidly shuttling through a built concrete environment (be it in Martinique, or elsewhere) enclosed in cars, offices, underground tunnels, and shopping malls.

In its descriptions of the relationships between people and nature, the novel builds a picture of a complex, interrelated community. This codified way of life comprises social traditions in which every member of the community must play their role. The presentation of childhood, in particular, has nothing in common with the western notion of 'childhood' as a time of separation, protection, and, increasingly, infant-targeted forms of consumerism. Instead, children are called on to undertake important 'grown-up' tasks, making a contribution which helps the wider community to function:

> la coutume étant que matin et soir les enfants, dès qu'ils sont capables de porter une calebasse de deux litres d'eau, commencent et terminent leur journée par la corvée d'eau qui donne lieu à des défilés de garçons et de filles de tous âges par les chemins, qui portant une calebasse au bout de chaque bras, qui défiant l'équilibre avec la rondeur d'un énorme *canari* sur la tête. (p. 41)

> the custom was that morning and evening, as soon as they could carry a calabash of two litres of water, the children would start and finish their day with the chore of fetching water, and so boys and girls of all ages

lined the paths, some carrying a calabash in their arms, others showing their superior balancing skills by carrying an enormous round *canari* pot on their head.

The children's labour is a subtle suggestion that a different kind of social organisation is at work in the Anse. In peppering his novel with Creole terms such as *canari*, Zobel was not only evoking a lost African heritage, but also a lost Amerindian past. The *calebasse*, or calabash, is a large fruit; it is not specific to the Caribbean, but here Zobel is describing a traditional Amerindian method of using the dried, hollowed-out fruit as a *coui* or bowl. In addition, the *canari* is a corruption of the Amerindian term *canálli*, which describes an earthenware cooking pot, and was recorded in 1665 by Père Raymond Breton in his remarkable *Dictionnaire Caraïbe-Français*. In the same work, Breton 'translates' the term as 'canari' and uses it in numerous examples throughout his dictionary; in the French Caribbean, this word is still in use.[17] This desire to use multiple layers of language to reconnect with a lost past is a further technique which places Zobel as a forerunner of the modern authors of Créolité. Patrick Chamoiseau describes the very same process that is at work in *Les Mains pleines d'oiseaux* in his extended essay *Écrire en pays dominé*, exemplified in his comments on how Creole language is the repository for many lost Amerindian words: 'J'ai rêvé-mots, *coui, yole, mabouya, waliwa, caye, ouicou* ... (I dreamed-words: *coui, yole, mabouya, waliwa, caye, ouicou* ...).[18] No other novel by Zobel includes such detailed descriptions of traditional practices which were directly transmitted from the Amerindian past. The recovery of this lost knowledge, and the social changes which its rediscovery has the potential to catalyse, are his second novel's true focus.

---

17 Edition consulted: Raymond Breton, *Dictionnaire caraïbe-français, 1665, révérend père Raymond Breton: édition présentée et annotée par le CELIA et le GEREC*, ed. Centre d'études des langues indigènes d'Amérique (Villejuif, France) and Groupe d'études et de recherches en espace créolophone et francophone (Schoelcher, Martinique) (Paris: Karthala, 1999), p. 56 (page number refers to given dictionary page number; it occurs on p. 170 of the book itself).

18 Patrick Chamoiseau, *Écrire en pays dominé* (Paris: Gallimard, 1997), p. 126.

'Growing' Change:
Les Jours immobiles and 'Considérations sur l'art local'

Zobel completed *Les Jours immobiles* on 25 April 1946, the day before his thirty-first birthday. The opening pages were reproduced in *Le Sportif* on 8 August 1946, alongside the information that the novel itself was due to be released the following week.[19] In the months leading to the manuscript's completion, Zobel prepared and delivered a public talk in which he reflected on the significance and potential of local art. Contemporary newspaper articles show that on Sunday 10 February 1946, Zobel gave the lecture as part of the Congrès de Tourisme Antillais (Antillean Tourism Congress).[20] The text was subsequently printed later in 1946 as the essay 'Considérations sur l'art local', in the fifth and final issue of *Martinique*, the review that had been launched by Georges-Louis Ponton. Zobel must therefore have been working on the novel and the essay concurrently. Interestingly, the three other articles that Zobel contributed to *Martinique* were short works of prose fiction. 'Considérations sur l'art local' is the only known critical essay published by Zobel, and it includes important reflections on the development of his thought regarding both the Amerindian past and the role of art and culture for marginalised groups in Martinican society, in turn casting new light on these themes in *Les Jours immobiles*. Zobel was aware of the emerging generation of Martinican artists being nurtured at the time, such as René Hibran, who provided the illustrations for *Martinique*, including the frontispiece, an abstract motif of a mermaid signed 'H'. Alongside René Menil's rather abstract essay in the first issue of *Tropiques* on 'Naissance de notre art' (Birth of our Art),[21] and Hibran's more pragmatic contributions to *Martinique* and *Tropiques*,[22] Zobel's essay forms one of the earliest works of art history criticism in Martinique.

---

19 'A Paraître: *Les Jours immobiles: roman antillais* de Joseph Zobel', *Le Sportif*, 8 August 1946, n. pag. Le Fonds Zobel: DD:JZ.B.246.
20 Th. M., 'Joseph Zobel', *Le Sportif*, 16 February 1946, n. pag, Le Fonds Zobel: DD:JZ.B.246.
21 René Ménil, 'Naissance de notre art', *Tropiques*, 1, April 1941; see Césaire et al., *Tropiques 1941–1945: collection complète* (Paris: Jean Michel Place, 1978), pp. 53–64.
22 René Hibran, 'Le Problème de l'art à la Martinique', *Tropiques*, 6–7, 1943, pp. 39–41 and 'Pour un art vraiment antillais', *Martinique: revue trimestrielle*, 1 (March 1944), pp. 21–25.

Zobel begins the essay by recognising that there is a problematic lack of local art in contemporary Martinican culture. He is thinking of the plastic arts and painting, and specifically references 'l'art nègre' (p. 34). This lack is not, he reminds his audience or readers, inherent to the island itself; prior to the arrival of Columbus, art had flourished in Martinique under the Amerindians:

> Ils avaient un art. Témoins les vestiges découverts dans les diverses fouilles effectuées en différents points de l'île et que ceux qui n'ont jamais eu l'occasion de les voir pourront examiner à l'une des expositions ouvertes sous l'égide de la Société Touristique.[23]

> They had an artistic tradition. The fragments discovered at various digs across the island bear witness to this, and those who have not yet had the opportunity to see them will be able to examine them at one of the exhibitions organised by the Tourism Society.

Much of this lost artistic tradition has literally lain buried after centuries of French colonial rule. It is clear from Zobel's words that in 1946 the Martinican Tourism Society was aiming to stimulate interest in this bygone era among Martinicans, through new exhibitions of Amerindian artefacts. Zobel then moves to the present era, to consider the specific case of the relationship between 'le Nègre' and art in Martinique. Again, he focuses on the link between artistic practice and the environment, arguing that transatlantic slavery rendered creative practices impossible in the island because its totalising brutality obliterated the material and spiritual conditions which are necessary to engender art:

> Jamais il [le Nègre] n'a savouré un bonheur quelconque de vivre, de travailler et de se reposer le cœur léger, l'estomac apaisé. Il n'a jamais pu jouir même des beautés naturelles qui l'entourent. Et jusqu'ici, très peu de Martiniquais sont capables de goûter les merveilles de leur pays.[24]

> He [the Negro] has never been able to take any pleasure in living, nor to work and to rest with a light heart, and a full stomach. He has never even been able to enjoy the natural beauty all around him. And to this day, very few Martinicans are capable of enjoying the marvels of their native land.

What is astonishing here is Zobel's conviction that Martinicans themselves were still, in 1946, blind to the natural beauty of the island

---

23 Zobel, 'Considérations sur l'art local', p. 33.
24 Zobel, 'Considérations sur l'art local', p. 34.

where they lived because of the legacy of slavery. He draws attention to the psychological damage wrought on the Martinican population, and argues that before they can create art, Martinicans must see their country anew. Until this shift occurs, the oppression and domination of the past will continue to curb any artistic impulses, leaving the Martinican unable to create anything meaningful:

> Son âme est un conflit entre la peur et l'ambition. Il est un être refoulé, et cet état est impropre à tout acte artistique vrai. Et qu'on veuille le reconnaître ou non, c'est un peu cet état qui rend notre population de couleur si manœuvrable, si facile à intimider et à mater, et qui autorise n'importe qui à nous mésestimer et à manquer de respect à notre égard quelquefois.[25]

> His soul is constantly in conflict, torn between fear and ambition. He is a repressed individual, and this condition impedes any true artistic act. And whether we wish to acknowledge it or not, it is this state of mind which makes our coloured population so easily manipulated, so easy to intimidate and subdue, and which at certain moments authorises absolutely anyone to underestimate us and fail to show us respect.

This quotation is also another instance of Zobel writing in a manner which anticipates the future work of Frantz Fanon. *Peau noire, masques blancs* appeared six years after this lecture was originally given, and the similarities in the ideas being expressed suggest that Fanon's extended series of essays in that publication is a brilliant synthesis of ideas which were very much part of the post-war Martinican cultural *zeitgeist*. In other words, Fanon was not writing in a vacuum. What is particularly remarkable about Zobel's intervention is the role which he ascribes to art as a healing force through which a new society may be forged, which contrasts with Fanon's focus on the potential of medicine, psychiatry, and psychoanalysis.

Zobel's essay builds to an unmistakably political climax (if this was also the case in the spoken lecture, then it has to be wondered what the Tourist Board made of this political outspokenness!). His final paragraph concludes that 'un mouvement culturel intelligent est le meilleur véhicule pour une révolution sociale constructive et bénéfique' (a well thought-through cultural movement is the best vehicle for a constructive and beneficial social revolution).[26] The belief that a cultural

---

25 Zobel, 'Considérations sur l'art local', pp. 35–36.
26 Zobel, 'Considérations sur l'art local', p. 38.

movement can bring about social revolution is the most explicitly political statement ever written by Zobel. He does not equate this comment with Négritude, nor is the movement mentioned in the essay; what he does do, however, is interrogate the concepts of *Nègre*, *élite*, and 'l'homme de couleur martiniquais' (the Martinican person of colour). The essay is an example of Zobel's intersectional Négritude, as it works its way through hierarchies of race, while always also drawing attention to the category of class.

This intersectional mode is most evident when he includes an autobiographical detail. Zobel explains that he is quite in awe when he attends 'ces petits bals rustiques, que les gens convenables ne peuvent pas voir ni même écouter décemment' (these small country parties, which decent people refrain from seeing or even listening to, for fear of impropriety) (p. 37). In contrast to these conservative reactions, he expresses his admiration for such parties over several paragraphs, jubilantly and defiantly proclaiming 'tout cela c'est la santé, la franchise, la force ignorée de ma race' (it all represents the health, the essence, the unrecognised strength of my race) (p. 37). The essay offers theoretical underpinnings for Zobel's career as a novelist, expressing his vision that literature, and his literature in particular, needed to promote alternative ways of living in the island of Martinique that would bring about a new manner of seeing its natural beauty and the incredible creativity of its peoples. This shift would both reshape social attitudes towards groups who had been marginalised by the intersecting colonial constructs of race and class, and rehabilitate the cultural heritage which had been suppressed and excluded by French colonialism.

Les Jours immobiles, like Zobel's essay, is steeped in an awareness that Creole culture owes a debt to both slavery and, more subtly, to the Amerindian culture which preceded it. He sets out a vision, quite without precedent in black Martinican literature of the time, of Creole culture as a continuum or set of interrelated systems. The novel demonstrates how the traditions of the inhabitants of the Martinican village reconcile past and present, slavery and abolition; just as the Martinican Tourist Board was conducting archaeological digs and creating exhibitions of the finds, Zobel is excavating the Creole culture which characterises the group known as *nègres* and displaying it as a complex composite of African and Amerindian cultures. The lines between different cultural elements are now quite blurred, as when he demonstrates the religious syncretism between Christianity and other spiritual practices; and so Cocotte is just as anxious for young Amboise to rub his arms, legs, and neck – areas of the body associated with strength – with bull's saliva (p. 57) as she is anxious to receive the ordained Christian *curé*'s blessing. The novel compellingly demonstrates that Creole culture became a repository for Amerindian knowledge after the Amerindians themselves were exterminated; indeed, in 'Considérations sur l'art local', Zobel refers explicitly to the Amerindians being 'exterminés sans merci' (mercilessly exterminated) (p. 33), in language which was intentionally loaded in the wake of the Second World War, and which drew an implicit parallel between the genocides perpetrated by Europeans, firstly through colonialism, and subsequently through the war and the Holocaust which had only ended a few months previously.

The area of Les Anses d'Arlet is particularly significant for its links to the Amerindian past. It takes its name from the Carib Chief Arlet, who continued to live in Martinique after the first decade or so of conquest around 1635–1648. According to some accounts, he was the brother of another legendary Carib chief, Pilote, who is immortalised in the northern town of Case-Pilote (literally, Pilote's Hut). The areas to which these chiefs gave their names are tragic historical markers; they indicate the places where the Amerindians took refuge as French colonisation efforts intensified.

The French settlement at Les Anses d'Arlet was significant enough for a parish to be founded there as early as 1665, followed by the construction of one of the first churches built on Martinique, L'Église Saint-Henri, which dates from 1671 and dominates the bay of Grande Anse.[27] The intensive and rapid development of Les Anses d'Arlet as an important French colonial settlement led to Chief Arlet and his group being driven out of the lands which they had once called home. This colonial pattern of removal and annexation was repeated throughout the Caribbean, and across the wider world more generally. Arlet retreated further south, to a bay called l'Anse Figuier (in a similar process, his brother Pilote also sought refuge in the south, in the area still known as Rivière-Pilote).[28] The bay of L'Anse Figuier remains an important site of memory for these acts of colonial genocide, and the modern-day Martinican Ecomusée is located there. This museum about the Martinican environment includes reconstructions

---

27 See: http://www.culture.gouv.fr/public/mistral/merimee_fr?ACTION=CHERCHER&FIELD_98=INSEE&VALUE_98=97202 (accessed 20 July 2015).
28 See: http://pnr-martinique.com/visiter/les-anses-darlet/ (accessed 21 July 2015).

of Amerindian villages and fragments of Amerindian pottery; it also includes a permanent installation dedicated to Zobel himself. The museum building is emblematic of another aspect of the island's history – slavery – as it is a former sugar refinery.

The south-west coast of Martinique is thus a site of great archaeological importance where significant Amerindian finds have been made. In 1946, Zobel discussed the legacy of the Amerindians and their art in his lecture and printed essay, and it appears highly likely that this knowledge shaped his understanding of Anses d'Arlet, particularly as he came to transcribe this knowledge in his novel. *Les Mains pleines d'oiseaux* includes the most significant reflections on the connections between Creole and Amerindian culture in all of Zobel's works. It is clear that the inhabitants of the remote bays which make up the area known as Les Anses d'Arlet are not burdened by the psychological complexes which Zobel would decry in his elite and bourgeois compatriots in his next novel, *La Rue Cases-Nègres*. There is no need for emancipation from a post-slavery present which still equates to a life of mental and physical slavery. There is, though, untapped potential for a more meaningful and more productive interaction with the natural environment. Yet in a community where everything appears still, *immobile*, and plentiful, how can anything significant change? In *Diab'-là*, the urgent need for change bristles from the opening lines about exploitation of *nègres* and finds expression through Diab'-là's own assertive voice, a voice which challenges the dominant social order and is a conduit for the opinions of the author himself. In contrast, *Les Mains pleines d'oiseaux* appears to depict a community where harmony and plenitude already reign. Nonetheless, the narrative does include a subtle critique of human relationships with the natural environment. It argues, through this burgeoning form of what would now be understood as ecocriticism, that a greater appreciation of the land and its potential to sustain the villagers of the Anse is possible, and should be a widely held aspiration:

> Cocotte sentait la possibilité de changer encore beaucoup de choses dans l'Anse, car, pensait-elle, on pouvait trouver un moyen d'avoir le cœur pareil à un *coui* rempli de fruits et qui ne désemplit pas, quel que soit l'empressement avec lequel on s'y rassasie. (p. 45)

> Cocotte felt that it would be possible to make many more changes in the Anse, because, she thought, you could find a way to make your heart as

full as a *coui* bowl full of fruits which never empties, no matter how great your appetite.

Change is implicitly connected with the past – here signified by the *coui*, a bowl made from a dried and hollowed-out calabash fruit, and a word which passed into Martinican Creole from the Amerindian language. The change comes about organically, and is fundamentally linked to the rediscovery of the island's Amerindian heritage.

In *Les Mains pleines d'oiseaux*, Zobel's use of social realism extends to depicting not only action, but also – and crucially – moments of inactivity. Moments of rest and quiet contemplation are shown as essential to allowing human creativity to ferment, allowing the subconscious mind to work through scenes, problems, and challenges at a level of which the conscious mind is unaware. The novel's pivotal moment is introduced in the most inauspicious manner, and involves precisely this play between activity and lethargy:

> Et puis, il y eut ce matin où, de son propre aveu, Géo n'eût pas fait l'effort de soulever un grain de sable; et Amboise, non plus, n'avait pas envie de bouger un pied. Il y a de tels jours dans cette vie qui ne se déroule pas à la cadence des aiguilles d'une montre, ni au rythme des délais et des échéances. Un besoin de se sentir comme une pirogue sans voiles et sans avirons sur une eau tranquille – au fond d'une crique oubliée. (pp. 84–85)

> And then came that morning when, by his own admission, Géo wouldn't even have taken the trouble to lift a grain of sand; and Amboise couldn't muster the energy to lift a finger either. There are days like that in this life which is not set to play out to the cadence of the hands of a watch, nor to the rhythm of limits and deadlines. Days when the overwhelming need is to feel as free as a *pirogue* boat without sails or oars on still waters – drifting down some forgotten creek.

Just as the natural world requires fallow periods to restore fertility to the soil, the novel argues that there is an instinctive human need to experience moments of rest, when thoughts can drift and wander. Contrary to the frenetic and increasingly regulated, orchestrated movements of the modern world, symbolised by the ominous ticking of a wristwatch, *Les Mains pleines d'oiseaux* argues for the recognition of the value of other kinds of activity. Every day must *not* unfold like clockwork to a set routine.

On the day in question, Géo, Cocotte, and Amboise decide to embrace their lethargy, and that their main accomplishment of the day will be nothing more than preparing 'un bon *féroce*, là, ce matin, et puis

… Ça va pour toute la journée' (a good *féroce* dip this morning, and then … That will do for the whole day) (p. 85). *Féroce* is a kind of dip or paste made from avocados, a Caribbean equivalent of guacamole (which is South American). This simple creative action brings about a sense of total satisfaction:

> Une belle matinée.
> Un bon *féroce*.
> On était bien. (p. 87)
>
> A beautiful morning.
> A good *féroce*.
> Life felt good.

The bold typography of these three short, descriptive sentences reduces the narrative's pace in line with the activity being described. Short, assertive sentences convey the characters' sense of utter contentment. They are absorbed in the moment, in the now, and this insistence on enjoying the present resonates with a phenomenon which has come to be known in western twenty-first century as 'mindfulness', and which itself is a diluted form of non-western, Buddhist practice. What was once denounced in capitalist society as wasteful, unproductive procrastination is increasingly being regarded as a creative necessity. It is becoming widely accepted that in allowing the brain to rest, unexpected connections may be made.

In the novel, the quiet, repetitive manual activity of preparing food together, and then eating together, in silence, acts as a period of incubation and enhances creativity. Suddenly, after being absorbed in these tranquil activities, Amboise is struck with an idea: 'Pourquoi ne ferions-nous pas de la farine nous-mêmes, puisque …' (Why don't we start to make flour ourselves, because …) (p. 88). There is a logical connection between the act of eating *féroce* and Amboise's idea, but this is not made explicit in the narrative and will only occur to those who are familiar with the French Caribbean context. *Féroce* is made from avocado, dried cod, chilli peppers, and manioc. This final ingredient is what triggers Amboise's sudden inspiration, as the flour to which he refers is not French wheat-based flour, but is a flour made from the starchy roots of the manioc plant.

The story of manioc, or *manihot esculenta*, which is also commonly known as cassava, arrowroot, tapioca, or yucca, depending on the region where it is consumed, reveals two fascinating transnational phenomena. First, it demonstrates how culinary practices demonstrate the circulation of Amerindian peoples; this starchy food was consumed across the Amerindian zone between Latin America and the Caribbean. Interestingly, the term 'manioc' was imposed by the French; it was not being used by the Amerindians of Martinique at the time of conquest. These Amerindians were a diverse group comprising Kalinago, a people who themselves had links with the Kalina groups on the South American continent, and Arawak members.[29] According to Breton's dictionary, they called the plant 'kiére';[30] he also lists the compound 'kierougánti', meaning 'il fait croître le manioc' (he grows manioc).[31] The word 'manioc' is itself a French adaptation of *manioka*, the term which was used by the Tupi people of Brazil.[32] It is a reminder of the earliest phase of French colonialism in the Americas, which saw the establishment of French *comptoirs* or trading posts in Brazil.[33] It is Breton who recognises and connects what he sees in Martinique with the crop grown by Amerindians in Brazil when he 'translates' *kiére* into 'manioc'. In Martinique, the flour derived from the *kiére* or manioc was a staple of the Amerindian diet, as evidenced by multiple entries in Breton's dictionary, including 'chibíba', which is glossed as 'farine de racines de Manioc' (flour from manioc roots) and 'kelétona', glossed as 'farine de manioc' (manioc flour).[34] In a second transnational development, the plant became even more intimately connected with colonialism: manioc is native to South America, but certain varieties were introduced to Africa by the Portuguese from their colonies in Brazil. In the twentieth century, it is a staple crop which feeds an estimated 500 million Africans.[35]

It is wholly significant that when Amboise's moment of inspiration strikes, the three friends are sitting in deep relaxation and enjoying the simple activities – eating, daydreaming, being together in contented silence – with which they are occupied at that moment. His idea to

---

29 Raphaël Nicole, *Histoire des Antilles françaises des Amérindiens à nos jours* (Trinité: Éditions de la Frise, 2012), pp. 8–17.
30 Breton, p. 164 (in dictionary; p. 278 of book).
31 Breton, p. 165 (in dictionary; p. 279 of book).
32 The Oxford English Dictionary lists the earliest usage of 'manioc' as 1544, in an account of Brazil.
33 Philippe Bonnichon, 'France et Brésil: apports réciproques aux XVIe et XVIIe siècles', *L'Année des outre-mer: Mémoires de l'Académie des Sciences, Arts et Belles-Lettres de Touraine*, 24 (2011), pp. 9–25.
34 Breton, p. 74 (of dictionary; p. 188 of book).
35 'The American Association for the Advancement of Science: Cassava-nova', *The Economist*, 20 February 2016, p. 70.

start making manioc flour will bring them even closer to the Caribbean environment, and to a forgotten aspect of their history. The scene furnishes the major example of the novel's attempts to rehabilitate the Amerindian heritage in Creole society, as the very words at stake here, manioc and *féroce*, and this practice of preparing flour, all originated in pre-Columbian history.

Several of the earliest French colonial narratives contain images which depict the preparation of manioc flour. The most famous is the incredibly detailed plantation vista called *Ménagerie* (Household; the term *ménagerie* can also designate a place where animals are kept, which suggests the denigration of the slaves who are pictured) included by Jean-Baptiste du Tertre in his *Histoire générale des Antilles habitées par les François* (1667).[36] Du Tertre shows a courtyard in full activity, with each stage of manioc preparation visible. These stages, removed from their surrounding context, are reproduced in the works of Père Labat. The reissued version of his *Nouveau voyage aux Isles de l'Amérique*, published in 1742, some years after his death, was expanded to include several illustrations. One illustrated insert shows the five stages of manioc preparation, including one depicting a *négresse* sitting with her legs wrapped around a large bowl and pressing grated manioc through a square screen to obtain flour.[37]

This *farine de manioc* was a staple of Amerindian diets which had also been adopted into slave diets as a simple method of nourishment. It is not, then, so much an innovation that strikes Amboise as a remembrance, or rather a moment of *remembering not to forget*. Amboise's plan derives all the more symbolism and urgency because in mid-1940s Anses d'Arlet, this traditional, local source of food has been forgotten in favour of imported flour from France. His idea is nothing less than a rapprochement, or re-entwining, of the multiple strands of the Caribbean environment and history, which the mercantilist logic of colonial modernity has systematically prised apart.

---

36 Père Jean-Baptiste du Tertre, *Histoire générale des Antilles habitées par les François, vol. 2* (Paris: Thomas Jolly, 1667), p. 419.

37 Père Jean-Baptiste Labat, *Nouveau voyage aux Isles de l'Amérique Contenant L'Histoire Naturelle de ces Pays, l'Origine, les Moeurs, la Religion & le Gouvernement des Habitans anciens & modernes [...] Ouvrage enrichi de plus de cent Cartes, Plans & Figures en Taille-douces. Nouvelle Edition augmentée considérablement, & enrichie de Figures en Taille-douces, Vol. I* (Paris: Cavelier, 1742), insert on p. 397. See: https://archive.org/stream/nouveauvoyageaux09laba#page/n491/mode/2up (accessed 16 November 2016)].

To carry out the plan, the men's method of transport again underscores their independence from French culture: Géo and Amboise travel in a *pirogue*, itself a word imposed by the French to denote the Amerindian canoe or *kanawa*, a small longboat that was paddled rather than sailed.[38] They head to Poirier, a small village at the mouth of the river known as La Rivière Pilote, a symbolic site of pre-Columbian heritage (a link explained above). In this historically charged place, they collect manioc shoots from a villager. He is most bemused by the pair, although whether he finds their idea comically outmoded, or comical because it is still commonplace to make manioc flour in his village, is unclear. A true representative of Zobel's vision of dignified humble Martinican society, the villager refuses to take any money in exchange for the manioc shoots. Eventually, out of sheer politeness, he accepts the fish that Géo and Amboise have brought with them, a subtle nod to a system of trade and barter which is itself an echo of the Amerindian structures of pre-monetised, pre-Colombian Martinique, and of the circuits of exchange which existed in slave plantation societies, held as they were in a deliberate state of economic dispossession.

The villager reassures Géo and Amboise that as they are making small quantities of manioc flour, they will not need any substantial machinery to grind it. It is he who explains the old Amerindian method: 'Vous grattez le manioc, vous le pressez dans un linge' (You grate the manioc, and then press it through a cloth) (p. 100), in terms that could describe the very same images from Labat's colonial literature discussed above. This is the specific method of preparing flour from bitter manioc. Moreover, in this traditional practice, no part of the manioc goes unused, and the old man elaborates:

> Vous n'avez qu'à laisser pauser le jus, et vous avez de la moussache pour amidonner. La pulpe, vous la grillez doucement dans un gros *canari* de la terre de Sainte-Anne; doucement, en remuant de temps en temps. Et vous avez une bonne farine à manger avec tout ce que vous voudrez. Vous pourrez faire aussi des *cassaves*, si vous aimez. (p. 100)

> Just let the juice rest, and there you are: it's starch for your clothes. Take the pulp and grill it over a gentle heat in a *canari* pot made from the clay of Sainte-Anne; gently, stirring it from time to time. Then you've got good flour, which will go with whatever dish you like. You can also make cassava bread, if you like.

---

38 Nicole, pp. 17–18.

The preparation of manioc flour, and the popular *cassave*, a flatbread similar to a tortilla, are fragments of Amerindian, pre-Columbian culture preserved under colonialism in slave society and through which African slaves learned how to survive in a new environment.

In the original version of the novel, *Les Jours immobiles*, the manioc plan unfolds in a similar manner, although the villager who gives them the roots provides even more practical details. In his description of how to prepare the manioc flour, the man uses the Creole term 'grage', which is glossed as a *râpe* or grater. The original novel also includes greater comment on the significance of this transmission of lost knowledge: 'c'était comme une langue qu'ils n'avaient pas parlée dans leur enfance, et qu'ils se mettaient à apprendre' (it was like a language that they had not spoken in childhood, and that they were just beginning to learn) (p. 113). This is a strikingly perceptive comparison of the environment to a foreign language, which figures it as a whole system with its own structures which must be learned, while also suggesting that there is something instinctive at work: it posits that learning to interpret the environment, like learning to speak languages, is an act which is intuitive to all humanity.

From *Les Mains pleines d'oiseaux* to the Original Novel: Rediscovering *Les Jours immobiles*

In *Les Mains pleines d'oiseaux*, when the flour plan has come to fruition, Cocotte exploits the full dramatic potential of the situation. In a characteristically flamboyant gesture, she astonishes the villagers by revealing a bowl of flour from a fold in her skirt (pp. 119–20), and asking the curate to bless it. This leads to the novel's climax, when the eponymous birds are drawn to the manioc plants in numbers never before witnessed in the Anse. Cocotte hears them before she sees them, sensing 'un léger bruissement pareil à un jeu de minuscules *chachas*' (a soft rustle which sounded like tiny *chacha* shakers) (p. 102). Yet again, manioc is equated with Amerindian heritage, as the *chacha*, a percussion instrument made from introducing seeds into a hollowed-out, firm-skinned vegetable, is part of this ancestry. The birds, too, have an Amerindian name: 'des *cicis*', a term for the species *tiaras bicolor*, known in English as the black-faced grassquit (p. 103). Two women villagers have observed the arrival of the *cicis* and assume from this unusual event that Cocotte has special powers. Their shocked faces prompt the comic, defiant outburst from the old lady which inspired the title of the rewritten novel: 'Et quoi encore [dites-vous]? Que j'ai planté du manioc? Oui. Que je commande aux oiseaux? Oui. Et vous allez voir' (What [are you saying] now? That I have planted manioc? Yes. That I can control the birds? Yes. Oh, you'll see) (p. 105). Here, and towards the end of the novel, glimpses of Cocotte's fiery temper become prominent. Zobel attenuated these moments in the rewriting process, and in *Les Mains pleines d'oiseaux* they can appear somewhat incongruous, yet they make more sense when read against the 'original' Cocotte, who is prone to angry, paranoid outbursts.

On its publication in August 1946, *Les Jours immobiles* received a similar level of support and promotion in local newspapers as *Diab'-là*. As the contemporary reviews of the time note, *Les Jours immobiles* is close to *Diab'-là* in its narrative style, but does not have the overtly political overtones of Zobel's debut novel.[39] In 1946, for the original Martinican reviewers, the novel's ingenuity lies in the fact that it holds up a mirror to Antillean society in which local readers cannot fail to recognise themselves: one review underscores the novel's realism in a discussion which places the word 'AUTHENTICITÉ' (AUTHENTICITY) in capital letters.[40] In a prescient comment, given the significance which Zobel's literature would go on to assume for Antillean cinema, another reviewer emphasises the filmic quality of the short chapters that structure the novel, and hails Zobel as 'un des premiers explorateurs' (one of the first explorers) of an indigenous Martinican post-war literature.[41] These reviewers all single out the original narrative style adopted by Zobel to describe his native society in such a way that the local people whom he depicts will not reject his literature as exoticism, but rather embrace it as representation. In the original version, or hypotext, the narrative style is indeed immediate and more directly comparable to that of *Diab'-là*; events are related from a position of proximity to the action, and direct speech abounds. Creole terms are frequent, and are helpfully glossed with brief footnotes, just as a greater number of songs are interspersed throughout the novel, given in their Creole original with a parallel French translation.

---

39 André Midas, 'Joseph Zobel et *Les Jours immobiles*', *L'Information*, 26 August 1946 (n. pag.). Le Fonds Zobel: DD:JZ.B.246.
40 See Midas.
41 Albert Adréa, 'Encore un des nôtres!', no publication name, issue number 1539, date 1946 (n. pag.). Le Fonds Zobel, DD:JZ.B.246.

In contrast, in *Les Mains pleines d'oiseaux*, the 32 years which have passed between 1946 and 1978 result in an increased distance between the narration and the events unfolding. In the original, the use of the third person is interrupted by the occasional use of the first person plural *nous* (we), which suggests the presence of an anonymous narrator who is part of the action. This proximity is diminished in *Les Mains pleines d'oiseaux*: several passages which were direct speech in the original become reported speech in the hypertext, and some songs which previously enlivened the novel have, regrettably, been removed. As a result, the rewritten narrative is laden with descriptions, and feels heavier and slower, lacking the deftness – and zeal – of *Les Jours immobiles*. It has also been sanitised: frequent references to *quimbois* (Martinican sorcery) and sex and sexuality in the original are almost eradicated. For example, a tender and erotic scene in *Les Jours immobiles* in which Néré and his wife slip away from their shack one night (where their many children are sleeping) to make love outdoors in the privacy offered by a *flamboyant* tree does not survive into the hypertext (p. 48). The juxtaposition of sexuality and natural imagery suggests that the natural cycles of life which structure life in the village are mirrored in the loving intimate relationships which the villagers form. Another example of this connection is found only in *Les Jours immobiles*, when Françoilise explains that she is not ashamed to be pregnant with Amboise's child despite the fact that they are unmarried (the marriage is duly announced). In the hypotext, Françoilise's pride leads to her imagining their growing child as the 'fleur de sa chair' (the flower of her body) (p. 164), a poetic variant on the French and English expression *fruit de mes entrailles* or fruit of my loins, which figures the child as a flower nurtured by her body, and as an extension of the natural life all around them.

Both versions unfold slowly, and yet the original has a more consistent pace and maintains a more constant narrative tension between characters, style, and plot. Moreover, small details in *Les Jours immobiles* lead to more rounded character development, particularly in the case of Cocotte. In the rewritten hypertext, Cocotte's angry outburst at the novel's conclusion comes as something of a surprise, as it is quite disproportionate to her other moments of bad temper. In the original, however, there are passages of direct speech in which Cocotte's inexplicable rages are used to full comic effect, as demonstrated by these early unprovoked outbursts which are directed at her innocent neighbours:

— Voici Cocotte! Bonjour Cocotte!

— Fouts-moi la paix, hypocrite? [*sic*]
— Cocotte bonjour, y a longtemps ...
— Tais-toi, saleté!
— Cocotte, quel jour j'amènerai ma tite fille pour que tu lui perces les oreilles?
— Perce-les lui toi-même avec ta langue, vipère! (p. 32)

'It's Cocotte! Why hello, Cocotte!'
'Will you leave me in peace, you hypocrite?'
'Hello Cocotte, it's been a while ...'
'Hold your tongue, hussy!'
'Cocotte, when can I bring my daughter to you to have her ears pierced?'
'Pierce them yourself with your tongue, viper!'

These angry outbursts are tolerated by all due to her advanced age and respected position in the community – she used to work as the village midwife and has an intimate bond with most families. In the hypotext, Cocotte actually emerges as a more idiosyncratic and endearing character, and in attenuating her outbursts Zobel loses much of her psychological complexity. Cocotte is only named as part of the Larcher family in the rewritten version. It is possible that Zobel based her character on a real person, and that at the time of writing in 1945, he did not wish to divulge such incriminating details. Three decades later, he decided to link Cocotte to the Larcher family – either he felt liberated by the passage of time to include this real-life detail, or he felt inclined to root his fictional creation more precisely in the landscape and history of the south-west of Martinique, an area for which he retained a deep affection.

Cocotte's angry outburst when the birds arrive is explicitly linked to *quimbois* in the original, which creates far stronger narrative coherence. Indeed, the original is richer in a subtle magical realism which conveys the way in which Christianity and other belief systems coexist in the daily lives of Martinicans in the Anse. She accuses the villagers of seeing the birds arrive, and immediately assuming that she has changed form by using her magical powers:

> Elles n'ont pas dit que çé moi qui suis tournée en cicis, non? ... Vous croyez que je ne connais pas votre langue? Vous êtes venues voir si cé pas moi qui suis tournée en manioc, si cé pas moi qui suis tournée en cicis, puisque le grand bourreau qui vous empoisonne avec son eau salée et son fruit à pain vert vous dit tous les jours que je suis gagée, que la nuit je survole la terre entière ... (p. 120)

They went and told you that it's me who turned into a *cici*, didn't they? You think I don't know your serpents' tongues? You came to see whether

I've turned myself into manioc, or into *cicis*, because that ole crook who's poisoning you with his dirty water and his unripe breadfruit tells you everyday that I'm a *gagée* [person with the magical power to transform into animals], and that at night I fly over the whole world ...

In the original, then, Cocotte seizes this opportunity to malign Sylva for his poor-quality water and breadfruit and for spreading rumours about her supernatural powers. In the revised text, Zobel truncates this outburst, removing the direct references to *quimbois*, which is now merely implied, leaving only a loose imprint of Cocotte's original speech. Read against the rewritten version, the original scene is far more compelling and evocative than its modified hypertext.

In both versions, the conclusion includes the rather surprising revelation that the animosity between Cocotte and Sylva is actually a manifestation of repressed sexual desire between the two cousins. Both *Les Jours immobiles* and *Les Mains pleines d'oiseaux* end with a scene in which Cocotte heads to Sylva's house and demands to dance with him. In the hypertext, this is related to Géo by Maïotte, whereas in the original hypotext, events unfold in real time and the narrative includes insights into the old lady's emotions. Cocotte is overcome with joy that Géo and Maïotte are reunited, and that Amboise and Françoilise are married, not to mention her delight at the success of the flour venture.

In the original, one of the final scenes sees Cocotte standing outside Sylva's house and singing a long song containing several pointed jibes aimed at him. The song, one contemporary reviewer noted, was a local '*bel air*'.[42] This refers to a particular style of music which, as Jacqueline Rosemain demonstrates, originated among slaves on rural plantations (Rosemain states that the *bel air* appeared in the era 1714–1789).[43] This song, then, provides another reminder of a Martinican Creole culture that runs counter to dominant European culture. Rosemain suggests that the term comes both from the French term *bel air* (literally a lovely melody) and the Yoruba term *bèlè*, a celebration marking the end of the harvest.[44] It is the transcription *bèlè* that is now found most frequently in Francophone Caribbean literature, to emphasise the musical style as a component of Creole identity.[45]

---

42   Adréa, 'Encore un des nôtres!'
43   Jacqueline Rosemain, *La Musique dans la société antillaise: 1635–1902* (Paris: L'Harmattan, 1986), p. 49.
44   Rosemain, p. 49.
45   This is evident in the name La Maison du bèlè, a prominent Martinican

Cocotte's *bel air* focuses on 'l'année-ta-là' or this year, and in it she enumerates her successes. When Sylva appears, furious, she kisses him on the cheek and he appears immediately softened, suggesting that he is indeed attracted to her. The assembled crowd begins to sing with Cocotte and Sylva, and the afternoon turns into a night of festivities. In one of the few published critical comments on *Les Mains pleines d'oiseaux*, Hal Wylie observes that this scene is an example of how 'festive activities, music and dance are major themes for Zobel', adding that 'Zobel is an optimist; his work shows more victories than defeats'.[46] This statement underplays the complexity, tensions, and tragedy of the conclusion, however. In both versions, this ability to dance and sing for long periods is described as a quality inherited from slave ancestors. In *Les Jours immobiles*, the narrative comments of Cocotte that 'elle dansait encore mieux que feue Ayotine, sa mère, l'esclave, la sorcière guinéenne!' (she danced even better than Ayotine, her dear departed mother, the slave, the Guinean sorcerer!) (p. 212), while the narrator of *Les Mains pleines d'oiseaux* passes the more circumspect comment: 'Elle est de la race de celles qui, dans le temps, dansaient toute une nuit et tout le lendemain, sans boire et sans manger' (She is of the race which, in times gone by, danced through the night and all the following day, without pausing to drink or eat) (p. 155). Blackness and the ancestral link to slavery, which were emphasised in the first version, are attenuated and come to be represented through euphemism in the rewritten text. Yet the rewritten comment only takes on its full significance when it is directly contrasted with the detail and tone of the original passage: it serves as something of a meta-narrative which passes comment on the original; without knowledge of that original, the new phrase falls rather flat. This suggests that Zobel rewrote his novels in a way which passes comment on the original novel, locking the two versions into a far more intimate relationship than he ever intended. The reader who compares the two versions is a literary archaeologist, comparing the different textual layers with which Zobel described the same event; each layer casts light on a different aspect, but it is only by accessing the earliest original layer and using it as a textual referent that the full potency of Zobel's narratives can be comprehended.

Cocotte will not be able to dance forever, and the clues as to her

---

museum and cultural centre in Sainte-Marie. See: http://www.lamaisondubele.fr/ (accessed 23 March 2017).
46 Wylie, p. 63.

ill health which are scattered throughout both versions of the novel are brought into sharp relief when she keels over mid-dance. While the hypertext *Les Mains pleines d'oiseaux* relates this from a third-person perspective, *Les Jours immobiles* includes insights into Cocotte's psychology in a far more ambitious narrative style. The final pages of the original are ominous, as her joy is juxtaposed with a repeated refrain, a fragmented voice which comes out of nowhere and must be Cocotte's internal monologue '… Pas la robe mauve!' (Not the mauve dress) (p. 215). This refers to the funeral dress which Cocotte has already prepared for her wake earlier in the novel. The final words of both accounts are identical and provide one of Zobel's most evocative descriptions, as Cocotte's lifeless face is 'scellé d'une expression que personne ne lui avait jamais vue' (sealed with an expression that no one had ever seen on it before) (p. 157/p. 217). The two versions of the text converge here, as at other points, and the narrative arc of both novels concludes with Cocotte's exuberant death.

* * *

In the Anse, human beings coexist, not without friction, but also in the company of its more positive counterpart, passion. The small community refuses to be defined by material wealth in the western sense. Money is present in the text, but its pursuit is rendered noble in Géo's ambitions for himself and Amboise, dignified through Maiotte's determination to be self-sufficient while winning back Géo's affections, and ironic through Cocotte's obsessive, petty desire to outdo Sylva. Even Cocotte's frenzied insults and dancing at the text's dénouement, remarkably, draw the community together as bemused spectators rather than dividing it. Zobel allows his cantankerous, dynamic, and unforgettable diva of Les Anses d'Arlet to depart from this life in a manner that will ensure her notoriety for generations to come.

In its depiction of natural resources and their management, and in the careful detail accorded to the traditional practices of growing food, *Les Mains pleines d'oiseaux* was ahead of its time in its interrogation of the Martinican population's relationship to the land. This enhanced understanding of natural cycles and indigenous crops allows the inhabitants of Petite Anse to enjoy an autonomy which, as the narrative highlights, is indeed rare. Read alongside the essay 'Considérations sur l'art local' with its call for local art, in all its forms, to help to generate a social revolution, it is evident that Zobel was offering up his novel as a means to spark a wider debate on how Martinicans might plan and develop a more autonomous future. Zobel carefully demonstrates that a Creole culture exists – quite apart from French culture – which is more closely attuned to the Caribbean environment; moreover, this Creole culture is a continuum, a living repository for different systems, which is enriched by knowledge passed down from the Amerindian past and the slave heritage.

As a pair, the texts *Les Jours immobiles* and *Les Mains pleines d'oiseaux* now stand as a testimony to a way of life in Martinique which would be challenged by a wave of post-war modernisation just years after the original 1946 publication. Although the rewritten version loosens the tension and coherence of the original, it remains a valuable document for its continued transmission of this moment in Martinican history. It can be considered an alternative account of *Les Jours immobiles* rather than a complete rewriting, because a reader of *Les Mains pleines d'oiseaux* will sense the uneven development of the narrative, and will undeniably benefit from greater knowledge of the first text. In this sense, *Les Mains pleines d'oiseaux* cannot be considered a complete artistic success as it sits in a complementary relationship with the first version, retold through the filter of a distance of three decades and drawing attention to different aspects, rather than standing alone.

Zobel's great achievement with his second novel, a success which endures in both of its iterations, is to present a view of an alternative kind of life in which the ways people live, love, think, and work are not measured and defined by the hoard of material goods which can be accumulated through monetised labour. Rather, fundamental to this way of existence is active involvement in a complex web of social interactions, which becomes its own system, or even ecosystem, through which labour is divided up equitably and rewarded through a complex and ancient system which cannot be reduced to a monetary value. Only this kind of system can lead to the personal and communal satisfaction of the full spectrum of human emotions, rather than just catering for those meagre needs which are valued – to the detriment of all others – in French colonial society. The novel depicts a vision of utopia; yet it is a modest utopia which relies on a quiet and constant appreciation of the wealth – both human and natural – that is already to be found in Martinique. Once Martinicans are able to perceive this bounty, the novel argues, it is theirs for the taking.

CHAPTER FOUR

Rereading *La Rue Cases-Nègres*

> Me voici entre deux lointains: celui qu'allonge à vue d'œil le sillage du paquebot – et que j'ai peur de ne pouvoir jamais récupérer – et celui vers lequel se laisse porter l'autre moi-même que je deviens chaque jour [...]
>
> Joseph Zobel, Private diary entry onboard the *Colombie*, 1 December 1946[1]
>
> Here I am between two horizons: one stretched out in the boat's foamy wake until it slips from view – and, I fear, perhaps now lost to me forever – and the other, towards which the new person I am becoming with each passing day is being carried [...]
>
> (my modified translation)

Zobel's name will forever be synonymous with his semi-autobiographical novel *La Rue Cases-Nègres*. Yet, read against the broader development of his career, this text is representative not of continuity, but of dissonance and rupture. It marks a break with his first two novels, *Diab'-là* and *Les Jours immobiles,* and the short story collection *Laghia de la mort,* all of which were written while Zobel was still living in Martinique and had never set foot outside his native island. While it is most frequently understood as a story rooted in Martinican society, *La Rue Cases-Nègres* is actually a novel of immigration. It is the work of a black Caribbean author who had, by the time he finished the

---

1 Charlotte Zobel, *Joseph Zobel photographies*, pp. 8–9.

manuscript, spent over three years living and working in Paris and the surrounding area. Zobel had realised that the unprecedented success of the Parisian edition of *Diab'-là* granted him a new visibility in mainland France, and this knowledge certainly influenced him as he began to draft what was to become his most famous novel. *La Rue Cases-Nègres* was written at a point in his life when he was finally in a position to reach an audience beyond Martinique. As a result, it is a quite different novel to his previous works.

Several critics, most notably Hal Wylie, have commented on the social realism which marks Zobel's early publications. Wylie, after György Lukács, traces the roots of the term 'social realism' to the nineteenth century, suggesting that the novelists Balzac, Dickens, and Flaubert were 'the first writers to focus on humanity as an economic entity, to show the relative functions of various classes and the dynamic emergence of the bourgeoisie'.[2] Zobel, Wylie argues, can be aligned with later nineteenth-century social realists Zola and Tolstoy, who brought 'the working class, the peasants and other have-nots into the literary picture'.[3] Zobel can also, as I have proposed in the opening chapters of this study, be aligned with metropolitan social realist authors such as Louis Guilloux. In a more recent continuation of this line of exploration, the Nigerian critic Zana Itiunbe Akpagu has suggested that *La Rue Cases-Nègres* owes a stylistic and thematic debt to Zola's *L'Assommoir*, tracing a number of parallels in the novels' themes, styles, and narrative arcs.[4]

Social realism does indeed shape Zobel's literature; yet *La Rue Cases-Nègres* marks a significant change. In his first three publications, the author had wielded the pen like a paintbrush or modelling clay. Indeed, he commented in interview that he would have liked to be a sculptor, but realised he had no means of accessing the necessary training in 1940s Martinique; his French state schooling, however, meant that he was already to some extent trained as a writer, and so he turned to literature. As a consequence, in his own words, 'je m'étais dit que ce que je voulais réaliser par la sculpture [...], je pourrais essayer de le faire avec des mots' (I told myself that what I had wanted to

2   Wylie, p. 62.
3   Wylie, p. 62.
4   Zana Itiunbe Akpagu, 'La Rencontre d'Émile Zola et de Joseph Zobel: un parallélisme thématique entre *L'Assommoir* et *La Rue Cases-Nègres*', *Neohelicon*, 27.2 (2000), pp. 287–308.

create with sculpture [...], I could try to do with words).[5] In his first publications, he transcribed quotidian Martinican scenes with careful attention to everyday passions and struggles, without neglecting to describe the enduring psychological and economic consequences arising from centuries of a transatlantic trade in human lives. The common denominator in his first novels and short stories is the fact that his leading protagonists are all united as members of the poorest group in society, the *petit-nègre* class. Because this is a situation shared by all, it actually receives little comment. *La Rue Cases-Nègres* is quite different. It is the first novel in which Zobel attempts to depict the conflict and discrimination at work within the black Martinican community itself that leads to groups – notably the *petit-nègre* group – being marginalised. His hero, José Hassam, is modelled on Zobel himself, and the novel charts the young boy's discovery that the combined factors of poverty and dark skin tone place him on the lowest rungs of the Martinican ethnoclass hierarchy. This leads him to realise that he is classed as a *petit-nègre* once he leaves the plantation space and comes into contact with the urban bourgeois world, a painful and pivotal experience which gives him a different perspective on modern Martinican life. *La Rue Cases-Nègres* represents the climax of Zobel's ambition to extend the scope of Négritude-inflected literature. In this audacious novel, Zobel develops Négritude's call for a reappreciation and re-evaluation of blackness and, in an original twist, he does so in order to turn a spotlight on the specific dynamics of the internal Martinican ethnoclass hierarchy. This in turn raises wider questions about global patterns of exploitation and uneven development.

La Rue Cases-Nègres is a strident defence of the *petit-nègre* class. In her magisterial close reading of the novel, Renée Larrier notes that the novel has 'three principal landscapes' and that in each of these, 'the structure of colonialism with its resulting discrimination and inequities is paramount [...] race, class, and color differences imposed by the colonial system determine and reflect an individual's economic condition'.[6] Part One, set in Petit-Morne (which literally means Small Hill), features just one journey beyond the confines of the plantation, when José and his grandmother M'man Tine walk to Petit-Bourg to attend church. There, they are too poor to contribute to the collection, prompting M'man Tine to reassure José that he must not be ashamed:

---

5 'Zobel: sa vie, son œuvre', p. 22.
6 Larrier, p. 36.

'tu n'as qu'à baisser la tête. Et surtout, n'aie pas peur' (p. 86) ('all you have to do is bow your head. And above all, don't be afraid') (p. 49).[7] Every inhabitant of the rue Cases-Nègres is a *petit-nègre*. It is also the only context in which José experiences a true sense of solidarity and community, qualities exemplified when the plantation workers unite to search for Médouze's body, and then to celebrate his funeral wake. In Part Two, José goes to school in Petit-Bourg (literally, Small Village) where he has his first experience of discrimination and racial prejudice. Moving from the countryside to the urban context of Fort-de-France, in Part Three, José's racial awakening becomes more complete as he is now immersed in bourgeois and so-called civilised, sophisticated society. Yet he cannot admire his teachers, who show him nothing but indifference, and he experiences pure revulsion at the sycophantic black Martinican servants who work in the capital's most prestigious avenue, route Didier, which is in every respect the antithesis of rue Cases-Nègres. These servants, he recognises, 'formaient une catégorie dévouée et cultivaient avec devotion la manière de server les *békés*' (p. 254) (formed a devoted category, developing ever more devoted ways of serving the *békés*) (p. 148; my modified translation). They have espoused white bourgeois French values and demonstrate no racial or class solidarity: moreover, they form an alienated group who have absolutely no concept of their own Négritude.

Why might this radical shift in narrative focus have occurred? Why did Zobel now choose to depict the discriminatory social structures of black Martinican society? The author's move to metropolitan France in December 1946 meant that the conditions in which he wrote *La Rue Cases-Nègres* afforded greater freedom to expose the Martinican ethnoclass hierarchy from afar. While he wrote the novel, he divided his time between central Paris, where he was a student and gave poetry recitals, and the refined town of Fontainebleau, where he worked as a teacher and established a home for his young family. Zobel commented that his awareness of these geographic and social distances greatly influenced him as he wrote the novel:

> Fontainebleau, c'est une ville extrêmement bourgeoise, et cela a intensifié tous les sentiments que pouvait susciter ce déracinement et je me suis mis à écrire *La Rue Cases-Nègres*.[8]

---

7 English translation from Keith Q. Warner's *Black Shack Alley* (Washington, DC: Three Continents Press, 1980).
8 'Zobel: sa vie, son œuvre', p. 28.

Fontainebleau is an extremely bourgeois town, and that intensified all the feelings caused by my move [literally: uprooting], and so I began to write *Black Shack Alley*.

Sensitive to these conflicting emotions, in the study *Caraïbales*, a pioneering work of Francophone Caribbean literary criticism, Jacques André identifies a paradoxical developmental arc at play in the novel's textual dynamics.[9] For André, Zobel's novel charts an obsessive drive towards progress, advancement, and forward movement, yet it simultaneously conveys to the reader a sense of longing for a 'remontée aux origines' (return to origins), leading André to describe it as an 'odyssée (le retour littérarie au pays natal)' (odyssey [the literary return to the native land]).[10] A return is only possible after a departure has taken place; without explicitly pushing his observation to its natural conclusion, André is receptive to the processes of distancing and migration that trigger the literary return to the native land which Zobel's novel actually represents.

Zobel's new status as an economic migrant coincided with the rapid social change of the post-war period across Europe. This is reflected in a visceral shift in narrative style when he embarks on *La Rue Cases-Nègres*: now Zobel's social realism, which had previously focused on characters rooted in Martinican society, evolves to reflect the paradoxes of his own lived experiences. From *La Rue Cases-Nègres* onwards, it is my contention that the author's social realism may be best understood with reference to Kristin Ross's definition of post-war realism as a 'mode [which] attempts to come to terms with, or to give an historical account of, the fatigue and exhilaration of moments when people find themselves living two lives at once'.[11] Ross is theorising the particular context of post-World War Two metropolitan France (her study considers the period up to the mid-1960s), and she charts France's transformation from an agrarian, insular, and empire-oriented nation, to a decolonised, industrialised country aspiring to Americanised consumer lifestyles. Drawing on literature and film, she discusses the rise of the ideology of the consuming couple, of whom one or both will be *cadres* (professionals), often occupying a nondescript and unclear 'professional' function in a burgeoning bureaucracy or in the nascent service

---

9 Jacques André, *Caraïbales* (Paris: Éditions caribéennes, 1981), pp. 55–56.
10 André, p. 100.
11 Kristin Ross, *Fast Cars, Clean Bodies* (Cambridge, MA: Massachusetts Institute of Technology, 1996), p. 13.

industries. Ross demonstrates that this group's increasing material prosperity is 'predicated on the conditions of generally and chronically uneven development'.[12] It is precisely these questions of development and inequality, at a global scale, which are implicitly posed by Zobel in *La Rue Cases-Nègres*. The novel is an uncompromising interrogation of the uneven patterns of development in the Antilles, and indeed the wider world. As Martin Munro has perceptively commented, not only do 'the opening descriptions of the plantation depict a world in which little has apparently changed since the time of slavery', but the plantation itself appears 'cut off spatially from the rest of Martinique'.[13] It is this disavowed space, which sits outside place and time, but is an undeniable aspect of modernity, which Zobel determines to represent in literature.[14]

Although it is most frequently understood as a testimony to Zobel's own individual experiences on his native island, *La Rue Cases-Nègres* must then also be understood as the work of a young migrant author who was himself 'living two lives at once', and who was facing, Janus-like, in two different directions. The quotation from Zobel's own diary which stands as the epigraph to this chapter demonstrates the author's awareness of this schism. When he comes to write *La Rue Cases-Nègres*, on the one hand, Zobel is staring back at his former life on his native island and, on the other, he is staring post-war modern metropolitan French society squarely in the face. Unsurprisingly, then, the idea of duality and 'doubles' is important to an understanding of the novel, and processes of 'doubling' are at play throughout. Photographs taken by Zobel himself to document his first years in metropolitan France illustrate some of these dualities. These images were recently discovered, developed, and published as *Joseph Zobel photographies* by his granddaughter, the photographer Charlotte Zobel. Zobel's photographs from his early years in France depict scenes such as Parisian streets, smartly attired white Frenchmen feeding swans on a lake, children climbing trees, and smiling school pupils in Fontainebleau. Several stylised self-portraits in

12 Ross, p. 148.
13 Munro, p. 149.
14 In the present era, the representation of the plantation space continues to be contentious. Larrier draws attention to the disturbing modern reappropriation and sanitisation of the space of the *rue cases-nègres* 'for Martinique's tourist-conscious economy', discussing the example of the Leyritz plantation, where tourists can stay in a restored plantation which includes a *rue cases-nègres* where the individual dwellings are referred to as 'bungalows', a name which, as Larrier observes, 'masks the former violent power structure'. See Larrier, p. 40.

the collection show Zobel in poses which self-consciously picture him alternately observing, thinking, or writing.

La Rue Cases-Nègres is more than a nostalgic recollection of childhood; it is an attempt to articulate the paradoxes and contradictions with which Zobel was grappling at a specific moment in his life. How could he make sense of a world in which his previous lived experiences in Martinique were the unacknowledged shadow of the French metropolitan prosperity which now lay within his reach – the kind of prosperity which, as Ross argues, can only arise through an ideology of 'uneven development' and 'exclusions'?[15] How might he reconcile the world of his grandmother, whose worldly possessions amounted to a shack, a pipe, and a bowl – the latter of which is acrimoniously broken in the opening pages of the novel – with the post-war turn to accumulation and consumerism (which, as *La Fête à Paris*, the sequel to *La Rue Cases-Nègres*, makes clear, was already gathering momentum in the immediate post-war period)? Ross convincingly argues that such parallel life trajectories constitute a defining feature of post-war modernity, and she demonstrates that the task of this era's double-visioned social realism was to render visible the aspects of modern life which risked being wilfully eclipsed and excluded from dominant discourses of 'progress' and 'modernity'. For Ross, after Raymond Williams, 'realism gives a shape to the experiences of those on the outer edges of modernisation's scope, the ones caught just outside or the ones who have been left behind, the ones for whom abundance is accompanied by a degradation in their conditions of life'.[16] The social realism of *La Rue Cases-Nègres* does just this; it is Zobel's attempt to provide a portal between two different worlds; between the world of dominant post-war French culture with its narrative of progress, prosperity, and modernity – which is also the aspirational cultural model for Martinican middle- and upper-class society – and the world of dominated Martinican culture, where endemic suffering and physical exhaustion is the price of these very same metropolitan narratives of progress.

15 Ross, p. 137.
16 Ross, p. 13.

First Publication of *La Rue Cases-Nègres*

La Rue Cases-Nègres was originally published in 1950 in Paris. This was another complete departure from Zobel's previous works, which had all first appeared with publishing houses based in Fort-de-France. Despite the success of the 1947 Parisian edition of *Diab'-là*, publishing *La Rue Cases-Nègres* in Paris was a challenge, and Zobel's manuscript was rejected several times, despite favourable opinions from influential contemporary critics such as Robert Kanters, Robert Sabatier, and Jean-Louis Bory.[17] The novel was eventually published by Éditions Jean Froissart, a publishing house launched by Charles Frémanger which provided a vehicle for friends such as Cécil Saint-Laurent, who used it to publish his Caroline Chérie (Darling Caroline) novels, a series of titillating historical bodice rippers focusing on what one online critic has euphemistically termed 'the horizontal progress' of a nubile young heroine in post-revolution Paris.[18] The novels were adapted into successful French films, the first of which appeared in 1951. Frémanger was displeased by the 1950 decision to publish *La Rue Cases-Nègres*, a text which deviated considerably from his vision for Jean Froissart. Presumably, his chief concern was that it risked alienating his established base of conservative white readers; it is difficult to imagine two more diametrically opposed works than *Caroline Chérie* and *La Rue Cases-Nègres*. After the initial print run of 35,000 was exhausted, no further reprints of *La Rue Cases-Nègres* were commissioned, effectively censoring the text in metropolitan France.[19] In Martinique, it was almost impossible to buy copies because the *békés* refused to stock *La Rue Cases-Nègres* in their bookshops, a decision which again all but amounted to censorship.[20] Possibly as a result of Froissart's hostility towards the novel, the first edition of *La Rue Cases-Nègres* was rapidly followed by a second edition in 1955 with the small publishing house Les Quatre jeudis.[21]

---

17 See Schaffer. I have amended the transcript, which reads 'Robert Granterce' and 'Jean-Louis Bories'; the original tape recording (now digitised) is clearly referring to Robert Kanters and Jean-Louis Bory.
18 See: https://www.kirkusreviews.com/book-reviews/cecil-saint-laurent/caroline-cherie/ (accessed 22 November 2016).
19 'Zobel: sa vie, son œuvre', p. 29.
20 James Ferguson, 'Uncomfortable Truth', *Caribbean Beat*, 82 (2006). See: http://caribbean-beat.com/issue-82/uncomfortable-truth#axzz30TcM5RiE (accessed 13 October 2015).
21 Joseph Zobel, *La Rue Cases-Nègres* (Paris: Les Quatre jeudis, 1955). Copy inspected on microfiche at the Bibliothèque nationale in Paris.

For reasons which remain unknown, the epigraph, dedications, and the *quatrième de couverture* (back-cover) text were all omitted from this second edition, and indeed from all subsequent editions, thereby lessening the visibility of the text's economic critique.[22] Suzanne Crosta has suggested that the scandal provoked by Frantz Fanon's attack on Mayotte Capécia, a scandal which resulted from the close association of author with protagonist, might have motivated the decision to remove the dedications and amplify the paratextual distance between author and protagonist in later editions of *La Rue Cases-Nègres*.[23] Nonetheless, it remains uncertain whether the decision to remove the original dedications was taken by Zobel or by his editors.

The Froissart edition of the novel enjoyed immediate success in metropolitan France. In July 1950, it won the 'Prix des lecteurs', a competition organised by the influential Parisian literary magazine *La Gazette des lettres*.[24] This prize was awarded through a democratic process whereby 1,000 *membres du prix des lecteurs* (members of the readers' prize committee) received copies of the shortlisted books and voted for their favourite. Zobel received a substantial prize of 400,000 francs.[25] It is wholly significant that *La Rue Cases-Nègres* gained prestige and visibility thanks to the support – and votes – of a significant sample of the reading public, a success which confirmed its appeal to the popular imagination. Decades later, the text's enduring public appeal was further borne out by the success of Euzhan Palcy's 1983 film adaptation.

As Zobel recalled in an interview, the editors who had rejected it had been concerned that a novel such as *La Rue Cases-Nègres* simply would not sell, as they considered that 'en 1950, il n'y avait pas en France une clientèle au point de vue commercial […] pour un tel ouvrage' (in 1950, there was no commercial market […] for such

---

22 Zobel's daughter Jenny, who has worked extensively on her father's life, was unable to shed any light on this. Unpublished private interview with Louise Hardwick at the Salon du Livre, Paris, 20 March 2016.

23 Suzanne Crosta, 'L'Enfance sous la rhétorique de l'édification culturelle: la poétique régénératrice chez Joseph Zobel', in *Récits d'enfance antillaise* (Sainte Foy, Quebec: GRECLA, 1998). See: http://www.lehman.cuny.edu/ile.en.ile/docs/crosta/zobel.html (accessed 14 October 2015).

24 'Chronique du Prix des lecteurs', *La Gazette des lettres*, 118, 8 July 1950, p. 1.

25 André Rétif, 'Review of *La Rue Cases-Nègres*', *Études*, 84.268, January 1951, p. 429.

a work).[26] The prestigious publishing house Albin Michel had been interested in the manuscript, which it submitted to René Maran for review. Maran, a staunch supporter of Zobel's earlier works, disliked *La Rue Cases-Nègres*, and felt that Zobel had failed to develop the talent and promise he had once shown. In a telephone conversation with their mutual friend, the Martinican novelist Raphaël Tardon, Maran had commented 'Zobel progresse à reculons' (Zobel is going backwards). During an interview decades later, Zobel repeated Maran's damning phrase, which suggests just how cruel a blow it must have been to his younger self.[27] The specific details of what Maran disliked about the text remain unknown. Compared to Zobel's experimental and self-assured literary debut novel, *Diab'-là*, however, there is no doubt that, from a stylistic point of view, *La Rue Cases-Nègres* lacks the brio and dynamism of his earlier writing. His radical decision to adopt the perspective of a child, and to write, for the first time, in the first person, lends the novel an exaggeratedly slow and earnest tone, in contrast to the deft changes in tempo and bawdy humour of his early novels and short stories.

Yet when *La Rue Cases-Nègres* is understood as a novel of rupture and dislocation, this stylistic shift becomes less puzzling. As a journalist, Zobel had honed his familiarity with a Martinican readership over a period of several years. In France, he had no such connection to his readers, who could not be relied upon to understand his native culture, hence the pronounced concern with clarity and cross-cultural communication in *La Rue Cases-Nègres*. This clarity ensures that the text continues to be a pedagogic staple to this day, attaining canonical status; no survey of Caribbean literature of the twentieth century is complete without a reference to *La Rue Cases-Nègres*. The work's central focus on the experiences of a young boy born into a colonial system, and its clear untangling of social, educational, and economic themes, also explains why it was adapted in 1983 with great success by Palcy into the internationally acclaimed film *Rue Cases-Nègres* (*Sugar Cane Alley*). To this day, *La Rue Cases-Nègres* – on page and on screen – represents Martinican culture on a global stage with a degree of success that no other Francophone Caribbean work has achieved. In 1950, attempting this act of cross-cultural communication, which would bring a challenging portrayal of the Caribbean to European readers,

26 'Zobel: sa vie, son œuvre', p. 29.
27 'Zobel: sa vie, son œuvre', p. 29.

was a significant ambition. In addition, Zobel knew that with this novel he would tackle the social injustices of the ethnoclass hierarchy with a pointedness he would not have dared use while still in Martinique. The combined factors of cross-cultural communication and socio-economic critique make the narrator of La Rue Cases-Nègres a very different, more circumspect, and less self-assured creation than the young male characters who had dominated Zobel's first novels.

Zobel's achievement in La Rue Cases-Nègres is substantial and has implications for the development of Caribbean literature more generally. With it he became the first black Francophone Caribbean author to undertake a semi-autobiographical account of his own childhood. In Packaging Post/coloniality, Richard Watts demonstrates how a number of 'cultural translations' are performed by the paratextual material to Césaire's Cahier d'un retour au pays natal; material which, depending on the edition consulted, tends to situate the prose poem at a crossroads of European, Caribbean, and Latin American cultures.[28] In contrast, the paratextual material to the original 1950 edition of La Rue Cases-Nègres is significant because the 'cultural translation' at work here has the sole purpose of attempting to render the text appealing to one group of readers: the metropolitan French public. The cover illustration of the original 1950 dust jacket capitalises on the novel's exotic appeal, showing José against the backdrop of the rue Cases-Nègres. The young lad depicted, however, has the features of a European boy whose skin is very olive, rather than a Caribbean child with African ancestry. José himself has been 'translated' into an image calculated to appeal to Europeans. The original 1950 illustrator (whose name cannot be traced) was likely to be inexperienced in drawing non-European characters. The main cover illustration, for all its drawbacks, does at least avoid the trap of straying into racist clichés of black figures. Yet a racist, gendered cliché adorns the book's spine, which of course is the only visible part of a book once it has been placed on a shelf. The spine illustration shows an attractive, amplebosomed black woman carrying a basket on her head, representing a stereotypical Creole washerwoman and *doudou*, the term used by elite white male discourse since colonial times to refer to a sexually desirable – and available – black Martinican woman. This image can be neither M'man Tine nor M'man Délia, and is a sexualised

---

28 Richard Watts, *Packaging Post/coloniality: The Manufacture of Literary Identity in the Francophone World* (Lanham, MD: Lexington, 2005), p. 101–15.

decorative addition more in line with exoticist French Caribbean writings by Lafcadio Hearn and Mayotte Capécia (whose own work was co-written with substantial input from white male ghost writers);[29] moreover, the image resonates with other Froissart publications, such as the sexualised *Caroline* series.

In complete contrast, the text on the *quatrième de couverture* resounds with sincerity and sobriety. It may have been written by Zobel himself, as is common editorial practice, although its direct references to 'Joseph Zobel' imply that a third party drafted it. This text foregrounds the novel's universal social realism and contains a direct appeal to metropolitan readers' compassion by underscoring the universality of the social struggle depicted in the novel. It immediately invites the reader to read this Martinican novel while keeping in mind a wider context of French poverty, both colonial and metropolitan. The novel, it claims, is testimony (*témoignage*) to all those living in:

> les rues Cases-Nègres de la Martinique, du Sénégal, de Madagascar; et même pour les rues Cases-Nègres, habitées par les blancs, de la banlieue parisienne, des mines du Nord ou des usines du Creusot.
>
> the Black Shack Alleys of Martinique, Senegal, Madagascar; and even in the Black Shack Alleys which are occupied by white people, in the Parisian outskirts, the mines of the north or le Creusot's factories.

This paratextual back-cover material indicates a doubling at work in the novel's marketing strategy. Visually, the images highlight *La Rue Cases-Nègres*'s exotic Caribbean otherness and include a glimpse of titillation in the generous forms of the washerwoman. Yet, paradoxically, the text of the *quatrième de couverture* is at pains to de-exoticise the text by underscoring the familiarity of its central theme: the struggle against oppression and poverty. It is quite possible that Zobel had no control over the images, which may have been commissioned by his editor, but that he did have some meaningful input into the lines on the back cover. These lines explicitly position the text as socially engaged writing, and strengthen comparisons between Zobel's novel and the social realism of other metropolitan French authors such as Guilloux.

The internal paratextual material in the 1950 publication is definitely supplied by Zobel himself, and is highly instructive as to how the author intended the book to be read. Regrettably, the removal of this material

---

29 Christiane Makward, *Mayotte Capécia ou l'aliénation selon Fanon* (Paris: Karthala, 1999), p. 158.

in all subsequent editions has rendered the original authorial intentions far less visible. The original edition of *La Rue Cases-Nègres* opens with dedications to Zobel's mother and grandmother, allocating them the same roles that they hold in the novel:

A MA MERE,
Domestique chez les Blancs.
A MA GRAND-MERE,
Travailleuse de plantation, et qui ne sait pas lire.

TO MY MOTHER,
A servant to the white folk.
TO MY GRANDMOTHER,
A plantation worker, who cannot read.

While suggesting an autobiographical proximity between the author and his child narrator, the original dedications also provide information which casts light on important differences between the life of José and that of Joseph Zobel himself. Most significantly, the original dedications to *La Rue Cases-Nègres* reveal that the text's tragic ending, in which José's academic success coincides with M'man Tine's death, is pure fiction. The dedication refers to the author's grandmother in the present tense and, indeed, Zobel's grandmother did live to witness his success at school and as a published author. This is clear evidence of the artistic licence at work in the novel. Most striking is the dedication's insistence on Zobel's grandmother's illiteracy, which stands as a poignant reminder of her vulnerability, exclusion, and subaltern status. It confronts the reader with the painful knowledge that this formidable woman will never be able to read the novel that she inspired.

The original paratext, then, provides alert readers with clues that what follows is not necessarily fact, and subtly suggests discrepancies between the lives of Joseph Zobel and José Hassam. These differences are particularly important where names are concerned. In the first part of the novel, set on the plantation, first names suffice for children, and even for José's grandmother M'man Tine, whose name bears no connection to a man, as her identity has never depended on any male. José's own surname, then, comes as a complete surprise when it is eventually stated at the beginning of Part Two on his first day at school, when his full name is revealed as José Hassam. The patronymic is an unsettling intrusion for the reader, who expects to find that the hero's name was José Zobel, or a close approximation thereof. The author's daughter Jenny Zobel suggests that the African or Arabic-sounding

'Hassam' may indicate Zobel's 'allegiance towards Africa as the land of his ancestors and a wish to associate himself with his African origins by selecting a surname which was not a slave master's name'.[30]

It does indeed appear that Zobel might have been aiming to forge a link with West Africa, and with Hausa culture in particular. The name Hassan is of Arabic origin, and is also a Hausa name for a twin boy; this borrowing of Arabic in Hausa reflects the fact that most Hausa speakers are Muslims. The meticulous composition of the documents in his personal archives reveals that Zobel constructed every aspect of his narratives with great care. From the archives, and his 1953 novel *La Fête à Paris* (republished as *Quand la neige aura fondu* in 1979), it is evident that in metropolitan France, Zobel took a strong interest in West African culture and had several acquaintances from the region (most famously Senghor, who was raised as a Christian, but whose mother was a Fula Muslim). This fascination with Africa and its cultural diversity would lead to Zobel's departure to live in Senegal in 1957, arranged by Senghor. It appears quite plausible that in Paris, the novelist became aware of the Hausa name and its nuance, and that this is why he chose to grant José the surname 'Hassam'; indeed, the spelling may well be a mistranscription of a term Zobel had only ever heard being spoken aloud. By implication, the name is a subtle confirmation of José as Zobel's literary twin. This adds a surprising new dimension to my arguments about the fundamental significance of the trope of doubling in the novel itself. What is certain is that the name Hassam, in a Martinican context, sounds quite unfamiliar, and even exotic; the official Martinican *état civil* database returns no search results for any citizens named Hassam or Hassan in post-abolition Martinique.[31] In contrast, Hassan is a name which is connected with areas such as Senegal and Chad. Read with an understanding of Hausa culture, the name bestows upon the character José Hassam a tangible connection with Africa, with which his creator was evidently preoccupied; the quest to affirm this very connection would compel the author to move to Senegal for almost 20 years.

Beyond any doubt, the name Hassam is intended to represent otherness and alterity; this might also be a reflection of Zobel's own relationship with his father, which was marked by rupture, lack, and the unknown.

---

30 Private email correspondence with Jenny Zobel, December 2011, cited in Hardwick, *Childhood, Autobiography and the Francophone Caribbean*, p. 40.
31 See: http://www.patrimoines-martinique.org/?id=chercher&formulaire=etat_civil (accessed 1 October 2016).

Raised only by female caregivers, José's connection to his father is in name only: and this name, when it is finally revealed as Hassam, is fittingly distant and strange. The author's father, Eugène Zobel, was a chauffeur, which corresponds with the brief details recounted by M'man Tine in *La Rue Cases-Nègres* about José's father, who is referred to only as 'Eugène' (p. 44). Other subtle changes reinforce the distance between author and narrator: Joseph Zobel's mother, Acélia Rocher, widely known as Man Célia, and grandmother, Marie, become Délia and M'man Tine in the narrative. In a further difference, *La Rue Cases-Nègres* makes no reference to José having any siblings, whereas Joseph Zobel spent part of his childhood being raised with Célia's other son, Zobel's younger half-brother, Michel Rocher.

The first edition of the novel also opens with an epigraph from the Epistle of Saint James (Saint Jacques in French) which unambiguously sets out the text's polemical intentions:

Voici, le salaire des ouvriers
qui ont moissonné vos champs,
et dont vous les avez frustrés, crie.

Behold, the hire of the labourers
who have reaped down your fields,
which is of you kept back by fraud, crieth.[32]

This quotation is taken from a section of the Epistle of Saint James entitled 'Warning to the Rich'; Zobel cites it as Chapter IV, when it is in fact located in Chapter V. The King James Bible rendering is most closely aligned with the complex syntax of Zobel's French quotation; the more fluid everyday English translation in the *Common English Bible* reads: 'Listen! Hear the cries of the wages of your field hands. These are the wages you stole from those who harvested your fields'.[33] The lines instruct the rich to weep and howl as miseries will befall them because they have fraudulently kept the wealth produced by the toil of the labourers. In short, they have grown rich by stealing the fruits of others' work; but the rich should now be fearful, as their fraud has been exposed. Judgement is nigh. Zobel's daring choice of epigraph, which takes aim at the wealthy in general and, in the context of his

---

32   King James Bible. A number of different translations of this complex phrase are compared at http://biblehub.com/kjv/james/5-4.htm (accessed 16 June 2016).

33   See: http://www.commonenglishbible.com/explore/passage-lookup/?query=james+5%2C4 (accessed 22 November 2016).

novel, appears to target Martinique's more affluent citizens – be they *békés* or middle class – reveals the full extent of his ambition for *La Rue Cases-Nègres*. The novel is both a denunciation of colonial and postcolonial exploitation and an act of vengeance for the downtrodden; 'ouvriers' (labourers) here resonates with several contexts: Marxist 'workers' and that colonially dispossessed group whom Fanon would later term 'les damnés de la terre' (the wretched of the earth). Buoyed by his physical distance from Martinique and relative material prosperity, Zobel dares to condemn outright the exploitation that he had witnessed – and experienced first-hand – in Martinique.

The removal of the original dedications and epigraph severely lessens the sociopolitical tenor of *La Rue Cases-Nègres* as they served as signposts to the multiple references to economic exploitation strewn throughout the novel. *La Rue Cases-Nègres* was intended to be nothing less than literary payback, an exposé of a centuries-old system of exploitation in which poorer individuals had severely limited prospects and suffered countless acts of physical and psychological violence in order to ensure the continued stable enrichment of a minority. José is, the novel emphasises, the only child to escape this cycle. All his friends from the rue Cases-Nègres, and others who grew up on similar plantations elsewhere in Martinique, are condemned to repeat their own parents' lives of servitude. In the early twenty-first century, the epigraph's damning condemnation of a system in which wealth is generated for the few, at the expense of the many, continues to have resonances in the contemporary context of renewed calls for Caribbean reparations,[34] and in the wider global context of growing inequality and exploitation.

These unmistakably polemical ambitions, and the novel's unambiguous critique of colonialism and oppression, may well explain why, after the 1955 edition, *La Rue Cases-Nègres* was not reprinted for 19 years. The novel became virtually impossible to find in both Martinique and metropolitan France. Moreover, Zobel himself was based in Senegal, where he had forged a new career as a radio presenter, and wrote occasional short stories. The author, and his most acclaimed novel,

---

34 In 2013, Caribbean heads of governments established the Caricom Reparations Commission with a mandate to prepare the case for reparatory justice for the region's indigenous and African-descendant communities. Since 2013, the case for reparations has been articulated with renewed frequency. See the report published by Institute of the Black World, 'CARICOM Reparations Ten Point Plan', at: http://ibw21.org/commentary/caricom-reparations-ten-point-plan/ (accessed 12 October 2015).

were slipping into obscurity. This only changed in 1974, when Présence Africaine obtained the rights to *La Rue Cases-Nègres*. The iconic publishing house, with joint offices in Paris and Dakar, where Zobel was working at the time, published their edition of the novel in 1974 to great success. This raised the novel's profile, and had implications in the Francophone and Anglophone spheres: the Trinidadian scholar Keith Q. Warner published his English translation *Black Shack Alley* in 1980, while the Martinican director Euzhan Palcy released her film adaptation in 1983. The Présence Africaine edition has been continuously in print (now bearing a still from Palcy's film as its cover), with new print runs commissioned to the present day.

La Rue Cases-Nègres is an archetypal *Bildungsroman*; more specifically, it is the work of a young man assessing his passage from one kind of life to another. How did he begin his life as an impoverished child in the cane fields, and come to be a published author in Paris? The text is written in the form of a semi-autobiographical novel, and can be further classified as a *récit d'enfance* or childhood memoir, terms which refer to that part of autobiography with a particular focus on childhood. As I have argued elsewhere, Caribbean authors turn to the genre of the childhood narrative in order to use childhood in both a politically and an aesthetically subversive manner to explore the representation of colonialism and slavery, and to offer new modes of resistance to this challenging historical legacy.[35] Zobel is a pioneer of the Caribbean childhood memoir genre, and *La Rue Cases-Nègres* helped to found a Francophone Caribbean tradition of *récits d'enfance* which rose to prominence at the turn of the millennium. The theme of childhood in this work is all the more appropriate given that *La Rue Cases-Nègres* is a literary début of sorts, as Zobel's first novel to be written and published in France, while also paradoxically being his fourth published book. The original 1950 edition represents a process of artistic rebirth and renewal for the author in metropolitan France, while its 1974 Présence Africaine counterpart 'relaunched' Zobel once again, and stands as a lasting indicator of the significance of his time living and working in Africa.

---

35 See Hardwick, *Childhood, Autobiography and the Francophone Caribbean*.

A Novel of Dualities

La Rue Cases-Nègres exemplifies Ross's argument that post-war social realism is a narrative mode which explores the conflicting emotions of 'fatigue and exhilaration' which result from the collision of two world views. The very opening of the novel is an indication that the reader must be alert to the dualities at play throughout, beginning as it does with two versions of how the day in the rue Cases-Nègres might end when M'man Tine comes home after labouring in the cane fields. The first account, or the 'positive' account, is typical of what happens on those days when José has been well behaved. He recalls how his grandmother would shower him with kind words and share with him the food she had taken to the fields, in a demonstration of her boundless self-sacrifice where her grandson is concerned: 'M'man Tine disait qu'elle ne pouvait porter quoi que ce soit à sa bouche qu'elle ne m'eût réservé une part' (pp. 9–10) (M'man Tine would say that she could not put anything whatsoever to her lips without keeping some of it for me) (p. 5; my modified translation). The strength of the bond between grandmother and grandson is established from the outset; but the device of the dual opening also allows a more nuanced psychological portrait of the old lady to emerge. This tranquil and bucolic version of life in the rue Cases-Nègres is quickly qualified by the narrator as a rare occurrence: 'Mais, le plus souvent, la journée se terminait mal' (p. 17) (But, on most occasions, the day ended badly) (p. 9). This alternative, more frequently occurring version emphasises M'man Tine's physical exhaustion and her exasperation with her infant grandchild should he have misbehaved. On such days, she does not spare José any detail of her difficult life: 'comme si j'en avais pas assez de mes coups de soleil, des averses, des coups de tonnerre, et de la houe avec laquelle il me faut gratter la terre coriace du béké' (p. 44) (as if I didn't already have enough problems, what with my sun strokes, the rain, the rolls of thunder, and scratching away with that hoe at the *béké*'s hard earth) (p. 25; my modified translation). José learns from his earliest days that just as M'man Tine is responsible for him, he too has a responsibility towards his exhausted yet formidable grandmother.

This dual opening subtly lays out Zobel's objectives: *La Rue Cases-Nègres* documents José Hassam's gradual awakening to the dualities, parallels, and double standards which structure his society. Born a *petit-nègre*, an ethnoclass grouping which occupies the lowest rungs of the social hierarchy, and which is defined as that group which is both very poor and very dark-skinned, José comes to understand that all the people around him have, through no more than an accident of birth, led lives which are the darker shadow of modern prosperity. Their toil, like the toil of the slave ancestors to which their way of life remains unmistakably similar, is the foundation for the accumulated riches of others. They are the *'ouvriers / qui ont moissonné vos champs'* (labourers/ who have reaped down your fields) of the novel's original epigraph; it is they who have been cheated of the fruits of their labour. José remains unequivocal in his admiration, respect, and love for the group of poverty-stricken *nègres* into which he is born. As he is propelled into different social situations, he seeks out people who remind him of those he grew up with, and retains a deep respect for manual labourers in both urban and rural contexts. Social success does not lead him to despise or deny his origins. Rather, from the beginning to the end of the novel, José continues to admire the humanity, community, and spontaneity which he experienced during his childhood on the plantation. The loss of direct contact with this part of society is the source of the melancholy which pervades the narrative.

As the original epigraph from the Epistle of Saint James makes clear, *La Rue Cases-Nègres* sets out to denounce economic exploitation in the French Caribbean. Accordingly, the novel offers a subtle economic critique of the Antillean ethnoclass hierarchy. Zobel's preoccupation with the construction of the ethnoclass hierarchy, and conversely with the 'mechanics of liberation' required to overturn this system, is analysed in the first critical article on Zobel published in English, by the Caribbean critic Randolph Hezekiah. Hezekiah draws attention to the emphasis on economic emancipation in *La Rue Cases-Nègres* and in *Diab'-là*, novels which exhort black Martinicans to take control of their own economic destiny. This is so that they might finally put an end to living in circumstances which had evolved very little since 1848, and which ensured the predomination of the white 'plantocratic' *béké* ethnoclass. However, in *La Rue Cases-Nègres*, it quickly becomes equally apparent that the situation is far more complex than a simple black-white dichotomy. Now, it is the black bourgeoisie – a group largely absent from Zobel's previous publications – who are shown to hold an antagonistic, racist attitude towards those black compatriots who belong to the *petit-nègre* class.

The novel achieves this denunciation by first establishing the limited parameters of the *petit-nègre* class's world and, in particular, the economic dependency in which this group is kept. On the plantation, payday is a mournful affair as each worker receives a pittance (p. 62), and these pitiful wages are spent in the shop run by the overseer's wife – significantly, the overseer is described as a mulatto, a status which confers a certain superiority in the ethnoclass hierarchy and is associated with wealth (pp. 19–20). After the children cause a fire on the plantation, M'man Tine draws José's attention to a decision which introduces yet another structure of exploitation. The fire serves as a pretext for the overseer to ban children from being left unsupervised while their parents are at work. As a result of this decision, the plantation workers are left with little choice but to send their children to work in the cane fields. M'man Tine is convinced that this same mulatto overseer has seized the opportunity to 'voir grossir les petites-bandes' (p. 79) ('swell the ranks of the *petites-bandes*') (p. 45), thereby increasing the number of children who are available to join the *petites-bandes*, the groups of young children who undertake simple manual work on the plantations. José cannot understand why M'man Tine flies into a rage when he makes what he considers to be the helpful suggestion that he, too, could work in the *petites-bandes*. To his young child self, any income appears an incredible bounty, and he is envious of his friends who suddenly appear more grown-up because they undertake paid work. This provokes one of M'man Tine's most memorable outbursts in the entire novel:

> Et de parler, ronchonner, bougonner! Je l'entendis mépriser les parents de mes camarades qui avaient envoyé leurs enfants dans les petites-bandes, les traitant de nègres sans orgueil et qui ne savaient pas s'attacher les reins solidement.
> — Hein! comment cela pourrait-il finir si les pères y foutent les fils là-dedans, dans le même malheur? Eh bé! si j'y ai pas mis ta mère, c'est pas toi que j'y mettrai. (p. 79)
>
> How she talked and fretted and grumbled! I heard her berating my friends' parents for sending their children to the *petites-bandes*, calling them shameless Negroes with no courage or backbone:
> 'Tell me, how will it all end if the fathers stick their sons into the *petites-bandes*, into the same misery? Well I didn't send them your mother, and I've no intention of sending you!' (p. 45; my modified translation)

The old lady makes no attempt to conceal her utter contempt for the neighbours who have sent their children to the *petites-bandes*. On a stylistic level, this passage is a fine example of Zobel's predilection for the historic infinitive, where infinitives are used to indicate completed actions. M'man Tine knows that entering the *petites-bandes* is not an opportunity, but a condemnation which will trap José in a cycle of poverty on the plantation. These children will now all be deprived of an education, and condemned to a future of punishing manual labour from which there is no escape.

José's socio-economic education thus begins in his earliest infancy. He is made aware of the violence and domination of his immediate environment before he is able to fully grasp the significance of his grandmother's recriminations. M'man Tine's speech is also an example of the hybrid language which Zobel forges: his *petit-nègre* plantation characters would have spoken Creole, and the author undertakes to transcribe their speech in a style which signals their linguistic otherness, while ensuring that their words remain accessible to readers accustomed to metropolitan French. The linguistics researcher André Thibault has established an insightful philological glossary of 'les régionalismes' (regional terms) used in the novel, which indicates the depth and breadth of Zobel's linguistic innovation.[36]

Through her inimitable utterances, M'man Tine makes José aware of the cycles of economic exploitation into which he has been born, and from which she is determined that he will escape. The strict financial education she imparts to José is discreetly laced through the narrative. She is shown walking all the way to Petit-Bourg to do her shopping to avoid the debt-inducing prices at the plantation shop (p. 105), and she forbids José to join his friends in asking adults for money for rides when the fair comes to town (p. 191). Thus emerges the portrait of a woman determined to live a life which is as autonomous as possible; M'man Tine embodies the old traditional virtues of godliness, cleanliness, and an aversion to debt. The education which she provides by example can be distilled into a set of moral and economic principles by which to lead a simple life, which focuses on securing the basics: shelter and food, all the while establishing, within a matriarchal framework, the importance of family and communal ties and, ultimately, love. Although her firm values and self-sacrifice will propel her grandson into new social and cultural spheres, her ethos of valuing simplicity is discernible throughout José's trajectory.

José also learns about sexual exploitation from his grandmother, although once again the full implications of her tales go beyond his

---

[36] André Thibault, 'Les Régionalismes dans *La Rue Cases-Nègres* (1950) de Joseph Zobel', in *Richesses du français et géographie linguistique*, ed. by André Thibault (Brussels: De Boeck-Duculot, 2008), pp. 227–314.

infant comprehension. M'man Tine's own experiences of plantation life provide clear echoes of the slave past through their insights into the sexual vulnerability of women. Children are often fascinated by stories of how their parents or grandparents met, but *La Rue Cases-Nègres* provides a brutal Caribbean counterpart to any romantic western narratives of courtship, as M'man Tine recounts her 'meeting' with the man who was José's maternal grandfather in the following terms:

> j'étais toujours baissée du matin au soir dans un sillon, ma tête plus bas que mon derrière, jusqu'à ce que le Commandeur, M. Valbrun, ayant vu comment j'étais faite, m'a tenue, m'a roulée à terre et m'a enfoncé une enfant dans le ventre. (p. 43)

> From morning till evening I worked bent over in a furrow, my behind higher than my head, until the Commander, Mr Valbrun, liking the look of me, grabbed me, rolled me over on the ground and drove a child into my belly. (p. 24; my translation)

M'man Tine thus reveals that she was raped at a young age while at work on a plantation. The matter-of-fact tone with which she relates her rape demonstrates how normalised such violent sexual assaults against women were. M'man Tine also reveals that she is the granddaughter of a *béké*, and this suggests that her own grandmother was likely to have been a slave who was raped by a white man. M'man Tine's own sexual assault, then, is an example of history repeating itself. This exemplifies the cyclic patterns and atemporality of the rue Cases-Nègres. The plantation is a closed, isolated space where life is a cycle of repetition defined by André, following the problematic but influential definitions of the pioneering structural anthropologist Claude Lévi-Strauss, as a 'société froide' (cold society): a community which has as its basis 'un système d'oppositions réglées' (a system of regulated oppositions) which André gives as hot/cold, old/young, life/death, crik/crak, and which ensure the repetition of the same patterns of life from generation to generation.[37] André helpfully draws attention to the closed, cyclical time and space of the plantation in the novel, although a more nuanced reading also reveals Zobel's attention to the socioeconomic factors and hierarchies of race and gender which have created such cycles.

M'man Tine offers José a broader perspective of history, and of socio-economic and gender exploitation.[38] She has decided that her

---

37 André, pp. 58–59.
38 For a reading of M'man Tine in the novel, see Eileen Julien, 'La Métamorphose

life's remaining task is to raise her grandson, which explains why she is more preoccupied with child-rearing and material struggles of an immediate nature in the present or near future than with wider existential questions. It falls to José's male role model to tell the more abstract stories which will introduce him to such existential questions, performing an initiation into the history of the Middle Passage, slavery, and abolition. The character who acts as a conduit for these stories is almost always referred to by the respectful form of M. Médouze (M. is the abbreviation for Monsieur, meaning Mister), demonstrating the esteem in which the young child holds the old man. From Médouze's first appearance, he is reminiscent of the *griot*, a captivating African oral storyteller. His character demonstrates the continuation of the African *griot* tradition and its metamorphosis into the Caribbean tradition of the *conteur* (storyteller); the principal difference being that the Caribbean *conteur* transmits the memory of slavery and performs a cathartic role for those held in a condition of domination and subjection on the plantations.[39] Médouze's surreal, fantastical stories initiate José into a more philosophical manner of considering his life, and alter the boy's perception of the plantation around him. In all his tales, Médouze articulates his longing for 'la Guinée' (West Africa), but his stories are decidedly Caribbean and Creole. As such, he personifies the Caribbean Négritude which Zobel espoused, and which he sought to develop from a working-class, *petit-nègre* perspective: a life lived in the full knowledge of the slave heritage, and a celebration of Creole black plantation culture. Médouze is the essence of how, for Zobel, Négritude could operate in the Caribbean: it offered an alternative set of values which have the power to transform an exhausted, exploited plantation pauper into a venerated, inspirational hero and teacher. The old man's riddles convey lessons about specifically Caribbean forms of subjugation and domination, as José learns 'comment une carafe en terre cuite qu'on tient par le goulot devient un domestique qui ne

---

du réel dans *La Rue Cases-Nègres*,' *French Review*, 60.6 (1987), pp. 781–87. While this article presents an excellent discussion of the education imparted by M'man Tine, it does not pay close attention to the astute financial critique she offers; in this, my own study builds on and goes beyond the work of Julien.

39 Again, this demonstrates that Zobel was ahead of his time; since the 1980s, the French Caribbean *conteur* has been accorded increasing literary prominence, particularly through the Créolité movement and in the fiction of Patrick Chamoiseau: his *Solibo magnifique* (1988) focuses on the life and death of the eponymous *conteur*, Solibo.

sert de l'eau à son maître que lorsque ce dernier l'étrangle' (pp. 53–54) ('How an earthenware water-bottle held by the neck became a servant who only served water to his master when the latter choked him') (p. 30). An inanimate everyday item comes to illustrate unwilling servitude – with a reminder that it is only functioning thus under physical duress.

Médouze provides the only direct discussion of slavery in *La Rue Cases-Nègres* when he relates his own father's lived experience of transatlantic transportation from Africa, and abolition. The account of his father's life emphasises that in 1848, once the euphoria of liberation had passed, the freed slaves discovered that the promised freedom was nothing but hollow words, for they had no choice but to return to the plantations (p. 57). This message encapsulates the main theme of *La Rue Cases-Nègres*; it provides, from the perspective of oppressed peoples, a socioeconomic history which differs from the official colonial narratives, and which is essential to understanding the lives of the poorest of the poor, the *petits-nègres*, from a position of empathy and compassion. In the passages featuring Médouze, the novel becomes an existential fable which proposes new ways to comprehend the dynamics of liberty and enslavement. Whenever José rushes to see Médouze, he knows that their abstract, interactive discussions will fuel his curiosity about the world:

> Notre conversation consistait en un long interrogatoire que je lui présentais, et auquel il répondait scrupuleusement. [...] J'avais aussi à cœur de savoir où les békés prenaient tout l'argent qu'on disait qu'ils possédaient. M. Médouze m'expliquait alors que c'était le diable qui le leur apportait. Or, je savais déjà par intuition que le diable, la misère et la mort étaient à peu près le même individu malfaisant, et qui s'acharnait après les nègres surtout. Et je me demandais en vain ce que les nègres avaient pu faire au diable et au béké pour être ainsi opprimés par l'un et l'autre. (p. 65)

> Our conversations consisted of a long series of questions which I put to him, and to which he replied scrupulously. [...] I was also very interested in finding out where the *békés* got all the money people said they had. Mister Médouze explained that it was the devil that had brought it to them. Now, I already knew by intuition that the devil, misery, and death were more or less the same evil individual, who persecuted Negroes relentlessly. And I wondered, quite perplexed, what on earth Negroes could have done to the devil and to the *békés* to be so oppressed by both. (p. 37; my modified translation)

As Larrier comments, 'Médouze's method contrasts with the rote learning, the memorization and recitation of names of rivers and kings that characterize the French school José will encounter'.[40] The child begins to understand the *békés*' involvement in maintaining the conditions of hardship which he has begun to detect on the plantation. Through Médouze, he comes to equate the *békés* with a devilish Faustian pact, in which incredible financial profit is obtained at the expense of black workers' lives: again, the epigraph from Saint James acts as a key to the reader to unlock the colonial man-made dualities which have created José's world.

Zobel states in the 1998 documentary *Joseph Zobel: d'amour et de silence* that Médouze was a real character from his childhood, and even locates the area where his shack once stood.[41] Médouze is also an archetype recognisable across the Caribbean. In 1943, the Guadeloupean poet Guy Tirolien, a writer who is also associated with the fringes of the Négritude movement, published 'Prière d'un petit enfant nègre' ('Prayer of a Little Negro Child'), which was later republished in his collection *Balles d'or (Golden Bullets)*.[42] Several parallels exist between Zobel's novel and Tirolien's poem: Tirolien's young narrator is explicitly named as a *petit-nègre*, thereby creating a strong parallel with José, and he is also described as a child who longs to listen to 'La voix cassée d'un vieux qui raconte en fumant / Les histoires de Zamba et compère Lapin' (The broken voice of an old man who smokes while telling / Stories of Zamba and Brer Rabbit [my translation]). There is a striking similarity between the presentation of the old man in Tirolien's poem and Zobel's depiction of Médouze, suggesting that both authors are seeking to depict an essential character of Caribbean plantation society. These figures are the repositories of memory on the plantation, and it is they who impart traditional folktales. The Francophone figure Compère Lapin, known in the Anglophone world as Brer Rabbit, is a trickster character whose origins lie in West African folklore.[43] He is

---

40 Larrier, p. 48.
41 See Kezadri and Codol.
42 Guy Tirolien, *Balles d'or* (Paris: Présence Africaine, 1961). A new edition has been published as *Golden Bullets/Balles d'or: a dual-language edition*, trans. by Micheline Rice-Maximin, Richard Sale, and Arthur Gionet (Paris: Les Éditions du ManGuier, 2014).
43 For further analysis of this 'Trickster' figure, see Ina Césaire, 'L'Idéologie de la débrouillardise dans les contes antillais: analyse de deux personnages-clé du conte de veillée aux Antilles de colonisation française', *Espace Créole: revue du*

the hero of pan-Caribbean legends which span plantation societies from the southern United States to the Caribbean, in which oppressed and disadvantaged characters manage to outwit those who are more powerful than themselves. Médouze's teachings might take place in his shack in the rue Cases-Nègres, but their scope is unlimited and they provide a diasporic education which helps José to begin to address the traumatic existential conundrum of why he and his friends and family are the descendants of Africans enclosed on a plantation on a small Caribbean island and kept in such abject poverty.

A pair of surrogate parents, M. Médouze and M'man Tine educate José about the world around him, and he learns from them that a remote group called the *békés* wield great power over his own *petit-nègre* group. Although no *béké* is ever seen on the plantation, their shadow looms large in M'man Tine's warnings and Médouze's stories. José is left to educate himself, however, about the rest of the ethnoclass hierarchy, which comprises intersecting matrices of social class and race, a phenomenon also sometimes referred to as the 'pigmentocracy' or 'colourism', or even as a 'caste' system. This education happens gradually, in a number of instances when José suddenly, instinctively senses that he is being treated in an inferior manner for a reason which he cannot grasp. Part One, set entirely on the plantation in Petit-Morne, is free of any such moments: here, José is surrounded by plantation labourers whose lives directly correlate with his own experiences. It is in Part Two, when he ventures out of the plantation to go to school in Petit-Bourg, that he first experiences racism. These incidents are never directly labelled by the narrator as racist. Rather, he presents the events with sufficient detail to guide the reader to an understanding of why he is being treated in an inferior manner: for no other reason than his dark skin and poor plantation origins.

In Petit-Bourg, the would-be benefactor Mme Léonce patronises and demeans José for no apparent reason. At Mme Léonce's house, where M'man Tine has arranged for him to eat lunch, the young boy is left to have lunch alone in a corridor, and twice equates his treatment to that of a dog. It is only when Mme Léonce decides that rather than ignoring him, she will exploit him, that her own racist and classist attitudes become fully apparent. As she asks him to do her a favour which he has no power to refuse, she patronises him with feigned affection using the loaded

---

GEREC (Groupe d'Études et de Recherches en Espace Créolophone), 1978, 41–48. See: http://www.potomitan.info/atelier/contes/ina1.php (accessed 23 March 2017).

words 'mon petit-nègre' (p. 118). In a telling decision, Warner leaves the term untranslated in *Black Shack Alley* (p. 68). Yet, in doing so, his translation fails to convey the explicitly racist pejorative nuances of the term and its direct link to slavery; 'nègre' here carries the nuances of the English terms 'Negro' and 'Nigger' (as discussed at length in Chapter Two of this study). One favour becomes another, until José is repeatedly late for afternoon classes because Mme Léonce is exploiting him without an afterthought. In her eyes, José is inferior. As a black woman, she experiences no guilt in satisfying her own desire for power by taking advantage of him, and handicapping his education in the process. Nor does she see any problem with using the term *mon petit-nègre*; she has accepted and internalised its use as a marker of racialised power which confers superiority upon the person uttering it, an indication of her own assimilation into the white colonial dominant hegemony. In other words, French colonialism has conditioned her to stereotype José, her fellow black Martinican and a young and vulnerable child, in this pejorative manner. This incident demonstrates the full extent of the psychological damage wrought on the Martinican population of African descent by slavery and colonialism. Mme Léonce follows her desire to wield a noxious power over those who are less fortunate than herself, and in so doing she furthers a perverse cycle of racialised domination which itself is the direct legacy of slavery.

Another inhabitant of Petit-Bourg, José's unfortunate, mistreated mulatto friend Georges Roc, better known as Jojo, is also surrounded by women whose behaviour is deeply racist. One of Jojo's carers, the abhorrent Mam'zelle Mélie, is another character who does not hesitate to brand José as 'ce petit-nègre'. Here, the narrator parenthetically objects to Mam'zelle Mélie's use of this term as particularly vexatious because: '[Mam'zelle Mélie, dis-je, est, telle que je la vois, noire comme moi, sinon comme un merle]' (pp. 175–76); ([To my eyes, I tell you, Mam'zelle Mélie seems just as black as me, even as black as the feathers of a grackle]) (p. 102; my modified translation). The 'merle' in question is the *quiscalus lugubris*, known in English as the Carib grackle, a tropical New World blackbird. This sentence is the sole use of square brackets in the novel, which draws further attention to this telling comment about race. The reasons for this anomalous punctuation (which also exists in the first 1950 edition) are unknown, but it is quite possible that the square brackets were inserted because a metropolitan editor noticed the passage's stark racial commentary and either suggested its removal or was seeking clarification of the dynamics and meaning of the passage itself. Such moments of racial tension are subtly interwoven into the narrative and prove quite decisive for José's development: as he begins to navigate the urban world, the boy becomes aware that Martinican society is not just plagued by binary, black-white antagonism, but also by deep ethnoclass divisions, as he encounters the discriminatory ethnoclass hierarchy at work. The text's deceptively naive narrative style, and its focus on the themes of education, friendship, and filial gratitude, do not diminish Zobel's acerbic critique of racial discrimination within the black community in Martinique, a critique to which he returns with renewed vigour in 1953 in the novel's sequel, *La Fête à Paris*.

The astute economic critique running through *La Rue Cases-Nègres* shows how money and race become interlinked in the ethnoclass hierarchies of colonial societies. Zobel demonstrates that money moves in cycles which – unfailingly – are geared to the advantage of those who are already wealthy, so that they might maintain and increase their fortunes. For example, housing is monopolised by the *békés*, who are revealed as the owners of Cour Fusil in Petit-Bourg (pp. 137–38) and Petit-Fond in Fort-de-France; a monetary function is even suggested by the name 'Petit-Fond', which calls to mind the French noun *fonds*, which means 'fund'. This black settlement is described as having been created by down-on-their-luck white landowners in order to generate income (pp. 252–53). Just as in the rue Cases-Nègres, where the labourers are constantly in debt to the plantation shop, in Petit-Bourg, wage money still moves in cycles. It is paid out to the *petits-nègres* for their manual labour, but instantly returns to the pockets of the *béké* classes through rent payments. As José's social ascent gains momentum and he passes the Certificat d'études (primary school leavers' qualification), and then – more importantly – the Concours des Bourses (scholarship competition) which entitles him to essential financial support, his awareness of the economic and political struggles ahead of him becomes more acute. The partial scholarship he has received from the colonial authorities to attend the *lycée* will only cover one-quarter of the fees. At this point, his mother Délia erupts into the novel with her own analysis of the situation, denouncing this partial scholarship as a deliberate form of racist and classist exclusion:

> *Ils* sont trop méchants! C'est parce que nous sommes des petits nègres, pauvres et seuls, qu'*ils* t'ont pas donné une bourse entière. *Ils* savent bien que je suis une malheureuse femme et que je ne pourrais pas te payer le lycée. *Ils* savent très bien que te donner un quart de bourse d'études, c'est rien te donner du tout. Mais *ils* savent pas quelle femme de combat je suis.

Eh bé! j'abandonnerai pas ce quart de bourse. Tu iras dans *leur* lycée! (p. 216; original emphasis)

They are too wicked! It's because we're black, poor, and alone in the world that *they* didn't give you a full scholarship. *They* know full well that I'm a poor unfortunate woman and that I won't be able to pay for you to go to the *lycée*. *They* know only too well that giving you a quarter scholarship is the same as not giving you anything at all. But *they* don't know what a warrior woman I am. Well! I'm not giving up this quarter scholarship. You will go to *their lycée*! (p. 125; emphasis original, my modified translation).

José's mother interprets the quarter scholarship as evidence of the animosity in black society between poor plantation workers – *petits-nègres* – and the bourgeoisie. Délia's speech, with its anaphoric oppositional patterns of 'them' and 'us', denounces the efforts of the black bourgeoisie to maintain the ethnoclass hierarchy, and she exposes the additional barriers against which the *petit-nègre* class must fight. Yet the partial scholarship is in itself miraculous, as mother and son are told that scholarships are usually 'une affaire de piston' (p. 215) ('a question of who you knew') (p. 125; my modified translation), another indictment of the unjust and biased administration of the colonial education system on the island. Délia's outburst marks her first appearance in *La Rue Cases-Nègres*, and in her anger and resourcefulness she resembles her own mother, M'man Tine. She is the second female character in José Hassam's life who will fight with incredible tenacity to help her *petit-nègre* son to far exceed society's low expectations of him.

It is through the theme of education, then, that the racial and class discrimination which Zobel exposes in the novel is brought into sharp focus. *La Rue Cases-Nègres* has all too often generated sweeping, reductive critical responses, which read the text as a monument to state education and as an elegiac celebration of the power of sacrifice and academic success to enable a determined individual to triumph over poverty. Yet such readings grossly underplay the novel's sophisticated critical stance towards the education system, and its denunciation of the rigid colonial and racial socio-economic structures which this system upholds and perpetuates. José suffers horribly in order to achieve an education. His origins as a *petit-nègre* mean that with each educational achievement, he becomes increasingly emotionally isolated. His progress from Petit-Morne to Petit-Bourg to Petit-Fond does not necessarily indicate an improvement in his socioeconomic status because, as Mary Gallagher has observed, 'the prefix "petit" characterises each one of these locations as lowly or inferior, its fateful recurrence denying hopes of social advancement and working against any notion of deep metamorphosis'.[44] José's overwhelming isolation on his arrival at the Lycée Schœlcher in Fort-de-France culminates in a painful outpouring, which again underscores the hierarchies and dualities at play in Martinican society:

> Personne ne me ressemble. Personne n'a d'ailleurs jamais fait attention à moi. [...] Certainement, s'il y en avait un qui fût né à une rue Cases-Nègres, un dont les parents maniaient la bêche ou le coutelas, je l'eusse reconnu et approché. Mais je suis le seul de mon espèce. (p. 221)

> There was no one like me. Furthermore, nobody paid me the slightest bit of attention. [...] If there had been another child who was born in a Black Shack Alley, another child whose parents wielded a spade or a cutlass, I'd have certainly recognised him and approached him. But I was the only one of my kind. (p. 128; my modified translation)

Zobel's *récit d'enfance* is not merely the tale of the dutiful *élève appliqué* (studious pupil) who, according to Roger Toumson, 'travaille d'arrache-pied, dans le pieux dessin d'occuper, au terme de ses études, une situation professionnelle qui lui permettra d'arracher M'man Tine ainsi que sa mère de la misère' (works as hard as he can, in the pious hope of obtaining a professional job at the end of his studies so that he can rescue M'man Tine and his mother from their life of misery).[45] This generalisation neglects to consider José's disillusionment with the Eurocentric syllabus and his increasing feelings of isolation at school, which result in him playing truant and even failing part of the *baccalauréat* (p. 285). For all his progress in the school system, each success cannot but remind him of his otherness and the distance which separates him from his peers.

José belongs to a generation of Antilleans who were among the first to have access to education, and with it the opportunity of social advancement to the bourgeoisie through a complicated system of examinations and scholarships. Symbolic of this struggle is the historic Lycée Schœlcher in Fort-de-France. The prohibitive cost of

---

44 Mary Gallagher, *Soundings in French Caribbean Literature since 1950: The Shock of Space and Time* (Oxford: Oxford University Press, 2002), p. 184.
45 Roger Toumson, *La Transgression des couleurs: littérature et langage des Antilles, XVIIIe, XIXe et XXe siècles*, vol. 2 (Paris: Éditions caribéennes, 1989), p. 326.

sending a child to the Lycée Schœlcher meant that it remained out of reach for the majority of poor families in rural areas, where most children would not continue their education to secondary level. A study published in the 1960s reported that even though only one-quarter of Martinique's school-aged children lived in Fort-de-France, they made up the overwhelming majority (two-thirds) of the island's secondary school pupils.[46] Such a disparity is borne out in *La Rue Cases-Nègres*. Zobel describes José's acute awareness of being the only child from his social background at secondary school in meticulous detail, thereby drawing attention to the dislocations, compromises, and isolation which accompany his academic progress.

In Part Three of the novel, José's social isolation becomes increasingly apparent. He realises that his world is very different to that of his better-off peers, whose French names – 'Serge' and 'Christian' – indicate their bourgeois origins. He is a fish out of water, sensing implicitly that while the black bourgeois pupils can enjoy calling the teachers nicknames behind their backs, he must not join in himself, because his lowly social position as a *petit-nègre* does not afford him the right to flippancy. He has internalised his inferiority, and is aware of the precariousness of his position at the bottom of the social hierarchy. The teachers are portrayed as uncompassionate and also exhibit a racial bias, as demonstrated in the infamous episode with the French teacher, M. Jean-Henri: a significant moment framed as a *mise en abyme*, in which José is shown writing a story about his life within his own narrative, as well as having to deal with the consequences of his innovative and unique literary style. The episode with M. Jean-Henri raises urgent questions about who has the right to write, and offers an important clue as to the sheer audacity of Zobel's own ambition to write Négritude-inspired literature about the experiences of humble *petits-nègres*.

In this brief but formative section of the novel, for homework, José is given the task of writing about 'votre plus émouvant souvenir d'enfance' (pp. 269–70) ('your most moving childhood memory') (p. 156). M. Jean-Henri refuses to believe that the boy's poignant account of Médouze's death can possibly be his own work. The teacher's sheer disbelief stems from his own racial and class prejudice: he is unwilling to contemplate that a *petit-nègre* such as José could produce work of such literary quality. At the very moment when José has found a

---

46 Christian Beringuier, *L'Espace régional martiniquais*, CERAG 3 (Fort-de-France: Centre d'Études Régionales Antilles Guyane, 1969 [1966]), pp. 11–12.

voice – a voice which, in its focus on the specificities of *petit-nègre* lives, bears the unmistakable imprint of Négritude – he is discredited and dismissed. The teacher, who stands for the dominant group of the black bourgeoisie, is unwilling to give credence to José's narrative, because he finds it guilty of being too eloquent, too articulate. He is unable to reconcile literary brilliance with the unabashedly *petit-nègre* narrative of Médouze's death. M. Jean-Henri therefore deduces that José's work must be plagiarised. It is against such ingrained prejudices within black society that the narrator José, and by extension the author Joseph, must struggle. The scene is an indication of the prejudice and preconceptions which Zobel himself faced for attempting to write literature about *petit-nègre* lives, and it demonstrates how unprepared the black Martinican bourgeoisie were to embrace their Négritude, and particularly the kind of popular, social realist Négritude prose pioneered by Zobel.

At the Lycée Schœlcher, José also becomes acutely aware that he lacks what his fellow pupils possess: his world is devoid of books, or fine pens, or excursions, or well-heeled political discussions at the dining table. In contrast to Serge's top-of-the-range school kit, which is obviously a gift from his family, José has for years been saving his pocket money so that he can buy his own school equipment and spare his mother and grandmother the extra expense (p. 191). Yet it is clear that José's sense of familial responsibility and self-sufficiency provides him with something that money cannot buy: an incredibly mature and reflective attitude towards learning. He realises that he is able to formulate his own independent responses to literature, but he is so disillusioned that he cannot bring himself to articulate his ideas in class, preferring to pass for a dunce while his peers trot out stock responses gleaned from study guides. Unsurprisingly, for reproducing rather than challenging the status quo, these unoriginal 'learners' meet with nothing but approbation from the teacher M. Jean-Henri, who can be best understood as a *mimic man*, after the model sketched out by Homi K. Bhabha in *The Location of Culture*.[47] Bhabha himself draws inspiration from a Caribbean literary source, V. S. Naipaul's Ralph Singh in the 1967 novel *The Mimic Men*.[48] A *mimic man* is intelligent and educated; he is assimilated and, as a result, he has internalised the dominant discourse of colonialism, and the messages of the *mission civilisatrice*, to the detriment of those

---

47 Homi K. Bhabha, *The Location of Culture* (London: Routledge, 1994).
48 V. S. Naipaul, *The Mimic Men* (London: Pan Macmillan, 2002 [1967]).

non-white, non-European aspects of his identity, which are repressed (I return to the figure of M. Jean-Henri in the pages that follow). Indeed, his educational, social, and political success is contingent upon such processes of repression, denial, and disavowal: it is these attitudes that Naipaul, and Zobel, are exposing and denouncing.

Despite the views of previous critics who have stated that *La Rue Cases-Nègres* champions education as a way to escape poverty, the novel is anything but a paean to increased access to colonial education and the social mobility which this can bring about. Instead, it is the reflective and mature chronicle of a series of important, if relatively modest, educational successes. The narrative is uncompromising in its insistence that these rare moments of success are accompanied by constant struggles and numerous disappointments; José's real education happens far away from the classroom as he learns to question the world around him, and observes a transition from the rural yet sincere world of the plantation, to the sophisticated and prejudiced 'educated' urban world. Zobel's commitment to describing and exposing these contradictions places a great focus on racial pride and race consciousness in *La Rue Cases-Nègres*, which becomes a strategy to resist dominant French culture, shaped by the author's own unique approach to Négritude.

Négritude: The Defence of the *petit-nègre*

Without the advances of Négritude, it would have been unthinkable for Zobel to write a novel with the title *La Rue Cases-Nègres*. In so doing, he gave literary representation to a marginalised space which holds a specific significance for Caribbean culture: the plantation. His novel resonates with similar cultures which arose in other areas of the globe where plantation society once thrived, from the Deep South to the Indian Ocean. A photograph taken by Charles E. Peterson in 1934 entitled *Slave Quarters at the Hermitage Plantation, Chatham County, Georgia* presents a row of basic, identical brick houses which echo the wooden shacks described in *La Rue Cases-Nègres*.[49] Zobel's novel is one of the first accounts by a black author of the world of the plantation – viewed from the inside. The word *nègres* in the title is a defiant declaration, and elevates a previously ignored, inconvenient locus of modernity to a

---

49 See: 'The Cultural Landscape of the Plantation', https://www.gwu.edu/~folklife/bighouse/panel15.html (accessed 22 June 2016).

leading role, along with the real, lived experiences of the group which inhabits this dispossessed space.

Zobel's novel aims to transform the popular understanding of dispossessed black people, and his reassessment is not confined to the rural world of the rue Cases-Nègres: in Fort-de-France, another marginalised group, the black dock workers, are rendered visible by the narrator. In Larrier's analysis of masculinity in the novel, she argues that 'José's subconscious search for male models in a society that denies black male authority draws him to the harbor in Fort-de-France'.[50] Larrier offers a detailed discussion of the performance of masculinity in *La Rue Cases-Nègres* and engages with previous criticism published by Keith Q. Warner and Jacques André on the topics of masculinity and homosexuality in the novel.[51] Like Warner, Larrier argues against André's assertion that José is homosexual by arguing that his preoccupation with different models of masculinity can be understood as a (heterosexual) response to the female-dominated world he inhabits.

In this section of the novel, without explicitly stating the parallel between the dockworkers and the labourers in the rue Cases-Nègres, the narrator specifies that there are no cranes or equipment to help load or unload the ships, and that the men work to a punishing quasi-mechanical rhythm. Despite their filthy bodies and foul language, José regards these workers as heroic 'nègres herculéens' (p. 246) (Herculean Negroes) (p. 143; my modified translation). Throughout the island, under José's watchful eye, black bodies are presented as incredibly strong, seemingly tireless, and exploited as though they were automatons. The narrator also intentionally fights back against any reductive equation of physical superiority with mental inferiority by emphasising the complexity of the tasks performed and the mental dexterity required not just to work, but to survive more generally. The reader is confronted with the undeniable humanity of the poorest black workers, and is compelled to see, and moreover admire, marginalised groups in society.

50 Larrier, p. 51.
51 See Keith Q. Warner, 'Emasculation on the Plantation: A Reading of Joseph Zobel's *La Rue Cases-Nègres*', *College Language Association Journal*, 32 (1988), pp. 38–44. See also André, pp. 77–103. For a more recent work of criticism which returns to these themes, see Keith B. Mitchell, 'Naming That Which Dare Not Speak: Homosexual Desire in Joseph Zobel's *La Rue cases-nègres*', in *Rhetoric of the Other: Lesbian and Gay Strategies of Resistance in French and Francophone Contexts*, ed. by Martine Antle and Dominique Fisher (New Orleans, LA: University Press of the South, 2002), pp. 115–30.

The ways in which different groups of people view, understand, and label each other is a theme which assumes increasing urgency as the novel develops. Zobel uses the emotive question of food to show how attitudes differ, as José goes to school hungry in both the second and third parts of *La Rue Cases-Nègres*. In Part Two, it is because M'man Tine falls ill. In Part Three, however, José's hunger offers an important chance to juxtapose the attitudes of the well-off town-dwellers with those of the *petits-nègres*. José has encouraged his mother to move out of their shack in the shanty town of Sainte-Thérèse on the outskirts of Fort-de-France, so that she can accept a better, live-in job on route Didier. He is now fending for himself in Sainte-Thérèse while completing his secondary education. Managing his meagre budget as best he can, he constantly finds himself short of food and suffers from acute hunger at school.

In depicting José's intense hunger, Zobel may have been inspired by Césaire's archetypal scene in *Cahier d'un retour au pays natal*, in which a boy described as 'le négrillon' (little nègre) is rendered mute by acute hunger 'car sa voix s'oublie dans les marais de la faim' (for his voice gets lost in the swamp of starvation) (pp. 76–77). In Césaire's poem, the child is physically debilitated by hunger, but the uncompassionate teacher wrongly interprets his silence as ignorance. In Part Three of his novel, Zobel further explores the socio-economic significance of food, starvation, and satiety. Vaguely aware that José is going hungry, his well-off friend Christian Bussi offers to share his sandwich. José steadfastly refuses, too proud to accept charity. Bussi continues to eat. Once he is full, he casually drop-kicks the rest of his sandwich across the playground. Unable to mask his horror at Bussi's wanton waste of food, José is suddenly overcome with hatred:

> Mais ce n'est plus contre la faim que je lutte en ce moment; c'est contre une soudaine et féroce impulsion de flanquer aussi, de toutes mes forces, un coup de pied à Bussi. (p. 229)

> But right then, it wasn't hunger I was struggling with – instead I was struggling to control my sudden, wild impulse to give Bussi a great kick too, with all my strength. (p. 133; my modified translation)

José deplores Bussi's wasteful gesture. Adding insult to injury, Bussi then buys a cake from the tuck shop, and again, after eating as much as he wants, he simply drops the rest of the cake into the drinking fountain. Food, a matter of life or death to José, is merely another form of entertainment, an expendable leisure commodity, for the Christian Bussis of the world. Zobel is mapping the duality in attitudes towards food between different socioeconomic groups which is exacerbated in hyper-consumerist post-war society.

Meticulously documenting José's world – the conditions in which he lives and his interactions with others – the novel arrives at its climax in Part Three, which draws together the narrative's overarching exploration of the ways in which people understand and label each other, and themselves. This final part of the novel discusses the racial codes and alienation which Frantz Fanon would famously explore two years later in his extended essay *Peau noire, masques blancs* (1952). Several of José's friends exhibit racial complexes and express a desire to be in close proximity to white French culture, disavowing and denigrating their own black identity. José is particularly disappointed to see that his great friend Carmen, who comes from a plantation background similar to his own, is stricken by 'ces complexes antillais, tellement contraires à toute dignité' (p. 278) ('all those West Indian complexes so contrary to all dignity') (p. 162). Zobel's choice of vocabulary here is significant; he uses the term 'complexes' and recognises that what he is describing is a psychological disorder. It would take the intervention of the trained medical doctor and psychiatrist Fanon to elucidate this in greater detail, but in 1950, Zobel is articulating through prose fiction those same psychopathological disorders diagnosed by Fanon in the essays of *Peau noire, masques blancs*.

Zobel's novel examines these complexes both in individuals, and as a wider social phenomenon. At the cafés which line La Savane, the central park in Fort-de-France, José observes the newly returned graduates of France, whose colonial scholarships – which, he states, will have been gained due to connections, not merit – have imbued them with a new confidence or, more accurately, arrogance. The obsessive desire for social mobility will lead to collective efforts to erase and deny a family's working-class origins:

> Pour commencer, la mère [...] répudiera son costume antillais, qu'elle porte pourtant avec dignité, et même beaucoup de grâce, mais qui, hélas! l'apparente encore trop aux gens du peuple; elle fera, pour l'avenir de son fils, le sacrifice de 'prendre le chapeau'. (p. 297)

> To begin with, the mother [...] would give up her West Indian style of dress, which she nevertheless wore with dignity and even with much grace, but which, alas, made her look too much like the lower class people; she would make the sacrifice, for her son's future, of 'wearing a hat'. (p. 173)

Even his own well-meaning mother attempts to inculcate a racial inferiority complex into José: 'Ma mère ne m'a-t-elle pas maintes fois répété que c'est déjà assez mal que je sois noir pour éviter de commettre la plus petite faute?' (p. 291) (Didn't my mother tell me over and over again that it was bad enough to be born black, and so I must avoid making the slightest mistake?) (p. 170; my modified translation). Like the well-meaning mothers at the park, his mother has internalised the dominant discourse, and lives out a simultaneous paradox of intense pride and extreme fear of persecution, because of her racial identity.

Despite his efforts to remain proud of his racial and socio-economic origins, José too begins to display signs of this complex. Social conditioning, imparted by his mother's anxious words as well as by the derision of figures such as Mam'zelle Mélie, Mme Léonce, and even the caretaker at the *lycée*, makes José keenly aware of his *petit-nègre* status. When a teacher at the *lycée* asks his pupils to state their parents' professions, he realises that it is imperative that he should translate – and conceal – his *petit-nègre* origins, to render himself acceptable to his bourgeois teacher and peers. The teachers at the Lycée Schœlcher make the mistake of assuming that all their pupils come from uniform socio-economic backgrounds, which leaves José lost for words. He quickly tries to find a French term for M'man Tine's role on the plantation which will be suitable for the classroom environment, recognising instinctively that the bourgeois school system is a space of 'modernity' and 'progress' which is contingent on the deliberate avoidance and disavowal of his grandmother's life of back-breaking manual labour. José hits on the term 'cultivatrice' (p. 234) ('farmer') (p. 136), which he intuits will be – just about – acceptable in this bourgeois context. He has internalised the idea that, as a *petit-nègre*, he must render his world 'acceptable' to the dominant group. He finds himself caught in a new world of translation, denial and anxiety, and his social mobility entails the navigation of taboos which simply do not cross the minds of his bourgeois classmates.

In this context of racial denial and psychological alienation, literature offers a lifeline. José is able to develop a sense of pride in his black identity thanks to his extracurricular reading of works which he describes as stories 'relatifs à la vie des nègres' (p. 293) ('pertaining to the lives of black people') (p. 171). Now, his ability to think independently, without recourse to study guides, will pay dividends. The authors he is reading include Claude McKay and René Maran, who represent the Anglophone and Francophone antecedents of Négritude. Césaire, Damas, and Senghor are not named; of course, at the time of José's adolescence these authors had not yet begun to write. But José is intentionally figured as responding to the same literary movements that would inspire Négritude. He cannot but be stirred by the literary cry of the black race, the cry of the oppressed. Literature enables him to take pride in his race, rather than accepting the ethnoclass hierarchy and retreating into racial denial: in short, he is shown developing his own Négritude. This literature counteracts the negative effects of the ethnoclass conditioning which is part of José's everyday lived experience. Literature galvanises him:

> Tout le passé de la race nègre, confronté avec son présent, se révéla ainsi à moi comme un défi jeté par les faits historiques à cette race, et une telle constatation me faisait tressaillir de ce vibrant orgueil qui fait lever les boucliers. (p. 293)

> The entire past of the Negro race, now brought into violent collision with its present, appeared to me like a challenge for this race posed by history, and this realisation made me quiver with the same vibrant pride that leads an army to raise its shields. (p. 171; my modified translation)

These literary encounters revitalise José and literally protect him – an idea clearly conveyed by the strident combat metaphor of shields being raised – from the psychological alienation which is repeatedly inflicted on him by Martinican society.

José realises that his love of literature can offer a way to develop and share his social and racial insights. He regularly lends books to his friends Jojo and Carmen, and even teaches Carmen how to read. For the critic Jacques André, Carmen is the decisive figure in the third part of the novel: he defies gender norms (he was given a girl's name by his superstitious father, to 'protect' him from the fate of his brothers who had all died in infancy) and at once upholds and destabilises traditional ideas of masculinity (promiscuity/indifference, exploitation/vulnerability).[52] After reading *Batouala* by René Maran, José relates that Carmen is 'littéralement bouleversé' (literally overwhelmed), and the Harlem Renaissance classic *Banjo* by Jamaican-born Claude McKay leaves him 'fou de joie' (p. 287) ('beside himself with joy') (p. 167).

Both novels influenced the development of Négritude. *Batouala: véritable roman nègre*, for which Maran had become the first black winner of the Prix Goncourt, denounced and challenged French colonialism. Here, intertextuality is a reminder of the relationship between the two Antillean authors; having previously supported Zobel, Maran refused

---

[52] André, p. 107.

to endorse the publication of *La Rue Cases-Nègres*. Nonetheless, Zobel includes this admiring comment about his former benefactor. McKay's *Banjo*, set in Marseilles and published in 1929, is a classic of the Negro Renaissance movement which depicts the troubled lives of poor black characters.[53] Its narrative intertwines an original combination of joyous, debauched celebration with unflinching, gritty realism; it also criticises those black French colonial subjects who live as immigrants in Marseilles and seek cultural assimilation into French society. To heighten the social realism, speech is transcribed in a hybrid linguistic form which evokes the vernacular and breaks grammatical standards and norms; a style which would prove influential for Zobel himself, as he strove to find ways of transcribing Creole. Where once M. Médouze's oral narratives helped José to analyse his world, it is now the printed word which develops his analytical powers. The new, contemporary literature by the authors of the Negro Renaissance movement and the precursors to Négritude such as Maran, builds José's awareness of the potential for black racial solidarity, and enables him and his friends to experience a nascent sense of a diasporic consciousness which unites oppressed black peoples across the globe. Zobel is explicitly documenting the same influences which would give rise to the Francophone phenomenon of Négritude, and showing that he was influenced in very similar ways when he began to write a different kind of Négritude literature.

As their private discussions of race develop, José, Carmen, and Jojo also undertake an angry deconstruction of cinematic representations of black men. They decry the stereotype of the 'nègre-grand-enfant' (pp. 287–89) ('the black man being a big child') (p. 168) who is overgrown, ungainly, and who has only a childlike intelligence. These later sections of the novel which critique art and culture appear to offer a glimpse of the author Zobel himself. In a veiled defence and explanation of his own book's title, José-Joseph condemns the films in which 'le style "rue Cases-Nègres" […] caractérise tout ce qui dans ce pays est destiné au peuple ou conçu par des gens de couleur' (pp. 288–89) (the 'Black Shack Alley' style that characterises all that in this country was destined for the people or conceived by persons of colour) (p. 168; my modified translation). This is an apparently contradictory statement that might seem to undo his own literary ambitions; but it actually works to demonstrate the extent of the differences between the stereotypes

---

53   Claude McKay, *Banjo: A Story Without a Plot* (New York & London: Harper and Brothers, 1929).

and his own novel. José's objection is that such films unfailingly aim to depict poor black people from environments like the rue Cases-Nègres in a pejorative manner, and thus actively work to discourage any notion of racial or class solidarity and social mobility. Here, the author seems to anticipate that these very same prejudices might colour the reception of his own novel, a work which is in fact intended to blast apart the bigotry which already exists *vis-à-vis* rue Cases-Nègres-like contexts. The 'nègre-grand-enfant' whom José abhors on the cinema screen, and who, racist film propaganda suggests, lives in poverty due to his own inherent intellectual deficiencies, is nowhere to be found in *La Rue Cases-Nègres*. Instead, Zobel paints the portraits of a series of men, women, and children who are involved in a daily struggle for survival – a struggle which is biased against them from the start, and which requires phenomenal physical and mental strength.

As the poor working-class figures José, Carmen, and Jojo develop their own critical acumen and discuss the racism they perceive in dominant social discourse, the narrative is aiming to encourage similar critical reflection in its readers: this non-elite debate is a shaping characteristic of Zobel's Négritude. Towards the end of the novel, José is unequivocal that his goal now is to fight back against the social prejudices which lead black people to '[se] désolidariser d'avec tous les nègres du monde' (p. 291) ('to dissociate [themselves] from all black people in the world') (p. 169). For him, this process, which leads black people to deny the inherent value of their own race and culture, and to equate social mobility with this very act of denial, is the most pernicious, harmful aspect of Martinican society. José – or Joseph – is now quite clear in his vision that the goals of art and culture from areas afflicted by such complexes must be to help the people: 'Toute entreprise dans un tel pays ne devrait-elle pas viser aussi à promouvoir le peuple!' (p. 289) (Surely every enterprise in such countries should aim to help the people?) (p. 168; my modified translation). Art can and must be put to the service of society, to encourage all Martinicans to work together towards greater racial pride, in short, towards solidarity.

These strident critical discussions about race and diaspora culminate in the narrator's increasingly urgent desire to communicate his life story – and, most importantly, the insights he has gained into racism and economic oppression – to a wider audience. And so José begins to dream of writing a book. Yet he wonders how to achieve this, because it appears to him that books may only feature the world of white people, the world of 'ces personnes à cheveux blonds, aux yeux bleus, aux joues roses [...] [l]es villes, avec leurs voitures automobiles, leurs grands hôtels, leurs théâtres, leurs salons [...] les trains, les montagnes et les plaines, les champs, les fermes' (p. 233) ('those people with blonde hair, blue eyes, pink cheeks [...] Towns, with their motorcars, their big hotels, their theatres, their salons [...] trains, mountains and plains, the fields, farms') (p. 135). This passage is echoed by the older Zobel's own words in the 2002 documentary *Joseph Zobel: le soleil d'ébène* (*Joseph Zobel: Ebony Sun*), where he explains that he began to write because he wanted to break with the conventions of the day, and depict people like himself in literature (discussed in the Introduction to this study).

José gradually realises that he too has a valid message to impart about class and race, and that literature offers him the means to communicate this message — a realisation triggered in Part Three of the novel, in a second pay scene at the rue Cases-Nègres when he returns to collect M'man Tine's wages, as she is too ill to go herself. This crucial scene is the double of the first pay scene and offers a glimpse of what José's life would have been had he not escaped to become a pupil at the *lycée*. The second pay scene illustrates how far José's life has diverged from the lives of his childhood friends, who have followed the narrow path designated for *petits-nègres*. He is the only part of this landscape to have changed. The wages are still doled out in the same manner, but now, instead of longing to be old enough to be paid like the *petite-bande* child labourers or the adults, José's double vision means that he is horrified by the terrible poverty in which the workers are intentionally held. This sickening recognition is accompanied by feelings of utter kinsmanship and solidarity with these workers. The inhabitants of the rue Cases-Nègres are astonished and delighted to see José again:

> Et parmi ce ramassis d'êtres puants, aux couleurs de fumier, des mains terreuses, mais les plus amicales qui fussent, se tendaient vers moi, à travers les sourires les plus lumineux que le contentement puisse allumer sur d'aussi sombres visages. (p. 266)

> And from that rabble of stinking, dung-coloured beings, many earth-stained hands came reaching out towards me — yet they were the friendliest hands imaginable, accompanied by the brightest smiles that happiness could bestow upon such sombre faces. (p. 154; my modified translation)

In this moment of reunion, José insists on the twin factors of extreme blackness and extreme poverty which mark out his own people. He connects their skin colour with negative adjectives which, for a second, suggest that he has indeed internalised the racist attitudes of the bourgeoisie of Fort-de-France. Yet these descriptions are an act of defiance; he purposely employs them to acknowledge the demonisation of darkness and poverty in Martinican society, and then deftly turns this assumption on its head by qualifying the inhabitants of the rue Cases-Nègres as the most genuine, sincere, and affectionate people he has ever known.

Overwhelmed, José is lost for words. It is only on the walk back to M'man Tine's home, when he is alone once again, that he begins to process his emotions – and those emotions are anger and shame. He reproaches himself for a cowardice of which he had previously been unaware: 'Il me semblait qu'il y avait eu des paroles qui s'imposeraient et que je n'avais même pas conçues …' (p. 266) ('It seemed to me that there had been something I could have said, that I hadn't even thought of …') (p. 155). His visit back to the rue Cases-Nègres triggers the realisation that his unique position of privilege also places a burden on him to testify to his experiences and share the benefits of his new education – or rather, the insights which he has gained away from the classroom. He suddenly becomes aware that he has political responsibilities, but the ellipsis in the narrative indicates his inability (as yet) to articulate his insights. It is the novel *La Rue Cases-Nègres* itself which expresses the compassionate and political voice that José is unable to summon on this return visit. He uses this voice to cast light on the connections between rich and poor in Martinique, and to expose, and disprove, ethnoclass disavowals of this poorer group's humanity. The more José witnesses of wealthy culture, the more he equates it with the inhumanity of the dominant hegemony.

This is nowhere more evident than in his apparently measured appraisal of the luxurious setting of the house where his mother works on route Didier. The exquisite Villa Mano lies 'au fond d'une petite allée blanche, gravée dans une spacieuse pelouse fleurie de roses et de zinnias' (p. 242) ('at the end of a small white avenue, set in a spacious lawn blooming with roses and zinnias') (p. 141). This perfectly composed image of tranquillity, harmony, and natural resplendence is intentionally paradisiacal. Yet in this same scene, a lone man – a gardener working on the immaculate borders, who is tellingly described as a *nègre* – serves as a visual reminder of the exploitation upon which this calm and splendour is contingent. This is nothing more than a latent invitation to the reader to perceive that such luxury and accumulated financial wealth for the few is dependent on the oppression and exploitation of many. José's double vision means that he is able to perceive that this wealth is actually the physical manifestation of the profit earned by workers such as M'man Tine in the terrible conditions of the cane fields: by the defrauded *moissonneurs* (harvest labourers) of the epigraph. He has already begun to question why his grandmother must struggle, and not even struggle for a life of luxury, but merely to survive: 'Et pourquoi? Pourquoi ne pas habiter une maison, porter des robes non déchirées [...] Et qui donc l'obligeait à être de la sorte?' (pp. 235–36) ('Why? Why not live in a house, why not wear dresses without holes [...] And who forced her to be like that?') (p. 137). This rhetorical question about the biased structures of modern society – one of many such questions which are scattered throughout the text – is a compelling invitation to reflect on social hierarchies and their role in the perpetuation of terrible injustices.

These rhetorical questions find their conclusion – and their audacious answer – in the novel's famous ending. José has learned of M'man Tine's death, and is inconsolable. He conjures up an image of her in his mind's eye, and homes in on her worn hands in obsessive detail. Now he makes the novel's double vision explicit. In a damning phrase, he makes it quite clear that he finally knows the reason why, every day of his grandmother's life, her hands were 'pincées, éraflées, et cramponnées au manche de la houe, en proie aux morsures féroces des feuilles de canne' (squeezed, scratched and clamped on to the handle of the hoe, an easy prey to the fierce cuts of the cane leaves); it was for no other reason than 'pour créer la Route Didier' (p. 311) ('to create Route Didier') (p. 181). His grandmother's hands have been deformed by a life of hard labour precisely so that the minority, symbolised by the route Didier, can prosper.

The novel's audacious conclusion explicitly equates white upper-class *béké* wealth with black *petit-nègre* suffering. José senses, however, that many people will not be ready to accept, or even acknowledge, the troubling insights of the terrifying double vision of modernity which he has presented. In his closing phrase, it is these groups whom he qualifies as the 'aveugles' (blind people), those 'qui se bouchent les oreilles' (p. 311) ('who block their ears') (p. 182). Zobel's ambition in *La Rue Cases-Nègres*, made explicit in the final line, reveals the full extent of the novel's double vision: it is a work which aims to make visible the hidden web of hypocrisies, double standards, exploitation, and abuse with which modern 'civilised' society has been constructed.

* * *

La Rue Cases-Nègres demonstrates that the contemporary myth of modernity is contingent on hierarchies of classification which ensure the physical separation of the rich and the poor. Zobel exposes this separation in order to collapse it, by showing beyond all doubt that it is the *petit-nègre* group's repetitive, endless, and improperly paid labour which has created the coveted riches that are enjoyed by the *béké*. It is easier for the alienated middle classes to look 'up' and aspire to their share of this wealth than to challenge the hegemony of the *béké* by turning their gaze 'down' and experiencing compassion for the exploited group. Zobel's novel is no less than a demand for a critical reconsideration of the most despised group in Martinican society. It is a true 'cri nègre' (Negro cry) which affirms the humanity of those who have been excluded from narratives of modernity and progress, and denied any chance of education, for no other reason than the terrible socio-economic circumstances into which they were born, where, to quote André, 'demain ne fait que répéter aujourd'hui' (tomorrow is but a repetition of today).[54]

To return to Ross, whose vision of social realism has guided the development of this chapter,

> realism offers a voice to those who live in a different temporality, who follow a pace of life that is nonsynchronous with the dominant one. In the post-war period realist fiction and film offered a critique of official representations of a uniformly prosperous France, surging forward into American-style patterns of consumption and mass culture. (p. 13)

Zobel's semi-autobiographical novel performs this critique of narratives of uniform development and consumerism, exposing dichotomies within Martinique itself which also work to reveal the dichotomies between Martinique and metropolitan France. On 1 January 1947, the island had cast off the status of a colony to become a *département d'outre mer* or overseas department, and the author wrote in full awareness that the contemporary era, and the end of 'colony' status, ushered in the potential for radical political change.

La Rue Cases-Nègres poses enduring questions about the very meanings which are ascribed to the terms 'progress' and 'civilisation'. The novel argues that having been denied the 'opportunity' to become

---

54 André, p. 57.

bourgeois, the people who live in the rue Cases-Nègres have in fact retained a deeper human culture. Their society is brutal and poverty-ridden, but is also based on simple and genuinely shared interactions, rather than individualistic and contrived superficial, egotistical, and materialistic urges. As a corollary of this 'lack' of 'opportunity', they have also been spared the process of extreme psychological racial alienation which begins to afflict José as soon as he leaves the space of the plantation. Throughout the novel, as he gradually becomes successful and improves his socio-economic prospects, José's dreams always lead him back to Petit-Morne, although his new-found status simultaneously makes any real long-term return impossible. This is the crux of the novel's double vision. Once he has been awakened to the realities of social injustice, José cannot aspire to live a life of poverty on the plantation, but neither he nor Zobel himself will ever stop searching for the unparalleled sense of community and humanity that he once experienced in the rue Cases-Nègres.

CHAPTER FIVE

Cultural Capital in the French Capital
From *La Fête à Paris* to *Quand la neige aura fondu*

> [L]e Noir, prisonnier dans son île, perdu dans une atmosphère sans le moindre débouché, ressent comme une trouée d'air cet appel de l'Europe.
>
> Frantz Fanon, *Peau noire, masques blancs*, p. 16
>
> The black Antillean, prisoner on his island, lost in an atmosphere without the slightest prospect, feels the call of Europe like a breath of fresh air.
>
> Frantz Fanon, *Black Skin, White Masks*, trans. Richard Philcox, p. 5

On 6 December 1946, Joseph Zobel arrived in Le Havre aboard the steam ship *Le Colombie*, and from there he made the train journey to Paris that was to become so many Antilleans' first experience of mainland France – and, indeed, of train travel. One year later, his wife Enny and the couple's three infant children joined him. The family spent Christmas together in Fontainebleau, a town in the metropolitan area of Paris which lies about 60 kilometres south-east of the city centre, where Zobel had found a teaching post. Thus began a completely new phase in the Zobels' life. Their move would anticipate the emigration patterns of hundreds of thousands of families who migrated to Europe from the Francophone and Anglophone Caribbean in the decades after the Second World War.

Zobel had obtained his *baccalauréat* in Martinique in 1935 and had then sought, and been refused, a colonial scholarship to study architecture in Paris. In 1939, the outbreak of the Second World War had imposed severe restrictions on Martinicans' mobility. As soon as these were lifted, Zobel was finally permitted to leave the island. Now, he was – at last – able to emulate the Négritude founding authors whose pre-war encounters in Paris had proved so significant to their understanding of racial identity. Mobility played a crucial role in the genesis of Négritude, as Malachi McIntosh's study of the literary – and material – significance of emigration for the development of Caribbean literature emphasises; for McIntosh, the movement is 'a clear product of emigration and a response to the Parisian context'.[1] The emigration in question is of course the wave of interwar migration from the French colonies to Paris which, as Jean Khalfa has observed, reached new levels in the 1920s.[2] It was this interwar migration which culminated in the Négritude movement of the 1930s.

McIntosh also draws attention to the social origins of that interwar generation of immigrants, noting that 'Négritude was [...] from the start, an inward-looking, emigrant elite-focused movement'.[3] Zobel stands in stark contrast to these 'elite-focused' emigrants. Denied the mobility which his peers had experienced, from his native Martinique he developed his own unique kind of Négritude which took a resolutely non-elite position. The move to Paris would bring about a new direction in the author's literary career, as he now attempted to test the extent to which his personal Martinican interpretation of Négritude could adapt and survive its transatlantic uprooting to Europe. The first fruits came in 1950 with the publication of *La Rue Cases-Nègres*, in which Zobel critically appraised the complexities and problems of his native island from his new home in Paris. *La Rue Cases-Nègres* explores the reasons that led Zobel to emigrate: it had become imperative for him to leave the colonial setting of his beloved yet repressive and prejudiced native island.

In the quotation which stands at this chapter's opening, Fanon observes that for Caribbean people, and Martinicans in particular, Europe represented a chance to escape the asphyxiating claustrophobia of the Antilles. Zobel experienced that exact same need to leave the

1 McIntosh, p. 112.
2 Khalfa, 'The Heart of the Black Race' (2008), pp. 15–24.
3 McIntosh, p. 112.

island space of the colony. He had enjoyed a brief period of rapid success in the mid-1940s – carving out a successful writing career at *Le Sportif*, then being catapulted into an administrative role for Governor Ponton, and publishing the novels *Diab'-là* and *Les Jours immobiles*. Yet, after Ponton's death, he had returned to his former school to work alongside his more successful teaching colleagues who had all benefited from their time studying in Paris as *boursiers coloniaux* (colonial scholarship holders), and who had experienced and directly contributed to Négritude's pre-war Parisian heyday: the very opportunity which had been denied Zobel. The fledgling novelist suddenly had to contend with regression and circularity.

It is therefore no surprise that Zobel applied for a *congé administratif* (administrative leave for civil servants) as soon as travel to metropolitan France once again became possible after the war. He was granted permission to move to Paris at the end of 1946 and in the capital he studied at the Institut d'ethnologie (Institute of Ethnology) at Césaire's suggestion;[4] indeed, this Parisian institution was itself a Négritude rite of passage, as Senghor and Damas had studied there before the war.[5] He also took courses on the dramatic arts at the Sorbonne, and supported himself financially with a teaching post at the Lycée François 1er in Fontainebleau.

In 2016, Zobel's photographs from this era were restored and brought together in the collection *Joseph Zobel photographies* by his granddaughter, the photographer Charlotte Zobel. This collection of images and diary entries offers a rare glimpse into Zobel's first years in metropolitan France. It includes portraits of his family and friends; a series of anonymous faces of different ages and different races, as well as an engaging series of scenes from the family's life in post-war France, which show boating excursions, rural walks, and grape picking. A comment from Zobel's personal diary in 1949 testifies to his readiness to embrace a new group of diverse friends in metropolitan France: 'Je songe encore à cette fatalité qui m'unit toujours à des gens qui quelle que soit leur race ou leur origine, me ressemblent comme à un frère' (I am still musing on this inevitable impulse that draws me to people who, regardless of their race or their origins, resemble me like a brother).[6] This comment conveys the young man's idealistic – and doubtless

---

4 Tarrieu, p. 29.
5 Miller, p. 13.
6 Charlotte Zobel, p. 90; my modified translation.

sincere – belief that in Paris, a sense of kinship, and a shared outlook on life, could transcend racial or social barriers; an attitude which is in evidence in his subsequent novels.

As the previous chapter has demonstrated, while it is set uniquely in Martinique, Zobel's seminal 1950 novel *La Rue Cases-Nègres* is actually the first work to arise from his experiences in Paris. The only clue to the author's new status as an immigrant is found on the final page of *La Rue Cases-Nègres*, where Zobel documents the date and place of completion as 'Fontainebleau, le 17 juin 1950', a paratextual detail which subtly indicates the novel's double vision. Indeed, that novel describes the Caribbean world he has left behind from his new, distant vantage point in Europe. This shift in viewpoint is never explicitly acknowledged in the narrative itself. Yet Zobel's painstaking efforts to produce a text which would render the opaque, other world of a rue Cases-Nègres visible and accessible to readers quite unfamiliar with the context – such as the new colleagues and friends who populate his photographs from the era – testify to the author's awareness that he is now writing for an entirely different, metropolitan, readership. It is in his next novel, *La Fête à Paris* (*Adventures in Paris*), originally published in 1953, that Zobel directly addresses this shift in perspective by fictionalising the life of a Martinican immigrant in the French capital, and documenting the cultural, racial, and political challenges which post-war immigrants had to navigate. The novel explores how Zobel's own home-grown, Martinican understanding of Négritude could be tried and tested in post-war metropolitan France.

Once again, Zobel was out of sync with his peers. The transatlantic voyage to Europe is the journey which heralds the beginning of so many canonical Caribbean authors' careers – particularly those who emigrated to pre-war France, and post-war Britain. Before the war, the transatlantic crossing had catalysed the creation of the Négritude movement, as the 'transplanted Caribbean intellectuals [broke] away from island assumptions about race and reorient[ed] their identification away from Europe toward their African peers'.[7] For Zobel, however, who had already developed a modest but successful career as an author in Martinique, leaving the Caribbean unsettled the pursuit of his literary vocation. It led to just two more original novels: *La Rue Cases-Nègres*, his acknowledged masterpiece, and its sequel, *La Fête à Paris*. Between 1954 and 1978, Zobel's only publications were short stories and poetry.

---

7   McIntosh, p. 112.

The reasons for this are complex and linked to another important decision to migrate once more. Unusually, Paris does not represent an end point in the development of Zobel's career; it was something of a staging post. Zobel did not settle in the French capital. He spent the majority of the years between 1957 and 1976 working in Senegal, in a move deeply influenced by his Négritude-inspired desire to reconnect with a lost African ancestry. In Senegal, however, as he commented in several interviews, he was too preoccupied with the need to earn a living and support his family to be able to write. In his retirement, he returned to the south of France, where he lived until his death. There, he published two more novels, but both were rewritten versions of earlier material: and so, in 1979, *La Fête à Paris* was rewritten and published under the new title *Quand la neige aura fondu*.

La Fête à Paris, in both its iterations, is the sequel to *La Rue Cases-Nègres*, and raises questions about the evolving relationship between the author and his literary surrogate, José Hassam. When Zobel decides to transpose his hero from Martinique to post-war Paris, it is a further instance of mirroring between the trajectories of Joseph Zobel and José Hassam. However, there is a crucial difference: while Joseph nurtured a successful career as a writer, José, despite the repeated clues in *La Rue Cases-Nègres* that he would become an author, has not taken this path. This increased distance between author and character casts José Hassam in a new light, suggesting that, by 1953, he is intended to be understood as an archetype, a composite character who represents the struggles of a whole class of Antillean people. Zobel suggests this in an interview given in 1957, some years after the publication of his two José Hassam texts:

> Ce que je puis affirmer, c'est que [...] si José Hassam n'est pas tout à fait moi, il n'en a pas moins existé, et je crois même qu'il existe encore aux Antilles des milliers de José Hassam.[8]
>
> What I can confirm is that [...] if José Hassam isn't exactly me, this doesn't mean he has never existed, and I certainly believe that thousands of José Hassams still exist in the Antilles.

José Hassam can only retain his status as a recognisable, relatable figure if his destiny remains relatively ordinary. To depict him living Zobel's life as an award-winning author – for by 1947, Zobel had become a

---

8   Hervé Bazin, '*La Rue Cases-Nègres*', RFO, dated 1 March 1957. Accessed at l'INA, Salle P, Bibliothèque nationale de France.

minor celebrity on the Parisian literary circuit[9] – would be irreconcilable with the character's 'everyman' status. As a result, in the sequel Zobel erases any traces of exceptionality, and instead has José do battle with the French capital without the help of any well-placed contacts.

This new distance between author and protagonist is indicated at the stylistic level by the novel's fragmented, episodic, and loose structure. Events are related in chronological order, but with far less sense of progression and purpose than in *La Rue Cases-Nègres*. There is also a significant shift in narrative perspective: the sequel novel is entirely related in the third person, thwarting attempts to establish the close, semi-autobiographical relationship between José Hassam and Joseph Zobel which the first-person narrative vantage point of *La Rue Cases-Nègres* had previously encouraged. As such, José becomes enigmatic, distant, even unknowable. In stark contrast to the clarity and focus of the José who narrates *La Rue Cases-Nègres*, the character is now mediated through an omniscient and impersonal narrator, a device which succeeds in conveying the unsettling, uncertain aspects of emigration, and his ambiguous adventures in Paris are shrouded in uncertainty and a sense of listlessness.

Following the pattern established throughout this study, this chapter's primary focus is the rewritten 1979 version, *Quand la neige aura fondu*. This is the novel to which Zobel intended readers to have access, and which remains most widely available to this day. As such, *Quand la neige aura fondu* is quoted whenever possible. If material refers explicitly to *La Fête à Paris*, this is clearly signalled in the analysis. There are, however, greater discrepancies between *La Fête à Paris* and *Quand la neige aura fondu* than in the case of Zobel's other rewritten works, and these differences repay closer investigation. In particular, my comparative approach reveals several passages in the original which the author chose not to include in the rewritten version. Strikingly, many of these deleted passages are sections which reveal much about Zobel's thinking on the dynamics of Négritude in the Caribbean, Africa, and France in the specific post-war context of the early 1950s. An important aim of this chapter is to concentrate on performing the first scholarly excavation of the 'lost' material for the specific insights it holds into

---

9 In February 1947, just before the publication of *Diab'-là*, Zobel complained in a letter to Enny that he had too many invitations, commenting that 'due to lack of time, I cannot answer them all'. See Emily Zobel Marshall and Jenny Zobel, 'Dans cette immensité tumultueuse', *Wasafiri*, 28.1 (2013), p. 29.

Zobel's authorial stance towards Négritude in the 1950s. In so doing, it paves the way for future scholarship on why the author may have decided to omit these remarkable earlier passages.

In *Quand la neige aura fondu*, the maturing racial awareness which textures José's interpretations of and responses to his new life in Paris is a strong indication of his increasingly sophisticated sense of his own Négritude, now put to the test in a new Parisian context. Yet in the intervening years between Négritude's heyday of the 1930s and José's arrival, the city of Paris, the cradle of Négritude, has been devastated by the Second World War. In my analysis, Stuart Hall's work on 'differential incorporation' proves helpful when analysing the emigrant experience in Paris, while Bourdieu's theory of cultural capital is used as the framework for investigating José's encounters with middle-class and elite circles in Paris. Zobel's final novel is also his final protracted reflection on the Négritude period, and it marks the culmination of the exploration of the psychology of race and class which informs all his novels. José faces untold challenges in the French capital and as *Quand la neige aura fondu* develops, it becomes evident that it is his own solid sense of his racial and social identity – his Négritude – which enables him to face, and overcome, adversity.

Situating the Sequel:
Post-war Emigration from the Caribbean to Paris

In October 1950, Zobel announced in a radio interview that he was writing 'la suite' (the sequel) to *La Rue Cases-Nègres*, and that this novel presented 'le milieu nègre à Paris' (the Negro *milieu* in Paris).[10] That novel was 1953's *La Fête à Paris*, which does indeed focus on the trials which José undergoes in the French capital as a black man. From the opening chapters, which privilege dismal, war-ravaged scenery and dank cityscapes, the title's suggestion of frivolity in the French capital emerges as heavily ironic.

The sequel explores race, language, identity, and nationality as intersectional, socially constructed phenomena in the post-war melting pot of Paris. In *La Fête à Paris*, Négritude offers a framework for José to weave

---

10 'Joseph Zobel lauréat du prix des lecteurs' (Joseph Zobel, Winner of the Readers' Prize), *Ondes courtes*, radiodiffusion française, service des émissions vers l'étranger, dated 22 October 1950. L'INA.

together these different, often conflicting aspects while maintaining an unshakeable attitude of racial pride. In *Quand la neige aura fondu*, this attitude endures, but the specific references which connected racial pride to Négritude in the original are now attenuated. The 1979 version is more muted, as reflected in its title, which offers the promise of gradual improvement and tentative hope. Both versions, however, close on a snowscape, thwarting any straightforward notions of progress and advancement, and presenting a more ambiguous future for Caribbean immigrants in the *métropole*; the snow might eventually melt, but so will it always return. What will change are the responses and reactions of the immigrant, whose experience grows with each passing season.

Originally written at a time when immigration from Martinique to Paris was about to become one of the defining features of France's post-war reconstruction efforts, Zobel's novel illustrates what would become established patterns of movement. It provides not only an account of post-war transatlantic migration from the Caribbean, but also of the transition from a predominantly rural Caribbean island to a rapidly modernising urban European centre. The migrant has to navigate trains, the *métro*, and large crowds for the first time, and José experiences Paris as an assault on his senses and even his body: 'brutal comme une gifle. La gifle qui conjure une syncope' (brutal as a slap in the face. The kind of slap that makes you pass out) (p. 19).

These new migration patterns between the Caribbean and France were also simultaneously occurring between the Caribbean and the United Kingdom. The post-*Empire Windrush* era, which took its name from the ship that brought the first group of Caribbean workers to the United Kingdom in 1948, saw the production of literary works by Caribbean emigrants that won critical recognition and acclaim. These include canonical novels by Barbadian author George Lamming (*The Emigrants*, 1954) and the Trinidadians Sam Selvon (*The Lonely Londoners*, 1956) and V. S. Naipaul (*The Mimic Men*, 1967), as well as later texts by future generations of British authors of Caribbean heritage, such as Andrea Levy (*Small Island*, 2004). These works are all recognised as constituting an important historical and psychological contribution to the understanding of Caribbean emigration. In the United Kingdom, this body of literature about the emigrant experience has attracted widespread attention from critics, reading publics, and other media alike.[11]

---

11 For example, through television adaptations such as the BBC's 2009 adaptation of Levy's *Small Island*.

Across the Channel, however, the experience of French Caribbean post-war migration to France remains severely under-represented in literature. *La Fête à Paris* and its rewritten form *Quand la neige aura fondu* are Zobel's contribution to this important corpus, and yet the novels have received little critical attention. Khalfa concludes his short study of Zobel in Paris with the comment that the Parisian-focused part of his career serves as a reminder that Zobel's entire *œuvre* 'truly needs rediscovering'.[12] The lack of scholarly attention to Zobel's novel of immigration is all the more surprising given that it is the first novel in either French or English about post-war Caribbean immigration to Europe and the related development of a Caribbean diaspora in mainland Europe, appearing before the works of Lamming and Selvon.

Migration from the Caribbean to Europe was not, of course, a wholly new phenomenon. In Martinique, as in the British colonies, specific kinds of patterns of migration to the *mère-patrie* or motherland had already been established around the turn of the twentieth century. For decades, a select group of elite and bourgeois Francophone pupils of black origin had been awarded colonial scholarships to study in metropolitan centres, and some had elected to make cities such as Paris their permanent home.

It was during the two world wars that this migration underwent a radical change as new policies prioritised the mass military deployment of working-class men to fight as soldiers. In the First World War, over 40,000 Martinicans fought in the French army.[13] In the Second World War, 2,000 Martinicans were deployed before the 1940 French defeat at the Battle of France.[14] After the Armistice, when the French islands fell under Vichy control, between 1940 and 1943, a further four to five thousand Martinicans and Guadeloupeans escaped by canoe to the neighbouring non-occupied islands of Dominica and Saint Lucia, travelling from there to North America to be trained to fight for De Gaulle's Free French forces.[15] These courageous men and women were known as La Dissidence (the Dissenters), and were the Caribbean equivalent of the French Resistance. Euzhan Palcy became the first

12 Jean Khalfa, 'Joseph Zobel in Paris', *Wasafiri*, 28.1 (2013), p. 26.
13 Paul Blanshard, *Democracy and Empire in the Caribbean* (New York: Macmillan, 1947), p. 251.
14 Richard D. E. Burton, *La Famille coloniale: la Martinique et la mère patrie: 1789–1992* (Paris: L'Harmattan, 1994), p. 148.
15 Eric T. Jennings, 'La Dissidence aux Antilles (1940–1943)', *Vingtième siècle: revue d'histoire*, 68 (2000), p. 60.

film-maker to focus on this remarkable episode in French Caribbean history with her 2006 documentary *Parcours de dissidents*.[16] This was part of a national campaign to recognise the sacrifice made by Antillean men and women who twice risked their lives in the name of freedom: first in their attempts to escape their islands, and then in the war itself.

The mass displacements of Martinicans and Guadeloupeans to the metropolitan centre brought about by the two world wars were not initially conceived of in terms of a French Caribbean diaspora. In Martinique, the French had 'built up among the inhabitants a loyalty to the mother country [...] quite unique among Caribbean territories'.[17] As Christine Chivallon has noted, the movement of French Caribbeans to mainland France was intended to be a seamless transition within a cohesive and secure cultural identity.[18] For Martinicans in particular, staunch adherence to the *mission civilisatrice* made this transition appear desirable, and unproblematic. The French policy had promoted the notion of a French Republic that was 'une et indivisible' (one and indivisible); therefore, French identity and French Caribbean identity were one and the same, and indissociable. In *Quand la neige aura fondu*, when José Hassam arrives in Paris, he is made aware that he is one in a long line of Martinican men to come to France. A café waiter recounts how a Martinican soldier fought alongside him in the First World War, and that they became good friends, remembering fondly: 'Quel chic type c'était!' (What a chic fellow he was!) (p. 49). A sense of kinship and a working-class solidarity is immediately established between José and this stranger, based on the white man's first-hand experience of Martinicans as fellow French soldiers.

In Paris, José remains anchored in working-class society, and is excluded from the considerable post-war black diasporic networks of the French capital. This presents a stark contrast to the experience of Zobel himself. In a diary entry made on 1 December 1946, during *Le Colombie*'s transatlantic crossing, the author jots down his intention to pay 'mes visites à toutes les personnes dont les noms et adresses remplissent un carnet qui fait partie de la panoplie de mes accessoires pour m'introduire dans Paris' (my visits to all the people whose names

---

16 Euzhan Palcy, *Parcours de dissidents* (France: JMJ Productions, 2006).
17 Blanshard, p. 251.
18 Christine Chivallon, 'De quelques préconstruits de la notion de diaspora à partir de l'exemple antillais', *Revue européenne des migrations internationales*, 13.1 (1997), p. 152.

and addresses fill the address book which is part of the panoply of my accessories to help me establish myself in Paris).[19] In contrast, José arrives in metropolitan France and experiences terrible isolation. He spends his first weeks in Paris in a tiny flat rented by his friend Carmen – the only character besides immediate family members to recur between *La Rue Cases-Nègres* and the sequel – and slowly builds up a wider number of acquaintances. On arrival in the *mère-patrie*, then, José Hassam is helped not by a network of middle-class contacts, but by his working-class peers such as Carmen, a character who shares his social origins and is more representative of the average experiences of men born into the *petit-nègre* class.

Carmen's arrival in France is also a legacy of the Second World War. He is described as having left Martinique in 1939 as a French soldier with 'le premier convoi' (the first convoy), a historical event which is woven into the novel in a small fleeting reference, but forms the focus of an entire short story, 'Le premier convoi', in Zobel's 1946 collection *Laghia de la mort*. After the Armistice, Carmen was held for several years as a prisoner of war in Nazi camps, before escaping and returning to fight for France's liberation in Alsace. This detail subtly frames Carmen as a war hero – although he modestly does not consider himself in such terms – and he stands as a symbolic reminder of the Antillean men and women who had shown great bravery and risked their lives to fight against Nazi rule just a few years previously.

Carmen is now a chauffeur in metropolitan France, and has decided not to return to Martinique. He is convinced that he has better prospects in Paris, both financially and, more importantly, as a human being. Carmen claims that although he is still only a servant in Paris, he is now considered a man. In *Quand la neige aura fondu*, he comments: 'Le patron est un homme et je suis un homme comme lui. La patronne est blanche, mais je ne suis pas son nègre' (The boss is a man, and I'm a man like him. The boss's wife is white, but I am not her Negro) (p. 22). Again, the nuances of the French term *nègre* are challenging to translate, due to the slippage in meaning it conveys – it might be rendered as either 'Negro' or 'nigger' in English. The original 1953 novel passes an even more explicit comment on the differences between race relations in France and Martinique, as Carmen goes on to comment: 'ici, on n'a pas besoin de se traîner à genoux pour servir' (here, we don't need grovel on

---

19 Zobel, *D'amour et de silence*, p. 8.

our knees as servants) (*La Fête à Paris*, p. 32); this suggests that the more pejorative nuances of *nègre* are indeed at the fore in the original passage.

Carmen's abject description of black Martinican servants' willing self-abasement underscores the continuities between the slave past and the post-slavery present in Martinique, particularly amongst the servants who work for the *békés* on the route Didier. In *La Rue Cases-Nègres*, José describes these black servants at length, and expresses his revulsion at the lack of dignity which he observes in their desperation to please the white people they serve. For José, this impulse is one of alienation, and is an explicit denial of the servants' Négritude. In Paris, this is no longer the case. Carmen is convinced that his role of servitude does not negate his autonomous identity as a black man; it does not deprive him of his racial pride and human dignity in the way it did in Martinique.

As a working-class man with no formal education, Carmen's immediate concerns are material, and he does not offer or participate in any further discussions on race in the novel. Instead, Carmen has high hopes for his future in Paris, and participates fully in the capitalist dreams of the post-war era. His attention has recently been drawn to newspaper adverts for courses to become an 'agent-comptable' (accountant) (p. 23). These adverts promise him social advancement through a new kind of long-distance study which can be undertaken at home. As a working-class immigrant, he does not know anyone who is an accountant, and has no real sense of what the profession entails, but he is convinced that the opportunity could be transformative. Yet he has unwittingly been ensnared by another predominant aspect of the post-war capitalist machine: a marketing ploy. These qualifications are not provided by a state-run educational establishment, but by private, fee-paying schools. After sending off for further details, he is swamped with offers, in several rounds of aggressive marketing: 'On l'avait harcelé de lettres. On lui offrait maintenant une importante remise sur le montant des cours; on lui accordait des facilités de paiement' (They kept bombarding him with letters. Now they were offering him a large discount on the course fees; they were also offering an advantageous payment plan) (pp. 23–24). It is the monetary aspect of this study transaction which is underscored. Carmen can obtain his mail-order qualifications as long as he is willing and able to be a paying customer.

While Carmen appears energetic, decisive, and the master of his own destiny in this post-war capitalist society where skills and knowledge have become a commodity to be marketed, rather than being a more idealistic and noble end in themselves, in contrast, José is exhausted, hesitant, unsure of himself, and troubled by his new role as a student in a society whose codes he does not understand. Although he comes to Paris with the ambition to study for study's sake, José is listless and overwhelmed. Lost, he experiences 'encore la sensation d'être un grain de poussière emporté par le vent vers des atterrissements incertains' (the sensation, yet again, of being a speck of dust carried by the wind and cast down somewhere quite out of his control) (p. 24). His lack of conviction is symptomatic of his otherness, or, to put it another way, his extraordinariness. Once again, his aspirations are well beyond the usual scope for someone from his racial and social origins as a *petit-nègre*; denied the support of his Martinican family and friends, this leaves him isolated and disoriented.

Quand la neige aura fondu provides a rather sad coda to *La Rue Cases-Nègres*. Despite having successfully completed his secondary schooling, the crowning achievement of the first José Hassam novel, it emerges that in the years which have elapsed between the end of *La Rue Cases-Nègres* and the beginning of the sequel, José has experienced bitter disappointments. He was unsuccessful in applying for a modest administrative post in Martinique, which he describes in the following terms:

> une de ces petites places auxquelles peuvent accéder moyennant bien des renoncements, certains petits nègres, dont le mérite n'est pas seulement d'avoir échappé à la rue Cases-Nègres pour aller suivre l'école laïque. (p. 31)

> one of these small positions which might be available, after many sacrifices, to certain *petits-nègres* who had not only managed to escape from the *rue Cases-Nègres* to receive a Republican schooling, but had then risen even further.

José is coming to realise that education and qualifications alone are not enough. To rise through the ranks of the rigid French Caribbean social order will take additional feats of determination and sacrifice. Although he had demonstrated an abundance of these qualities, José's progress in Martinique was still blocked. The clear implication is that his *petit-nègre* origins and low position in the ethnoclass hierarchy still held the young man back, despite his educational successes.

In *Quand la neige aura fondu*, it is his failure to secure a relatively modest administrative position in Martinique which pushes José to emigrate and pursue a university education. José recalls his mother's conviction that he must go to university, because once this final educational hurdle was overcome, then 'personne ne pourrait dire qu'il n'y a pas de place pour toi ...' (nobody would ever be able to say that there isn't a position for you ...' (pp. 31–32). In an intentional parallel with Zobel's own life, José made his first attempt to emigrate before the outbreak of the Second World War. Despite his outstanding academic achievements, however, José was denied a colonial student bursary in the interwar years, because he unwisely revealed his dreams of studying architecture in Paris to the bursary committee. In Paris, José recounts this painful rejection to his Martinican friend Alexandre, commenting that when he told the committee chair that he wanted to be an architect, 'son indignation était telle que je fus presque convaincu d'avoir effectivement mal agi' (so great was his indignation, that I was almost convinced that I really had done something wrong) (p. 32). In interwar Martinican society, José's university scholarship application is rejected because his career aspirations are deemed incompatible with his *petit-nègre* ethnoclass identity. This episode resonates with comments Zobel made in interviews about this real event, particularly in Gallet and Makki's documentary film *Joseph Zobel: le soleil d'ébène*. The author, in his own words, was made to feel that it was nothing less than 'fou et scandaleux' (crazy and scandalous) for someone of his social extraction to aspire to becoming an architect (discussed in the Introduction to this study).

This rejection is a direct echo of an important scene in *La Rue Cases-Nègres*. At the beginning of Part Three, José's mother makes her first appearance. She erupts into the narrative by denouncing the decision to award her son only a partial high school scholarship to the Lycée Schœlcher as nothing other than a classist and racist attempt to deny *petits-nègres* access to an educational system which the black bourgeois and elite are determined to keep for themselves. In a further parallel, both novels document the attempts to induce the *petit-nègre* José to accept his inferior status, and he teeters on the brink of accepting and internalising this discrimination. Yet in both novels, José is almost convinced, but not quite. Almost browbeaten into admitting his place as a *petit-nègre*, but not quite.

José refuses to accept the narrow parameters in which Martinican society strives to enclose him as a *petit-nègre*. So much so that, as he relates in *Quand la neige aura fondu*, after several years spent teaching in Martinique, and a wartime administrative post, he applied for a scholarship for civil servants as soon as the war was over. José's trajectory to Paris is thus not so dissimilar to that of Carmen: both are working-class men from the *petit-nègre* class whose arrival in the capital is a direct result of the Second World War, albeit on different terms. The aftermath of this global catastrophe permitted a certain fluidity and movement which the rigid social and racial hierarchies of the pre-war era had previously denied.

The novel's publication history also reveals the surprisingly fluid publishing dynamics that were at work in post-war France. Zobel obtained a contract for *La Fête à Paris* from La Table ronde, a controversial publishing venture comprising both a review and a publishing house, the latter of which had been launched in 1944. A more usual choice might have been Jean Froissart, the publisher of *La Rue Cases-Nègres*. Yet, as I have discussed in the previous chapter, that publisher's wealthy owner had been greatly displeased that his employees had agreed to publish Zobel's novel, meaning that Jean Froissart was never a viable avenue for the sequel text.

Jean-Yves Mollier and Patrick Louis have demonstrated that following the Liberation of France, La Table ronde provided a publishing outlet for authors who had been blacklisted by the Conseil national des écrivains (National Council of Writers) due to accusations of collaboration or pacifism during the war.[20] The inclusion of a black Martinican author in a publisher with apparently pro-fascist sympathies would appear to be as much an anomaly as Zobel's involvement with Jean Froissart. It may also, however, signal a strategic shift in La Table ronde's immediate post-war direction: after the war had ended, its publications included the 1948 French translation of *Der Friede* (*Peace*) by Ernst Jünger, a book which testified to German resistance to Hitler.[21] The back cover of the 1953 edition of *La Fête à Paris* promotes other titles by La Table ronde by then up-and-coming authors and literary critics, such as Antoine Blondin, Pierre de Boisdeffre, André Brincourt, and Jean Freustié, as well as Paul Bodin's erotic *Les Amants du Theil* (*Theil's Lovers*) and *Le Dimanche musulman* (*The Muslim Sunday*) by G. M. Dabat. Dabat's title implies a cross-cultural focus on explaining Muslim traditions to metropolitan French readers, which might, broadly speaking, align his work with Zobel's novel. The focus on post-war Paris in Zobel's novel, and the fact that one prominent character is revealed to have worked for

---

20   See Patrick Louis, *La Table ronde: une aventure singulière* (Paris: La Table ronde, 1992), pp. 26–27; Jean-Yves Mollier, *Édition, presse et pouvoir en France au XXe siècle* (Paris: Fayard, 2008), p. 268.
21   Ernst Jünger, *La Paix*, trans. by Armand Petitjean and Banine (Paris: La Table ronde, 1948).

the French Resistance, might be other factors which led La Table ronde to favour its publication. Nonetheless, Zobel's inclusion in the catalogue remains unusual; all the more so given La Table ronde's later staunchly right-wing position on the Algerian War. Viewed against the wider context of Zobel's publications, however, it confirms a pattern of one-off contracts with a variety of publishing houses. Publishers in metropolitan France did not know what to make of Zobel, and he in turn struggled to find a 'natural' outlet for his novels.

Decades later, in 1979, *Quand la neige aura fondu* also appeared with what at the time was a small fledgling publishing house, Éditions caribéennes. Although the rewritten novel remains an engaging exploration of Caribbean immigration to post-war Paris, it is the least successful of Zobel's attempts to rewrite his earlier work. The rewritten passages comprise a combination of new inserted phrases, minor descriptive changes (for example, changing adjectives and adverbs), and substantial deletions. Although these changes do not impede the development of an individual's character arc (a problem which afflicts the character of Cocotte in the transition from *Les Jours immobiles* to *Les Mains pleines d'oiseaux*, discussed in Chapter Two), they do result in a number of narrative inconsistencies. For example, certain characters appear without any introduction in *Quand la neige aura fondu*, and yet are referred to as though they have played a role in the action – which they had indeed already done in *La Fête à Paris*. These narrative weaknesses indicate that the author himself became confused during the rewriting process. The publishing house's editorial team either failed to spot these inconsistencies, or left them unchallenged. Both possibilities are likely. An article in *Libération* in 1982 emphasised Éditions caribéennes's gratitude towards Zobel for supporting their new venture:

> Les 'grands' écrivains antillais déjà connus n'ont pas daigné apporter leur concours à cette entreprise, excepté Zobel, qui a compris la nécessité d'une maison d'édition antillaise pour la communauté.[22]
>
> The 'great' Antillean authors who were already well known did not deign to lend their support to this enterprise, apart from Zobel, who understood the need for an Antillean publishing house for the community.

Éditions caribéennes had only launched in 1978. In 1974, after Présence Africaine had obtained the publication rights for *La Rue Cases-Nègres*

---

22 Marie-France Ozée and Alex Carotine, 'Les Éditions caribéennes: comment me prouver que je suis Antillais?', *Libération*, 28 May 1982, p. 35.

– finally rescuing the novel from the obscurity in which it had languished for two decades – Zobel's star was once again in the ascendant. He was Éditions caribéennes's best-known author, and he provided one of their very first novels. This would explain their keen artistic and commercial interest in Zobel, and their willingness to publish a manuscript which in reality would have benefited from closer proofreading, and deeper dialogue between author and editor about Zobel's ambitions for his rewritten novel.

Despite these editorial inconsistencies, it is important not to downplay the significance of *Quand la neige aura fondu*. Zobel's original 1953 novel, a pioneering account of Antillean migration, had exhausted its print run and virtually disappeared. While Zobel lent his support to Éditions caribéennes in an important gesture of Caribbean solidarity, the publishing house in turn helped to ensure that this important, neglected novel about Caribbean migration to Paris was reissued, and could reach new audiences.

In a final significant publication detail, it is important to note that Zobel's last novel has borne three titles. The original working title, as announced by Zobel in a radio interview given in December 1952, was *L'Amertume que vous m'avez donnée* (*This Bitterness You Gave Me*).[23] This is a cryptic reproach; from the title alone, it is unclear which individual or group might have caused a feeling of bitterness. At some point in the intervening two months, Zobel changed his mind and the novel was published in February 1953 as *La Fête à Paris*. The decision to change the title repays further consideration. Read in the light of the two subsequent titles, the working title *L'Amertume que vous m'avez donnée* might be assumed to refer to the bitterness experienced by an immigrant who is disappointed by his reception in metropolitan France, and there is ample evidence of the mistreatment of immigrants in the text itself to support this reading.

It is more likely, however, that the bitterness to which the working title refers was actually caused by the poor treatment which Zobel had received in Martinican society, an important push factor that led emigrants to leave their native society. In his previous novel, *La Rue Cases-Nègres*, Zobel had documented the hardships and discrimination he had experienced from his own compatriots in Martinique

---

23 'Vente du livre de la mer et de l'outre-mer', RTF, dated 12 December 1952. L'INA. In *La Transgression des couleurs*, Roger Toumson also refers to this original title (p. 328).

due to his *petit-nègre* status. In an extension of this line of critique, it is Martinique's elite and bourgeoisie who appear to be targeted in the sequel. This, then, is the group which caused the bitterness that can still be detected throughout the narrative, despite the late change of title. It is this discrimination that makes José determined not to return to Martinique. There is a strong parallel here with the life and work of the Jamaican-British cultural theorist Stuart Hall, whose own struggles with Jamaica's ethnoclass hierarchy or pigmentocracy have been documented by critics. Grant Farred has argued that it was internal racism which triggered Hall's decision to leave Jamaica, commenting that 'the indigenous form of colonial racism was [...] a brand more potent and vituperative than its European variety'.[24] Such indigenous, vituperative racism is the cause of the bitterness to which Zobel's original title refers, and this invites a reading sensitive to the racism to which José Hassam was subjected long before leaving Martinique. The exposé of colonial racism in Martinique aligns what is otherwise a surprisingly different sequel more firmly with *La Rue Cases-Nègres*, and continues that text's excavation and excoriation of the Martinican ethnoclass hierarchy.

The novel begins and ends with transatlantic crossings, the first being José's emigratory journey, which is a largely maudlin affair. On arrival in Le Havre, José ensures that he is well attired, a common trope in the cultural representations of Caribbean emigration which aligns his image with the iconic images of the Caribbean passengers arriving aboard the *Empire Windrush* in the British port of Tilbury in Essex on 22 June 1948. For José, his clothing is a ritual, and a kind of armour, to better prepare himself to do battle with the French: 'José s'habillait comme pour une fête. Une fête ou un combat' (José had dressed to impress, as though he was off to a party. A party or a battle) (p. 14). This is an image which takes on its full significance in the light of the original title, *La Fête à Paris*. José's clothing is a conscious reflection of his mental preparations for the challenges of integrating into metropolitan society. Indeed, *La Fête à Paris* places great significance on metaphors of battles and games. Such metaphors occur at moments of significant racial tension, and offer Zobel an opportunity to reflect on the various forms which racism assumes in metropolitan France and in Martinique. In the opening pages, as José carefully dresses for his arrival in France on board

---

24 Grant Farred, 'You Can Go Home, You Just Can't Stay: Stuart Hall and the Caribbean Diaspora', *Research in African Literatures*, 27.4 (1996), p. 34.

the ship, the scene announces the novel's equation of emigration to the idea of a struggle and a fight. These metaphors of combat are crucial to understanding Zobel's vision of Négritude, a theme to which I return later in this chapter, after undertaking a more thorough interrogation of how the author presents the experience of emigration.

Emigration and Differential Incorporation

The optimistic idealism and promise of Fanon's 'trouée d'air' (breath of fresh air) offered by metropolitan life away from a small colony gives way in *Quand la neige aura fondu* to a more circumspect understanding of what it means to live far from one's land of origin, and between two or more cultures. *Quand la neige aura fondu* is heavy with loss. There is the loss of a local native language, Creole, and the loss of friends and family, some of whom will die before the migrant has a chance to return. More generally, there is the loss of the country of origin, which is represented through metonymy-by-negation in the snow of the title, snow which suggests its very opposite: the Caribbean sunshine that the protagonist has left behind.

The novel depicts the migrant's struggles to adapt to the French climate at length, and excels in evoking the dismal Parisian winter which, in a nod to the 1979 title, lasts for no fewer than nine of the 13 chapters, drawing the reader into a European winter *sans fin*. Winter, of course, is a new season for José. For the first time, he is able to apply the Eurocentric knowledge which he learned during his French Caribbean schooling. On his windowpanes, he recognises the icy substance which sticks to his fingers as frost, an exotic word he had uncomprehendingly learned by rote through the pages of 'son livre de science' (his science textbook) in his home village of Petit-Bourg (p. 25). Whereas Zobel's other novels, all set in Martinique, are rich in descriptions of characters interacting with flora and fauna, in Paris there is scant space for nature. When it is present, it is horribly deformed and even menacing: 'Il n'y avait pas d'arbres, mais des rangées de potences le long des boulevards; José ne les regardait plus lorsqu'il marchait dans cet hiver qui n'en finissait pas' (These were not trees, but so many rows of gallows lining the boulevards; José no longer so much as glanced in their direction as he walked through this never-ending winter) (p. 103). José's gaze deliberately reverses a European perspective, and France itself is positioned as strange and other. The sense of depression is compounded by compelling descriptions of poorly heated rooms, murky daylight which is barely distinguishable from night, and a stove which is deemed so important that it is personified: 'Rougeaud ... C'est le père de tous les nègres ...' (Old Red ... The father of all Negroes) (p. 33). The stove is humorously ascribed a protective role for the black race; indeed, it is the focal point around which José and his Antillean friends huddle to exchange stories about their experiences in Paris.

Stuart Hall's concept of the Caribbean migrant's 'differential incorporation' into mainstream (British) society provides a helpful framework for understanding the challenges which José experiences.[25] Hall argues that the arriving Caribbean subjects constitute a group that is segregated within the culture of the subordinate working class. In particular, he notes, Caribbean immigrants were assigned substandard accommodation. Indeed, in Zobel's novel, trepidation and uncertainty about where José will live hang heavy in the opening chapters, when the new migrant is at his most vulnerable. Growing increasingly concerned about his personal accommodation crisis, José relies on racial solidarity and unburdens himself with uncharacteristic frankness to any black strangers he meets. This pays off when a black man he encounters in the Parisian *métro* suggests that José should enquire at the Foyer des étudiants d'Outre-Mer (Centre for Overseas Students). The black stranger, himself a student, has heard a rumour that 'le Ministère des Colonies vient de mettre à sa disposition quelques "maisons" désaffectées' (the Ministry of Colonies has just obtained several disused 'houses') (p. 38). Crucially, in a further marker of the new migrant's vulnerability, José is too naïve to understand the full cultural significance of the term *maisons*. He duly makes enquiries, and is delighted when the authorities assign him a room. On arrival, however, he discovers that his 'official' lodgings are in fact in a seedy hotel run by a woman suspected of being a backstreet abortionist, an episode which demonstrates the dynamics of differential incorporation at work.

José has his first experiences of metropolitan racism at these tawdry lodgings in Paris. He is not shown that there is a lift, despite his bulging suitcases – and is treated with a cold indifference. In contrast, white residents are received with fawning courtesy. The realisation that he is being treated differently suddenly reactivates his memory of the tales

---

25 Stuart Hall, Chas Critcher, Tony Jefferson, John Clarke, and Brian Roberts, *Policing the Crisis: Mugging, the State and Law and Order* (Basingstoke: Palgrave Macmillan, 2013 [1978]), p. 344.

of the racism which Martinican soldiers had encountered during the Second World War:

> Des soldats, qui étaient revenus de France après la guerre, lui avaient affirmé, en Martinique, que les Français n'aimaient pas les nègres. 'D'ailleurs, presque partout où nous passions, les gens nous accusaient d'avoir quitté notre pays pour venir nous battre chez eux, alors qu'ils ne voulaient pas la faire, cette guerre-là'. (p. 41)

> Soldiers who had come back from France to Martinique after the war had told him that the French did not like Negroes: 'And pretty much everywhere we went, people accused us of having deserted our own country to come and fight in theirs, even though they themselves didn't want to fight this here war'.

The narrative does not use the term *racisme*, and this reflects José's own naïve confusion at what is happening. He, too, will need more experience in Paris before he can assert with confidence that such incidents are manifestations of racism, and that they indicate the very real divisions between certain groups of French citizens, while giving the lie to narratives of French republican unity. These moments and tensions are examples of Hall's differential incorporation at work.

For example, the street where José is lodged is initially described as 'une petite rue tranquille' (a small, quiet street) (p. 38). This is, however, a deliberate narrative ploy which presents the hotel through José's naïve, exhausted, and relieved eyes. Only later does the novel provide the street's name: and then it emerges that through the intervention of the official colonial administration, José has been lodged in the rue Joubert, a Paris street renowned for prostitution, even to the present day. The *maison* is shorthand for the French term *maison close*, or 'closed house', a euphemism for a brothel. José's vulnerability and ignorance of Paris have been exploited by the French authorities, as summed up by his Martinican friend Alexandre, who exclaims: 'c'est dans une rue de retape et dans un bordel qu'ils t'ont envoyé, tes types du Ministère!' (those chaps from the Ministry have sent you to live in a brothel in a red-light district!) (p. 60). The phrase hangs heavy with the suggestion of a betrayal of the very French republican values which had encouraged José's optimism and belief in the prospect of a better life through immigration to France. The depiction of racism in the novel is nuanced through intersectionality, however. The racism of the hotel staff in the rue Joubert is presented as a symptom of the depravity of a section of French society which is marked out as being a degenerate underclass, the 'subordinate working class' to which Hall refers. Down at heel and engaged in illegal activities, the dispossessed working-class white French staff at the hotel derive a perverse pleasure from the arrival of a new group over which they can assert cultural superiority, for the first time.

José's girlfriend, an enigmatic white French woman named Marthe, provides a far more positive example of metropolitan attitudes towards other groups. The character of Marthe is perhaps the most significant way in which José Hassam's life deviates strongly from Zobel's own experiences, for at the time of writing, Zobel was married to Enny, a black Martinican woman, and the couple had three young children. As the author's daughter and granddaughter have proposed in their own study of his work, José may well be 'a projection of the young man Zobel would have liked to have been when he came to France, unshackled by family responsibilities and free from the sense of guilt and remorse Zobel evidently felt in leaving his young family behind'.[26] While every day in Paris is a struggle for survival for José, he is not afflicted by the crippling guilt that Zobel experienced in being torn 'between his love of writing and the necessity to provide for his family'.[27]

Marthe is one of the most significant characters in the novel. She serves as a reminder that both black and white people can endure horrific suffering, and have done, and she symbolises the potential for all races to experience abject, horrendous brutality. This point was utterly pertinent in the novel's original post-war Parisian context. A quiet and self-contained young woman, towards the novel's close, it emerges that Marthe was in the French Resistance and, having been captured, was deported to Ravensbrück. In her longest dialogue in the novel, in which she finally opens up to José, she recalls how, in the Nazi camp, a terrible tension and hostility arose between the female prisoners. In hindsight, she ascribes this to the fact that they had been utterly dehumanised: 'Nous étions dénaturées. Nous n'avions plus nos règles; les cheveux ni les ongles ne poussaient plus. [...] Nous étions traitées comme des bêtes; nous étions devenues des bêtes' (We were denatured. We stopped having our periods, and our hair and nails no longer grew. [...] We were treated like animals; we became animals) (pp. 126–28). This significant account of processes of dehumanisation, in which humans lose their dignity as an inevitable result, creates clear parallels with the dehumanisation of black people under slavery. Marthe, a troubled but courageous young woman,

---

26 Zobel and Marshall Zobel, p. 5.
27 Zobel and Marshall Zobel, p. 5.

is a character whose insertion demonstrates that terrible suffering can be inflicted on anyone, regardless of race. Here is a white French woman who has known fear, starvation, and abject suffering. Moreover, she has experienced first-hand what it means to be suddenly and brutally stripped of her status as a human being by fascist authorities. Indeed, the novel also opens with José befriending a Jewish man returning to France from exile in Brazil (discussed in detail below). The narrative strongly urges that the historical event of the Second World War is indicative of the potential for authoritarian governments to inflict untold harm on any groups of individuals, regardless of skin pigment. In this manner, *Quand la neige aura fondu* juxtaposes the suffering of transatlantic slavery with this modern French trauma of the Holocaust, and subtly argues for the unification of oppressed peoples of all races in the aftermath of the war. Zobel was always wary of politics, particularly in the post-war years; in 1947, he wrote to his friend Valbrun, 'I don't believe in anything [...] politics will bring us the next war'.[28] Instead of proposing political solutions, the author is more content to imagine unification at a personal level, through lived experiences, as represented through the mixed-race relationship between José and Marthe which forms an understated backdrop to the novel. Far from being a couple which conforms to a model of Antillean desire for whiteness as depicted in other colonial works of the era, Zobel's novel presents a far more nuanced portrait of two young people who are gradually and tenderly brought together by their distinct, yet not dissimilar, experiences of suffering.

Cultural Capital

The previous chapter of this study argued for a new reading of *La Rue Cases-Nègres* as a novel in which Zobel's use of social realism resonates with a wider post-war metropolitan French use of social realism in literature. In my analysis, I turned to Kristin Ross and her study of how, in the post-war era, social realism becomes a mode with which to emphasise the double vision of modernity, and to give voice to an extraordinary historical moment which was at once conscious of past ways of living and of new patterns being introduced by a rapidly industrialising future. Ross shows that this startling double vision gives

---

28 Letter to Valbrun 7 May 1947, cited in Zobel and Marshall Zobel, p. 28.

rise to moments of exhilaration and fatigue in post-war social realist fiction, a hypothesis which forms the analytical framework for my rereading of *La Rue Cases-Nègres*. In *Quand la neige aura fondu*, Zobel continues to document the paradoxes of modernity, in all its exhilaration, contrasts, and inequalities. While the narrative styles differ, he employs the same transcultural and transnational social realist mode which he had pioneered in *La Rue Cases-Nègres*; that is to say, he seeks to make a culturally specific set of experiences accessible to audiences in a way that transcends barriers of culture and nationality.

Quand la neige aura fondu also unmistakably continues the exploration of the intersectionality of race and class that runs through *La Rue Cases-Nègres*, and the sequel includes a remarkable juxtaposition of working-class and middle-class perspectives on post-war Paris. Zobel's final novel is a fascinating study of how José sets about acquiring what the French sociologist Pierre Bourdieu would later identify in his seminal 1979 work *La Distinction* as 'le capital culturel' (cultural capital).[29] Bourdieu's theory posits the existence of cultural capital in three states: *l'état incorporé* or *embodied*, such as knowledge; *l'état objectivé* or *objectified*, such as possessions; and *l'état institutionnalisé* or *institutionalised*, such as qualifications with national or international valence. Bourdieu argues that individuals acquire cultural capital from very different starting points, and so it is a framework with which to understand disparity of achievement. Cultural capital itself feeds into social capital as it creates a group of people who share the same constellations of knowledge, and even economic capital, as these groups may work together. This capital also confers a self-assurance or confidence, or indeed arrogance, upon the bearer. Bourdieu's three states of cultural capital – embodied, objectified, and institutionalised – are all in evidence in Zobel's novel; moreover, all three become further complicated through the introduction of racial identity, which exerts an influence on each category as José constructs what can be understood as his own racial capital.

The most significant category of cultural capital in *Quand la neige aura fondu*, particularly when read against the material poverty of *La Rue Cases-Nègres*, is objectified capital. In that earlier novel, José's grandmother M'man Tine's possessions are contained in a small shack, and this cycle of material poverty is repeated by her daughter Délia in

---

29   Pierre Bourdieu, *La Distinction: critique sociale du jugement* (Paris: Minuit, 1979).

her own shanty town home in a converted shipping container. In *La Rue Cases-Nègres*, it is the route Didier which represents the nexus of objectified cultural capital. *Quand la neige aura fondu* moves the gaze to consider the Parisian bourgeoisie, a group which provides the example *par excellence* of the objectified cultural capital which José and his family so keenly lack. Early in the novel, José is invited to spend his first Christmas in Paris with a white French family. The family live in the *commune* (town) of 'Villemonble', a thinly disguised rendering of the *commune* of Villemomble which lies some 12 kilometres east of central Paris. The head of the family, André Dorgenne, is an architect, as is his son-in-law Jacques Favier. This pattern of intergenerational repetition conforms to the model of an 'endlessly self-reproducing' new middle-class in the post-war era, as proposed by Ross.[30] It simultaneously reinforces the fact that José is positioned far outside of this self-reproducing middle-class professional model and, most poignantly, serves as a reminder that his desired access to this *milieu* was explicitly barred by the Martinican scholarship committee. The novel derives heightened pathos and dramatic irony from this brief episode in Villemonble, because architecture was the dream profession of José Hassam, and indeed of Zobel himself. The articulation of this dream, however, drew the strongest reprobation from the Martinican colonial authorities in the infamous episode in which José/Zobel is denied a scholarship.

While André Dorgenne shows José his office, the apparently neutral narrative tone is in fact deliberately sparse, inviting the reader to consider the chasm – or cultural capital deficit – which separates José from Dorgenne. The older man talks José through a collection which represents the immeasurable objectified cultural capital acquired by his family, over several centuries:

> des bibelots, des souvenirs de famille, des armes anciennes, des miniatures, un assignat encadré sous verre ainsi qu'une lettre autographe d'un soldat du Second Empire.
> — Elle est de mon arrière-grand-père qui était un Cent-Gardes … (p. 57)
>
> trinkets, family souvenirs, centuries-old weapons, miniatures, an *assignat* banknote [dating from the French Revolution] in a glass frame as well as a handwritten letter from a soldier under the Second Empire.
>   'The letter is from my great-grandfather, who was in the *Cent-gardes* Squadron' [an elite cavalry corps of the Second French Empire].

---

30 Ross, p. 137.

These personal treasures and the wider networks of power in which they are situated continue to procure social advantages for their owner. Dorgenne relates how, on a trip to Alsace, the mere mention of his surname won him the admiration of the local people, who were familiar with the story of his illustrious ancestor (p. 57). Significantly, his cultural capital is directly connected to a secure knowledge of filiations and provenance. In the colonial context, dominated and subjugated peoples were systematically robbed of this very knowledge through transatlantic deportation and plantation slavery. As narrated in *La Rue Cases-Nègres*, José's knowledge of his own family tree extends to his maternal grandfather, named as M. Valbrun, who raped his grandmother M'man Tine in the cane fields, and ends with his great-grandfather, who was a *béké* and therefore also occupied a position of racial superiority and sexual dominance over his black maternal great-grandmother. In the scene in Dorgenne's office, the narrative silence at this show of wealth and lineage reflects José's stupefaction. It also firmly implies, in line with Ross's self-reproducing model, that this is the kind of environment in which professional elites, symbolised here by architects, can develop and thrive. In the office, José is confronted with a smorgasbord of objectified cultural capital and, at this early point in the text, it stands as a stark reminder of all that he lacks.

Dorgenne's personal *cabinet de curiosités* (cabinet of curiosities) does not elicit any specific narrative comment. Yet a number of stylistic devices convey José's personal distance from this bourgeois setting. He is figured as detached and separate from the main action, and becomes a spectator or voyeur to the family as they make arrangements around him:

> Par la fenêtre de la cuisine, José les voit marquer la neige de leurs pas et avec les roues du landau, puis s'arrêter, se parler, se séparer, comme dans un film muet. (p. 55)

> Through the kitchen window, José can see them as they make traces in the snow with their steps and the wheels of the pram: he watches them stop, speak to each other and then move apart, as though in a silent movie.

José is mute, passive, and separated from this happy scene by panes of glass, while the secure white European family unit is active and self-assured. It is they who make an imprint in the snow, and who hold the bourgeois signs of future prosperity, of which the ultimate symbol is the pram which contains their infant child, born into this self-replicating cycle of success. Even the family's Christmas tree, a common European object, is a rare luxury to José. The material opposition between him and the family is now highlighted more explicitly, as he is enraptured by the spectacle of the tree being decorated. He chooses to watch in silence:

> afin de mieux jouir, pour la première fois, de la création, sous ses yeux, d'un arbre de Noël. Car il n'y a pas eu d'arbre de Noël dans son enfance sans étrenne et sans anniversaire. (p. 55)

> all the better to enjoy, for the first time, the process of decorating a Christmas tree, here, right before his very eyes. For there had been no Christmas trees in his own childhood, which had been unencumbered by New Year gifts or birthday presents.

The narrative's gentle but eloquent insistence on the lack of material objects, or objectified cultural capital, in José's life – Christmas trees, birthday gifts, not to mention heirlooms providing a tangible familial link with major historical events – provides the frame through which the detailed description of the architect's office is to be read. The simple symbol of the Christmas tree is a measure of the *décalage*, the gap or abyss, which separates José from the European bourgeois culture which the Dorgenne family take for granted. The narrative contrasts opulence with poverty and encourages the reader to consider the inverse of these European scenes – the office, the front garden, the Christmas tree. Indeed, these scenes act rather like a photographic negative: the true emphasis is not on the actual objectified capital being displayed and described, but on the distinct lack of objectified capital which it implies for José Hassam himself.

Throughout the novel, José is watching, observing, and learning. By its close, he has started to get to grips with the codes of western society, and this is most visibly symbolised by his actual gain in objectified cultural capital. Now, his once-bare student room is decorated with books and images:

> Les murs ponctués de photographies de masques nègres, de gravures. Tout ce qui s'est accumulé pendant trois ans et que, pendant trois ans, José a rangé, dérangé, pour avoir plus de place, plus de clarté, et qui, dans son eurythmie a composé de lui une sorte d'autoportrait. (pp. 134–35)

> The walls were dotted with photographs of Negro masks and engravings. Everything that he had accumulated over three years and that, in those three years, José had arranged and rearranged, to free up space, or let in more light. The whole unpredictable and clashing mix formed a kind of self-portrait of him.

These objects and images are tangible manifestations of José's new urban sophistication and cultural cosmopolitanism. Moreover, he has begun to use cultural capital to construct and consolidate his racial identity in a material extension of his Négritude which displays or stages his desire to reconnect with the lost continent of Africa (and, indeed, anticipates – or from the perspective of the rewritten text, echoes – his move to Africa in 1957). The photographs of Negro masks proclaim his interest, and pride, in his racial heritage, and are evidence of his desire to project aspects of his personality through his décor, an idea which has assumed ever-greater prominence in post-war modern societies in the western world. Moreover, they are representative of the essential connections between Négritude and visual culture, particularly the rediscovery of Negro Art in the late interwar years and during the Second World War. This is exemplified by Cuban artist Wifredo Lam, in whose work the motif of the Negro Mask assumed great prominence in this period. Lam was a close associate of the French surrealists who influenced Césaire's Négritude, and was himself a direct influence on Césaire.

José's time in Paris also endows him with new knowledge and institutional awareness which constitutes significant embodied and institutionalised cultural capital. The novel includes a meticulous level of detail about the places and locations José visits, and the institutional networks of which he becomes a part, such as the Institut d'ethnologie; the Sorbonne; the Musée de l'Homme; the Foyer des étudiants d'Outre-Mer (Centre for Overseas Students); the Maison des Lettres (House of Letters), an impressive house on the rue Férou which became a centre for Parisian students of literature and the arts in the post-war era; the Musée des Colonies; and the Maison de la Mutualité, the headquarters of a federation of non-profit mutual insurers which is also a well-known conference, concert, and seminar centre, often used to hold important meetings of national political parties, and public concerts. Through his wider network of friends, José learns about the Faculté de droit (Faculty of Law) and the Institut des hautes études cinématographiques (Institute for Cinematography) (p. 83), and becomes aware of the cultural heritage of the city where he is now based, including a litany of actors and avant-garde artists and composers who had been the toast of turn-of-the-century Paris, such as Bartet, Mounet-Sully, Sylvain, Ravel, and Marie Laurencin (p. 93).

Embodied cultural capital is now his. José has acquired confidence as he has gained physical, spatial knowledge of these places and where they are located, and, more significantly, he now feels able to pass judgement on these institutions and the roles which they fulfil. As he acquires this knowledge, he apprehends it from a perspective which complicates Bourdieu's theories of cultural capital by introducing a racially aware perspective, as represented by the objectified capital of Negro masks. Those moments at which cultural capital and race intersect become examples of what can be termed 'racial capital', and in *Quand la neige aura fondu*, this inflects all three of Bourdieu's original categories, most significantly institutionalised and embodied capital. For example, the Musée de l'Homme is singled out for particular praise. An anonymous voice, which may be that of José, or one of his friends, remarks:

> Je dirais même que le terme de Musée est un peu vulgaire pour ce lieu. Il faudrait une désignation qui exprime le respect avec lequel chaque chose a été recueillie, rapportée, souvent de très loin, dans le but de faire connaître à l'humanité toute entière, chaque aspect de l'humanité; rien ici n'était pour satisfaire la superficielle curiosité ni pour officier une consécration à la célébrité. Une invitation à comprendre, admirer, respecter l'homme dans sa race et dans sa culture. (p. 78)

> I'd go as far as to say that the term 'museum' is too vulgar for the place. There should be another term which expresses the respect with which each item has been located and collected, often from distant regions, in the aim of presenting every aspect of humanity in such a way that it can be appreciated by all of humanity. Nothing was included merely to gratify superficial curiosity or to induce some kind of infamy. It was an invitation to understand, admire, and respect mankind through race and culture.

This museum displays and categorises different races and cultures in a manner which Zobel's black characters judge dignified and helpful to the advancement of positive knowledge about ethnic diversity. Despite such praise in the novel, the displays of non-white culture at the Musée de l'Homme have a controversial history. At the time when Zobel was writing *La Fête à Paris*, the exhibit of Sara Baartman's skeleton and plaster cast 'greeted any visitor passing case 33 at the Musee de l'Homme'; indeed, this display of the remains of the woman who was objectified and exploited as the Hottentot Venus remained in place 'until the late 1970s'.[31] The Musée de l'Homme was inaugurated in 1938 and its organisation was intended to reflect the vision of the French ethnologist Paul Rivet, who believed 'l'humanité est un tout indivisible, non seulement

---

31   Sadiah Qureshi, 'Displaying Sara Baartman, the "Hottentot Venus"', *History of Science*, 42 (2004), p. 245. Baartman's remains were finally repatriated to South Africa in 2002.

dans l'espace, mais aussi dans le temps' (humanity is an indivisible whole, not only in space, but also in time).[32] In *Quand la neige aura fondu*, the unnamed speaker's praise for the respectful manner in which different cultures have been brought together at the museum has to be understood as a view of its time which neglects the specific racial and gendered violence inflicted on Baartman's dissected body, and the interpretative framework within which that body was placed on display. The exhibition was finally removed following a feminist campaign in the 1970s.[33]

In Zobel's novel, praise for the Musée de l'Homme, although problematic when appraised (in a necessarily anachronistic manner) by a contemporary reader, is not an indication of the author's uncritical acceptance of institutionalised French republican racism. It is actually included in the narrative to act as a foil, and to pass a strident and daring 1950s critique on another museum: the Musée des Colonies. This museum is rejected outright by the young black students as nothing more than an imperialist defence of colonial conquest and a thinly veiled defence of racism. The nationalist, imperialist nature of the museum is denounced in the strongest terms: 'Que de mensonges et d'infâmies!' (What lies and infamies!) (p. 78) in *Quand la neige aura fondu*. The original version, *La Fête à Paris*, went even further, as another anonymous young black speaker underscores this museum's binary, inferiorising, and imperial presentation of other cultures:

> Il est vrai que j'y étais allé surtout pour voir ce qu'entre eux, ils pensent de nous. Or je n'aime pas ce mémorandum impudent de leurs 'victoires' sur nous autres qu'ils ont souillés de tous les maux et des épithètes les plus infâmes. (p. 117)

> It's true that I went there mainly to see what they really think of us, among themselves. Well, I didn't appreciate this impudent account of their 'victories' over us, nor did I appreciate how they have sullied us with all manner of outrageous slurs.

The Musée des Colonies, located in the Palais de la Porte dorée which was built for the World Fair of 1913, was from its construction intended to be a paean to French colonialism. Zobel's final novel, in both its forms, offers an audacious challenge to the official French

---

32 Paul Rivet quoted by the Musée de l'Homme. See: http://www.museedelhomme.fr/fr/musee/histoire-musee-homme/creation-musee-homme-1937 (accessed 5 November 2015).
33 Qureshi, p. 246.

public repository of colonial memory, as the museum is decried by black students as a repulsive project of colonial propaganda. The name used in the novel is anachronistic; between 1935 and the end of the 1950s, it was actually called the Musée de la France d'Outre-Mer. The fact that José and his friends still use the older name, which is more transparently imperialist, might suggest that the museum's vision (and reputation) had not changed, even if its new name appeared to be progressive. This building's relationship with the colonial period endures into the present era. The Palais de la Porte dorée has, since 2007, been the location of the Cité nationale de l'histoire de l'immigration, a major museum of immigration.

For all his growing cultural capital, José does not attain the gold standard of institutionalised capital: a university degree from an elite institution. Although he frequents the Sorbonne and the Institut d'ethnologie, and he passes several exams, he refuses to make a degree his main goal. In the original 1953 novel, José discusses his lack of academic success with a youthful flippancy, commenting with pride that he is different from his student peers: 'Par mon non-conformisme à la vie universitaire d'abord. Parce que, somme toute, je suis et m'efforce d'être un amateur' (In my non-conformism to university life, first and foremost. Because, all in all, I am, and go to great pains to be, an amateur) (p. 218). No trace of this juvenile boast remains in the 1979 rewritten novel, however, in which José sighs: 'Je perds mon temps à Paris' (I am wasting my time in Paris), prompting the narrator to comment, 'Au demeurant, il n'était pas satisfait de l'amateurisme volontaire avec lequel il menait ses études' (Moreover, his deliberately amateur approach to his studies left him dissatisfied) (p. 130). José fails to become truly integrated into the Parisian elite educational system, much as he failed to become fully integrated into the Lycée Schœlcher in Martinique. He remains an outsider. Yet it is precisely this difference and external viewpoint which enables him to retain a critical distance from major institutions, and, more importantly, to develop, quite independently, his own analytical understanding of race and Négritude.

Négritude: At Home and Away

In 1950, Zobel gave a radio interview for the programme *Ondes courtes* (*Short Wave*) to mark the publication of *La Rue Cases-Nègres* and to celebrate its new status as winner of the Prix des lecteurs. He was asked directly by a radio presenter whether he had experienced racism in metropolitan France. Zobel's answer is illuminating, and bears reproduction:

> Personnellement pas. Quand on écoute les discussions à la Chambre concernant les colonies, on devient un peu inquiet. On se demande si, au point de vue politique, il n'y a pas des préjugés, certains complexes qui règlent, dictent certaines mesures. Mais dans la vie, les rapports entre individus, je crois qu'il est peut-être difficile de trouver des manifestations flagrantes de racisme.
>
> Personally, no. When you listen to the discussions in the *Chambre* [French Parliament] about the colonies, it is rather concerning. You start to wonder whether, from a political perspective, there are certain prejudices and complexes which decide and dictate certain measures. But in everyday life, in the relationships between individual people, I think that it might be more difficult to find flagrant examples of racism.

Zobel's initial response to this pointed question is to deflect its invitation to divulge personal information about his own experiences of racism, by offering criticism of the racism which he detects in political discussions of the 'colonies'. (At the time of the interview, there were no longer any Caribbean colonies as the 1946 Loi de la départementalisation had come into force on 1 January 1947, which suggests that Zobel may have had colonies in Africa or Indochina in mind.) Returning to his personal interactions, the author offers the opinion that racism in France is not flagrant; yet his tentative wording is heavy with the implication that racism is present, and that it actually takes more insidious, covert forms. At this, the presenter seizes the opportunity to lecture the young author on the inclusive and enlightened model of equality which, to his mind, the French Republic embodies:

> Je crois qu'en France, le problème ne se pose pas, et que nous ne faisons jamais aucune différence entre les Français, quelle que soit leur couleur, quelle que soit leur appartenance, et c'est peut-être un des traits essentiels de la vie actuelle en France, cette égalité absolue entre tous les nationaux.[34]
>
> I believe that the problem does not exist in France, and that we never differentiate in the slightest between French people, whatever their colour, whatever their affinities, and this is probably one of the fundamental features of life today in France, this absolute equality between all French nationals.

34 'Joseph Zobel lauréat du prix des lecteurs'. L'INA.

This condescending intervention offers Zobel no opportunity to elaborate on any forms of racism in France, flagrant or subtle, without directly contradicting the zealous republican rhetoric of the radio presenter. Zobel responds by deflecting the comment, as follows:

> C'est peut-être aussi ... c'est certainement la raison pour laquelle tous les peuples de couleur, et en particulier les peuples de couleur de langue française, se trouvent chez eux en France, même plus à l'aise que dans leurs territoires d'origine.
>
> It is perhaps also ... it's certainly the reason why all peoples of colour, in particular the peoples of colour who speak French, find themselves at home in France, and even more at ease than in their countries of origin.

Rather than focus any further on racism in France, which the presenter has just asserted to be a categorical impossibility in the French Republic, Zobel skilfully turns his comment on its head. Although he tactfully leaves unchallenged the presenter's claim that racism is not a major issue in France, he also avoids agreeing outright with his statement. Instead, he uses the presenter's republican diatribe as an opportunity to pass comment on an area of racism of which the presenter almost certainly had no knowledge: racism in the land of origin. This interview encapsulates the racial tensions onto which the author will cast a spotlight in *Quand la neige aura fondu*, which repeatedly juxtaposes the subtle (and not-so-subtle) forms of racism which José encounters in Paris with a discussion of racism in Martinique. True to Zobel's individual use of Négritude throughout his career as a manner of excavating the socio-economic racial biases which formed the social structure of the Caribbean colonies, *Quand la neige aura fondu* seeks to denounce these local racisms in the strongest terms.

Zobel's final novel is a challenge to the French republican framework. If in 1950 he had been corralled into agreeing with the radio presenter's bold claim of racial harmony in the Republic, in 1953 *La Fête à Paris* explicitly calls this into question, and goes into great detail about the republic's failings towards its colonial citizens of colour. While staunch republicans might find comfort in the lack of flagrant racism in the text, the covert and insidious forms of racism which Zobel presents throughout the novel work to unsettle and challenge any claims to a united colour-blind republic. Nonetheless, as Zobel's 1950 radio interview suggests, discrimination in Martinique is the real push factor. This is what catalyses José's decision to emigrate to Paris.

The novel's opening, on board the ocean liner, immediately presents a deft sketch of the Martinican ethnoclass hierarchy, and of José Hassam's place within it. There is a reference to three or four *békés* who, most unusually, appear willing to leave the confines of first class, and to mingle with the black passengers. José's own dark skin tone is foregrounded when he is mistaken for a Guadeloupean, a mistake which he takes with good humour, joking that he is one of the rare Martinicans who have not been 'délayé' (diluted) (p. 8). More seriously, however, his racial difference within his own society is now signposted to the reader. From the outset, it is clear that the voyage itself carries not only geographic but also racial significance:

> Le bateau s'éloignait des terres coloniales, il semblait déjà que les nègres devenaient des hommes pareils aux autres, et les blancs rigoureusement conformes à l'image que les leçons d'Histoire de France inculquent aux petits enfants noirs. (p. 8)

> As the boat drew further away from colonial lands, it already seemed that Negroes were becoming men like any others, and the whites were conforming without exception to the image with which little black children are inculcated in their History lessons from France.

The idea of the Antillean ethnoclass hierarchy is thus deftly introduced, and any reader, regardless of their own cultural background, finishes the first chapter with an understanding that there is a pigmentocracy running from the white *békés* down to darker skin tones, and that José belongs to the latter group. All onboard seem to share the view that this journey represents a great levelling and a new beginning. The novel sets up a comparative perspective which suggests parallels between racial and religious persecution in the wake of the Second World War and the Holocaust, as José befriends Gaston Chiminder, a Jewish refugee who is returning from wartime exile in Brazil, and who also sees the transatlantic crossing as the beginning of a new era for men such as himself in Europe. Both José and Gaston hope that as members of oppressed groups whose humanity has previously been denied, by colonialism and Nazism respectively, they will find in post-war metropolitan France a society in which they are finally treated with equality. For the black passengers in particular, there is a real optimism that their arrival in Europe will liberate them from the racial prejudices which structure the colonies. This process is couched in terms which allude to René Maran's semi-autobiographical novel *Un homme pareil aux autres* (*A Man Like Any Other*), about a black man who strives for acceptance in white society. As this work appeared in 1947, just six years before Zobel published *La Fête à Paris*, the timely allusion would not have been lost on his original audience. Maran's initial support for Zobel had helped him to publish *Diab'-là* in France; the subsequent withdrawal of this support – Maran did not like *La Rue Cases-Nègres*, and refused to endorse its publication – was a snub which Zobel felt keenly (discussed in the previous chapter). The subtle allusion to his one-time patron may also have been an attempt to show deference to, and build bridges with, Maran.

José is adamant that he has come to Europe to '[m]'affranchir des tabous et des préjugés de chez nous' (emancipate myself from the taboos and prejudices of back home) (p. 33). In the original 1953 novel, the psychological and racial harm inflicted on José in Martinique is stated as a catalyst for emigration in more forceful terms: 'J'ai besoin de me désintoxiquer, de me vider de tous les miasmes dont les Antilles m'ont infecté et contre lesquels l'accoutumance ne m'a pas immunisé' (I need to detoxify myself, and purge myself of all the miasmas with which the Antilles have infected me, and to which I am habituated, but not immune) (p. 49). Racial alienation is analysed in the narrative as a medical, psychopathological disease in terms highly reminiscent of Fanon's *Peau noire, masques blancs*, which had been published in Paris just one year before *La Fête à Paris* (it is quite possible that Zobel was aware of Fanon's text when he was completing his novel in 1952, although he does not directly refer to it).[35]

Indeed, of all the changes and omissions which occur between the two versions, the most significant difference is Zobel's decision to tone down the repeated references in *La Fête à Paris* to Martinican citizens as suffering from a 'complexe d'infériorité' (inferiority complex) in *Quand la neige aura fondu*. Again, Zobel's careful discussion in 1953 of this phenomenon is reminiscent of Fanon's own diagnosis of the intense alienation of the colonial subject: a subject who has been inculcated with French culture and a belief that he is French, but who arrives in the

---

35 I have not located any archival evidence that Zobel knew Fanon, although it seems highly likely that in Paris or in Martinique, Zobel would have had some awareness of his work. However, Zobel's words here develop the comments made in his 1946 essay 'Considérations sur l'art local' (discussed at length in Chapter 3). Zobel's thinking on the psychopathology of racial alienation is most likely to have been strongly influenced by the articles in *Tropiques*, the literature of the Negro Renaissance, particularly McKay's *Banjo* (which criticises black French colonial subjects who seek assimilation into French society and deny their racial origins), and his own personal experiences.

métropole to discover the racial and cultural paradoxes, contradictions, and denials upon which his own identity has been formed. The idea that Martinicans suffer from a 'complexe d'infériorité' is a leitmotif in both versions of Zobel's final novel. For example, in *Quand la neige aura fondu* Alexandre remarks that José is likely to end up in arguments with the metropolitan French from time to time, as there are some French who think that 'par nous, la France ternit plus ou moins l'éclat de sa blancheur' (through us, France is more or less tarnishing its dazzling whiteness) (p. 34). Yet, for Alexandre, it is not José's skin colour but his 'peau orgeuilleuse' (proud skin) (p. 34) that will lead to challenging situations, as it means that José will rise to the occasion and fight back when he encounters racist discourse, precisely because, as Alexandre notes, José does not have a 'complexe d'infériorité' (p. 34). José's own personal Négritude manifests as his staunch pride in his racial identity, a factor so significant that it is recognised by his peers – be they Antillean or white – as quite exceptional.

In a later passage in *Quand la neige aura fondu*, another black Martinican character, Maurice, expresses his admiration for the Senegalese because they do not have any complexes, a comment he quickly qualifies as follows: 'Pas de complexe d'infériorité, en tout cas' (No inferiority complex, at least) (pp. 122–23). The implication is that while Martinicans struggle to accept their black racial identity – their Négritude – because of the complex centuries-old history of colonialism and slavery, in Senegal, where French colonialism was a different phenomenon, and plantation slavery was not the dominant social structure, black people were more comfortable with, and saw no reason to deny, their Négritude.

Why might José have been spared this inferiority complex? Or rather, how has he succeeded in overcoming the prevailing psychological malaise which afflicts the vast majority of black, socially mobile Martinicans? The reason is evident in both versions of the novel: as a lowly *petit-nègre*, José has battled all his life against the Martinican ethnoclass hierarchy, and this has led him to develop, from a very young age, his own critical reflections on the racism which pervades Martinique. He is, as noted in *Quand la neige aura fondu*, already exceptionally adroit at detecting racial prejudice in the Antilles:

> L'habileté de Joseph Hassam à déceler les préjugés de couleur aux Antilles était grande. Rompu à toutes les nuances de leur manifestation, il pouvait se vanter de la sûreté de son flair à les localiser, les analyser. (p. 77)

Joseph Hassam's skill for sensing the colour prejudices in the Antilles was finely tuned. Well acquainted with all the nuances with which they manifested themselves, he could boast of his flair for detecting and analysing them.

In the original novel, there is an additional clause which provides greater detail on how and why José has developed this instinct: 'à la longue la répétition des choses crée un instinct de défense infiniment subtil' (over time, the repetition of certain things creates an incredibly subtle defence instinct) (p. 116). José has developed a defensive reflex against the repeated incidents of racism which he had experienced in his own country. This defence mechanism operates to articulate José's pride in his identity as a *petit-nègre*. Although he can appraise, not without horror, the abject suffering and paltry opportunities of the *petits-nègres*, and although his education has set him on quite a different course, he cannot bring himself to turn his back on his humble roots. This is an intrinsic aspect of José's – and Zobel's – own variant of Négritude, in which racial awareness always intersects with an awareness of class. José is secure enough in his own identity as a *petit-nègre* to recognise that the poverty in which his family and friends still live is not a sign of their inherent inferiority; it has been constructed by an unjust colonial order, and inflicted on them.

Other immigrants' reminiscences of Martinique are similarly tainted by the painful memory of the ethnoclass hierarchy. Pauline is a Martinican woman suffering from severe psychological difficulties. She, José, and some friends go to the well-known Paris *bal nègre* (Negro Ball) in the rue Blomet, a night club which symbolises the acceptance – and indeed fetishisation – of certain kinds of black culture by the fashionable Parisian nightlife scene. For white Parisians, this club offers the promise of exoticism and the unknown, in the comfort and safety of central Paris. For Pauline, however, an immigrant who has been away from Martinique for two decades, it is too much to bear. On the way home, she is overcome by loss and longing for her native island. She is gently warned by her Caribbean friends that she must stop this nostalgic reminiscing because she 'oublie ce que c'est' (is forgetting what it is) (p. 96): she is forgetting what it means to exist in a racist Caribbean society where your place is clearly defined, and controlled, by the colonial race-class hierarchy maintained by the *békés* and the black bourgeoisie. Yet Pauline refuses, with a stubbornness which belies her mental turmoil, to believe that the situation in the Antilles cannot have changed and evolved:

> Oui, mais les choses ont dû changer, réplique Pauline sur un ton plaintif. Il y a eu la guerre, et tout le reste. Les *békés* sont peut-être plus aussi arrogants; d'ailleurs, je me suis laissée dire qu'ils envoient leurs enfants au lycée, maintenant. C'est donc plus comme au temps où, plutôt que de fréquenter l'école laïque, ils auraient préféré ne pas apprendre à lire et à écrire. Et puis, l'île va devenir un département français. Dans un département, tout de même ... (pp. 96–97)

> 'Yes, but things must have changed', Pauline replies in a plaintive tone. 'There has been a war, and all the rest. Perhaps the *békés* are no longer as arrogant; besides, I've heard that they are now sending their children to school at the *lycée*. So it's no longer how it was back in the days when they would have preferred to remain illiterate rather than set foot in the republican schools. And what's more, the island's about to become a French Department. In a Department, after all, ...

Pauline's speech reminds the reader of the *békés'* essential traits: they enjoyed almost total control over the French Caribbean colonies, and were notorious for despising the French Republic. Having remained elitist monarchists, they avoided secular schools, in a snub to egalitarian republican values of equality. Pauline hopes that in the current era things will change, particularly after the Second World War, and in the light of the administrative change represented by impending departmentalisation (which came into effect on 1 January 1947). Her words express the political hopes of the black Martinican population at this turning point in the island's history; more generally, she represents the turmoil of long-term immigrants, rendered weary from struggles in a new city and caught between two cultures.

Pauline's extreme mental turmoil echoes the real-life cases which Zobel documented in his personal letters. He wrote of Antilleans he knew who were repeatedly hospitalised in Paris due to immigration-induced depression.[36] *Quand la neige aura fondu* investigates the dynamics and forces at work on black immigrants in uncompromising detail: black people find that they must not only wear their black skin with modesty, but must also adhere to unrealistic and idealistic social standards. The novel exposes those white people who believe that they are not racist because they are prepared to accept the presence of black people among them, but only if these groups uphold exceptional standards:

---

36 Zobel Marshall and Zobel, p. 29.

Ils nous souffrent parmi eux à condition que nous leur soyons reconnaissants et que nous fassions preuve à tout instant de trois à quatre fois plus de qualités que les meilleurs d'entre eux. Malgré cela, les meilleurs d'entre eux gardent, avec toute la sympathie qu'ils puissent nous témoigner, la conviction que notre mentalité est primitive, que nous sommes vulnérables à la plus légère pression et que tout ce que nous pourrions posséder ou acquérir est susceptible de s'écrouler à la moindre épreuve. (p. 77)

They tolerate us among them as long as we are grateful and demonstrate, at all times, an abundance of good qualities – three or four times more than the best men among them. Despite all that, the best men among them remain convinced, for all the kindness that they might profess towards us, that our mentality is primitive, that we are susceptible to the slightest persuasion, and that anything we are capable of possessing or acquiring is quite likely to crumble at the first sign of difficulty.

These (double) standards are critiqued by an unnamed voice which is attributed to an immigrant who has spent two decades in Paris. The speaker comments that for all their declarations of equality – calling to mind, once again, the pompous declaration by the white French *Ondes courtes* radio presenter to Joseph Zobel himself – white people do not truly see black people as equals; they tolerate them, as long as they remain obliging and servile. The black citizen in France must adhere to a set of white expectations in order to be accepted, and even then there is an underlying assumption of an inherent weakness and susceptibility to cave in under the slightest pressure. In the narrative, this is suggested by the loaded word 'primitive', which evokes the colonial era and thinkers like Gobineau, whose theories of racial inferiority were used to justify the colonial venture. As *Quand la neige aura fondu* demonstrates, the black immigrant in Paris is anything but weak, and must draw on incredible strength. He or she is placed under the constant and conflicting pressures of the need to adapt to a new culture and to quell any melancholy for the lost land of origin, while simultaneously confronting endemic racial bias.

Through a series of portraits of individual immigrants, some of whom are black Caribbean while others are Vietnamese, Eastern European, Algerian, and sub-Saharan African, the novel casts a spotlight onto the metropolitan experiences of a wide range of marginalised groups, and the racism which they encounter. While racist individuals receive short shrift, so too does institutional racism. This is exemplified by an incident at the Institut d'ethnologie. To José's dismay, during an academic lecture, 'le professeur de physiologie avait insinué que la capacité respiratoire du nègre, plus faible que celle du blanc, est une des preuves de l'infériorité de la race noire!' (the physiology lecturer had insinuated that the Negro's respiratory capacity was weaker than that of the white man, which was further proof of the inferiority of the black race!) (p. 78). That a university lecturer teaching in one of the most prestigious institutions in France could openly make such a claim and go quite unchallenged, demonstrates the extent of the difficulties faced by José, and by immigrants more generally. This racist discourse leaves the three black students in the lecture theatre in shock: 'Hassam et les deux autres nègres de l'auditoire, un Haïtien et un Togolais, s'étaient regardés sans rien dire, avec le sentiment d'avoir été victimes d'une trahison ou d'un abus de confiance' (Hassam and the two other Negroes in the lecture theatre, a Haitian and a Togolese, looked at each other in silence, feeling that they had just been victims of a betrayal or an abuse of trust) (pp. 78–79). The sense of betrayal shared by these men underscores their previous faith in the French republican education system. Yet, to their dismay, even after the genocides of the Second World War this system is still disseminating racist propaganda as scientific fact.[37] The pseudo-scientific argument that black peoples' respiratory system differs from that of white people, and is inherently weaker, originated in the nineteenth century in America to support the claim that 'blacks [in America] should be returned to Africa, where the warm climate better suited them'.[38] This discourse was based on flawed scientific data which had recorded higher occurrences of illness and death from tuberculosis and other infectious diseases in black populations. The studies did not acknowledge the poor living conditions or inadequate nutrition which underpinned these mortality rates.[39]

In the face of this institutionalised racism, José's reaction moves from stunned shock, to action. His response is to promote open dialogue between black and white people. At the professor's racist words, the white Frenchman sitting next to José turns to him and asks sardonically:

37 For a detailed discussion of French colonialism and scientific racism, see 'Scientific Racism', in William B. Cohen, *The French Encounter with Africans: White Response to Blacks, 1530–1880* (Bloomington, IN: Indiana University Press, 2003 [1980]), pp. 210–62.

38 Leslie M. Harris, *In the Shadow of Slavery: African Americans in New York City, 1626–1863* (Chicago, IL: University of Chicago Press, 2004), p. 154.

39 Harris, p. 154.

'Cela ne vous fait pas peur?' (Must be rather worrying for you?) (p. 79). José immediately gains the upper hand by using humour and responding in a similarly mocking tone, although his words go unreported in the novel. The student is Jean-Claude Pelletier (originally named Gaston Pelletier in *La Fête à Paris*), and he symbolises the conservative white French bourgeoisie. From that moment, José and Jean-Claude form an unlikely friendship in which race plays a defining role, as they take pleasure in heated debates which offer the chance to 'se renvoyer toutes les absurdités dont ils avaient étés gorgées sur les races, et devinrent, à leur réciproque étonnement, de bons camarades' (bombard each other with all the absurd comments which they had been forced to swallow about race, and, to their mutual surprise, became firm friends) (p. 79). José's courageous choice of humorous dialogue offers others a paradigm or coping mechanism which applies beyond the immediate space of the novel. His embodied Négritude is intended to assist others experiencing similar situations, testimony to the author's belief that open intercultural dialogue can create mutual respect and understanding.

Jean-Claude Pelletier is both a mouthpiece of and a foil for western racism. He takes a malign pleasure in taunting José with a range of racist clichés, some of which he has garnered from his cousin who works as a 'chef de chantier dans une exploitation forestière en Côte d'Ivoire' (site manager of a logging operation in Ivory Coast) (p. 79). This cousin opines that 'il n'y a rien à tirer des nègres. Qu'est-ce que la civilisation peut attendre de gens qu'on n'arrive pas à faire travailler autrement qu'à coups de trique sur le dos ou à coups de pied?' (Negroes are good for nothing. What can civilisation expect from a people you can only get to work with lashes of the whip or a kick up the behind?) (p. 79). The belief that 'il n'y a rien à tirer des nègres' pervaded colonial culture, and features in Césaire's *Cahier*: 'Et il n'y a rien, rien à tirer de ce petit vaurien' (And there is nothing, really nothing to worm out of this little good for nothing) (pp. 76–77). In his poetry, Césaire deconstructs racist colonial clichés through heavy irony: what really holds back the black child, he demonstrates, are the conditions of acute hunger and abject poverty which colonialism has created. In Zobel's novel, the comments made by Pelletier's cousin replicate the very same colonial prejudices, which represent a widespread French view that the imperial *mission civilisatrice* was nothing less than a duty, and had been imposed for the reason that human civilisations elsewhere in the world were inferior to European civilisations. José strives to challenge such ingrained racist views among the bourgeois metropolitan French population.

Moreover, through Pelletier, the divisive effect of the *mission civilisatrice* for any idea of black solidarity and a black diaspora is exposed, and José's Négritude emerges as central in addressing these colonially inflicted schisms. Pelletier is adamant that José cannot speak for, or defend, Africans, and he reminds José of his difference: 'lui qui était de Martinique, "vieille colonie française" où les problèmes n'étaient pas les mêmes; lui que la colonisation avait déjà définitivement arraché à la barbarie' (he who was from Martinique, 'an old French colony', where the problems were quite different; he whom colonisation had already raised out of barbarism once and for all) (p. 79).

Pelletier is determined to view the French Caribbean citizen José as 'une création des blancs, élevé au mode de raisonnement des blancs, accessible à la confiance des blancs grâce aux bienfaits de la colonisation' (the creation of white men, raised to the same level of intelligence as white people, thanks to the benefits of colonisation) (p. 79). José completely refutes this line of thought. His ability to withstand and challenge such divisive claims gives credence to the comments made throughout the text that José does not have an inferiority complex: that is to say, he refuses to believe that his self-worth and intelligence are solely contingent on that part of his identity which is French. By the time of *Quand la neige aura fondu*, however, his response has been altered so that it is rather muted and vague: 'Vous vous laissez tromper par des théories pseudo-scientifiques, argumentait José' (You are allowing yourself to be deceived by pseudo-scientific theories', argued José) (p. 79). In *La Fête à Paris*, José's rebuke offers more explanation of his thinking; it is far more spirited, and more convincing: 'Vous n'allez pas croire que la culture des Blancs ait fait de moi un être meilleur que celui que je devais être, non? D'ailleurs, je refuse d'être un cas justificatif du colonialisme' (You are not really going to claim that White culture has turned me into a more superior being than I would have otherwise been, are you? Besides, I refuse to be a justification for colonialism) (p. 120).

This impassioned rejection of the *mission civilisatrice* and cry for solidarity across the black diaspora finds an echo in a later passage which exists in both versions of the novel, and which again accuses black Martinicans of being too quick to assert their superiority over other colonised peoples as proof of their advanced assimilation into French society. In *Quand la neige aura fondu*, José gradually befriends his Vietnamese neighbours, who confide in him that they had never had a positive impression of Antilleans in Paris, because 'Ils se complaisaient tellement à jouer aux bons Français, et la plupart d'entre eux étaient si fiers d'êtres intégrés dans le système colonial!' (They were oh so content to play at being good little French people, and most of them were so proud of being integrated into the colonial system) (p. 111). In *La Fête à Paris*, however, the analysis is made in far more forceful terms, as the Vietnamese criticise the Antilleans in greater detail:

> nous n'aimons pas les Antillais. A cause du rôle qu'ils jouent chez nous, sous le cul des Blancs. Parce que les Blancs sont en train de faire des Antillais les dépositaires de tous leurs préjugés, leurs plus dociles complices, et de pires colonialistes qu'eux-mêmes. Un peu comme les chiens de garde de leurs colonies! (p. 174)

> we don't like the Antilleans. Because of the role that they play back home, always fawning around the Whites' arses. Because the Whites are turning the Antilleans into the repositories of all their prejudices, making them their most compliant accomplices and even worse colonialists than themselves. Rather like the guard dogs of their colonies!

From this strident critique of racial conditioning and alienation, it is evident that the original novel reflected Zobel's own frustrations at the prejudiced Martinican society he had just left behind. In the original, the Vietnamese also praise José as the first Martinican whom they have been able to view as a friend. In a further revealing change, a sentence is inserted in *Quand la neige aura fondu* which credits Aimé Césaire, in a speech given at the Maison de la Mutualité conference hall in Paris, with changing the Vietnamese students' perceptions of black Antilleans. In the rewritten version, then, it is Césaire, not José, who has shown the Vietnamese that the Martinicans have an identity separate from a French identity, and are capable of compassion and solidarity with other colonised peoples. In the original, José acts as a proxy for a Négritude-inspired dialogue and the changes in intercultural understanding which it brings about, whereas in the rewrite, he is substituted and literally overwritten with the universally recognised founder of the movement, Césaire. Nonetheless, in both versions it is Négritude, be it through José's lived example of racial awareness or through Césaire's rhetoric, which is credited with promoting enhanced solidarity between colonised peoples.

Martinicans in Paris are critiqued from a variety of angles, from the 'external' perspective offered by the Vietnamese to the internal critique of each other which takes place within groups of Martinican immigrants. Both versions of the novel contain an important protracted discussion of race between José and his Martinican friends Bambam and Alexandre. An astute additional voice is provided by Alexandre's Romanian girlfriend Anca (in the original, she is called Anak, and is Hungarian). In a section of the original which survives in *Quand la neige aura fondu*, Alexandre mocks the Martinicans arriving in Paris. Too many of them, he laughs, arrive with the arrogant belief that their status in the Martinican ethnoclass hierarchy – described as 'des vanités qui sont l'apanage de la petite bourgeoisie de couleur – que les nègres des villes adoptent comme des règles de savoir-vivre' (those superior airs which are the prerogative of the *petite bourgeoisie* of colour, and which are adopted by the town-dwelling Negroes as a code of conduct for life) (p. 89) – will entitle them to the same ethnoclass privileges in Paris. These Martinicans are 'furax de ce que cela n'ait pas cours à Paris' (hopping mad when this turns out not to be the case in Paris) (p. 89). For characters such as José and his friends, who were at the bottom of the ethnoclass hierarchy in Martinique, this reversal could not be more welcome, and they experience clear *schadenfreude* at this levelling.

Immigration, moreover, brings about a more considered reflection on the land of origin. Alexandre judges that one of the most significant effects of migration for an Antillean in Paris is that the city acts as a distant vantage point which opens up new perspectives on the possibilities – and problems – of the Antilles:

> Franchement, ce que j'aime dans ce pays-ci, c'est qu'il me donne des tas d'idées qui pourraient faire des Antilles le plus beau pays du monde ... Mais les Antilles sont des coins empoisonnés. Les blancs y vivent, puisque le poison, c'est eux-mêmes. Tandis qu'ici, on a l'impression que nous nous désintoxiquons et que le blanc est un contre-poison. Bizarre, n'est-ce pas? (p. 89)

> Frankly, what I like about this country is that it gives me heaps of ideas which could turn the Antilles into the most wonderful country in the world ... But the Antilles are poisoned corners. The whites live there, because the poison, well, it's them. Whereas here, it feels as though we are ridding ourselves of the toxins, and the white man is himself an antidote to the poison. Strange, eh?

Yet again, the Antillean inferiority complex is diagnosed in medical language; the islands are poisoned by their colonial history, a poison which pervades contemporary culture, and which emanates from the white elite. The narrative is identifying a specific racial and socio-economic sector of the population, the *békés*, as having exerted a toxic effect on the social fabric of the Antilles. For black men such as themselves, the antidote to this malaise is to leave the islands and meet a different group of white people who do not exhibit the same level of engrained racial discrimination. In *La Fête à Paris*, this discussion is amplified by José's comments that he has met white people in Europe who are horrified by the crimes committed under colonialism:

> Et puis, ajouta José, il me semble qu'ici en Europe, nombreux sont les Blancs qui feraient *mea culpa*, devant nous, et qui nous demanderaient pardon pour les crimes de leurs ancêtres, envers nous. Vous ne croyez pas? Tandis que là-bas, le maintien de leur tout-puissance de leur infaillibilité ne les rend que plus féroces. (p. 138)

> 'And what's more', added José, 'it seems to me that here in Europe, there are numerous Whites who would admit their guilt before us, and who would ask our forgiveness for the crimes which their ancestors inflicted on us. Don't you think? Whereas back home, their determination to maintain their all-powerful infallibility only serves to make them even more ferocious'.

The psychopathology of the *békés*, José suggests, is an attitude specific to their own ruling caste, and has everything to do with their ferocious grip on the island's biopolitical power: their control and governance of all other sectors of the population. A power they are not prepared to relinquish, and will defend at any cost.

In another section omitted from *Quand la neige aura fondu*, the José of *La Fête à Paris* observes, with sincere consternation, how the effects of the colonial racial conditioning with which Martinicans have grown up endure and persist even when they move to metropolitan France. He explains that, as a black man, he is hurt most deeply not by white racism, but by the endemic racism of the black community, citing the example of a black Martinican woman who cannot tolerate the idea of her brother marrying his white girlfriend. José points out the hypocrisy in this situation, as the same sister has just refused to marry 'un jeune médecin dahoméen qui, à ce qu'elle dit partout, était trop noir pour son gout …' (a young doctor from Dahomey who, according to what she's telling everyone, was too black for her liking) (p. 201). The young man in question is eminently eligible and holds the aspirational professional status of a doctor: it is his darker skin alone which has disqualified him in the young black Martinican woman's mind.

José's friend Maurice defends the sister's attitudes, saying that she is only concerned for her brother because when the romance turns sour, his white wife will unfailingly resort to the racist insult 'sale nègre' (dirty nigger) (p. 201). Maurice continues by linking the Martinican woman's refusal of a black African suitor to a sociological study undertaken in the US, where black children preferred to play with white dolls (pp. 201–02). This is an allusion to the famous study 'Racial Identification and Preference among Negro Children' by Kenneth Bancroft Clark and Mamie Phipps Clark, the African-American psychologists who became known for their 1940s experiments using dolls of different skin colours in order to study children's attitudes towards race.[40] José remains unconvinced of the validity of such scientific studies, pointing out that the black dolls made by white people can appear crude and repulsive. He then continues to say that were he to go to a brothel, described as 'certaines "maisons" ou les poupées sont de chair' (certain 'houses' where the dolls are real) (p. 202), he might also be tempted by a real-life white doll, but that his choice results from human curiosity, and does not automatically mean that he wants to be white. The conflation of women, dolls, and prostitutes is surprising, and the remark is uncharacteristically sexualised. Although this is a novel in which José Hassam embarks on a sexual relationship with a white French woman, Marthe, his student experiences include very limited discussion of sexuality. Indeed, the third part of *La Rue Cases-Nègres* contains more bawdy detail of sexual experiences, as related by the charming charmer, Carmen. The leap from dolls to women in the sequel may be a nod to the most famous admirer of 'poupées noires', the Négritude poet Léon-Gontran Damas, with whom Zobel was vaguely acquainted. His poem 'Limbé' (a Creole word meaning spleen) includes a plea to be left to play with his 'poupées noires', just one example in the poem which argues that black people be allowed to develop unimpeded by social conditioning towards a preference for 'white' society. Indeed, the spleen of his title echoes the 'amertume' of Zobel's original title for the novel. In his poem, Damas praises the beauty of black women, and critiques the Antillean alienation which results in an impulse towards 'lactification', or whitening of the race. Zobel's musings on black and white dolls made flesh go further, as José argues that an interest in the

---

40 Kenneth B. Clark and Mamie P. Clark, 'Racial Identification and Preference among Negro Children', in *Readings in Social Psychology*, ed. by Theodore M. Newcomb and Eugene L. Hartley (New York: Henry Holt, Rinehart, and Winston, 1947), pp. 169–78.

other is an intrinsic component of human curiosity. Rather grandly, and with the self-assurance of a young male student, he issues a sweeping rejection of scientific work on both race and the unconscious, by major authors including the psychoanalyst Freud, and the aristocrat and theorist of the Aryan race Gobineau (p. 202). In another echo of Fanon, José is adamant that true liberty means rejecting any fixed notion of a racial identity. It means allowing people of all races to choose their destiny according to the inclinations of free will. Zobel had little time for theorists and did not consider himself to be one; however, this original passage shows his characters debating racial theories from the United States and Europe, and indicates the high level of interest in these theories among black people in Paris in the 1950s. José is aware that racial identity is the subject of scientific studies, yet he experiences an overwhelming feeling of frustration at any such attempts to generalise and to impose fixed, over-determined identities upon him.

Négritude as a Battle, Négritude as a Game

In Zobel's novels, Négritude's specific function is to challenge and change the understanding of a marginalised group within black Martinican society, the *petit-nègre* class. *Quand la neige aura fondu* liberates this group by transposing its hero, José Hassam, from the repressive context of Martinique to Paris, where his struggles against racism and classism continue, but in different ways. Intriguingly, sections which were integral to *La Fête à Paris*, but subsequently deleted from *Quand la neige aura fondu*, actually contain the most unambiguous discussions about the Martinican racism which shaped José Hassam's Négritude. Despite these deletions, both versions of the novel provide a blueprint for how others who can relate to José's suffering in the Caribbean and in metropolitan France might react, survive, and even gain the upper hand in situations of racial and class combat.

In the French capital, alone and far from friends and family, the combined pressures of racism and immigration take a great toll on José. It is Négritude which offers both a support network and a strategy for survival. In a pivotal scene in *Quand la neige aura fondu*, when he can no longer endure the racism at the hotel in the rue Joubert, José erupts in an angry outburst. Sensing danger, his African neighbour Ousmane Koné quickly takes charge of the situation. He ushers José away, and the two men sit together in private while Ousmane sets out the rules of the game, or battle, of life for a black immigrant in a racist environment. As a new arrival, José is at his most vulnerable – and, symbolically, it is an African student who comes to his assistance. First, Ousmane outlines the pernicious forms of discrimination which José will have to face at the hotel:

> Ils feront tout pour nous dégoûter: pas d'ascenseur, défense d'avoir un réchaud électrique ou à alcool, pas de visites. Ils ne transmettront pas les coups de téléphone qu'ils auront reçus pour vous en votre absence. (pp. 43–44)

> They'll do whatever they can to upset us: no lift, a ban on electric heaters or alcohol, no visits allowed. They won't pass on any telephone messages that came in for you when you were out.

More than just a warning, however, Ousmane's explanations offer José a practical survival guide. He provides tactics which directly anticipate the theory of the battle and the game which José goes on to elaborate at a later stage in the original novel:

> faites le mort, sans toutefois vous laisser marcher sur les pieds ... Vous venez de débarquer, vous n'êtes pas encore assez fort pour les avoir. Il ne faut pas vous faire bafouer sans pouvoir vous défendre. (p. 44)

> play dead, without letting them walk all over you ... You've only just arrived, you're not yet strong enough to have them. Don't let yourself be trampled on while you are unable to defend yourself.

The African student sketches out the lines of battle. To survive, José will need to adapt his behaviour, and not make the slightest request of the white staff who run the hotel, so as to be beyond reproach:

> Au début j'ai eu des histoires, moi aussi, mais j'y resterais encore des années que je n'en aurais plus. Pourtant ce n'est pas moi qui céderais, au contraire. Le tout est de les posséder, vous comprenez?' (p. 44)

> In the beginning, I had trouble too, but now I could stay here for years, and quite trouble free at that. But that's not to say that I would yield. Quite the contrary. The trick is to get them where you want them, see?

This important section is almost identical in both versions of the novel. The character of Ousmane is another form of Négritude personified, that of an African Négritude, quite different to the Caribbean Négritude of Médouze in *La Rue Cases-Nègres*. Spared the trauma of slavery and transatlantic deportation from Africa, Ousmane has a secure relationship with his racial identity, which confers on him a regal grandeur. Cloaked in a simple dressing gown, '[il] avait la majesté sereine d'un jeune roi dans sa pompe' (he had the serene majesty of a young king in all his finery) (p. 44). José feels immediately drawn to Ousmane and, by extension, to the continent which he represents, a fact expressed by the novel's most telling remark about his relationship with Africa as a black Caribbean man: 'José aimait l'Afrique avec la tendresse et la nostalgie de celui qui ne connaît de sa mère que des photographies ou des objets personnels laissés en souvenir' (José loved Africa with all the tenderness and nostalgia of someone who knew their mother only through the photographs and personal items she had left behind) (p. 45). Indeed, in this significant scene, Ousmane represents Africa, placing the Caribbean under the tutelage and protection of a nurturing mother Africa, an idealised relationship which was frequent in pre- and immediately post-war Négritude writings by Caribbean authors such as Césaire and Damas.

Ousmane explains that José cannot afford to give the hotel staff the slightest excuse to find fault with him; otherwise they will be quick to attack. By playing this strategic psychological game, José will eventually gain the upper hand, and come to 'les posséder', to possess them. Put in more informal language, he will then have them where he wants them. This strategy, which argues that the black man will win the struggle against racism through an attitude of humility and by countering overt racism with a show of impeccable dignity, anticipates Martin Luther King's Civil Rights policy of non-violent protest in the United States in the 1950s and 1960s. José is being forced to 'prove' his superior humanity and, above all, maintain his calm in the face of repeated racial harassment, which in the hotel manifests itself through a series of passive-aggressive refusals to treat him equally and with respect. Ousmane's advice functions as a reminder of the extreme psychological stress which a black immigrant has to bear, and strive to overcome, in metropolitan France, and he provides José with a 'game plan' for life in Paris.

At moments of racial tension, the original novel *La Fête à Paris* places huge significance on metaphors of battles and games. Any act of rewriting will lead to changes in the balance of a piece, and what is most conspicuous about *Quand la neige aura fondu* is that it greatly diminishes these metaphors. The José of *La Fête à Paris* is unequivocal in his belief that he stands a fighting or game chance of success in France – where he has journeyed with the aspiration to become, as the early deliberate allusion to Maran suggests, 'un homme pareil aux autres' (a man like any other), precisely because he feels that the scales are weighted too heavily against him in Martinique, where he is not viewed as a man, and where society is structured in such a way that he is constantly denied a fair chance.

In both versions of the novel, this theme is explored in depth in conversations with his friend Maurice, who is an alter ego for José: he comes from the same ethnoclass, the *petits-nègres*, and as a consequence he experiences Martinican racial struggles from the same perspective. In *Quand la neige aura fondu*, the narrative explicitly qualifies Maurice as a 'nègre', and includes a highly telling comment on that section of the poorest, darkest-skinned Martinicans whose attributes came to signify how wider society viewed them. Although Maurice is from Macouba, in the north of the island:

> la noirceur du teint apparentait plutôt Maurice Perrin aux gens de Trois-Ilets, de Diamant ou de Sainte-Anne, localités où il y a de grandes plantations, de grosses *habitations*, et dont on ne dit pas des habitants qu'ils sont gens d'ici ou de là, mais nègres de Petit-Bourg, de Sainte-Anne ou de Ducos.

> the darkness of his complexion suggested that Maurice Perrin was likely to be related to the people of Trois-Ilets, Diamant, or Sainte-Anne, places where there are large plantations or, as they are locally known, huge *habitations*, and whose occupants are not called people from here or there, but referred to as Negroes from Petit-Bourg, Sainte-Anne, or Ducos.

Maurice and José (implied through the reference to his native town of Petit-Bourg) come from that group who were more frequently referred to as *nègres* than *gens* or people. This derisory use of *nègres* was a further way of denigrating their humanity; Zobel the author will marshal his version of Négritude to fight back, and to urge people from this group, the group with which he identifies most closely, to wear their racial identity with pride.

The development of José's understanding of race, and of the role of Négritude for people like him in Antillean society, is illustrated by a lengthy, pivotal section in *La Fête à Paris* which is omitted in *Quand la neige aura fondu*. In another lively discussion, while Maurice explains that he is badly affected by the racism he encounters in France, José offers quite another perspective: 'Pour moi', dit José, 'ce n'est pas ce qui presse; parce que vous savez, à ce point de vue, je ne découvre pas grand-chose que je n'aie déjà enduré là-bas' ('It doesn't bother me all that much', said José, 'because you know, in that regard, I'm not discovering anything that I hadn't already endured back home') (p. 197). José then relates two anecdotes about the extreme racism directed at the *petit-nègre* class in Martinique. The first concerns a real-life experience he had at the Savane park in Fort-de-France, when during a playful conversation, a so-called friend who was a mulatto suddenly 'pulled rank' on him with the cutting racist remark 'Attention [...] sachez surtout que je ne plaisante pas avec les petits-nègres!' (Careful [...] know that above all, I don't joke around with *petits-nègres!*) (p. 198).

José goes on to recount a tale told by his (unnamed) grandmother which functions as an allegory for the racism that structures Martinican society, and which explains the psychology of the categories of *nègre*, mulatto, and *béké* (pp. 197–99). In the fable, a mulatto stands in his well-tended garden and passers-by from these three categories admire it. As their skin hues become lighter, moving from the *nègre* to the *béké*, the mulatto's behaviour moves predictably from scorn to fawning adulation. The tale places the mulatto's wish to be white at the epicentre of Martinique's racial problems. So the mulatto flatters the *béké*, hoping for greater social recognition, although this flattery is received with nothing but disdain as the *béké* wishes to maintain his elite social privilege. Most troubling of all is the mulatto's quickness to exploit the *petit-nègre* class in order to further his sycophantic ambitions: at the tale's climax, he offers to send flowers to the *béké*'s wife, and vaunts his own power by emphasising that the flowers will be delivered 'par mon petit Nègre …' (by my Negro [the French here has clear pejorative nuances, approaching the term nigger]) (p. 200). The slave heritage of Martinique means that power and social status are inherently equated with the domination of darker groups in society. This allegorical fable represents the psychological dilemmas of the Antillean population, and stands as an illustration of Fanon's *masques blancs* phenomenon in action. The unspoken message is that the only way to resolve this racial dilemma is for the mulatto to stop despising that part of his identity which unites him with his darker compatriots, and instead to embrace his Négritude.

In *La Fête à Paris*, José explains why he prefers the game offered by metropolitan France to that of Martinique. He finds that metropolitan France offers freedom from the constraints of the ethnoclass hierarchy which had plagued his life in the former colony. It is his firm belief that in Paris, 'on peut jouer avec n'importe qui, avec tout le monde' (we can play with anyone and everyone) (p. 200). On metropolitan soil, he can battle against racism, and both defend his position and attack in this game or battle: 'on peut rendre les coups que l'on reçoit et on trouve même des gens qui vous aident à rendre les coups que vous recevez, et à marquer des points' (you can give as good as you get, and you even find people who will help you return the blows that you have received, and to score points) (pp. 200–01). The troubling implication of this rousing speech is that Négritude is actually a more potent force in Paris, because debate is possible there. In the streets of colonial Fort-de-France, however, the rigid enforcement of the ethnoclass hierarchy precludes any such discussion.

Maurice lacks José's will to test and break through rigid boundaries of class and race. He is following the conventional pathway for the rare *petits-nègres* who have managed to gain a superior education: he is returning to Martinique and – in a detail in the original, but not in the rewritten version – he has found a post as a teacher (p. 235). In other material in *La Fête à Paris* which does not survive in *Quand la neige aura fondu*, José's conversation with Maurice returns to his idea that people such as them are able to 'play' in metropolitan France, that is to say to be included in the wider world in a manner which is impossible in Martinique:

> La vérité, je crois, c'est que je ne pourrais plus vivre dans aucun pays colonisé. Ni Afrique, ni Madagascar, ni Antilles ... C'est, vois-tu, comme une chose dont on a mangé ou bu une fois, et qui t'a rendu malade, et dont la seule vue, après, et même la seule pensée, te fait te sentir mal. Tu me comprends? Eh bien, maintenant, il en est ainsi pour moi. Et puis encore, à cause de ce que je t'ai dit une fois: leur refus de jouer avec nous, là-bas ... Ici je joue; pourquoi n'aurais-je pas l'espoir de gagner? (p. 237)

> The truth is, I believe, that I could never again live in a colonised country. Not in Africa, or Madagascar, or the Antilles ... You see, it's like something you've eaten or drunk once, and which made you terribly ill, and then afterwards, just the sight of it, or even the thought of it, makes you feel ill. Understand? Well, now, that's how it is for me. And moreover, as I've said to you before, it's to do with their refusal to let us play and have a fair shot at it, back home. Over here, I am playing: and indeed, why shouldn't I hope to win?

Maurice has just announced that he is going home, and this decision leads to José's reflections on why he does not wish to return to Martinique, or any other colony. He is adamant that his prospects to develop, both professionally and as a human being, will forever be thwarted in a colonial society, because in a colony, as a member of a dark-skinned, poor ethnoclass, the game of life is forever biased against him.

In Paris, José feels he has a real chance of winning, and *La Fête à Paris* depicts a series of victories which are omitted in *Quand la neige aura fondu*. The most significant deleted material is in his debates with Pelletier. A pivotal section in *La Fête à Paris* which does not survive into *Quand la neige aura fondu* sheds more light onto how Zobel was conceptualising Négritude as a battle and a game in 1950s Paris. In this episode, Pelletier tells José how much he enjoys their debates on the question of race. Most significantly, Pelletier comments, in his characteristically arrogant style, that he takes great pleasure in bombarding José with racial clichés and prejudices, because he knows that a heated debate will inevitably ensue – and that José will prove an adroit sparring partner. Indeed, Pelletier recognises José's superior manner of handling such racial needling: 'tu gardes toujours une dignité imperturbable. Tu n'as pas de complexe d'infériorité, en tout cas' (You always retain your unshakeable dignity. You don't have an inferiority complex, at any rate) (p. 228). José's imperturbable Négritude – once more equated with his lack of inferiority complex – is what enables him to take on opponents such as Pelletier and, for the first time in his life, win.

In *La Fête à Paris*, his success in challenging, and then convincing, his racist friend is a victory which the narrative links directly to Négritude. In their final conversation in the novel, Pelletier acknowledges the admiration and respect which he now has for José, because José has succeeded in changing his perception of black people. Pelletier's conceding phrase explicitly attributes José's success to the power of his Négritude, for he expresses his admiration of his friend in the following terms:

> tel que tu vois ma face de Blanc, je dois avoir l'air cynique de te parler de mon amitié pour toi qui fais de ta négritude, comme tu dis, un sujet de vanité. (p. 228)

> as you look at my face, the face of a White, I must appear rather cynical to profess my friendship for you, you who make your négritude, as you call it, a matter of pride.

Although the term *nègre* abounds in the novel, this is the first and only reference to Négritude, and the telling possessive adjective 'ta' (your) indicates José's individual, personal response to the movement, which manifests itself in José's way of living his life. Years later, in an interview with Raymond Relouzat, Zobel would employ this same technique, referring to 'ma' (my) Négritude (as discussed in Chapter One). Négritude is a lived phenomenon in Zobel's novels, a Négritude of acts and deeds, of everyday practice. Moreover, Pelletier comments that José has also defeated the stereotypical ideas about black people with which he had been inculcated by his prejudiced family:

> tu jetterais la confusion, la panique dans ma famille! Tu démolirais trop brutalement ses idées et ses conceptions raciales. On se sentirait tout à coup à la veille d'être dépouillé, exproprié, domestiqué par les Nègres! Car, à vrai dire, ce n'est pas tant d'être mangés ou salis par les Nègres que craignent les négrophobes, mais plutôt de les voir s'échapper de la place qu'on leur avait assignée et se placer d'eux-mêmes tel qu'on ne puisse plus gagner de l'argent sur leur dos. (p. 231)

> You would throw my family into panic and confusion! You would demolish their ideas and racial prejudices with the utmost brutality. We would suddenly feel as though we were on the eve of being plundered, expropriated, and domesticated by Negroes! For the truth of it is that negrophobes are not so much worried about being eaten or sullied by Negroes as they are about seeing them escaping from the fixed role we have assigned them, and creating a new position for themselves so that we can no longer earn money off their backs.

Through his lived Négritude, which manifests as eloquence, wit, and a dignified attitude, José has managed to convince Pelletier that black people cannot be pigeonholed as inferior, and nor will they accept being consigned to exploitative economic roles, a comment which echoes the sentiments expressed in Zobel's first novel, *Diab'-là*. Now this debate is relocated from the rural framework of a colony to the urban metropolitan centre. For Pelletier, a man like José has untold political potency, and he goes as far as to conclude: 'tu constituerais un danger pour notre civilisation occidentale' (you would be a danger to our western civilisation) (p. 231). José's Négritude has broken down engrained attitudes around race and racial identities in Pelletier. José himself is overjoyed at his victory, telling Pelletier: 'c'est comme si tu venais de me donner de l'or' (It's as though you'd just given me a gift of gold) (p. 232). At the chapter's close, he is pictured alone in the process of 'jubiler, tel un homme qui vient de gagner' (celebrating, like a man who has just been victorious) (p. 232), an important and rare scene of success.

The image of a mixed-race relationship concludes both *La Fête à Paris* and *Quand la neige aura fondu*. The novels end with the fragile image of José and Marthe at the docks, waving farewell to friends who are returning to Martinique, and then heading back into central Paris, hand in hand. In *La Fête à Paris*, José's recent 'victory' over Pelletier lends the closing chapters a greater air of triumph. This brings the original novel to a climax which suggests that José, who chooses to stay in Paris, is slowly winning the difficult 'game' of immigration. Although it is clear that further difficulties lie in store, he has begun to win the respect which had eluded him in Martinique due to his racial identity. Most importantly, this dignity has been won not by suppressing that part of his identity as a *nègre* and *petit-nègre*, but rather by steadfastly nurturing these aspects, and through the unwavering proclamation of his Négritude.

* * *

Zobel's final novel, in both versions, is a visionary work which rejects and refutes the definition and categorisation of human beings according to narrow definitions of race or social class. *Quand la neige aura fondu* develops the working-class Négritude which Zobel had documented in his other novels, transposed now to a metropolitan French context. It shows José Hassam living out moments of intercultural contact, and tension, with dignity and intelligence – expressions of José's maturing Négritude.

The original 1953 novel is more strident in its racial critique, and it directly addresses racial struggles as a battle or a game. It includes a direct use of the term 'Négritude', and unpicks in greater detail this movement's antithesis, the 'complexe d'infériorité', a concept which, intentionally or not, creates a clear parallel with Fanon. Significantly, the force of such critiques is almost completely attenuated or omitted in the rewritten version – most tellingly in the episode with the Vietnamese students, where José's eloquence is substituted for that of Aimé Césaire himself. This reflects the wider change in tone between the two novels. The original is written with the pride and arrogance of a young man ready to take on the world with 'sa Négritude' (his Négritude); the second version is more hesitant and less sure of itself, which points to Zobel's more mature awareness of social complexities, and new perspectives. His many intervening experiences, in Africa, the Caribbean, and Europe, appear to have triggered a loss of confidence in what the figure of José Hassam actually represents; this would seem to mirror the author's own uncertainty about, and frustration with, the realities of decolonisation.

Nonetheless, despite these notable changes, the novel in both its iterations continues the journey which commenced in *La Rue Cases-Nègres*, by documenting the life of a young *petit-nègre* who seeks to go beyond the underprivileged destiny mapped out for him. To do so, an excellent school career is not enough; José must become aware of, and acquire, cultural capital. Zobel's final novel complicates Bourdieu's paradigm by introducing race as a fundamental point in the constellations of cultural capital available to young Antilleans newly arrived in Paris. As José's Négritude gathers momentum, it comes to constitute a kind of racial capital and informs every aspect of his burgeoning cultural capital. Yet he is adamant about refusing to follow the well-trodden path of using his education to return to Martinique as a new member of the black bourgeoisie. He regards life in Martinique as a game whose rules ensure that he, a *petit-nègre*, will never be given a fair shot. This attitude is explicit in 1953, and implicit in 1979. Instead, his own personal fulfilment is predicated on a series of unpredictable, spontaneous meetings with people from all over the world, from all kinds of backgrounds. The cultural capital José derives from his encounters with diverse groups of people, who differ in race, gender, and age, is not about gaining economic connections, but personal capital. For all their differences, both versions of the novel depict José Hassam growing into his Négritude, that is to say, growing into his role as a black man whose formidable courage in the face of countless trials and challenges, in the Caribbean or continental Europe, is contingent on his unshakeable pride in his identity as a *nègre*.

Afterword

In his 1993 Reith Lectures, broadcast on BBC Radio 4, Edward Said defines the intellectual as an 'individual endowed with a faculty for representing, embodying, articulating a message, a view, an attitude, philosophy or opinion to, as well as for, a public'.[1] I have undertaken to re-examine Joseph Zobel – the novelist and his novels – in a mode which, after Said's model, considers both the author's conceptual innovations and the ways in which he transmitted these ideas to, and for, wider public audiences. To do so, I have brought Zobel's novels into dialogue with several literary traditions to which they undoubtedly make important contributions – Caribbean literature, European literature, Négritude, the Negro Renaissance, and black literature more broadly, and I have demonstrated his significance for World Literature. My close readings, supported and contextualised by references to the author's wider *œuvre* and career, and through extensive original archival research, reveal the lasting importance of Zobel's interventions on the transnational construction of black identity, black politics, and black philosophy between continents.

The afterlives and legacies of Zobel's novels across the world demonstrate that his reputation has been subject to constant processes of reinterpretation and redefinition, and this continues to the present day. The multiple ways in which Zobel is represented is an indication of his varied transnational and transdisciplinary contributions to literature and the audiovisual arts. Indeed, Zobel's international reputation owes a great debt to the popular appreciation of *La Rue Cases-Nègres* and its afterlives, particularly Euzhan Palcy's celebrated film adaptation *Rue Cases-Nègres*. Strikingly, my study has shown that this popular

---

[1] Edward Said, *Representations of the Intellectual: 1993 Reith Lectures* (London: Vintage, 1994), p. 9.

appreciation has, to date, far surpassed the academic analyses of Zobel's work, a public impact quite unique among Caribbean authors.

Through undertaking the first comparative reading of all of Zobel's novels, and by paying attention to the specific ways in which they dialogue with the Négritude movement, I have drawn attention to previously unacknowledged aspects of the author's innovative, subversive literature. My reconsideration of Zobel makes a substantial and original contribution to the recent wider scholarly turn to reconsider Négritude by arguing for a shift in how his novels, and Négritude more generally, are understood. Zobel aimed to hold up a mirror to his native Martinican society, and his literary vision extended Négritude's scope to make it relevant to people from every social background. Zobel's novels may be considered complementary to the work of Césaire, Senghor, and Damas, with the specific difference that the novelist aimed to reach, and indeed did reach, a wider audience. If anything, my study shows that Zobel's literature and its afterlives need to be reframed as an essential contribution to promoting intellectual and public discourse into Négritude, filtered through his particular lens, and ensuring the movement's continued international visibility. My analysis of Zobel's novels also draws attention to hitherto under-explored connections between the Francophone Négritude and North American Negro Renaissance movements; indeed, a broader ambition of this study is to generate new insights into the complexity of Caribbean literature, and its inherently transnational, transcultural nature.

Zobel's earliest novels, *Diab'-là* and *Les Jours immobiles*, the latter of which was rewritten as *Les Mains pleines d'oiseaux*, forge a new tradition of Caribbean novels written for Caribbean audiences through their focus on depicting black working-class culture in its mores, traditions, and socio-economic conditions. I have demonstrated how these novels announce Zobel's literary ambition of expanding Négritude's critical framework so that it might include subaltern and marginalised Martinicans for the first time. The political consequence of this bold move was the publishing ban imposed on *Diab'-là*. In reappraising these first two novels and their significance to the contemporary era, I argue that Zobel also raises specific debates about the land which constitute an important contribution to the rapidly developing field of ecocriticism. Both works render visible the multiple, transnational tensions exerted on the very earth of the Caribbean as a direct result of colonialism and its enduring legacy, and in a revolutionary gesture, Zobel encourages Martinicans to work towards a different relationship with their native land.

After this close excavation of his neglected early novels, I have demonstrated why Zobel's later novels, written after he had immigrated to metropolitan France, must be reconsidered. Developed in Paris, they are at once Caribbean and part of a wider tradition of post-war European social realism. Ross's concept of the 'double vision' of post-war French social realist literature provides a critical framework for the development of my radical new reading of *La Rue Cases-Nègres*. My original analysis demonstrates the novel's uncompromising determination to recover and represent the disavowed space of the Caribbean plantation for wider audiences in Europe and the Caribbean. This new approach culminates in my reframing of *La Rue Cases-Nègres* as both a paean to plantation society and a denunciation of how modern civilisation has developed. Western civilisation's very existence is predicated on the exploitation of invisible, abject 'plantation' spaces. Zobel's novel reveals these connections, making the invisible visible, and in doing so issues a bold challenge to re-evaluate modern 'developed' societies.

My final chapter moves from *La Rue Cases-Nègres* to examine how the sequel novel, *La Fête à Paris*, rewritten as *Quand la neige aura fondu*, undertakes a critique of post-war migration from the Caribbean to Europe. In his final novel, Zobel crafts an innovative and uncompromising exploration of cultural capital, which I have explored through Bourdieu's paradigm. While showing how Zobel's novel illustrates Bourdieu's three states of cultural capital (embodied, objectified, and institutionalised), my reading of the novel complicates this paradigm by arguing that Zobel introduces a fourth category, that of racial capital, which operates in a Négritude-inflected, transnational framework. This complex approach enables the novelist to critically assess racial and socio-economic intersections in both Martinique and metropolitan French society.

The overall ambition has been to move the field of Zobel studies forward, going beyond *La Rue Cases-Nègres*, and to reconsider each of his novels in turn; in many cases, my study represents the first significant scholarly analysis of these works. Having redefined the parameters of Zobel's career as a novelist, it becomes evident that the novel *La Rue Cases-Nègres*, considered to be quintessentially *zobelien*, requires urgent critical reframing in the light of this new wider analysis. This leads to my radical new reading of *La Rue Cases-Nègres*, which breaks with conventional scholarly opinions to demonstrate that Zobel's best-known novel is nothing less than an attempt to decry the dualities, hypocrisies, and contradictions of which modern society is constructed, using Martinique's specific island space in order to interrogate social inequalities more broadly, with repercussions in both the Caribbean and Europe. For readers throughout the circum-Caribbean regions of the Americas which were directly affected by colonial plantation systems, the novel is a foundational, canonical text, as it is for those readers from other parts of the world where plantation society was a dominant structure; beyond this, any reader who wishes to understand more about the development of plantation societies in the slavery and post-slavery eras will not find a more accessible or insightful starting point than *La Rue Cases-Nègres*.

* * *

Joseph Zobel is still very much a presence in Martinique. In the southern town of Rivière-Salée, near the author's birthplace of Petit-Morne, the local high school was renamed the Lycée Joseph Zobel on 14 April 2000. After Zobel's death in 2006, his daughter Jenny Zobel organised the gift of his archives to the people of Martinique. To display the sheer range of important documents and artefacts in this collection, a dedicated Espace Joseph Zobel (Joseph Zobel Installation) was created at the regionally administered Écomusée (Museum of the Local Environment) in the south-west of the island. This museum, housed in a former distillery, and just metres from the beach in Anse Figuier, is a fitting location given its focus on the specificities of Martinican local spaces. While the building itself stands as a reminder of the colonial past, inside it hosts significant displays about the Amerindian heritage and transatlantic slavery. Zobel's impact is also evident at the living museum La Savane des esclaves (The Slaves' Savannah). This privately run site created by Gilbert Larose is close to Anse Mitan, one of the island's main tourist centres. All visitors take a guided tour of this outdoor site which includes a visit to a simple wooden hut called La Case de Médouze (Médouze's Shack) – Larose was so impressed by the figure of Médouze in Palcy's film that he included a reference to the character in his museum.[2]

Several recent Martinican publications also owe a great debt to Zobel. Local historian Ludovic Louri's *Habitation Trénelle 1948–1974: les travaux et les jours* (2010) is a memoir of life on one of Martinique's last

---

[2] Unpublished interview conducted with Gilbert Larose at *La Savane des esclaves* in April 2015; I would like to record my thanks to Larose.

working plantations, inspired in part by Zobel's belief that disappearing traditions needed to be recorded for future generations.[3] Louri's subsequent publication, *Rivière-Salée 1943–1974*, applies the same approach to Zobel's home town.[4] In the field of literature, the Martinican author Mérine Céco's 2016 collection of stories *Au revoir Man Tine* (*Goodbye, Man Tine*) foregrounds Zobel's iconic grandmother figure in order to explore the complex and fraught transmission of historical memory in the French Caribbean.[5]

Zobel's legacy continues to exert an influence over the cultural life of his native island, in ways which the author himself could not possibly have anticipated. This enduring popular appeal is a reflection of Zobel's talent for describing local scenes and everyday people. His first novels, *Diab'-là* and *Les Jours Immobiles*, were inspired by real characters and situations in Martinique, and a letter written in Paris in 1947 shows that Zobel's desire to celebrate everyday Martinican people endured after he emigrated to the French capital:

> Et quand Ennare arrivera, quand je vais recevoir des amis chez moi, je leur parlerai de Petite-Anse, de ces personnages [...] Et cela m'a donné l'idée de faire un de ces jours une conférence intitulée 'Rencontre avec mes héros' et je parlerai de tous ces braves gens qui m'ont inspiré.[6]

> When Ennare arrives or when I have friends over to my place, I will tell them about Petit-Anse, about these characters [...] In fact, this has given me an idea for a paper that I would like to give one of these days, called 'A Meeting with my Heroes', and I will speak of all these wonderful people who have inspired me.

That Zobel's first novels have yet to be reissued, and have not been made accessible to wider audiences through translation into languages such as English, Spanish, and Portuguese, has left a notable gap in the scholarly understanding of the development of the Caribbean novel, and the Francophone Caribbean novel in particular. An important development occurred in 2015, when *Diab'-là* had a central part in the metropolitan

---

3 See Ludovic Louri and Florence Gauthier, *Habitation Trénelle 1948–1974: les travaux et les jours. Mémoires* (Fort-de-France: K Éditions, 2010). I would like to record my gratitude to Louri for taking me on a guided tour of Petit-Bourg in 2015, and for the information that in several conversations, Zobel encouraged him to record vanishing aspects of traditional Martinican heritage in print.
4 Ludovic Louri, *Rivière-Salée 1943–1974* (Fort-de-France: K Éditions, 2016).
5 Mérine Céco, *Au revoir Man Tine* (Paris: Écriture, 2016).
6 Private letter from Joseph Zobel to Valbrun, 23 October 1947; my translation.

French celebrations of the centenary of Zobel's birth. To commemorate the centenary, a new *bande dessinée* (graphic novel) adaptation by Roland Monpierre was published. This was financed by a crowd-funding initiative organised by the cultural network Passions partagées (Shared passions) under the leadership of cultural activist Patricia Thiéry.[7] This twenty-first-century initiative includes a highly successful new exhibition curated by Thiéry, *Joseph Zobel: le cœur en Martinique et les pieds en Cévennes* (*Joseph Zobel: Heart in Martinique, Feet in the Cévennes Mountains*),[8] which has to date travelled around various locations in metropolitan France. The graphic novel *Diab'-là* was launched at the 2015 Salon du Livre in Paris, and formed the centrepiece of Le Stand Martinique (the Martinican Stand) at that event. Several panels, debates, and interviews, with academics (including myself) and creative artists who are engaging with Zobel's work, took place during that edition of the Paris Book Fair, and reports were broadcast across the Francophone world. The graphic novel, currently available only in French, contributes to a welcome and timely broadening of the international Francophone public understanding of Zobel.

In Martinique, the official celebrations of the centenary of the author's birth were led by the town of Rivière-Salée, where 2015 was commemorated as L'Année Zobel (The Year of Zobel). Over several months, a series of public readings, debates, lectures, art exhibitions, activities with local schools, most notably the Lycée Joseph Zobel and its feeder schools, and television interviews took place, and I was honoured to play a part in these activities. I would like to single out for further praise a remarkable exhibition organised by Raphaëlle Bouville at the Médiathèque de Rivière-Salée (the public multimedia library) which displayed to local citizens the literary talents and international significance of their town's most famous author.[9]

The centenary was also the occasion for numerous special screenings of Palcy's *Rue Cases-Nègres* across Martinique, France, and the UK. The legacy of that 1983 film has ensured that *La Rue Cases-Nègres* holds an enduring public and scholarly appeal although, as the Cameroonian

---

7 The official *Passions partagées* website can be found at: http://www.exposition-joseph-zobel.fr/ (accessed 13 July 2015).

8 The title of the exhibition alludes to a memoir by José Lemoigne which is discussed overleaf.

9 Bouville developed this exhibition in collaboration with international partners including myself and Jenny Zobel.

critic Jacques Etoundi Ateba has remarked, the film has taken on an extraordinary cultural life of its own, to such an extent that it is not necessarily associated with Zobel. In 2006, Ateba claimed to speak for a generation of African viewers when he commented that:

> Au nom de tous les jeunes universitaires et lycéens des années 1980, nous voulions nous excuser d'avoir longtemps ignoré Joseph Zobel en nous méprenant sur l'auteur de *La Rue Cases-Nègres*, film qui nous a tant émus; dont nous avions pensé qu'il avait été écrit par Euzhan Palcy.[10]

> In the name of all the young university and high school students of the 1980s, we want to apologise for having been ignorant of the identity of Joseph Zobel for so long, failing to realise that he was the author of *La Rue Cases-Nègres*, a film which had touched us so greatly and which, we believed, had been written by Euzhan Palcy.

By bringing the novelist to the fore, my study has attempted to go some way to redressing the uneven relationship between Zobel and Palcy's film *Rue Cases-Nègres* which Ateba so aptly summarises, in a sentence which itself elides Zobel's novel and Palcy's film. While Sylvie César's 1994 comparative study of the novel and film remains an important reference work, my research draws attention to new areas of analysis such as the complex depiction of themes including education, the environment, and gender. This points the way for future scholarship into how Palcy's film adaptation can be brought into dialogue not only with *La Rue Cases-Nègres*, but all of Zobel's novels.

In another recent development, the provenance of Zobel's unusual surname has been explored by critics, and what emerges would seem to further align the novelist with his Creole plantation subject matter. In his preface to *Joseph Zobel: le cœur en Martinique et les pieds en Cévennes*, a memoir by José Lemoigne which offers an account of Zobel's final years in Anduze, Raphaël Confiant explains that for many years, the origins of the surname Zobel had perplexed him.[11] Finally, he discovered the term in a poem by the Martinican poet Monchoachi, in the Creole phrase 'bèl-bèl/ Zobèl/ Solèy bèl' (Beautiful-Beautiful/ Flash/ of Sunshine).[12] Confiant translates the term into French as *éclat*, a term

---

10 Jacques Etoundi Ateba, 'Zobel l'Africain', *Le Français dans le monde*, 348 (2006), p. 24.
11 Raphaël Confiant, 'Deux mots quatre paroles à propos du "Nègre totémique"', in José Lemoigne, *Joseph Zobel: le cœur en Martinique et les pieds en Cévennes* (Matoury: Ibis Rouge, 2008), p. 12.
12 Confiant, p. 13.

which carries the nuances of a flash or dazzling effect. He goes on to imagine that an ancestor of Zobel may have deliberately chosen this term as his surname, in a defiantly Creole flourish which unmistakably anchored him and his descendants in the world of the Creole plantation. This leads to Confiant's jubilant decision to hail Zobel as 'un Nègre créole', the implication being that Zobel's work should be read as a visionary moment in which the struggles of Négritude of his contemporary era, and the much later linguistic turn to local languages of the 1990s Créolité movement, converge.

* * *

Rediscovering Zobel the novelist has entailed a rigorous recontextualisation of his works in the light of the Négritude movement. My final chapter in particular draws attention to a significant difference between Zobel's last original novel, *La Fête à Paris*, published in 1953, and the 1979 rewritten version, *Quand la neige aura fondu*. By undertaking the first close comparative reading of both iterations of the novel, my study has established that when rewriting, Zobel attenuated much of the Négritude-influenced, strident racial critique of his original work. This appears to indicate that the author's attitudes towards Négritude had undergone a shift in the intervening years, the majority of which Zobel had spent in Senegal. While it is beyond the scope of this analysis to fully excavate Zobel's substantial career in Africa, the following pages offer reflections on the subsequent developments in his thinking on Négritude.

The years in Africa were the culmination of Zobel's relationship with Négritude. He lived a significant part of his life in the *terre-mère* itself, a decision informed by his personal Négritude-inspired quest for racial discovery, and so he became one of only a handful of Martinican and Caribbean authors to live on three continents: North America (in Martinique), Europe, and Africa. Yet the rewritten sections in *Quand la neige aura fondu* suggest that these experiences also herald a more circumspect understanding of Négritude. The complexities of Zobel's lived experiences in Senegal took precedence over what had previously been a more abstract, intellectual Négritude-inflected desire to assert a distinct Caribbean identity while recovering lost African origins.

The exploration of blackness commenced in his novels remains an important theme in the short story collections which Zobel published between his move to Africa in 1957 and his death in 2006. Although he would not write another original novel, a number of his short stories return to questions of Négritude, identity, and blackness in highly significant ways. A recently discovered journal extract from his first year in Senegal, 'Sabar', written in May 1958, was made available for the first time in *Joseph Zobel: écrits inédits* (*Joseph Zobel: Unpublished Stories*) as part of the 2015 centenary celebrations by the Région Martinique. The narrative illustrates the young Martinican's admiration of the forms of Négritude he believed he witnessed in African culture. The tale deftly captures Senegalese music and dance on the page, in a manner reminiscent of Zobel's vivid descriptions of the Martinican *laghia* dance one decade earlier in *Laghia de la mort* (1946). By his return from Senegal to retire in Anduze, however, this initial tone of awe was tempered by a new sense of political awareness. The 1983 collection *Mas Badara* includes the short story 'Voyage de noces' (Honeymoon), which focuses on African decolonisation and the jubilation or 'honeymoon' which it ushered in. From this sombre narrative, however, it becomes clear that the optimism of this period gave way to terrible, tragic disappointments, symbolised by a destitute, mentally ill character whose suicide concludes the story, and the whole collection.

That is not to say that Zobel's belief in Négritude had waned; rather, his comments on the movement become more complex and reflective. In another collection, *Et si la mer n'était pas bleue…* (1982), Zobel considers the Martinique of his youth in the late 1930s and early 1940s. In the final short story, 'Nardal', he offers an important homage to the Nardal family, and particularly focuses on that neglected female forerunner of Négritude, Paulette Nardal (pp. 81–89). Decades later, this remarkable woman's legacy for Négritude has now finally begun to be addressed by scholars, and Zobel's 1982 story makes an important contribution to reconstructing the prehistories and pluralities of Négritude.

'Nardal' stands 'en guise de postface' (by way of an afterword) (p. 81), and represents a shift as it is written in an autobiographical mode, unlike the other stories in *Et si la mer n'était pas bleue* …. It opens by raising a painful, racist question that the author himself had repeatedly endured from other black Martinicans during his adolescence: 'Comment ça se fait que tu sois si noir, si laid?' (Why is it that you are so dark-skinned, and so ugly?) (p. 81). This traumatic question, which is now, at last, uncompromisingly transcribed by Zobel, reveals the reasons for the protracted exploration of the ethnoclass hierarchy which the author had undertaken decades earlier in the novels *La Rue Cases-Nègres* and *La Fête à Paris*. The short story ends by emphasising the debt which

Zobel felt towards the Nardal family in general, and to Paulette in particular, for their exemplary, inspirational, lived form of Négritude. Moreover, the tale offers a rare moment of reflection on the significance of Négritude for intellectuals, and for the wider population:

> Le concept de la Négritude jeta le trouble dans l'esprit de certains intellectuels; mais plus nombreux furent ceux pour qui il joua le rôle de passeur vers une sorte de marronage [sic] spirituel ou un retour à soi. Et ceux-là de s'interroger. (p. 88)

> The concept of Négritude troubled certain intellectuals; but for an even greater number of people, it led to a kind of spiritual *marronnage* or a return to oneself. And it led those people to ask themselves key questions.

For Zobel, the lived Négritude embodied by the Nardals inspired other individuals to work towards a complete personal acceptance of, and pride in, their black identity. He suggests, however, that at the time of writing in 1982, Négritude's work is not yet complete. He concludes the same paragraph on a more ambiguous note: 'C'est d'ailleurs, la non-réponse à leurs questions, qui donne à la Martinique son visage crispé d'aujourd'hui' (It is, moreover, the lack of responses to their questions which renders the face of Martinique so tense today) (p. 88). This brief sentence passes an uncomfortable political comment on modern Martinican society. For Zobel, on an individual level, the working through of the paradoxes and traumas which structure Martinique's identity has, thanks to Négritude, been commenced, and in some cases has led to a more complete, nuanced understanding of racial identity. This process, however, has not yet resulted in wider changes at the scale of the radical social movements which, several decades earlier, the author had dared to imagine and depict in his Négritude-inspired novels.

* * *

Zobel has a gift for description which avoids the trap of sentimentality or the exotic, all the while drawing the reader, Caribbean or otherwise, into Caribbean contexts. His Négritude demonstrates an enduring optimism in the capacity of human nature to create transcultural connections which are based not on exploitation, but on mutual exchange. He thus infuses painful subject matter and everyday tales of ordinary people, *le peuple*, with humanity and compassion. His six novels are narrated in clear and persuasive language; they resolutely refuse to reproduce the discourse of 'elite' and 'highbrow' culture. In such a way, the author fully achieves his aims of depicting the societies which influenced his own life. He produces a literature in which his Négritude becomes an offering to these very same societies, and an invitation to reflect, and to act.

My study has uncovered the intersectionality inherent to Zobel's novels, in which discourses of race are complicated and nuanced by the analysis of socio-economic structures. Zobel carves out a literary space for subaltern, voiceless people who are oppressed both by the pigment of their skin and the economic systems into which they were born, and he does so in a unique style that aims to engage all readers, regardless of their background. He gives voice to the experiences of the poorest group of *nègres*, the *petits-nègres*: plantation labourers who not only fight against the racial bias imposed upon them by white society, with which they have scant contact, but who are also forced to confront the daily racial prejudices of their mixed-race, economically advantaged neighbours and compatriots. In Zobel, it is the struggle for dignity and autonomy, for self-determination and independence in the face of abject poverty which truly shapes depictions of oppression. This confirms the novelist's cultural legacy as the champion of those human interactions which are shaped by the unmistakable articulation of humanity's capacity for compassion and altruism, in even the most unfavourable conditions. Zobel's novels pass urgent social comment on colonialism's material and spiritual legacy. While this is irrefutably a legacy of racism, oppression, and poverty, it is also, as Zobel so compellingly demonstrates, a legacy of indomitable human courage.

Bibliography

Works by Joseph Zobel

[writing as Kay-Mac-Zo], 'Mon Village', *Le Sportif*, 138, 27 December 1940, pp. 3–4. Archives départementales, Martinique. PER 156/1938–1950.
Diab'-là (Fort-de-France: Imprimerie officielle de Fort-de-France, 1945).
Les Jours immobiles (Fort-de-France: Imprimerie officielle de Fort-de-France, 1946).
'Considérations sur l'art local', *Martinique: revue trimestrielle*, 5 (1946), pp. 33–38.
Laghia de la mort (Fort-de-France: Bezaudin, 1946).
Diab'-là (Paris: Nouvelles Éditions Latines, 1947).
La Rue Cases-Nègres (Paris: Éditions Jean Froissart, 1950).
La Fête à Paris (Paris: La Table ronde, 1953).
La Rue Cases-Nègres (Paris: Les Quatre jeudis, 1955).
Le Soleil partagé (Paris/Dakar: Présence Africaine, 1964).
Incantation pour un retour au pays natal (Anduze, Gard: Imprimerie de Languedoc, 1965).
Incantation pour un retour au pays natal/ Joseph Zobel dit trois poèmes de Joseph Zobel (Voxigrave VX6845, no year). Bibliothèque nationale de France: FRBNF38067745, stamped 1966 [handwritten date added: 1965].
La Rue Cases-Nègres (Paris/Dakar: Présence Africaine, 1974).
Les Mains pleines d'oiseaux (Paris/Dakar: Présence Africaine, 1978).
Laghia de la mort (Paris/Dakar: Présence Africaine, 1978).
Quand la neige aura fondu (Paris: Éditions caribéennes, 1979).
Et si la mer n'était pas bleue... (Paris: Éditions caribéennes, 1982).
Mas Badara (Paris/Dakar: Présence Africaine, 1983).
Poèmes de moi-même (Fort-de-France: Désormeaux, 1984).
D'Amour et de silence (Fréjus: Éditions Prosveta, 1994).
Gertal et autres Nouvelles – Suivi de Journal 1946–2002 (Guyane: Ibis Rouge, 2002).
Le Soleil m'a dit. Œuvre poétique (Guyane: Ibis Rouge, 2002).

Posthumous Publications and Adaptations of Works by Zobel

Beuze, Lyne-Rose and Gabrielle Chomereau-Lamotte (eds), *Joseph Zobel: écrits inédits* (Fort-de-France, Martinique: Région Martinique, Collection connaissance du patrimoine, 2015).

Monpierre, Roland, *Diab'-là, d'après le roman de Joseph Zobel* (Paris: Nouvelles Éditions Latines, 2015).

Zobel, Charlotte, *Joseph Zobel photographies* (Graulhet: Charlotte Zobel/Région Martinique/Escourbiac, 2016).

Zobel's Novels in Translation

Čertův chlapík: Román z Antil, trans. by Miroslav Vlček (Prague: Pavel Prokop, 1949) [Czech translation of *Diab'-là*].

Černošská ulička, trans. by Miroslav Vlček (Prague: Svoboda, 1951) [Czech translation of *La Rue Cases-Nègres*].

Мальчик с Антильских островов: повесть (Malchik s Antilskih ostrovov: povest), trans. by Татьяна Иванова (Tatyana Ivanova) (Москва: Детская литература, 1967) [Russian translation of *La Rue Cases-Nègres*].

Black Shack Alley, trans. by Keith Q. Warner (Washington, DC: Three Continents Press, 1980).

Via delle capanne nègre: romanzo, trans. by Andriana Crespi Bortolini (Milan: Jaca Letteraria, 1983) [Italian translation of *La Rue Cases-Nègres*].

Negerhuttenweg, trans. by José Rijnaarts (Brussels: Baarn/Ambo/Den Haag/NOVIB, 1991) [Dutch translation of *La Rue Cases-Nègres*].

Zobel's Short Stories in Translation

'The Gramophone', trans. by P. Gering and J. Nicholas, *The Classic*, 2.2 (1966), special issue on 'French African Writing', guest editor Dorothy Blair (pp. 34–43) [English translation of 'Le Phonographe', in *Le Soleil partagé*, originally published in the Francophone Senegalese women's magazine *Awa!*, 5 (May 1964)].

'Huwelijksreis', in *Moderne Caribische verhalen*, ed. by Arie Sneeuw, Elly Orsel, and Robert Dorsman (Amsterdam: Van Gennep, 1987). [Dutch translation of 'Voyage de noces' (Honeymoon) in *Mas Badara*].

'Lágia, életre-halálra', trans. by Kun Tibor Fordítása, *Ezredvég* (September 1999), pp. 33–36 [Czech translation of 'Laghia de la mort'].

Works Cited

Akpagu, Zana Itiunbe, 'La Rencontre d'Emile Zola et de Joseph Zobel: un parallélisme thématique entre *L'Assommoir* et *La Rue Cases-Nègres*', *Neohelicon*, 27.2 (2000), pp. 287–308.

Alliot, David, *'Le Communisme est à l'ordre du jour': Aimé Césaire et le PCF, de l'engagement à la rupture (1935–1957)* (Paris: Pierre-Guillaume de Roux, 2013).

André, Jacques, *Caraïbales* (Paris: Éditions caribéennes, 1981).

Arnold, A. James, *Modernism & Negritude: The Poetry and Poetics of Aimé Césaire* (Cambridge, MA: Harvard University Press, 1998).

Ashcroft, Bill, 'Bridging the Silence: Inner Translation and the Metonymic Gap', in *Language and Translation in Postcolonial Literatures: Multilingual Contexts, Translational Texts*, ed. by Simona Bertacco (New York: Routledge: 2014), pp. 17–31.

Ateba, Jacques Etoundi, 'Zobel l'Africain', *Le Français dans le monde*, 348 (2006), p. 24.

Badiane, Mamadou, *The Changing Face of Afro-Caribbean Cultural Identity: Negrismo and Negritude* (Lanham, MA: Lexington, 2010).

Beringuier, Christian, *L'Espace régional martiniquais*, CERAG 3 (Fort-de-France: Centre d'Études Régionales Antilles Guyane, 1964).

Beuze, Lyne-Rose, *André Maire (1898–1984): un peintre voyageur à la découverte de l'âme martiniquaise* (Fort-de-France: Musée Régional d'Histoire et d'Ethnographie, 2006).

Bhabha, Homi K., *The Location of Culture* (London: Routledge, 1994).

Blanshard, Paul, *Democracy and Empire in the Caribbean* (New York: Macmillan, 1947).

Boittin, Jennifer Anne, *Colonial Metropolis: The Urban Grounds of Anti-Imperialism and Feminism in Interwar Paris* (Lincoln, NE: University of Nebraska Press, 2010).

Bonnichon, Philippe, 'France et Brésil: apports réciproques aux XVIe et XVIIe siècles', *L'Année des outre-mer: Mémoires de l'Académie des Sciences, Arts et Belles-Lettres de Touraine*, 24 (2011), pp. 9–25.

Bourdieu, Pierre, *La Distinction: critique sociale du jugement* (Paris: Minuit, 1979).

Breton, Raymond, *Dictionnaire caraïbe-français, 1665, révérend père Raymond Breton: édition présentée et annotée par le CELIA et le GEREC*, ed. Centre d'études des langues indigènes d'Amérique (Villejuif, France) and Groupe d'études et de recherches en espace créolophone et francophone (Schœlcher, Martinique) (Paris: Karthala, 1999).

Burton, Richard D. E., *La famille coloniale: la Martinique et la mère patrie: 1789–1992* (Paris: L'Harmattan, 1994).

Bush, Ruth, *Publishing Africa in French: Literary Institutions and Decolonization 1945–1967* (Liverpool: Liverpool University Press, 2016).
Butel, Paul, *Histoire des Antilles françaises, XVIIe–XXe siècle* (Paris: Perrin, 2007).
Calverton, V. F., *An Anthology of American Negro Literature* (New York: The Modern Library, 1929).
Camus, Albert, 'Préface', in Louis Guilloux, *La Maison du peuple* (Paris: Grasset, 1953 [1927]).
Céco, Mérine, *Au revoir Man Tine* (Paris: Écriture, 2016).
Césaire, Aimé, *Cahier d'un retour au pays natal/Notebook of a Return to My Native Land*, trans. Mireille Rosello with Annie Pritchard (Newcastle upon Tyne: Bloodaxe, 1995 [1939]).
—— et al., *Tropiques 1941–1945: collection complète* (Paris: Jean Michel Place, 1978).
Césaire, Ina, 'L'idéologie de la débrouillardise dans les contes antillais: analyse de deux personnages-clé du conte de veillée aux Antilles de colonisation française', *Espace Créole: revue du GEREC (Groupe d'Études et de Recherches en Espace Créolophone)*, 1978, 41–48.
Césaire, Suzanne, *Le Grand Camouflage: Écrits de dissidence (1941–1945)*, ed. by Daniel Maximin (Paris: Seuil, 2009).
——, *The Great Camouflage: Writings of Dissent (1941–1945)*, ed. by Daniel Maximin and trans. by Keith L. Walker (Middletown, CT: Wesleyan University Press, 2012).
César, Sylvie, *'Rue Cases-Nègres' du roman au film, étude comparative* (Paris: L'Harmattan, 1994).
Chamoiseau, Patrick, *Écrire en pays dominé* (Paris: Gallimard, 1997).
—— and Maure, *Émerveilles* (Paris: Gallimard Jeunesse/Giboulées, 1998).
Chivallon, Christine, 'De quelques préconstruits de la notion de diaspora à partir de l'exemple antillais', *Revue européenne des migrations internationales*, 13.1 (1997), pp. 149–60.
'Chronique du Prix des lecteurs', *La Gazette des lettres*, 118 (8 July 1950), p. 1.
Clark, Kenneth B. and Mamie P. Clark, 'Racial Identification and Preference among Negro Children', in *Readings in Social Psychology*, ed. by Theodore M. Newcomb and Eugene L. Hartley (New York: Henry Holt, Rinehart, and Winston, 1947), pp. 169–78.
Cohen, William B., *The French Encounter with Africans: White Response to Blacks, 1530–1880* (Bloomington, IN: Indiana University Press, 2003 [1980]).
Condé, Maryse, *Le Cœur à rire et à pleurer* (Paris: Laffont, 1999).
——, *Tales from the Heart*, trans. by Richard Philcox (New York, NY: Soho Press, 2001).

Confiant, Raphaël, 'Deux mots quatre paroles à propos du "Nègre totémique"', in José Lemoigne, *Joseph Zobel: le cœur en Martinique et les pieds en Cévennes* (Matoury: Ibis Rouge, 2008), pp. 11–18.

Cooper, Thomas, *Facts illustrative of the Condition of the Negro Slaves in Jamaica: with notes and an appendix* (London: J. Hatchard & Son, 1824 [1823]).

Crosta, Suzanne, 'L'enfance sous la rhétorique de l'édification culturelle: la poétique régénératrice chez Joseph Zobel', in *Récits d'enfance antillaise* (Sainte Foy, Québec: GRECLA, 1998). See: http://www.lehman.cuny.edu/ile.en.ile/docs/crosta/zobel.html (accessed 14 October 2015).

Curtius, Anny Dominique, 'Cannibalizing *Doudouisme*, Conceptualizing the *Morne*: Suzanne Césaire's Caribbean Ecopoetics', *The South Atlantic Quarterly*, 115.3 (2016), pp. 513–34.

D'Arboussier, Gabriel, 'Une dangereuse mystification: la théorie de la négritude', *La nouvelle critique* (June 1949), pp. 34–47.

Dash, J. Michael, *The Other America: Caribbean Literature in a New World Context* (Charlottesville, VA/London: University Press of Virginia, 1998).

Diagne, Souleymane Bachir, *African Art as Philosophy: Senghor, Bergson and the Idea of Negritude* (Chicago, IL: University of Chicago Press, 2011).

Douglas, Rachel, *Frankétienne and Rewriting: A Work in Progress* (Lanham, MD: Lexington, 2009).

Du Tertre, Père Jean-Baptiste, *Histoire générale des Antilles habitées par les François, vol. 2* (Paris: Thomas Jolly, 1667).

Dumont, Jacques, 'La "famille" sportive aux Antilles françaises', *Outre-mers*, 96.364–65. Special issues 'Le Sport dans l'Empire Français. Un instrument de domination coloniale?' ed. by Driss Abbassi (2009), pp. 107–25.

Edwards, Brent Hayes, *The Practice of Diaspora: Literature, Translation, and the Rise of Black Internationalism* (Cambridge, MA: Harvard University Press, 2003).

Fanon, Frantz, *Peau noire, masques blancs* (Paris: Seuil, 1952).

——, *Black Skin, White Masks*, trans. by Richard Philcox (New York, NY: Grove Press, 2008).

Farred, Grant, 'You Can Go Home, You Just Can't Stay: Stuart Hall and the Caribbean Diaspora', *Research in African Literatures* 27.4 (1996), pp. 28–48.

Fauquenoy, Marguerite (ed.), *Atipa revisité ou les itinéraries de Parépou* (Fort-de-France: Presses Universitaires Créoles/Paris: L'Harmattan, 1989).

Ferguson, James, 'Uncomfortable Truth', *Caribbean Beat*, 82 (2006). See: http://caribbean-beat.com/issue-82/uncomfortable-truth#axzz30TcM5RiE (accessed 13 October 2015).

Filostrat, Christian, *Négritude et Agonistes: Assimilation against Nationalism in the French-Speaking Caribbean and Guyane* (Cherry Hill, NJ: Africana Homestead Legacy, 2008).

Fonkoua, Romuald, *Aimé Césaire* (Paris: Perrin, 2013 [2010]).
Fontaine, Thomas and Denis Peschanski, *La Collaboration, Vichy Paris Berlin, 1940–1945* (Paris: Tallandier/Archives nationales/Ministère de la Défense, 2014).
Franklin, Albert, 'La Négritude: réalité ou mystification?', *Présence Africaine*, 14 (1953), pp. 285–303.
Frazier, Edward Franklin, *The Negro Family in the United States* (Notre Dame, IN: University of Notre Dame Press, 2001 [1939]).
Gallagher, Mary, *Soundings in French Caribbean Literature since 1950: The Shock of Space and Time* (Oxford: Oxford University Press, 2002).
Gautier, Arlette, *Les Sœurs de Solitude: femmes et esclavages aux Antilles du XVIIe au XIXe siècle* (Rennes: Presses universitaires de Rennes, 2010).
Glissant, Édouard, *Le Discours antillais* (Paris: Seuil, 1981).
Glotfelty, Cheryll, 'Introduction: Literary Studies in an Age of Environmental Crisis', in Glotfelty and Fromm, *The Ecocriticism Reader: Landmarks in Literary Ecology* (Athens, GA: University of Georgia Press, 1996), pp. xv–xxxii.
Gouvernement de la Martinique, *Le Gouverneur Georges-Louis Ponton: sa carrière administrative et militaire. Sa mort et ses funérailles* (Fort-de-France: Imprimerie du Gouvernement, 1944).
Gyssels, Kathleen, *BLACK LABEL ou les déboires de Léon-Gontran Damas. Essais.* (Paris: Passage(s), 2016).
Hall, Stuart, Chas Critcher, Tony Jefferson, John Clarke, and Brian Roberts, *Policing the Crisis: Mugging, the State and Law and Order* (Basingstoke: Palgrave Macmillan, 2013 [1978]).
Hardwick, Louise, *Childhood, Autobiography and the Francophone Caribbean* (Liverpool: Liverpool University Press, 2013).
——, and Alessandro Corio (eds), 'Race, Violence and Biopolitics', a special issue of the *International Journal of Francophone Studies*, 17.3–4 (2014).
Harris, Leslie M., *In the Shadow of Slavery: African Americans in New York City, 1626–1863* (Chicago, IL: University of Chicago Press, 2004).
Hayot, Émile, *Les Gens de couleur libre du Fort Royal (1679–1823)* (Paris: SFHOM and Société d'Histoire de la Martinique, 2005 [1971]).
Hezekiah, Randolph, 'Joseph Zobel: The Mechanics of Liberation', *Black Images*, 4.3–4 (1975), pp. 44–55.
Hibran, René, 'Le Problème de l'art à la Martinique', *Tropiques*, 6–7 (1943), pp. 39–41, in Césaire et al., *Tropiques 1941–1945: collection complète* (Paris: Jean Michel Place, 1978).
——, 'Pour un art vraiment antillais', *Martinique: revue trimestrielle*, 1 (March 1944), pp. 21–25.
hooks, bell, *Ain't I a Woman? Black Women and Feminism* (Boston, MA: South End Press, 1981).

Jack, Belinda, *Negritude and Literary Criticism: The History and Theory of 'Negro-African' Literature in French* (Westport, CT: Greenwood Press, 1996).

Jennings, Eric T., 'La Dissidence aux Antilles (1940–1943)', *Vingtième siècle: revue d'histoire*, 68.1 (2000), pp. 55–72.

Jones, Donna V., *The Racial Discourses of Life Philosophy: Négritude, Vitalism and Modernity* (New York: Columbia University Press, 2010).

Julien, Eileen, 'La Métamorphose du réel dans *La Rue Cases-Nègres*', *French Review*, 60.6 (1987), pp. 781–87.

Jünger, Ernst, *La Paix*, trans. by Armand Petitjean and Banine (Paris: La Table ronde, 1948).

Kesteloot, Lilyan, *Les Écrivains noirs de langue française: naissance d'une littérature* (Brussels: Université Libre de Bruxelles, 1963).

——, *Black Writers in French: A Literary History of Négritude*, trans. by Ellen Conroy Kennedy (Philadelphia, PA: Temple University Press, 1974).

Khalfa, Jean, 'The Heart of the Black Race: Parisian Négritudes in the 1920s', *Wasafiri*, 23.4 (2008), pp. 15–24.

——, 'Joseph Zobel in Paris', *Wasafiri*, 28.1 (2013), pp. 25–26.

Labat, Père Jean-Baptiste, *Nouveau voyage aux Isles de l'Amérique Contenant L'Histoire Naturelle de ces Pays, l'Origine, les Moeurs, la Religion & le Gouvernement des Habitans anciens & modernes [...] Ouvrage enrichi de plus de cent Cartes, Plans & Figures en Taille-douces. Nouvelle Édition augmentée considérablement, & enrichie de Figures en Taille-douces*, 8 vols (Paris: Cavelier, 1742).

Langellier, Paul, 'Review: *Diab'-la, roman antillais* [sic] by Joseph Zobel', *The French Review*, 19.5 (1946), p. 322.

Largange, Alfred, 'Lire et relire Diab'-là', *Potomitan*, 2006. See: http://www.potomitan.info/bibliographie/zobel/diabla.php (accessed 13 July 2015).

Larrier, Renée, *Autofiction and Advocacy in the Francophone Caribbean* (Gainesville, FL: University Press of Florida, 2006).

Lewis, Shireen K., *Race, Culture and Identity: Francophone West African and Caribbean Literature and Theory from Négritude to Créolité* (Lanham, MD: Lexington, 2006).

Locke, Alain (ed.), *The New Negro: An Interpretation* (New York: Albert and Charles Boni, 1927 [1925]).

Louis, Patrick, *La Table ronde: une aventure singulière* (Paris: La Table ronde, 1992).

Louri, Ludovic, with the collaboration of Florence Gauthier, *Habitation Trénelle 1948–1974: les travaux et les jours. Mémoires* (Fort-de-France, K Éditions, 2010).

——, *Rivière-Salée 1943–1974* (Fort-de-France, K Éditions, 2016).

Makward, Christiane, *Mayotte Capécia ou l'aliénation selon Fanon* (Paris: Karthala, 1999).

Maran, René, 'Un Plaidoyer contre l'esclavage. Destins de l'empire', *Gavroche*, 11 October 1945, p. 1 and continued on p. 6.

——, 'La Martinique, bastion littéraire française des Antilles', *Les Lettres françaises*, 3 May 1946, p. 5.

——, 'Le Mouvement littéraire aux Antilles et à la Guyane', *De West-Indische Gids*, 33 (1952), pp. 12–22. The article was reproduced with permission of the review *Eldorado*, where it had originally appeared in 1949.

Marshall Zobel, Emily and Jenny Zobel, 'Dans cette immensité tumultueuse', *Wasafiri*, 28.1 (2013), 27–35.

Maximin, Daniel, *Tu, c'est l'enfance* (Paris: Gallimard, 2004).

McIntosh, Malachi, *Emigration and Caribbean Literature* (New York: Palgrave Macmillan, 2015).

McKay, Claude, *Banjo: A Story Without a Plot* (New York & London: Harper and Brothers, 1929).

Ménil, René, 'Naissance de notre art', *Tropiques*, 1 (April 1941), in Césaire et al., *Tropiques 1941–1945: collection complète* (Paris: Jean Michel Place, 1978), pp. 53–64.

Mercier, Vivian, 'The Uneventful Event', *The Irish Times*, 18 February 1956, p. 6.

Miller, Bart, *Rethinking Négritude through Léon-Gontran Damas* (Amsterdam: Rodopi, 2014).

Mitchell, Ernest Julius II, '"Black Renaissance": A Brief History of the Concept', *Amerikastudien / American Studies*, 55.4, special issue 'African American Literary Studies: New Texts, New Approaches, New Challenges' (2010), pp. 641–65.

Mitchell, Keith B., 'Naming That Which Dare Not Speak: Homosexual Desire in Joseph Zobel's *La Rue cases-nègres*', in *Rhetoric of the Other: Lesbian and Gay Strategies of Resistance in French and Francophone Contexts*, ed. by Martine Antle and Dominique Fisher (New Orleans, LA: University Press of the South, 2002), pp. 115–30.

Moitt, Bernard, *Women and Slavery in the French Antilles, 1635–1848* (Bloomington, IN: Indiana University Press, 2001).

Mollier, Jean-Yves, *Édition, presse et pouvoir en France au XXe siècle* (Paris: Fayard, 2008).

Munro, Martin, *Different Drummers: Rhythm and Race in the Americas* (Berkeley, CA: University of California Press, 2010).

Myers, Norman, Russell A. Mittermeier, Cristina G. Mittermeier, Gustavo A. B. da Fonseca, and Jennifer Kent, 'Biodiversity Hotspots for Conservation Priorities', *Nature*, 403, 24 February 2000, 853–58.

Naipaul, V. S., *The Mimic Men* (London: Pan Macmillan, 2002 [1967]).

Nicole, Raphaël, *Histoire des Antilles françaises des Amérindiens à nos jours* (Trinité: Éditions de la Frise, 2012).

Ozée, Marie-France and Alex Carotine, 'Les Éditions caribéennes: comment me prouver que je suis Antillais?', *Libération*, 28 May 1982, p. 35.
Parépou, Alfred, *Atipa: un roman guyanais* (Paris: Auguste Ghio, 1885).
Price, Richard, *The Convict and the Colonel: A Story of Colonialism and Resilience in the Caribbean* (Durham, NC: Duke University Press, 2006).
Qureshi, Sadiah, 'Displaying Sara Baartman, the "Hottentot Venus"', *History of Science*, 42 (2004), pp. 233–57.
Relouzat, Raymond, *Joseph Zobel: La Rue Cases-Nègres* (Fort-de-France, Martinique: Librairie Relouzat, n.d.).
Rétif, André, 'Review of *La Rue Cases-Nègres*', *Études*, 84.268 (January 1951).
Robert, Amiral Jean, *La France aux Antilles (1939–1943)* (Vaduz, Lichtenstein: Calivran Anstalt, 1978 [1950]).
Rosemain, Jacqueline, *La Musique dans la société antillaise: 1635–1902* (Paris: L'Harmattan, 1986).
Ross, Kristin, *Fast Cars, Clean Bodies* (Cambridge, MA: Massachusetts Institute of Technology, 1996).
Roumain, Jacques, *Gouverneurs de la Rosée* (Port-au-Prince: Imprimerie de l'état, 1944).
Rueckert, William, 'Into and Out of the Void: Two Essays', *Iowa Review*, 9.1 (winter 1978), pp. 62–86. Republished as 'Literature and Ecology: An Experiment in Ecocriticism' in Cheryll Glotfelty and Harold Fromm, *The Ecocriticism Reader: Landmarks in Literary Ecology* (Athens, GA: University of Georgia Press, 1996), pp. 105–23.
Said, Edward, *Culture and Imperialism* (London: Vintage, 1993).
——, *Representations of the Intellectual: 1993 Reith Lectures* (London: Vintage, 1994).
Sartre, Jean-Paul, 'Orphée noir', in Léopold Sédar Senghor, *Anthologie de la Nouvelle Poésie nègre et malgache de langue française* (Paris: Presses Universitaires de France, 1948), pp. ix–xliv.
Scheel, Charles W., 'Introduction au dossier "Zobel" retrouvé dans la bibliothèque universitaire de l'UCAD à Dakar', *Continents manuscrits* 8 (2017), published 15 March 2017. See: http://coma.revues.org/857 (accessed 6 August 2017).
Sharpley-Whiting, T. Denean, *Negritude Women* (Minneapolis, MN: University of Minnesota Press, 2002).
Taher, Amode, *La Rue Cases-Nègres de Joseph Zobel: analyse critique* (Vacoas, Mauritius: Le Printemps, 1989).
Tardon, Raphaël, *Bleu des îles: récits martiniquais* (Paris: Fasquelle, 1946).
Tarrieu, Véronique, '"Je suis comme eux et ils sont comme moi": un entretien avec Joseph Zobel, Fonds Masson, 14 March 1995', *INDIGO: North American and Caribbean Studies Newsletter of the Université des Antilles-Guyane*, 22–23 (1999), pp. 29–41.

'The American Association for the Advancement of Science: Cassava-nova', *The Economist*, 20 February 2016, p. 70.

Thibault, André, 'Les Régionalismes dans *La Rue Cases-Nègres* (1950) de Joseph Zobel', in *Richesses du français et géographie linguistique*, ed. by André Thibault (Bruxelles: De Boeck-Duculot, 2008), pp. 227–314.

—— and Patrick Drouin, 'Le Lexique de Joseph Zobel, auteur antillais: extraction semi-automatique des particularismes lexicaux', paper presented at XXV edition of the *Congrès International de Linguistique et de Philologies Romanes*, Innsbruck, 3–7 September 2007. See: http://www.rose.uzh.ch/seminar/personen/glessgen/actes_cilpr_Thibault_Drouin_section17.pdf (accessed 19 July 2016).

Tiffin, Helen and Graham Huggan, *Postcolonial Ecocriticism: Literature, Animals, Environment* (London: Routledge, 2009).

Tirolien, Guy, *Balles d'or* (Paris: Présence Africaine, 1961).

——, *Golden Bullets/Balles d'or: a dual-language edition*, trans. by Micheline Rice-Maximin, Richard Sale, and Arthur Gionet (Paris: Les Éditions du Manguier, 2014).

Toumson, Roger, *La Transgression des couleurs: littérature et langage des Antilles, XVIIIe, XIXe et XXe siècles, tome 2* (Paris: Éditions caribéennes, 1989).

Warner, Keith Q., 'Emasculation on the Plantation: A Reading of Joseph Zobel's *La Rue Cases-Nègres*', *College Language Association Journal*, 32 (1988), pp. 38–44.

Watkins, Sylvestre C. (ed.), *An Anthology of American Negro Literature* (New York: The Modern Library, Random House, Inc., 1944).

Watts, Richard, *Packaging Post/coloniality: The Manufacture of Literary Identity in the Francophone World* (Lanham, MD: Lexington, 2005).

Wood, Peter, 'Slave Labor Camps in Early America: Overcoming Denial and Discovering the Gulag', in *Inequality in Early America*, ed. by Gardina Pestana and Sharon V. Salinger (Hanover, NH: University Press of New England, 1999), pp. 222–38.

Wright, Richard, *Native Son* (New York & London: Harper and Brothers, 1940).

——, *Black Boy* (New York & London: Harper and Brothers, 1945).

Wylie, Hal, 'Joseph Zobel's use of Negritude and Social Realism', *World Literature Today*, 56.1 (1982), pp. 61–64.

'Zobel: sa vie, son œuvre', *Les Cahiers de l'U.G.T.M. Education*, 6 (October 1985), pp. 19–32 [transcription of radio interview with Radio Asé Pléré Annou Lité on 24 February 1985].

Zobel, Jenny and Emily Marshall Zobel, '"Lorsque je vais dans mon village" (When I Return to My Village): Joseph Zobel's Visions of Home and Exile', *Wasafiri*, 26.3 (2011), pp. 1–8.

Audiovisual Works Cited

(audiovisual archival material is referenced in next section)

BBC1, *Who Do You Think You Are: Liz Bonnin*, 9 December 2016.

Condé, Maryse, 'Joseph Zobel', propos recueillis par Annette M'Baye d'Erneville. Interview followed by readings of selections of *La Rue Cases-Nègres* by Jenny Alpha and Robert Liensol (co-production CLEF – Radio France Internationale. Non commercialisé. En prêt au Service Culturel de l'Ambassade de France dans les États d'Afrique francophone et de l'Océan Indien). (No date – Worldcat places the date between 1978 and 1980. See: http://www.worldcat.org/title/joseph-zobel/oclc/29033391].

Gallet, Dominique and Mona Makki, *Joseph Zobel: le soleil d'ébène* ('tv-francophonie' production, 2002).

Kezadri, Kamel and Olivier Codol, *Joseph Zobel, d'amour et de silence* (Mona Lisa, RFO, 1998).

Léardée, Ernest, 'Dans trou crab'-là', *Quand Paris biguinait: orchestres créoles 1930–1940*, CD (1991).

Palcy, Euzhan, *Rue Cases-Nègres*, 1983. English: *Sugar Cane Alley*. An alternative English title is *Black Shack Alley* (see Introduction).

——, *Aimé Césaire. Une parole pour le XXIème siècle / A Voice for the 21st Century* (Paris: JMJ productions, 1994–2006). Box set of three films, including the booklet *Aimé Césaire, un recueil de textes* (no place or editor, 1994).

——, *Parcours de dissidents* (France: JMJ Productions, 2006).

Schaffer, Matt, 'Interview with Joseph Zobel, 23 June 1969', unpublished original cassette recording (digitised) and transcript held at MARBL, the Woodruff Library, Emory University, Atlanta. Audio cassette reference: ID: q4gtr (side A); ID: q4gvw (side B). MSS 755 Matt Schaffer Collection Box 2, Folder 4.

Stellio, Alexandre, 'Ah Gade chabine-là', *Au bal antillais: Franco-Creole Biguines from Martinique*, CD (1992).

Archival Sources
Martinique

Archives départementales, Schœlcher

Miscellaneous issues of *Le Sportif*. Earliest is no. 21, Thursday 29 September 1938. PER 156/1938-1950.

Zobel, Joseph writing as Kay-Mac-Zo, 'Mon Village', *Le Sportif*, 138, 27 December 1940, pp. 3–4. PER 156/1938-1950.

Bibliothèque Schœlcher, Fort-de-France

Relouzat, Raymond, *Joseph Zobel: La Rue Cases-Nègres* (Fort-de-France, Martinique: Librairie Relouzat, no year). Copy is stamped 21 June 1972 (p. 3). The lectures, and interview with Zobel, must therefore date from between 1969 and 1972. 843.009-2ZOB.

Le Fonds Zobel, Musée régional d'histoire et d'ethnographie, Fort-de-France

Clippings from *Le Sportif, Les Cahiers de la libération*, DD:JZ.B.246.

'A Paraître: *Les Jours immobiles: roman antillais* de Joseph Zobel', *Le Sportif*, 8 August 1946, n. pag. DD:JZ.B.246.

'Acte de naissance de Joseph Zobel: extrait du registre des actes de l'État Civil de la commune de Rivière-Salée, 1915'. On display at the Écomusée de la Martinique (at the time of inspection in 2013).

Adréa, Albert, 'Encore un des nôtres!', no publication name, issue number 1539, date 1946, n. pag. DD:JZ.B.246.

'*Diab'-là* par Joseph Zobel', *Le Sportif*, 24 mars 1945 (p. 3). DD:JZ.B.246.

'Échos des Lettres et des Arts', *La Croix*, stamped 15 and 16 February 1948. DD:JZ.B.246.

'Le beau livre que voilà' *Le Clairon*, 10 July 1945. DD:JZ.B.246.

M., Th., 'Joseph Zobel', *Le Sportif*, 16 février 1946, n. pag. DD:JZ.B.246.

Midas, André, 'Joseph Zobel et *Les Jours immobiles*', *L'Information*, 26 August 1946 (n. pag.). DD:JZ.B.246.

'School Photograph with Stephen Rose', on display at the Écomusée de la Martinique (at the time of inspection in 2013).

Tarrieu, V[éronique] *Indigo*, MS:DD:JZ.B, 1995.

Zobel, Joseph, *Chants de la Négritude: 14 poètes, 20 poèmes de la Négritude*. Boite: Poèmes. 2014.17.3; No. 2014.17.3.15. A.

——, *Cocotte ou les jours immobiles* [manuscript] 2014.17.4.9.

Patrimoines Martinique Online Database

Eugène Zobel. Record 2E8/19, actes 1384–1389, dated 1849–1857. See also record E_d_8/E30, actes 1384–1389, dated 1849–1857: http://www.patrimoines-martinique.org/?id=chercher&formulaire=etat_civil (accessed 8 January 2015).

Metropolitan France

ANOM (Archives nationales d'Outre-Mer), Aix-en-Provence

Césaire, Aimé, letter to Georges-Louis Ponton, dated 17 July 1944, ANOM: FP 173APOM/1 PONTON.

Bibliothèque Mazarine, Paris

Césaire et al., *Martinique: revue trimestrielle*, 1 (March 1944). Fort-de-France: Service général d'information des Antilles françaises. ANT 4°164.

Bibliothèque nationale de France, Paris

Zobel, Joseph, *Incantation pour un retour au pays natal / Joseph Zobel dit trois poèmes de Joseph Zobel* (Voxigrave VX6845, no year). Bibliothèque nationale de France: FRBNF38067745, stamped 1966 [handwritten date added: 1965].

L'INA, accessed at Salle P, Bibliothèque nationale de France, Paris

Bazin, Hervé, '*La Rue Cases-Nègres*', RFO, dated 1 March 1957.

'Joseph Zobel lauréat du prix des lecteurs', *Ondes courtes*, Radiodiffusion française, service des émissions vers l'étranger, dated 22 October 1950.

'Vente du livre de la mer et de l'outre-mer', Chaîne nationale, RTF, dated 12 December 1952.

Musée du Quai Branly, Paris

Martinique, 2 (1944) – 5 (1946). Magasins P1660, PERIODIQUE.

Zobel, Joseph, 'Considérations sur l'art local', *Martinique*, 5 (1946), pp. 33–38: Magasins P1660, PERIODIQUE.

United States

Stuart A. Rose Library (MARBL – Manuscripts, Archives and Rare Book Library), Emory University, Atlanta, Georgia

Relouzat, Raymond, *Joseph Zobel: La Rue Cases-Nègres* (Fort-de-France, Martinique: Librairie Relouzat, n.d.). Part of Michel Fabre collection. Barcode: 010002394902.

Schaffer, Matt, 'Interview with Joseph Zobel, 23 June 1969', unpublished original cassette recording (digitised) and transcript. Audio cassette: ID: q4gtr (side A); ID: q4gvw (side B). Transcript: MSS 755 Matt Schaffer Collection Box 2, Folder 4.

Index

Abetz, Otto 20
abolition 39, 61, 66, 79, 88–89, 120, 126, 155, 164–65
Achille, Louis 17, 26
Achille, Louis-Thomas 26
Adréa, Albert 135n41, 138n42
Africa 2, 5, 7, 11, 21–22, 26, 28, 31n1, 35, 39–40, 46, 53, 70, 79, 84–85, 93, 105, 107, 118, 122, 126, 131, 134, 152, 154–55, 157n34, 158, 164–68, 190–92, 214, 215n31, 218, 225–26, 228, 232–35, 238, 241, 249–51
African American 5n9, 33, 50, 54, 77, 226n38, 232
Akpagu, Zana Itiunbe 143
Algeria 202, 225
alienation 67, 116, 177–79, 186, 198, 221, 229, 232
Aliker, André 92–94
Alliot, David 93
Amerindian 39, 104, 122–24, 126–29, 131–34, 141, 246
André, Jacques 146, 163, 175, 179, 185
Anglophone 6, 21, 33, 52, 158, 166, 178, 187
L'Anse Figuier 127, 246
Les Anses d'Arlet 17, 107–08, 110, 113–14, 119, 121, 127–28, 132, 140
anthology, anthologie 12, 49–50, 52–55
antillanité 39–40
D'Arboussier, Gabriel 54, 100

Arlet, Chief 127
Arnold, A. James 51
Ashcroft, Bill 64
assimilation 7, 9, 168, 173, 180, 221n35, 228
Ateba, Jacques Etoundi 249
Aubéry, Eugène 94
audience 3, 5, 9, 18, 45, 47, 62, 63, 69, 71, 81, 124, 143, 181, 203, 210, 221, 243–47
autobiography 2, 10, 58, 126, 142, 152, 154, 158, 185, 192, 220, 251

Baartman, Sara 215–16
baccalauréat 15–16, 19, 94, 171, 188
Badiane, Mamadou 7–8n13
bal nègre 33, 223
Bayle, Henri 95
Bazin, Hervé 191n8
Beckett, Samuel 103
béké 13, 65–66, 71, 87, 92, 94, 109–110, 119–120, 145, 149, 157, 159, 160, 163, 165–67, 169, 184–85, 198, 212, 220, 223–24, 231, 237
bèlè 138
Bénard, Pierre 98
Benjamin, Moïse 'Benzo' 64
Beringuier, Christian 172n46
Beuze, Lyne-Rose 29, 76–77
Bhabha, Homi K. 173
Bildungsroman 158
biodiversity 81, 102

biopolitics 61, 77–78, 231
Bissol, Léopold 94
Black Shack Alley (film) *see* Euzhan Palcy *Rue Cases-Nègres*
Black Shack Alley (translation) *see* Keith Q. Warner
Blanshard, Paul 195n13, 196n17
Boittin, Jennifer Anne 7–8n13, 31
Bonnichon, Philippe 131n33
Bonnin, Liz 120n16
Bory, Jean-Louis 149
Bourdieu, Pierre 30, 193, 210, 215, 242, 245
bourgeois 8, 11, 15, 62, 85, 115–16, 128, 143–46, 160, 170–73, 178, 183, 186, 195, 200, 204, 211–13, 223, 227, 230, 242
Bouville, Raphaëlle 248
Brazil 131, 209, 220
Brer Rabbit *see* Compère Lapin
Breton, Révérend Père Raymond 122, 131
Burton, Richard D. E. 195n14
Butel, Paul 20n36, 94n41

Calverton, V. F. 52–53
Camus, Albert 58–59
Canada 47, 49
Capécia, Mayotte 150, 153
Caribbean *see individual island entries*
Carotine, Alex 202n22
Céco, Mérine 247
Césaire, Aimé 1, 7, 8, 14–16, 18–23, 26–27, 31, 34, 36, 42–44, 51, 53, 56, 62–63, 67–69, 72, 78, 82, 84, 86, 90, 93, 96, 99, 106, 152, 176, 178, 189, 214, 227, 229, 235, 241, 244
    Cahier d'un retour au pays natal 18, 34, 44, 68, 86, 152, 176, 227
Césaire, Ina 166–67n43
Césaire, Suzanne 8, 31, 48, 51, 56
César, Sylvie 115, 249
Chamoiseau, Patrick 61–62, 122, 164n39

Chivallon, Christine 196
Chomereau-Lamotte, Gabrielle 29
Clark, Kenneth Bancroft 232
Clark, Mamie Phipps 232
Le Code noir 119
Codol, Olivier *see Joseph Zobel, d'amour et de silence*
Cohen, William B. 226n37
colonial, colonialism 5, 7, 10–12, 16, 23, 29, 32, 35–38, 46–47, 52n42, 56, 79, 81, 91–93, 95, 104, 114–15, 124, 126–27, 131–34, 141, 144, 151–53, 157–58, 165–66, 168–69, 170, 173–74, 177, 179–80, 188–89, 195, 200, 204, 207, 209, 211–12, 216–17, 219–23, 225, 226n37, 227–31, 238–39, 244, 246, 253
colony 6, 21, 24–25, 82, 185, 189, 205, 228, 237–40
communism 93–94, 100
Compère Lapin 166
Condé, Maryse 1, 17n28, 104n3–n4, 107n7, 114n11
Confiant, Raphaël 249–50
Cook, Mercer 81
Creole 24, 27, 36, 39, 63–65, 69–73, 88, 91–92, 101, 113–14, 117, 120, 122, 126–29, 132, 134–35, 138, 141, 152, 162, 164, 166–67n43, 180, 205, 232, 249–50
créolité 7n13, 39, 64, 71–72, 122, 164n39, 250
Crosta, Suzanne 150
Cuba 53, 83, 214
Cupidon, Antoine 53
Curtius, Anny Dominique 8, 31
Czech 3, 64

Dadié, Bernard B. 53
Dakar 24n46, 26, 97, 158
Damas, Léon-Gontran 7, 8, 31, 34, 42, 78, 178, 189, 232, 235, 244
Dash, J. Michael 83

Index 269

decolonisation 36, 241, 251
département d'outre-mer 6, 185, 218, 224
Desportes, Georges 53
Dewitte, Philippe 35
Diagne, Souleymane Bachir 35n7
Diakhate, Lamine 53
Le Diamant 17, 65, 67, 73, 76, 77n22, 78–79, 81, 88, 107, 121, 236
diaspora 2, 84, 167, 180–81, 195–96, 204n24, 228
Diop, Birago 53
Diop, David 53
disability 111–12
Dominica 21, 195
doudou 34, 152
doudouiste, doudouisme 8n16, 56
Douglas, Rachel 105–06
Duhamel, Marcel 55
Dumont, Jacques 52
Dutch 3

ecocriticism 10, 29, 56–57, 60–102, 128, 244
École des Beaux-Arts 16
École Normale Supérieure (Paris) 18, 51
Écomusée de la Martinique 13n20, 14n24, 127, 246
Éditions caribéennes 202–03
education 11, 14–17, 35, 38, 91–92, 113–14, 151, 162, 163–64n38, 167–72, 174, 176, 183, 185, 198–200, 217, 223, 226, 238, 242, 249
Edwards, Brent Hayes 7n13, 31
elite 5, 15–16, 20, 22–23, 35–36, 45, 59, 63, 67, 73, 92, 97, 126, 128, 152, 181, 188, 193, 195, 200, 204, 211–12, 217, 230, 237, 253
emigration *see also* immigration; migration 35, 187–88, 192–209, 221

environment 2, 10, 29, 56–57, 62, 67, 76, 79, 81–82, 102, 106–07, 111, 121, 124, 127–28, 132, 134, 141, 162, 178, 181, 212, 234, 246, 249
état civil 13–14, 155
ethnoclass 12, 42, 77, 144–45, 152, 159–61, 167, 169, 170, 179, 183, 199–200, 204, 220, 222–23, 230, 236–39, 251
Eurocentric 16, 171, 205
Europe 2, 4–6, 35–36, 44, 53, 70, 80, 127, 138, 146, 151–52, 174, 187–88, 190, 194–95, 204–05, 212–13, 220–21, 225, 227, 231, 233, 241–43, 245–46, 250
évolué 11
exile 60, 209, 220
exotic 54, 56, 63, 98, 121, 135, 152–53, 155, 205, 223, 252
exploitation 2, 47, 61, 65–66, 81–83, 117, 120, 128, 144, 157, 160–63, 179, 183–84, 227, 245, 252

Fanon, Frantz 26, 38, 88–89, 125, 150, 157, 177, 187–88, 205, 221, 233, 237, 241
Peau noire, masques blancs 38, 88–89, 125, 177, 187, 221
Farred, Grant 204
Ferguson, James 149n20
Festival mondial des arts nègres 26
film 2, 5, 6n10, 14–16, 28, 43–44, 62, 115, 135, 146, 149, 150–51, 158, 180–81, 185, 196, 200, 212, 243, 246, 248, 249
Filostrat, Christian 7n11
fishing 17, 44, 62, 64–70, 77n22, 78, 80, 103, 107–09, 111, 121, 133, 172
Le Fonds Zobel 13n20, 14n24, 24n46, 24n49, 53n45, 81n28, 97n49–50, 99n62, 108n8, 123n19–20, 135n39, 135n41
Fonkoua, Romuald 14n23, 15n25, 18n29, 21n39, 35n6

Fort-de-France 8–9, 11, 13n20, 15, 17–18, 20–22, 24, 49, 53, 80, 92, 94, 96, 98, 104, 145, 149, 169, 171–72, 175–77, 183, 237–38
Foucault, Michel 77
Francophone 1–6, 21, 26, 32–33, 36, 39, 45–46, 52–53, 63, 68, 81, 138, 146, 151–52, 158, 166, 178, 180, 187, 195, 244, 247–48
Franklin, Albert 100–101
Franklin Frazier, Edward 77
Frémanger, Charles 149
French Guyana 5, 64
Froissart (Éditions Jean Froissart) 149–50, 153, 201

Gallagher, Mary 170–71
Gallet, Dominique *see* Joseph Zobel: le soleil d'ébène
De Gaulle, Charles 20–21, 195
Gauthier, Florence 247n3
Gautier, Arlette 117n13
gender 2, 5, 8, 73–78, 109, 152, 163, 179, 216, 242, 249
Générargues 25, 27, 104
genocide 60, 127, 226
Ghana 21
Glissant, Édouard 6, 26, 60, 73, 106
Glotfelty, Cheryll 56–57
De Gobineau, Joseph Arthur 225, 233
grandfather 14, 110, 119, 163, 211–12
grandmother 13, 15, 108–09, 144, 148, 154, 156, 159, 162–63, 173, 178, 184, 210, 212, 237, 247
griot 164
Guadeloupe 5, 63, 166, 195–96, 220
Guillén, Nicolás 53
Guilloux, Louis 58–59, 143, 153
Gyssels, Kathleen 8, 31

Haiti 1–2n4, 21, 23, 32, 81–82, 84, 90, 106, 226
Hall, Stuart 193, 204, 206–08

Hardwick, Louise 10n18, 55n50, 77–78n24, 150n22, 155n30, 158n35
Harlem Renaissance *see* Negro Renaissance
Harris, Leslie M. 226n38–n39
Hausa 155
Hayot, Émile 120n15
Hezekiah, Randolph 41, 47–48, 67, 88–89, 91, 100, 160
Hibran, René 123
Holocaust 127, 209, 220
homosexuality 175
hooks, bell 117–18
Huggan, Graham 57n54
Hughes, Langston 51, 53, 81

immigration *see also* emigration; migration 2, 44–45, 142, 194–95, 202, 207, 217, 224, 230, 233, 241
indigénisme 32
Indochina *see also* Vietnam 218
inferiority complex (also referred to as complexe d'infériorité) 12, 178, 221–22, 228, 230, 239, 241
Institut d'ethnologie 25, 189, 214, 217, 225–27
intertextuality 106, 179–80
Italian 3

Jack, Belinda 100
Jamaica 37n9, 179, 204
Jennings, Eric T. 195n15
Jew, Jewish 22, 46, 209, 220
Jones, Donna V. 35n7
Julien, Eileen 163–64n38
Jünger, Ernst 201

Kane, Cheikh Hamidou 31n1
Kanters, Robert 149
Kay-Mac-Zo 51–52, 99
Kennedy, Ellen Conroy 45
Kesteloot, Lilyan 45–47, 59, 93
Kezadri, Kamel *see* Joseph Zobel, d'amour et de silence

Khalfa, Jean 7n13, 31, 188, 195
Khaly, Néné 53
King, Martin Luther 36, 235

Labat, Père Jean-Baptiste 132–33
laghia 24, 27, 75, 85–86, 116, 142, 197, 251
Lam, Wifredo 214
Lamming, George 194–95
Langellier, Paul 97
Larcher family 119–21, 137
Largange, Alfred 71, 98n58
Larose, Gilbert 246
Larrier, Renée 55, 144, 147n14, 166, 175
Laye, Camara 31n1
Léardée, Ernest 72
Lemoigne, José 248n8, 249
Lévi-Strauss, Claude 163
Levy, Andrea 194
Lewis, Shireen K. 7n13, 31
Locke, Alain 50–52, 54
Lorion, Paul 53
Lotaut, Eustache 97
Louis, Patrick 201
Louri, Ludovic 246–47
Lycée Schœlcher 15–19, 23, 26, 50, 62–63, 67, 93–94, 96, 171–73, 178, 200, 217

Maire, André 77
Makki, Mona *see Joseph Zobel: le soleil d'ébène*
Makward, Christiane 153n2
manioc 130–35, 137–38
Maran, René 7, 60, 97n54, 98–99, 151, 178–80, 220–21, 235
  Batouala 99, 179
  Un Homme pareil aux autres 220, 235
marron, marronnage (also referred to as maroon) 80, 89, 93, 252
Marshall Zobel, Emily 1n1, 1n3, 192n9, 208n26–n27, 209n28, 224n36

Martinique 3–6, 8–9, 12–14, 16–18, 20–25, 27, 29, 31–32, 38–40, 42, 44, 49–52, 57–60, 62–63, 65, 68–69, 72, 76–79, 81–83, 89, 93–98, 101, 103–07, 110, 112, 113n9, 114–15, 117, 119, 121, 123–24, 126–28, 131, 133, 137, 141–43, 147–49, 152–53, 155, 157, 169, 172, 183, 185, 188, 190–91, 194–200, 203–05, 207, 217, 219, 221–23, 228, 230, 233, 236–38, 241–42, 245–52
Martiniquais/Martinican 1, 4, 5–6, 9–14, 16–23, 24n49, 25–26, 28, 32, 36–37, 39, 44–45, 50–52, 54, 56–57, 60–63, 65, 68–71, 76–77, 79–81, 83, 85–86, 88–89, 91–99, 101–03, 106–109, 111–112, 116, 119–121, 123–27, 129, 133, 135–38, 140–42, 144–46, 148, 151–53, 155, 158, 160, 168–69, 171, 173, 179, 181, 183, 185, 188, 190, 195–96, 198–201, 203–04, 207–08, 211, 220–24, 228–233, 236–37, 244, 246–52
Maure 61
Maximin, Daniel 8, 31, 55n50
M'Baye d'Erneville, Annette 17n28, 104n3
McIntosh, Malachi 35, 188, 190n7
McKay, Claude 32, 36, 49, 50–52, 55, 58, 71, 178–80, 221n35
  Banjo 36, 49–50, 55, 99, 179–80, 221n35
Melet, Pierre 81
Ménil, René 16, 19, 51, 123
Mercier, Vivian 103n1
metonymic gap 64, 71
Midas, André 135n39
Middle Passage 118, 164
migration *see also* emigration; immigration 30, 146, 188, 194–95, 203, 230, 245

Miller, Bart 7n12, 8, 31, 189n5
mimic man 173–74, 194
mindfulness 130
mission civilisatrice 35–36, 39, 95, 117, 173, 196, 227–28
Mitchell, Ernest Julius II 5n9, 50n36–n37
Mitchell, Keith B. 175n51
Moitt, Bernard 117n13
Mollier, Jean-Yves 201
Monchoachi 249–50
Monnerot, Jules 93–94
Monpierre, Roland 28, 67, 98n56, 248
mother *see also* grandmother 13–15, 110, 139, 154–56, 161, 169–70, 171, 173, 176–78, 183, 196, 199–200, 235
Munro, Martin 48, 147
Musée des Colonies 214, 216
Musée de l'Homme 214–16
Myers, Norman 102n67

Naipaul, V. S. 173–74, 194
Nardal, Andrée 7–8, 31, 251–52
Nardal, Jane 7–8, 31, 251–52
Nardal, Paulette 7–8, 31, 51, 251–52
Nazi 197, 208, 220
nègre see also petit-nègre 4, 12, 16–17, 26, 33–40, 42–45, 51, 54, 61, 67–70, 76, 87–89, 91–92, 95, 99, 101, 115–16, 118, 124, 126, 128, 160–61, 165–66, 168, 174–76, 178–79, 180–81, 183, 185, 193, 197–98, 206–07, 213, 220, 223, 226–27, 230, 232, 236–37, 239, 240–42, 249n11, 250, 253
négresse 38–39, 54, 76, 115, 117, 132
Négritude 2, 4–5, 7–12, 26, 29–59, 63, 67–70, 72, 75–76, 78–79, 84–85, 87–88, 90–91, 98–101, 116–17, 119, 126, 144–45, 164, 166, 172–86, 188–94, 198, 205, 214, 217–45, 250–53

Negro Renaissance 4–5, 29, 32–33, 36–37, 49–55, 58, 71, 93, 99, 180, 221n35, 243–44
New Negro movement 5, 50
Nicole, Raphaël 131n29, 133n38

Obama, Barak 37
Oyono, Ferdinand 31n1
Ozée, Marie-France 202n22

Palcy, Euzhan 2, 6n10, 28, 43, 44n18, 115, 150–51, 158, 195, 196n16, 243, 246, 248, 249
  Rue Cases-Nègres (film) 2, 5, 14, 28, 115, 151, 243, 248–49
Pan-africanism 7, 53
Parépou, Alfred 64
Paris 1, 3–4, 7–11, 14–16, 18–20, 24–28, 30, 33, 35–36, 43, 49, 51–53, 63, 64n7, 68, 72, 81, 93, 97–99, 101, 104–05, 107, 113n9, 143, 145, 147–50, 153, 155, 158, 169, 187–242, 245, 247–48, 250–51
Paris Salon du Livre (Paris Book Fair) 28, 64n7
Pétain, Philippe 17, 20, 81
Peterson, Charles E. 174
petit-nègre 16–17, 25, 38, 45, 115, 144–45, 159–60, 162, 164, 166–68, 170, 172–86, 197, 199, 200, 204, 222–23, 233, 237, 241–42
Philcox, Richard 1n2, 89n35, 187
Pillement, Georges 97–98
Pilote, Chief 127, 133
plantation (also referred to as habitation) 5, 13–14, 37, 44, 55, 60–62, 65–67, 77, 83–84, 101, 112, 114, 116–20, 132–33, 138, 144–45, 147, 154, 157, 160–67, 169–70, 174, 175n51, 177–78, 186, 212, 222, 236, 245–47, 249–50, 253

poetry 2, 4, 25, 27–28, 31, 33, 36, 43–44, 50–51, 53–54, 60, 68, 70, 72, 78, 87, 93, 100, 103, 105, 111, 136, 145, 152, 166, 176, 190, 227, 232, 249
politics 4–8, 10–12, 18–20, 21n37, 22–23, 31, 33, 35, 37, 42, 49, 52, 55, 57, 59, 68–69, 78–101, 103–04, 106, 110, 116, 125–26, 135, 157–58, 169, 173–74, 183, 185, 190, 209, 214, 218, 224, 240, 243–44, 251–52
Ponton, Georges-Louis 21–25, 82, 85, 96–97, 123, 189
postcolonial 9, 10, 29, 56–57, 64, 102, 157
Présence Africaine 26n53, 27, 100, 158, 202
Price, Richard 79
Price-Mars, Jean 32
Prix des lecteurs 150, 193n10, 217–18
Prix Goncourt 99, 179
psychoanalysis 88–89, 125, 177, 221, 233, 241

quimbois 136–38
Qureshi, Sadiah 215n31, 216n33

racism 7, 12, 37–38, 99–100, 115, 152, 160, 167–69, 181, 183, 200, 204, 206–07, 216, 218–19, 222–27, 231–37, 239, 251, 253
radio 2, 17, 19n31, 20–23, 25–26, 85, 94, 95n43, 97, 104, 107, 157, 193, 203, 217–19, 225, 243
Relouzat, Raymond 39–41, 55, 240
Republic 13, 196, 199, 207, 216, 218–19, 224, 226
Rétif, André 150n25
rewriting 3, 10–11, 27, 30, 105–08, 135–39, 141, 191–92, 195, 202–03, 214, 217, 229, 235, 238, 241, 244–45, 250
Rivet, Paul 215–16
Rivière-Salée 13–14, 246–48

Robert, Admiral Georges 17, 20–21, 24, 62, 80, 95–96
Roblot, Madeleine 120
Rose, Stephen 14
Rosemain, Jacqueline 138
Ross, Kristin 146–48, 159, 185, 209, 211–12, 245
Roumain, Jacques 81–83
Rueckert, William 56
Russian 3

Sabatier, Robert 149
Said, Edward 46, 243
Saint-Laurent, Cécil 149
Saint Lucia 195
Sartre, Jean-Paul 12, 36, 58, 100
Schaffer, Matt 26n52, 42n16, 149n17
Scheel, Charles F. 24n46, 97n49
Schœlcher, Victor 13, 88
Second World War 8, 17, 19, 49, 80, 93, 127, 146, 187–88, 193, 195, 197, 200–01, 207, 209, 214, 220, 224, 226
Selvon, Sam 194–95
Senegal 7, 24n46, 26, 40, 45, 56, 97, 104, 153, 155, 157, 191, 222, 250–51
Senghor, Léopold Sédar 7–8, 12, 26, 31, 35n7, 36, 42, 53, 56, 78, 155, 178, 189, 244
sexuality 55, 73–75, 77, 82, 100, 118, 136, 138, 152–53, 162–63, 175, 212, 232
Sharpley-Whiting, T. Denean 7n13, 31
slave, slavery 7, 13–14, 32, 34–35, 37n9, 38–39, 44, 46, 60–2, 64, 66–67, 77, 79–80, 84, 89, 93, 101, 104, 109, 116–20, 124–26, 128, 132–34, 138–39, 141, 147, 155, 158, 160, 163–65, 168, 174, 198, 208–09, 212, 222, 226n38, 234, 237, 246
Socé, Ousmane (also known as Ousmane Socé Diop) 7
Sorbonne 18, 22, 25, 189, 214, 217

Le Sportif 18–19, 22, 24, 43, 51–52, 62–63, 75, 97, 99, 123, 189
Stellio, Alexandre 72
Sugar Cane Alley see Euzhan Palcy Rue Cases-Nègres
surrealism 11, 36, 44, 70, 84, 100, 164, 214

Taher, Amode 47n28
Tardon, Raphaël 98, 151
Tarrieu, Véronique 24–25n49, 49n33–n34, 71n16, 72n17–n18, 189n4
Du Tertre, Père Jean-Baptiste 132
Thibault, André 47, 162
Thiéry, Patricia 248
Tiffin, Helen 57n54
Tirolien, Guy 53, 166
Togo 100, 226
Toomer, Jean 51
Toumson, Roger 171, 203n23
tourist, tourism 123–26, 147n14, 246
translation 2–4, 7n13, 29, 33–38, 42, 45, 50–51, 53, 55, 58, 63–64, 81, 103, 122, 131, 135, 145n7, 152, 156, 158, 168, 178, 197, 201, 247, 249–50
transnational 2, 4, 6, 28, 30, 53, 130–31, 210, 243–45
Trinidad 3, 158, 194
Tropiques 19–20, 21n37, 23, 42, 50–52, 56, 96, 123, 221n35

Valère, Laurent 79
Vichy 17, 20, 21n37, 29, 42, 47, 49, 51, 62, 68, 80–82, 94–96, 195
Vietnam 225, 228–29, 241

wake (also referred to as 'veillée') 108, 115, 140, 145
Warner, Keith Q. 2n6, 3, 42, 145n7, 158, 168, 175
Watkins, Sylvestre C. 52
Watts, Richard 152
Weldon Johnson, James 51, 53
West Indies 41, 97n54, 177
Windrush 194, 204
Wood, Peter 61n2, 66
working class 10, 58, 116, 143, 164, 177, 181, 195–96, 198, 200, 206, 208, 210, 241, 244
World Literature 37, 45n20, 46, 243
World War Two see Second World War
Wright, Richard 32, 36, 55, 71, 93
    Native Son 36, 49, 55
    Black Boy 36, 55
Wylie, Hal 45–48, 113, 139, 143

Zobel, Charlotte 29, 113n9, 142n1, 147, 189
Zobel, Emily Marshall see Emily Marshall Zobel
Zobel, Jenny 1n1, 13n21, 25, 150n22, 154–55, 192n9, 246, 248n9
Zobel, Joseph see also Kay-Mac-Zo
    Black Shack Alley (translation) see Keith Q. Warner
    Black Shack Alley and Sugar Cane Alley (film) see Euzhan Palcy Rue Cases-Nègres
    'Considérations sur l'art local' 23, 104, 123–27, 140, 221n35
    Diab'-là 2, 3, 9–11, 20, 23–25, 28–29, 36, 43, 46, 49, 54, 56, 60–102, 103–05, 107–08, 111–12, 116, 119, 121, 128, 135, 142–43, 149, 151, 160, 189, 192n9, 221, 240, 244, 247–48
    Et si la mer n'était pas bleue… 8n14, 27, 251–52
    La Fête à Paris 3–4, 10–11, 25, 27, 30, 43, 63, 101, 105, 107, 148, 155, 169, 187–242, 245, 250–51
    Laghia de la mort 24, 27, 75, 85–86, 116, 142, 197, 251
    La Rue Cases-Nègres 2–3, 6, 10–11, 15–16, 17n28, 25, 27, 30, 36, 39–40, 47n28, 48, 50, 54–55, 66, 92, 101, 105, 108–11, 128, 142–86, 188, 190–93, 197–204, 209–212,

217, 221, 232, 234, 242–43,
245–46, 248–49, 251
Les Jours immobiles 3, 9–10, 24,
27, 29, 54, 56, 103–41, 142,
189, 202, 244, 247
Les Mains pleines d'oiseaux 3, 9,
27, 29, 103–41, 202, 244
Quand la neige aura fondu 3,
10–11, 27, 30, 33, 44, 52, 107,
155, 187–242, 245, 250

Joseph Zobel, d'amour et de silence (documentary) 15n26, 43n17, 63n4, 107, 166n41
Joseph Zobel: le soleil d'ébène (documentary) 9n17, 16n27, 182, 200
Zobel, Pauline Ennare (also known as Enny) 25, 187, 192n9, 208, 247
Zola, Émile 143